The Pentagonists

Books by
A. ERNEST FITZGERALD

The High Priests of Waste

The Pentagonists

The
Pentagonists

An Insider's View of Waste,
Mismanagement, and Fraud
in Defense Spending

A. Ernest Fitzgerald

1989

HOUGHTON MIFFLIN COMPANY · BOSTON

For information about permission to reproduce selections
from this book, write to Permissions, Houghton Mifflin
Company, 2 Park Street, Boston, Massachusetts 02108.

Library of Congress Cataloging-in-Publication Data

Fitzgerald, A. Ernest (Arthur Ernest)
The Pentagonists : an insider's view of waste,
mismanagement, and fraud in Defense spending.
Includes index.
1. United States—Armed Forces—Procurement.
2. United States—Armed Forces—Appropriations and
expenditures. I. Title.
UC263.F57 1989   355.6'212'0973   88-32036
ISBN 0-395-36245-8

Printed in the United States of America

V 10 9 8 7 6 5 4 3 2 1

The author is grateful for permission to quote from the following sources. The
editorial "What to Make of the C-5A Affair" (May 14, 1969); and excerpts from
"Presidential Panel to Assess Defense Purchasing Practices" (June 8, 1985), by
Michael Weisskopf; "Breaking the Bank and the Sound Barrier" (Apr. 4, 1973), by
Nicholas von Hoffman; and "Arms Firms See Postwar Spurt" (Dec. 8, 1968), by
Bernard Nossiter, are reprinted from The Washington Post © The Washington Post.
The excerpt from "Believing in Grace" (Feb. 3, 1985), by George F. Will, © 1985
Washington Post Writers Group, is reprinted with permission. The excerpts from the
editorial "The Fitzgerald Affair" (Apr. 2, 1973), and from "Curb Sought on Mollenhoff
Testimony" (Mar. 22, 1973), by Anthony Riple, are copyright © 1973 by the New
York Times Company and are reprinted by permission. The excerpts from "Firm
under Scrutiny Paid Carlucci $96,000 (July 6, 1988), by Dave Evans, military affairs
correspondent for the Chicago Tribune, is reprinted with the permission of the
author. Quotations from The Defense Management Challenge: Weapons
Acquisition, by J. Ronald Fox with James L. Field, are reprinted with the permission
of Harvard Business School Press (Boston, 1988).

Contents

Acknowledgments

Robie Macauley, my editor, is a veritable blacksmith of books. He has beaten many rough slabs of prose into readable and successful books. He did some of his best hammering on my manuscript. Any success this book achieves will be another tribute to Robie's editorial genius.

I am also indebted to Chris Coffin, Peg Anderson, and the other kind, patient, and skillful people at Houghton Mifflin. Less sympathetic and insightful partners would have abandoned me long before this work was finished.

None of these folks would have had anything to work with, though, if my son, John Patton Fitzgerald, had not put his own career on hold to help me with research and manuscript preparation.

My daughter Susan's writing suggestions were invaluable, and all of us were supported and kept within reasonable bounds of both rhetoric and schedule by my most severe but caring critic, my wife, Nell.

The Pentagonists

1

☆ ☆ ☆

Code of Silence

RICHARD NIXON SEEMED to be at the top of his game. At 4:17 on the afternoon of January 31, 1973, he was relaxing and chatting confidently with his assistant Charles Colson in the Oval Office of the White House. He had breezed masterfully through a noontime press conference where the only bothersome question had come from Clark Mollenhoff, who had served for a year in 1969–70 as a trouble-shooter on Nixon's staff.

Iowa native Mollenhoff, now a well-known Washington journalist, had won the Pulitzer Prize and numerous other awards for investigative reporting, and he was not a man to let go of a scandal once he got his teeth into it. So even the supremely confident Nixon, just inaugurated after his 1972 election landslide, had to be careful in dealing with the Boomer, as the big-voiced, six-foot-four, 250-pound Mollenhoff was known.

"Like, out there, I was very informal today," Nixon said to Colson. "I just, you know, talked quite a while when I wanted to. Kidded around with Mollenhoff. He sure presses, though." (The whole conversation was faithfully recorded on the president's tapes.)

Right.

Mollenhoff had used his first question to set up his old boss on the question of executive privilege, a presidential excuse often used to avoid answering questions about official wrongdoing. A lawyer as well as a reporter, Mollenhoff had been the scourge of presidents since Dwight Eisenhower when they resorted to the privilege dodge.

At the press conference Mollenhoff had asked, "Did you approve the use of executive privilege by Air Force Secretary Seamans in refusing to disclose the White House role in the firing of air cost analyst Fitzgerald?"

Mollenhoff went on to explain the reason for his question: "It came up yesterday in the civil service hearings. He [Seamans] used executive privilege. You had stated earlier that you would have to approve all these uses of executive privilege, as I understand it, and I wonder whether your view still prevails in this area or whether others are now entitled to use executive privilege on their own in this type of case?"

The president was wary; he assumed Mollenhoff was trying to trap him on the privilege issue, which would later be the cornerstone of his Watergate bastion. He failed to grasp the significance of "the White House role in the firing of . . . Fitzgerald."

"Let me explain," he answered Mollenhoff. "I was totally aware that Mr. Fitzgerald would be fired or discharged or asked to resign. I approved it, and Mr. Seamans must have been talking to someone who had discussed this matter with me.

"No, this was not a case of some person down the line deciding he should go. It was a decision that was submitted to me. I made it and I stick by it." Nixon had then evaded the executive privilege question by promising "a precise statement" in writing.

Colson, though, had picked up Mollenhoff's subtler purpose. As he chatted with Nixon after the press conference, he said, "I was so relieved when you did that because Mollenho — I could tell what Clark was doing. He was, he was working around the Fitzger — "

" — this guy that was fired," Nixon interrupted. "I'd marked it in the news summary. That's how it happened. I said, get rid of that son of a bitch. You know, 'cause he is, he's been doin' this two or three times. So Seamans, who isn't much of a sandbagger, uh, will get rid of him, I understand, uh, claimed executive privilege because he knew I had ordered it."

"Right," Colson said.

Why would the president of the United States take the trouble to reach down into the bowels of the Pentagon to pluck out a middle-level bureaucrat — a mere "air cost analyst" — and personally see that the man was fired? What made the president angry enough to say, "I said, get rid of that son of a bitch"?

A few minutes later John Ehrlichman came into the Oval Office. He wanted to know about the "precise statement" on executive privilege.

"You should have the most god-awful gobbledygook answer prepared," Nixon ordered. "Just put it out on executive privilege. Something that will allow us to do everything that we want."

As the conversation continued, it began to dawn on Nixon and his aides that he might have made a blunder in speaking out so explicitly about my firing. Nixon, concerned more with the question of privilege, kept drifting off the Fitzgerald problem and occasionally seemed to confuse me with other government employees he had savaged. Ehrlichman, though, kept bringing the focus back to the importance of putting me down and keeping me there. At one point he interrupted to say, "No, no, no, no, this is the guy that, uh, ratted on the C-5A overruns."

I had indeed violated the unwritten code of silence — by testifying truthfully to Congress in 1968 and 1969 about the concealed cost overruns and the technical problems of the giant Lockheed C-5A transport plane (I wrote about how I was harassed and fired for publicly committing these truths in my book *The High Priests of Waste*, 1972.)

Freshly reminded of my sins, Ehrlichman and Nixon got to the major point.

"He was a, he was a thorn in everybody's side, you see — " Ehrlichman began.

Nixon interrupted. "Yeah, well, the point was not that he was complaining about the overruns, but that he was doing it in public."

"That's the point. And cutting up his superiors," Ehrlichman said. "That's right."

"Yeah," said Ehrlichman.

"And not, and frankly, not taking orders."

In addition to committing the unforgivable Washington sin of telling truths that embarrassed powerful special interests, I had refused my bosses' instructions to alter my testimony about the C-5A disaster, thus undermining their "artful exercise to rescue hard-pressed Lockheed," as the *Wall Street Journal* (December 1, 1970) described it.

Years later, as I read the transcript of the White House tapes from that January afternoon, I began to feel — as Yogi Berra once put it — that this was "deja vu all over again." And as I read the records my lawyers had put together for my reinstatement after being fired, I began to understand the many complications in what had happened — in a small way to me personally and in a much bigger way to the whole moral fabric of the United States government.

As President Nixon made perfectly clear in that 1973 conversation with Colson and Ehrlichman, his administration's code of silence about military waste was enforced as effectively as the Mafia's code of *omertà* (though without the bloodshed). Nixon apologists might reply that this didn't start with him — and they would be right; both the wrongdoing and the cover-up were there when he came into office. The situation has gotten even worse since then, and today it is the primary cause of the United States' emergence as the world's largest banana republic.

Our military establishment may not have won a war in forty-three years, but it has managed to pull down the world's greatest industrial colossus. This could not have happened without the concomitant disintegration of institutional checks and balances in business, government, and society. When the tribunes and the senate neglect their vigilance, the Praetorian Guard takes over the treasury for itself.

The collapse of management controls and moral standards radiated outward from the Pentagon's acquisition community, the ripened fruit of the noxious military-industrial-complex weed that President Eisenhower warned us about. The problem is that the fruit, though deadly to liberty and lasting prosperity, is addictive. Almost all who partake are hooked, and the addiction has spread far beyond the military and its suppliers. The weed now chokes formerly productive industrial fields not directly involved in supplying the military. Greed, institutionalized dishonesty, and legalized stealing have corrupted not only the military but also segments of Congress, prestigious universities, and even whole civilian communities that have become dependent on military money. Many who have hardly known honest work live in luxury on the sweat of their conned, exploited fellow citizens. Wallowing in the taxpayers' money, the acquisition community became so inefficient during the Reagan years that the huge infusions of money have actually produced fewer useful weapons.

When this process becomes so repugnant that even some of its beneficiaries are repelled, the secrecy necessary for it to prosper may break down, and the public is then treated to juicy scandal — like the well-publicized allegations of Pentagon bribes, kickbacks, and bid rigging that woke up so many people in June 1988 and shook official Washington "to its shoes," as one official said. Usually, damage-limiting propaganda campaigns and pro forma "reforms" follow, secrecy is tightened, and the acquisition community continues on its merry, larcenous way.

Washington is essentially a one-industry town. Anyone who grew up, as I did, in a mill town, will understand how things work in Washington. Our mill town's product is not steel or textiles but politics, and the lifeblood of politics is patronage. Patronage in the forms of import quotas, tariffs, tax laws (especially the ones that benefit powerful special interests), selective prosecution, regulatory rulings, decisions about the location of government facilities, about grants, appointments, and — most potent of all — contracts, especially military contracts. Although it is impolite to talk about it publicly, both the executive and legislative branches are preoccupied with distributing patronage. All branches of our government prize employees who are "responsive" to the never-ending work of paying out or paying off. The judicial branch understands this and, as we shall see, often cooperates.

Sometimes the patronage distribution process gets messy. It requires lying, stealing, cheating, and then covering up for any or all of the above. The Pentagon, as the dominant patronage machine — the largest money dispenser the world has ever seen — needs more of such behavior than other departments. Therefore it has to shield itself very carefully from disclosures. So even though many laws and regulations exist commanding all military and civilian bureaucrats in the federal government to come forth and "expose corruption wherever discovered," woe to the man or woman who obeys these laws.

Richard Nixon was most especially aware of his obligation to protect me for telling the truth about the C-5A overruns. In 1951, when he was still a senator, Nixon carried on a noisy and vigorous campaign against then-President Harry Truman for Truman's firing of General Douglas MacArthur and Admiral Louis Denfeld on the grounds, at least in part, that they had told Congress embarrassing things about Truman's conduct of military affairs.

Nixon spoke of impeaching Truman. He also offered an amendment to strengthen Title 18, Section 1505, of the U.S. Code, the statute that supposedly protects congressional witnesses from interference and retaliation. This criminal statute carries penalties of up to five years in jail and a $10,000 fine for anyone convicted of retaliating against such a witness or obstructing a congressional inquiry. Senator Nixon's amendment failed to pass, but Nixon had violated even the basic law when he retaliated against me.

Four other presidents — one earlier (Lyndon Johnson) and three to come — were equally determined to silence me or get rid of me. Because of Nixon's uniquely candid record of unsavory conversations in the Oval Office, we tend to think of him as something of an anomaly, a singularly amoral politician who somehow was able to con his way into the Oval Office while we weren't looking. I can't agree. His attitudes and actions in regard to the problems that have always concerned me were quite consistent with the actions of his predecessors and successors. All five presidents, under the guise of national security, systematically exploited the American people. And all five were equally fierce in concealing what was going on. Richard Nixon was part of a continuum.

There is, however, by great good fortune, a disparity between the policy of these men and the order of government set up by the founders of the republic. No matter who is in the White House, the fundamental principles are still there — and that was how my lawyers, through years of skillful, dogged work, were able to pry out the evidence to substantiate my case. This narrative is heavily dependent on their discoveries.

Those revelations could not have occurred, nor would I have coped as well as I did personally without the early assistance of the National Capitol Chapter of the American Civil Liberties Union (not to be confused with the national ACLU, whose policies and priorities became quite different). After Nixon fired me, Florence Isbell and Ralph Temple of the local ACLU recruited a series of excellent lawyers to represent me without pay for themselves or their firms. (By 1982, at normal rates, they would have earned a million dollars from my legal actions.) John Bodner, Jr., in particular, represented me for more than eighteen years out of sheer public-spirited altruism.

After years of digging, my lawyers had enough evidence to sue the Lion of Whittier for his role in destroying my career. Nixon himself proposed to testify before a jury of citizens of the District of Columbia and to be cross-examined by my lawyers. His proposed witnesses for the trial included a number of his former staffers, among whom were such familiar names as Robert Haldeman, John Ehrlichman, and Charles Colson; assorted Pentagon bureaucrats — generals, colonels, and civilians, including some defense secretaries; various defense industry executives; and, perhaps surprisingly to innocent readers, Jimmy Carter and Ralph Nader. Nixon's long and varied list of witnesses reflected his justifiable confidence that the nation's leaders in business and government would rally to support the right of a president — even a disgraced one — to break yet another law in defense of Pentagon concealment.

2

☆ ☆ ☆

*Carrying Out
the Contract*

AT THE END of 1968, as the Johnson administration gave way to that of Richard Nixon, the old Pentagonists handed on the message to the new: get rid of Fitzgerald. The man who passed the word was Air Force Secretary Harold Brown, described by his admirers as "the smartest man in the world."

Not demonstrably true, perhaps, but Brown certainly had a good claim to being smart.

In 1961, before his thirty-fourth birthday, he had been appointed director of defense research and engineering by President Kennedy. In this job he was one of the highest-ranking and most powerful of Secretary of Defense Robert McNamara's "whiz kids," whose reason for being was to bring the big military spenders to heel and make sure our defense got "more bang for a buck."

Although a fair number of his associates couldn't stand Harold personally because of his arrogance, he was generally considered to have performed brilliantly in his job. On October 1, 1965, just ten days after I, a civilian, joined as management systems deputy in the Air Force Secretariat, President Johnson appointed him secretary of the Air Force. I was delighted to be working for a man who was both brilliant and so critical of dubious military schemes that he had earned the nickname "Dr. No." I wanted to help him live up to that nickname.

Brown was aware of my intention — at least I thought he was. When I filled out the standard government employment form before being hired, I appended a dense, six-page supplement that described some of my most successful cost-cutting assignments. I wanted to lay out my intentions from the very first. At the time I was president of a small but highly successful management consulting company, and I didn't want to interrupt a flourishing career if the top managers at the Pentagon had reservations about the aggressive approach to improving quality and cutting costs that my associates and I practiced. I had just turned thirty-nine, and I figured I could spend a few years shaping up the Air Force if Harold Brown had the stomach for it.

Brown didn't flinch. After looking at my papers, he wrote a note to retiring Air Force Secretary Eugene Zuchert — in the small, clear hand I would come to know only too well — "Gene, Sounds very good. Let's get him. H.B."

In the beginning all of us had great confidence in Brown. We respected him for his quick mind and his ability to isolate problems, and we worked very hard for him. I used to start early in the morning and finish late at night, and I worked many weekends.

After a promising start, though, Brown began to change course. He seemed to back away from the fundamental improvements recommended by our more-bang-for-a-buck staff. Our labors began to be Sisyphean. With great effort, we would bring projects to a point where his decision was needed — to enforce a contract, endorse a directive, or support a stand on pricing — and Brown would let the boulder roll back down the hill. His failure to support cost cutting was devastating. It wasn't long before the word got out to the big-spending military contractors on the outside and the open-handed generals on the inside that Harold Brown would not lift a hand to stop the "cannibals from eating our missionaries."

On November 13, 1968, I testified to Senator William Proxmire's committee (the Joint Economic Committee of the Congress) about the C-5A with hopes that Brown would support me. He had professed to support my management control initiatives, and he had been critical of the C-5 overruns in Pentagon meetings. As those familiar with this historic disaster will recall, Lockheed's giant C-5A transport plane, nicknamed "the tin balloon," had a tendency to shed parts in flight. At the time I testified, it looked as if the 120-airplane program would cost about $2 billion more than the original estimate.

A scandal such as the one caused by my testimony on the C-5A is usually a five-day wonder. Ordinarily, members of Congress lose interest once the headlines are forgotten. But Senator Proxmire and his assistant, Richard Kaufman, were made of sterner stuff. Proxmire scheduled another hearing for the following January, and Kaufman kept digging into the dirty details of the C-5A.

I didn't realize it fully at the time, but my testimony set off a big cover-up in the Air Force. Harold Brown tried to make my C-5A testimony appear inaccurate by allowing one of his assistant secretaries, Robert Charles, to alter the official Air Force C-5A cost estimates after my testimony. He tried to palm these off on Senator Proxmire as the genuine article.

When the new set of figures arrived at Proxmire's office, Richard Kaufman called me to ask why I'd changed my testimony. I hadn't, of course, but it took a lot of effort to get Brown and company to reveal the truth. When I got the original worksheets, they showed that my figures were correct and the secretary's were doctored. I requested that the evidence be forwarded to the congressional committee, but Brown stubbornly refused. It was only after Proxmire scheduled the January 16, 1969, hearing to find out why the Air Force was obstructing a witness and tampering with evidence (both of these are felonies punishable by big fines and long prison terms) that the secretary forwarded the real figures. When the hearing occurred, Brown copped out by sending Assistant Secretary Charles to testify in his place.

What, then, was Brown's solution to the scandals of the C-5A? It seemed obvious to him that the first course of action was to fire Ernest Fitzgerald. The time seemed right; the new Nixon administration was just about to come into office and Robert Seamans was to replace Brown. On January 9 — as I learned ten years later through legal discovery — Brown gave his advice to Seamans and dictated a memorandum about it for the record:

(a) With respect to Mr. Fitzgerald, I pointed out that, though some of his ideas about procurement practices and financial control of contractors had merit, his practices were unacceptable. These include speaking to the press against Air Force decisions, discussing internal Air Force matters with Congressional Committee staffs, and providing them with documents without going through Legislative Liaison channels. This behavior has greatly lessened, if not eliminated, his value as an employee of the Air Force. I drew the distinction between advocating one's views vigorously within the department before a decision was taken, and public non-support, or volunteering and advocating contrary views to the press and the Congress. . . . I indicated that his actions up to now probably do not constitute sufficient reason for us to take removal action against Fitzgerald, but that we would act to make it clear to Fitzgerald that we considered his usefulness to the Air Force to be negligible if not negative. In the interest of discipline, it was important that the new Air Force Secretariat take a similar position in subsequent months. Dr. Seamans indicated that he understood this principle and that, in the light of the facts I had described, he recognized that Fitzgerald is of no use to the Air Force; though his rights must be protected, he is to be discouraged from remaining.

Then came the most important part of the memo — something that involved many millions of dollars rather than my personal fortunes. Brown wrote, "I described to Dr. Seamans the C-5 technical progress and its satisfactory performance and contrasted them with the financial problems of the C-5." Brown then proceeded to argue that the Air Force should buy a fourth squadron, but suspend a decision on a fifth and a sixth, before he left office. Thus Brown's second action to solve the C-5A problem was to buy more of the flimsy tin balloons, thus helping to bail Lockheed out of its gross errors. Seamans agreed that it was Brown's decision to make.

Harold Brown was not content to simply pass the word about me to his successor. About a week before their discussion, Brown had decided to work out a strategy for firing me. As a merit-system employee, I was theoretically protected against arbitrary dismissal, so he had asked John Lang, his assistant, "What are his rights?" This was a little like Henry II's seemingly rhetorical question about Thomas à Becket, "Who will free me from this turbulent priest?" What Brown really meant (as testimony in my firing hearings later brought out) was, "How can I fire him?" Less bloody than Henry Plantagenet, but in the same robust spirit.

Lang's memo in answer outlined three ways to fire Fitzgerald, only one of them frankly described as "underhanded," although they all were. There was also a suggestion from Thomas Nielson, my immediate boss, as to how he could reorganize his office so as to get rid of me.

Through the process of legal discovery we also obtained a record of these events as seen by the new secretary of the Air Force. Seamans, an engineering professor at Massachusetts Institute of Technology, was a worthy successor to Brown. A few years after these events, in the recollections he tape recorded for the official Air Force historian, he said:

I never heard of a guy named Ernie Fitzgerald until either the last week in December or the first week of January, 1969. . . . At that very first meeting, [Brown] told me something about [him], and I'm pretty sure that by then Proxmire had written me a letter. . . . It talked about this "wonderful public servant" . . . and he was sure I would want to rely on him heavily because he was one of the "greatest public servants" that ever came down the pike. So I wrote him back a short letter and said, "Thanks very much, and I'll look into this matter when I become Secretary of the Air Force." The facts of the matter are that Ernie did testify on the C-5; that he was certainly not encouraged to do so; that this was bigger than just the Air Force. . . . Between Fitzgerald and Proxmire, they were "coony" enough to make it well-known publicly that he was up there testifying even though the Defense Department hadn't wanted him to. Of course that made it all the more exciting and everything appeared more valid and the Air Force and DOD looked more like conspirators deceiving the public.

Then, of course, a few strange things happened . . . the most amazing being the memo that John Lang (of Personnel) wrote to Harold Brown on three ways for separating Fitzgerald from the Air Force. One was to fire him for cause; one was to abolish his job; and the third one, which he [Lang] said would be a little deceitful, would be to — and I can't remember what the third one was offhand, but it's all in the record. It took about 24 hours from the time Lang wrote the memo until Proxmire had [it].

(The third method was to convert my job to the "career service" and fill it through a competitive examination. The Air Force could then invite "all the eligibles from the executive inventory and an outside search" to compete.)

In all this, a fundamental principle was at stake: could a citizen employed by the government communicate information directly to Congress about serious errors or malfeasance in the executive branch? Many presidents hated the thought of such a situation. In 1906 Teddy Roosevelt promised instant dismissal for anyone caught in the act. In 1910 William Howard Taft made the rule a little stiffer by forbidding any employee even to answer a congressional request except through the head of his department. This clear violation of the First Amendment inspired the Lloyd-LaFollette Act (now Title 5, Section 7211, of the U.S. Code):

> The right of persons employed in the civil service of the United States either individually or collectively to petition Congress or any member thereof or to furnish information to either House of Congress, or to any committee or member thereof, shall not be denied or interfered with.

The January hearing on the C-5A was notable for three things: Senator Proxmire revealed Lang's memo to Brown describing the three ways of firing me; I testified about the phony C-5A figures Brown had tried to hand the committee; and Assistant Secretary Charles stuck to the official party line that the C-5A was in great shape and that Lockheed was doing splendidly. All of this made it clear that the new Nixon administration would have to bring about some reforms in the Pentagon. It was also clear that I would need some political help to save my job.

Senator Len Jordan of Idaho, a Republican on Proxmire's committee, proved to be sympathetic. He asked me in for a talk. A tough old cowboy who had been governor of Idaho, Jordan had a shrewd idea of what I was up against. He told me that those forces were bigger and more powerful than anything my friends in Congress could muster, but that he would do what he could to help.

I also called on two Republican congressmen from my home state of Alabama, Bill Dickinson and Jack Edwards. They were willing to help arrange the one thing I wanted at the time — to meet with some of the new administration's Pentagon appointees and explain my case.

This resulted in a short, unsatisfactory meeting with Secretary Seamans, whose most memorable comment was that "the staff" didn't like me. I already knew that. And, in his later confidential memoir dictated to the official Air Force historian, Seamans voiced his distaste for my public testimony about C-5A cost overruns and added, "He [Fitzgerald] is terribly good at playing the Southern Boy from Alabama, the country boy taking on the big corporations and all these big-money spenders and the generals — 'the high priests of waste.'" (Seamans either had not read my book or had not understood it. The "high priests of waste" of my title were the economists, mostly neo-Keynesians, who preach that military spending, wasteful or not, makes the nation prosperous.)

The Seamans oral history memoir went on to note that my boss, Tom Nielson, was still hoping to reorganize his office in such a way that I would be out of a job. But Seamans knew that Nielson was going to depart in a few months, so he delayed his decision about me until Spencer Schedler (whose best-known contribution to the national welfare was helping to get Spiro T. Agnew elected vice-president in 1968) was sworn in as assistant secretary of the Air Force for financial management. By then Seamans, with advice from on high, had decided that I should leave the Air Force.

That same period, late spring of 1969, saw a new turn of events in the congressional wars. Congressman William Moorhead of Pennsylvania, a member of Proxmire's joint committee, had picked up some cues about the Pentagon follies. He carried his suspicions to the powerful House Committee on Government Operations, of which he was a member. Representative Chet Holifield was acting chairman of the committee. His southern California district included influential contractors for the Pentagon, NASA, and the Atomic Energy Commission. The last thing they wanted to read about in the newspapers was more about the C-5A and other corporate scams.

Holifield fell back on an old Washington strategy: if you have a problem that you want to deep-six, you simply study it into oblivion. After lengthy committee hearings, a blue-ribbon commission is appointed to study the matter; sometime before all the commission members die of old age, they authorize a report, which takes an extended time to write; and finally committee hearings are held to consider the report. A capable chairman can keep the process going for three or four years, but the talented Holifield managed to stave off action on the procurement scandals for a full six years.

The Holifield commission avoided the specific problem we had pinpointed, but "studied" the truly worldwide problem of government — not just Pentagon — procurement. (Part of the death-by-study strategy is to change the subject.) Any nasty particulars of waste, fraud, and abuse that managed to leak out during the Holifield commission's lengthy stalling process could then be referred to that august body for decent burial.

Peter Stockton, Congressman Moorhead's designated staffer on Holifield's committee, was an unassuming thirty-one-year-old whose life had committed him to no narrow category. His B.A. and M.A. degrees were in economics, and he had worked at the Bureau of the Budget, but he didn't look the part of a government economist. The lawyers and corporate officials in pinstripes who showed up at his office found a casual man in shirtsleeves, khakis, and running shoes. They knew very well how to deal with a slick congressional staffer on the make, but Stockton appeared invulnerable to their blandishments, and they couldn't fathom him.

There is nothing a representative or senator loves to talk about more than "oversight" — checking up on the executive branch to find out what the special interests (mostly big corporations) are getting away with. The checking up is done by staff investigators, however, most of whom are political hacks whose specialty is finding no evidence of anything wrong. But once in a while we taxpayers get lucky. We were lucky when the people of Wisconsin elected William Proxmire and lucky when he chose Richard Kaufman as his investigator. And we were equally lucky with Moorehead and Stockton. A congressional investigator who really wants to benefit the United States has to have both a powerful elected protector and superb survival instincts. As an old-time congressional staff director once told me, "The ideal congressional investigator is a highly motivated, very intelligent . . . savage."

Moorhead unleashed Peter Stockton on the C-5A scandal, and he slowly began to strip away the Pentagon camouflage. Using my C-5A testimony and working with the "closet patriots" in the Pentagon,

The Washington Post

AN INDEPENDENT NEWSPAPER · SUNDAY, MAY 4, 1969 · PAGE B6

What To Make of the C-5A Affair

Word of Defense Secretary Laird's plan to review the Air Force's contract with the Lockheed Aircraft Corp. to build the giant jet transport C-5A would be more reassuring if it had come unaccompanied by evidence that the Secretary is preoccupied with putting the best face on things. While promising a "thorough" inquiry about the contract, Mr. Laird asked his top aides to design ways to combat what he called "adverse commentary" on the rising costs of the C-5A. In any case, the results of "in house" investigations, even one conducted by a Republican Administration of actions during a Democratic one, are seldom as persuasive as those obtained by full-scale congressional hearings. In the case of the C-5A (also known as the Galaxy), a number of questions—if not allegations—of impropriety have been raised about the contract and about defense procurement policy itself.

Under probing by Rep. William S. Moorhead, an Air Force colonel told a House Government Operations Subcommittee last week that his civilian superiors had approved an effort to cover up huge cost increases in building the Galaxy because public disclosure "might put Lockheed's position in the common (stock) market in jeopardy." The civilians named by the colonel are Robert H. Charles, Assistant Secretary of the Air Force for Installations and Logistics, and Robert N. Anthony, a former Defense Department Comptroller. Whether, in fact, Messrs. Charles and Anthony glossed over cost increases to shield Lockheed's stock has yet to be determined. What is clear is that if they did, they should not have; the Pentagon's responsibilities do not include protecting the market value of stock of firms with which it contracts.

But that is only part of the matter, which really goes to the fundamental question of how the Pentagon buys its hardware. For one thing, the Galaxy contracts involve a $2.1 billion miscalculation on a $3.1 billion project. For another, the terms of the contract would seem to reward inefficiency—and at a premium rate.

Without getting engulfed in the esoteric language of cost analysis and weapons procurement it is important to understand a few basic things about the Galaxy contract. In 1964, the Air Force estimated that 120 C-5A aircraft would cost $3.1 billion. Now the Air Force figures the Galaxy will cost at least $5.2 billion, or $2.1 billion more. Excesses of actual costs over estimates, called "overruns" at the Pentagon, are not unique in weapons development and procurement, although a $2 billion overrun seems on the high side. But the Galaxy contract, which was designed by Assistant Secretary Charles, contains a novel feature which provides that losses suffered by Lockheed on the first installment of 58 planes it produced could be recovered and turned into profits—by a price adjustment—if the Air Force decided to order a second batch of 62 aircraft.

Just how much of the overrun can be attributed to inefficiency on the part of Lockheed or inflation or unforeseen, but normal development problems with the aircraft itself is not known. And it is not easily determined just how much of a loss Lockheed anticipated on the first batch of 58 planes. Rep. Chet Holifield, the California Democrat who heads the House Committee, not only ordered a witness not to answer that question, but threw in a challenge to attendant newsmen to make what they could of it.

What we make of it is that the instinct for the cover-up in these matters is as strong in certain quarters in Congress as it is in the Pentagon, and that some Congressman or Senator with more courage and candor than Mr. Holifield ought to step in on the taxpayers' behalf and investigate not only the Galaxy affair but the whole procurement process at the Pentagon.

Stockton learned of a sensational document hidden away in the safe of a high Pentagon official. The document, which became notorious as the "Trenton Boyd memo" after the Air Force auditor who wrote it, showed explicitly how top Pentagon officials had conspired to falsify official government records to cover up the C-5A cost overruns. The memo said in part, "They [System Program Office personnel] stated that verbal direction was received on or about June 6, 1968, that the anticipated overrun on the C-5A program should not be reflected in routine management-type reports. It was indicated that this direction was by Mr. Charles and Mr. [Bob] Anthony and was received by SPO through channels." If proven, such an action was, of course, a felony punishable by a stiff fine and a long prison sentence.

Stockton blind-sided Holifield. He waited until the night before Holifield's climactic whitewash hearing on April 29 and 30, 1969.

Representative Moorhead suddenly requested that the General Accounting Office (GAO) procure the document and turn it over to the committee. Secretary Seamans, weak-kneed at the summons, opened the safe. With great reluctance, Comptroller General Elmer Staats complied with Moorhead's request.

Holifield had pointedly not invited me to the hearing, but it did him little good. In the midst of self-serving testimony by the C-5A program

"Air Cover" from Herblock's State of the Union *(Simon & Schuster, 1972).*

manager, Colonel Kenneth Beckman, Moorhead and Stockton fired their ground-to-air missile. Faced with the Trenton Boyd memo, Beckman began to stammer. Then, even worse, he began to tell the truth: he admitted that official records had been falsified, then compounded the felony by revealing that the purpose was to protect Lockheed's interests in the stock market.

Congressman Holifield, seeing a lot of hard-won obfuscation go down the drain, blew up. He ordered the Air Force witnesses not to answer any further questions about Beckman's admissions. Then, in a voice clearly audible to members, staffers, and reporters, he told Moorhead, "You're a son of a bitch to bring that document in."

The American press almost unanimously condemned the Pentagon procurement practices. Their views are well represented by the *Washington Post*'s lead editorial and cartoon on May 4, 1969. The next day Senator Proxmire had the editorial inserted in the *Congressional Record*. He also gave a speech in which he said, referring to me and Kenneth Beckman, "I intend to do anything I can to see that these men and any other government employees who testify to the truth at the request of Congress are insulated from petty retaliation on the part of the higher-ups who were at fault."

As is the usual outcome of such congressional dramas, everybody got his unjust reward. The Pentagon, Lockheed, and C-5A got off scot-free, and Stockton was fired. Holifield told Moorhead, "You're elected and I have to swallow you. But I don't have to swallow Stockton."

So began Peter Stockton's career as an outcast and a maverick, a fate all too common among us "whistle blowers" who violate the Pentagon code of silence. But if his Trenton Boyd missile had failed to shoot down the tin balloon, at least it drew a lot of attention in the neighborhood. Moorhead and Proxmire demanded that the Securities and Exchange Commission (SEC) investigate efforts by Pentagon and Lockheed officials to affect the financial markets. Nixon's secretary of defense, Melvin Laird, tried to limit the damage by throwing Harold Brown's two holdover assistants, Tom Nielson and Bob Charles, off the sleigh — but without breathing a syllable of "C-5A." Wily Melvin got his message through by announcing these departures at the same press conference in which he defended the Pentagon against Stockton's disclosures.

Seamans also disapproved of my having taken part in some seminars designed to educate congressional staffers on how we all could do a better job in acquisitions management. He described it as "Ernie up there [on Capitol Hill] conducting seminars for staff people on the poor job the Air Force was doing on its weapons systems program." Actually, these seminars, which Richard Kaufman organized, were one of the few positive results of the C-5A affair. For my part, I explained how the management systems my associates and I had been pushing for many years could give us the defense we needed without bankrupting the country. The simplest of these initiatives was a "should-cost" approach to contract pricing, which means we would pay only what goods and services should cost, according to industry standards. This contrasted with the Pentagon's idea of pricing based on past experience, which permits building in fat, inefficiency, fraud, and management abuse by the contractor.

My second major recommendation was for a comprehensive set of military-industrial indicators to show where we actually stood on big weapons buying programs. Pentagon buyers like to keep the bad news a secret until it is too late to correct mistakes, so they try to avoid making timely reports of the facts. In one of my seminar talks I compared the federal government to a corporation, of which Congress is the board of directors and the citizens are the stockholders. The directors and shareholders have every right to get timely, accurate reports from the operating divisions — the federal agencies — so that incipient problems are revealed before they become disasters. Full disclosure also depersonalizes the transmittal of information so that whistle blowers do not have to set their hair on fire just to shed light on the situation (and so they can't then be sacked for not having a proper military haircut).

The opposition to full reporting was represented by Holifield's assistant, Herb Roback, who argued that "Congress doesn't want all those facts." He explained that most members of Congress preferred to vote on military contract matters on the basis of "who gets the contracts, where are the jobs, and where the money is to be spent."

In May 1969 the Joint Economic Committee (JEC) issued a report titled "The Economics of Military Procurement." It endorsed should-cost, real competition for contracts, and ten other sweeping reforms — ideas that my friends and I had been trying to promote. Any responsible steward of the public purse, such as the secretary of the Air Force, would welcome the JEC recommendations, right? Wrong. At the moment, Seamans and his administration colleagues were too worried about protecting Lockheed and its kind.

The SEC investigation that Stockton's disclosures had forced was also getting under way in May. My friends and I had serious hope that it would unwrap the C-5A cover-up, but the Nixon administration was worried. The government documents my lawyers extracted years later showed that this inquiry was the last thunderhead in a rainy week for the administration. They decided I had to go, and Seamans was the man to do the job. He called the president's counselor, Bryce Harlow, at the White House for the heavyweight support he needed.

Harlow, one of Nixon's most trusted barons, was his second appointee when he entered the White House. The two men had met in 1948 when Nixon was a freshman representative and Harlow was a staffer on the Armed Services Committee. Harlow's other close ties were with Lyndon Johnson and the congressmen who loved big military budgets. Pat Buchanan used to say that Harlow had the most intimate knowledge of Capitol Hill of any high official in the Nixon White House. (Much later, in 1979 when my lawyers took a deposition from him, Harlow made a funny Freudian slip in describing his administration role. He said, "I was sort of resident guru. . . . I was sort of his [Nixon's] transgressional savant and a stroker." On viewing the record, he changed "transgressional" to "congressional.")

In the early spring of 1969, Representative Bill Dickinson had invited me to speak on military spending to a group of his conservative Republican colleagues who called themselves the Good Guys. Dickinson, a very junior member of Mendel Rivers's generally awful Armed Services Committee, usually voted for the Pentagon's requests, but he had a certain sympathy for my proposal to sweat some of the lard off the great Pentagon stalled ox.

About forty of the Good Guys had gathered at Costin's restaurant in downtown Washington; I was seated next to their chairman, an affable Ohioan named Sam Devine. The diminutive, smiling man on my left was introduced as Bryce Harlow. When it was time to give my pitch, I pointed out that we kept coming up against a false choice of alternatives: either "support the military" by giving them whatever they asked for or be a "unilateral disarmer" by cutting the budget wholesale. I said that the third, and reasonable, alternative was to make the Pentagon a lot more efficient so that we could defend the country without bankrupting it.

One small, elderly — and fairly drunk — congressman was so infuriated by this message that he wanted to slug Bill Dickinson for sponsoring me. His friends restrained him. Dickinson, an ex-football player, was a very large man, much younger and soberer than the challenger.

The other Good Guys seemed receptive to what I'd said — but not Bryce Harlow, who spoke next. Years after the event he recalled it this way in his deposition to my lawyers:

And, I said . . . the statement of Mr. Fitzgerald was, in aggregate, an attack on the Defense Department leadership. I said, "Gentlemen, I don't know what to say about Mr. Fitzgerald's observations because I don't know anything about them . . . All I can say now is that you all know Melvin Laird. . . . He is a former colleague of yours and he is enormously admired by all of you. . . . [And] he's the President's appointee in this area."

My own recollection is that Harlow was not nearly so milk-toasty as his deposition pretended. He suggested much more strongly that I was attacking the personal integrity of the new secretary of defense and was disparaging our brave lads who were out there holding the Bolshevik hordes at bay. Angrily, and no doubt against the coaching of his lawyer, Harlow accused me of "lese majesty" for my remarks at Costin's.

On May 6 Proxmire publicly demanded that the Justice Department conduct a criminal investigation of the C-5A scandal.

That same day saw something of a confrontation during a secret hearing of Rivers's Armed Services Committee. When Bill Dickinson reproached Melvin Laird for the way I had been treated for telling the truth, Laird was stung. He replied that the office of the assistant secretary for financial management was going to be reorganized and that the new chief of FM would make any decisions about me.

On May 7, again in secret testimony to the same committee, Seamans fulminated about the congressional staff seminars I'd been participating in and accused me of releasing classified information — a very serious offense, or at least it used to be. (Seamans's accusation, he later told the official historian's tape recorder, was inspired by Herb Roback of Holifield's staff and General John Murphy of his own staff.)

Later, after I was fired, Proxmire forced Seamans to retract this accusation. In his *apologia pro vita sua* to the official tape, he produced this wonderful waffle:

> At the time I was testifying, I really thought that Ernie had given them classified material, marked "Confidential." Later on, when we still had the opportunity of going over the testimony, it wasn't clear as to whether any of the material was classified or not. So we changed the word from Confidential with a capital C to confidential with a small c.

Since I hadn't given Congress any classified material, I thought I had nothing to fear. Little did I know how far my detractors would go in falsifying the record and just plain lying about me.

On May 8 the *Washington Post*'s Bernard Nossiter, their designated C-5A hitter, published a brilliant analysis of the Golden Handshake, his name for the grotesque repricing formula by which Lockheed was able to reap rich profits by increasing their overruns. He backed the accuracy of my testimony on the C-5A overruns and suggested that the Pentagon use rubber slide rules to make the overruns look smaller — and pay Lockheed with checks that could shrink in the same way. But it is not good to laugh at military establishment officials. It makes them unstable.

General Joseph Cappucci, head of the Air Force Office of Special Investigations (OSI), was in charge of compiling the "dirt file" — the derogatory information that could be used against me. The dirt file was carefully organized to destroy evidence showing I had done nothing wrong and to circulate baseless gossip that harmed me. One of the detrimental contributors was my former assistant, Lieutenant Colonel Hans "Whitey" Driessnack, a secret informer (designated T-1) against me for the OSI. The downright silly OSI investigation charged that I worked late at night and was a "pinchpenny." Evidence for the latter charge was that I drove an old Rambler automobile. OSI's attempts to suggest that I had a conflict of interest involving my old consulting firm, Performance Technology Corporation, proved that I didn't, but that didn't bother OSI. They just discarded the proof of my innocence.

In mid-May Seamans unleashed Cappucci, who set out to smear me to justify my firing. Then Seamans called in Thomas Nielson and Spencer Schedler to discuss the plan that would reorganize me out of the Air Force. Far from being the objective, impartial protector of the merit system for the taxpayers' employees, the Civil Service Commission, or at least its chairman, Robert Hampton, was an active participant in the secret conspiracy to get rid of me, if we can believe Seamans. As he told the story to the historian's tape recorder:

> The people that I talked to outside the Department of Defense were first of all, Bob Hampton, who runs the Civil Service Commission. I did check with him about this in May [1969] and asked him, "What are you supposed to do when you're managing a large government program, and you've got a guy like A. Ernie Fitzgerald on the payroll?" He said, "It's frankly one of the problems we face in running the government, and there's no very good answer to it." He said, "On the basis of what you've told me, I don't believe you could ever sustain a separation for cause. So your only alternative is to abolish his job."

Hampton never revealed this conversation during all the years he was sitting in judgment on my case, and Seamans kept it secret for ten years.

The case against me worked its way up to the highest of kangaroo courts on May 17 at a high-level meeting in the White House. The roll call included the president, Secretary Laird, Air Force General Stewart, the head of the Bureau of the Budget, Robert Mayo; and National

Security Adviser Henry Kissinger. James Schlesinger later insisted that he was there, but his name does not appear on the original invitation list. The primary subject for discussion was the Manned Orbiting Laboratory (MOL), a very secret and very dubious Air Force boondoggle, an early attempt to take over control of space from the civilians. Nixon had decided to kill MOL, but Seamans was still pleading for it. The abolition of Ernest Fitzgerald came up as a secondary matter.

Years later, in a deposition to my lawyers, Schlesinger spoke of the "general feeling" of that White House meeting that "Mr. Fitzgerald had transcended the normal bounds of an executive branch employee." Schlesinger added that they "were concerned about the leaks that had occurred and the detrimental effect this was having on the image of the military overall . . . and the effect it might have directly on requests to Congress regarding defense appropriations." He further deposed that Nixon had referred to the "Fitzgerald sort of thing" and had used my name "in an agitable way."

The Pentagon and White House position was that exposures of waste and mismanagement were actually attacks on the military motivated by unpatriotic sentiments. Unfortunately, this simple view has been held by most of our recent administrations, but President Nixon expressed it best in his June 4, 1969, speech to the Air Force Academy: "It is open season on the armed forces. Military programs are ridiculed as needless if not deliberate waste. The military profession is derided. . . . Patriotism is considered by some to be a backward, 'unfashionable' fetish of the uneducated and unsophisticated."

But the presidential declaration did not make the issue disappear; the news kept getting worse. In the Proxmire committee hearings of June 10, 11, and 13, my former associate Mert Tyrrell testified that the Minuteman program — theretofore regarded as a model of good management — was hugely overrun and full of other troubles. Additional testimony pointed to serious problems in the Mark II avionics system for the F-111 fighter-bomber. The Short Range Attack Missile (SRAM) was revealed as another fiasco. Shipbuilding contracts were said to be in shambles.

The last straw for the Nixon administration, apparently, was a long article by Richard Harwood and Lawrence Stern on Robert McNamara's legacy, published in the *Washington Post* on June 15, 1969. It inspired a long Special Report written by John Charles Huston, an assistant to Patrick Buchanan, which was included in the president's daily news summary. According to the report the *Post* article made the point

> . . . that McNamara's reputation is being placed on trial by virtue of the current investigation of defense spending practices, most of which were developed during his tenure. The article notes that he is accused by

former Kennedy administration colleagues . . . of having helped create . . . *a military machine of such size and power that it is not responsible to political control.* These critics say that "we should be clear on one point: *it is not the uniformed military which has created the present situation,* but the civilian leadership and the institutions they have created to centralize and expand the performance on national security functions" [emphasis added; even as he was writing this, the military were well on their way to taking control of those institutions — and thus of the distribution of patronage].

McNamara has declined to testify before the Proxmire committee, but he has his defenders — General David Shoup, the Marine dove; General Maxwell Taylor; and Rosewell [*sic*] Gilpatric among them. Even Dave Packard "expresses the common view" — "he (McNamara) made great contributions. . . . You might criticize some things with hindsight, but I don't know that I would have done anything different at the time."

Huston's "even Dave Packard" is interesting. The chairman of Hewlett Packard, a big supplier to the military and their contractors, was currently deputy secretary of defense under Laird. The procurement policies of McNamara and his predecessors had made Packard rich. So it was hardly surprising that he wouldn't have done anything differently. Huston quoted Harwood and Stern's assertion that when McNamara took over the Pentagon, the "operative word was rationalize." In this the authors were a bit naive. They didn't quite understand the nuance of meaning in what they were writing: a secondary meaning of "rationalize" is "to devise self-satisfying but incorrect reasons for one's behavior." One of the things McNamara rationalized was waste. His whiz kids had seized upon the cost-justifying mathematical procedures in wide use and had extended them throughout the vast establishment. Except for a small circle of spoilsports — mostly my associates and me — no one had resisted them. In fact, the spending coalition loved them.

The Special Report continued:

It would, I think, be a serious mistake to take lightly the impact of the Proxmire hearings. He has been very effective, particularly on television. The administration, however, had not come off well. Witnesses from the Pentagon, with the exception of Barry Shillito and Johnny Foster, have been indecisive, defensive, and often ill-prepared. Except for Senator Goldwater and Congressman Rivers, the friendly forces in Congress have been conspicuously quiet. . . . And the Pentagon's muzzling for 72 hours [a vain attempt to keep me from testifying before Proxmire again] of the Air Force civilian who first exposed the C-5A overrun was a classic case of poor public relations, exceeded only by the five large defense contractors who refused to appear before the committee to present their case. . . .

While the buck stops at the President's desk, the heat ought not to be concentrated there. The attack on ABM and on defense spending has centered on the President because DOD, congressional and party officials are not doing the appropriate thing — sticking their necks out. Every time some obscure critic belches, *The New York Times* reports it on page one. We have to expect that, but surely we can generate a little support among our friends if some initiative and good judgment and toughness is displayed. We have noticed among our friendly columnists and papers an attitude of lying low which suggests to us that they don't know what line to take . . . about the Proxmire hearings. Surely Secretary Laird must have some goodies stashed away over there on the McNamara years that Mollenhoff and others could use with some effectiveness.

Richard Nixon drew a half circle around the last sentence and noted in the right-hand margin, "Check this." But Mollenhoff told me later that he was never asked to check anything. The truth was that McNamara and the whiz kids didn't start the mess in Pentagon management; they simply made it worse, especially in the later years, when the Johnson administration was preoccupied with the war in Southeast Asia.

The report went on:

Perhaps this sort of thing is inappropriate — dirty politics and unstatesmanlike. But it strikes me that we have a tough fight on our hands, and it strikes me that we ought to fight like we are used to power and know how to use it.

Our opponents will scream bloody murder if we really turn the heat on them, but they will know we mean business, that we're not soft, and that they cannot expect to fire away with immunity.

Right below this passage Nixon wrote "E — have Huston and Buchanan work with defense and congress to stir up some activity." (Nixon, in his second deposition to my lawyers, said that the E stood for John Ehrlichman.)

Those who remember Watergate will scarcely be astonished to find Huston recommending "dirty politics and unstatesmanlike" deeds and Richard Nixon endorsing it. Henry Kissinger and his assistant, Colonel Alexander Haig, had already started their wiretapping campaign against dissidents and suspected "leakers." As William Safire recounted in his book *Before the Fall*, Haig gave the names of his suspects to William "Crazy Billy" Sullivan of the FBI, who then arranged the wiretaps.

Sullivan, said to be Nixon's favorite FBI agent, was one of those involved in an attempt to pin something — perhaps an espionage rap — on me. On May 29, 1969, Alexander Butterfield, a retired Air Force colonel and former schoolmate of Robert Haldeman, and at that time a kind of doorkeeper for the Oval Office, wrote Ehrlichman and Colonel Hughes of the White House staff a memorandum:

> It has come to my attention — by word of several mouths, but allegedly from a senior AFL-CIO official originally — that a civilian named A. Ernest Fitzgerald, presumably employed by the Department of the Navy, is about to blow the whistle on the Navy by exposing to full public view that service's "shoddy purchasing practices." Evidently, Fitzgerald attended a recent meeting of the National Democratic Coalition and, while there, revealed his intentions to a labor representative who, fortunately for us, was unsympathetic.
>
> I believe that this information has already been passed to Bill Sullivan at Justice (FBI), but I thought I should alert each of you to the facts as they were presented to me.

When I first read this memo many years later, I was charmed with its pure silliness. Why would I plan to "blow the whistle" on the Navy? My special knowledge was Air Force boondoggles. Why would I be "about" to do that, when I had testified six months earlier? The whole report baffled me. (I have never, incidentally, liked the newspaper term "whistle blower," because it tends to set apart and isolate taxpayers' employees who do what they're paid to do — tell the truth.)

I finally figured out some of it. In May a minister from Connecticut named Joe Duffy had phoned me with an invitation to join him at a banquet for Senator Edward Kennedy. We met at the hotel, had dinner with about a thousand other people, and listened to some forgettable speeches. That was all.

But many years later, through a Freedom of Information request, I got a heavily censored copy of an FBI report in reply to Butterfield's memorandum. This fruit of "Crazy Billy" Sullivan's investigations, dated June 20, 1969, was addressed to J. Edgar Hoover. Its subject was, in part, "miscellaneous information concerning espionage." The first page is largely blanked out; the second page reveals only the site (the Sheraton-Park Hotel) and the sponsor of the dinner (the New Democratic Coalition). The third page, after censorship, yields only the information that Ernest Fitzgerald was "third in command of top civilians in the Air Force, and the man who had exposed USAF for excessive contract costs." Fortunately, I was never hanged on charges of espionage for exposing excessive contract costs.

On June 17, at the final session of Senator Proxmire's hearings on military waste, I presented information on more C-5A problems and other embarrassing failures. (A few days earlier the Air Force had tried to keep me from doing this by muzzling me for seventy-two hours.) After I returned to the Pentagon, Secretary of Defense Laird called me in. Present also were his military assistant, Colonel Robert Pursley and — to impress me — Deputy Secretary of Defense David Packard. Laird, friendly and smiling, said that Jack Edwards and Bill Dickinson had spoken highly of me (Proxmire and Moorhead had also tried to intervene). He said Dave would have things under control in short order.

When I asked Dave how he planned to go about it, Packard stared at me, apparently incredulous that a nobody industrial engineer would dare question one of the eminent industrialists of the age. After spending some time puffing on his pipe, he said, "I'm going to select good people, the best people I can find, and put them in charge and let them alone — just like I did at Hewlett Packard."

It was foreordained that the "good people" whose names would be sent to Packard would be the military officers who had been in charge of big Pentagon programs. The ones who had excelled in getting and spending money, not necessarily in acquiring useful products, and certainly not in operating with economy and efficiency. Packard was going to put the biggest-spending officers in charge and "let them alone."

I was appalled. I had seen other highly regarded businessmen fail as Pentagon managers because they did not understand — or so I thought — how fundamentally the Pentagon differs from private business. In a truly competitive private business, each branch manager has the job of maximizing revenues and minimizing costs. The profit and loss statement is the Book of Judgment. But the Pentagon has no profit and loss statements. The job of Pentagon managers is to get money and to spend it on schedule. The two financial management indicators are obligations, which commit monies to be spent, and outlays, which record the spending. Meeting the goals of these two is called "executing the program."

I thought then that Packard was naive. How wrong I was. Gently, I tried to explain why his plan had to be reinforced with some other measures. My suggestions were not welcomed. Packard, incensed, puffed furiously on his pipe. After about twenty minutes Laird ended the meeting, saying we would get together another time. He left the problem of what to do with me in the hands of Colonel Pursley. They were going to go through the motions, at least, of placing me in a job somewhere.

I had become acquainted with Bob Pursley, one of our more intelligent

Air Force officers, when he was an assistant to Robert McNamara and I was working on the faltering F-III program. I had a high regard for him, but unfortunately he was a product of his conditioning. Military *omertà* was part of his code. After the meeting he wrote a memorandum to Laird:

> The more I reflected on our meeting Tuesday, the bigger plus it became. Ernie's analysis of weapons system management has so much merit it would be a shame to lose the value of his insights. The danger of a maverick in our midst is clear, however. I wonder if it would be useful on Monday June 23 to ask him to reduce some of his *key concepts* to writing. It would be a brief paper outlining:
> — major problem areas
> — organizational changes desirable
> — procedural changes desirable
> — the utility or disutility, as he sees it, of going to the Hill, as he has, versus working through (a) the old administration and (b) the new administration.
> The last policy is the key. If he feels his contacts have continuing value, that would be a factor in deciding whether to keep him on the team. If he signs a paper disavowing — in any way — his current *modus operandi*, such a paper could be of great value if he were to jump the fence again.

My *modus operandi*, of course, was simply to speak about problems and propose solutions. My sin was that I was doing it in public. Pursley wanted me to sign a paper stating that I would agree to gag myself, a statement that could be used against me if I ever again said anything in public. The man was way ahead of his time.

Pursley's career was on the rise. He later became important enough to have his phones tapped on Henry Kissinger's orders, but he passed the telephone loyalty test. His promotion to three-star rank in the Air Force presumably gave him more scope for his ideas about loyalty tests to protect the system of big spending.

Pursley followed up with a series of memorandums to Laird, all raising the question of my loyalty. Loyalty to the Army, Navy, and Air Force in the field? No, he was speaking of loyalty to "the team" that was ripping off the public treasury for the benefit of some giant corporations and their allies in government. The armed forces were getting less equipment than the expenditure warranted, and in many cases equipment that didn't perform very well. What about loyalty to the taxpayers who paid the bills?

On July 11, 1958, Congress had passed a Code of Ethics, ten commandments for every person in government service. The first was to "put loyalty to highest moral principles and to country above loyalty to persons, party, or government department." Commandment four was to "seek to find and employ more efficient and more economical ways of getting tasks accomplished." The shortest was number nine: "Expose corruption wherever discovered." A cynic might note that most congressmen didn't mean a word of it. And "the team" counted on that.

After my meeting with Laird in June until I was fired in November, I kept trying to do my regular job. Little by little, however, I was stripped of important functions and excluded from meetings. I persisted in trying to complete the reports on C-5A technical performance I'd promised the Joint Economic Committee and SEC investigators interviewed me several times in connection with their probe of insider trading and Lockheed's C-5A debacle.

Meanwhile the tide had turned in favor of Richard Nixon. The moon landing in July was a public relations bonanza, even though his administration had little to do with it. His hard line attacks on critics of military spending paid off; he won every round against congressional attempts to cancel dubious weapons systems.

Melvin Laird prospered as well. His standing was so high that he could afford to make long-range plans to boost Pentagon spending even though the war in Southeast Asia was supposedly winding down. Opponents of the war had assumed that its end would bring a "peace dividend," a $30 billion reduction in an $80 billion military budget. Laird and his friends laid plans to head off this dangerous development.

His first move was deceptive. On October 18, 1969, he wrote to Paul McCracken, chairman of Nixon's Council of Economic Advisers, to discuss the impact of defense spending on the economy. He summarized military-contracting activity for the past June and July: DoD outlays for the military and for national defense were the highest since 1967; shipments of defense products were the highest since 1953; DoD procurement outlays were the highest since 1954; manufacturers' inventories for defense products were the highest in history.

Laird admitted that "it does appear that the defense spending is contributing toward overheating the economy at an unprecedented rate"; as a result, he said, he was cutting $4.1 billion from outlays. The truth was that the administration — despite some victories on behalf of wasteful programs — had lost a battle on Capitol Hill. In an effort to get Nixon to end the war, a congressional consensus had formed to essentially freeze the military budget. Laird was making a virtue of necessity.

All this called for some modest budget trimming and some careful shielding in the Bureau of the Budget and the Pentagon to protect the core group of big contractors as much as possible. Budget director Robert Mayo and his deputy, James Schlesinger, worked on the Pentagon budget problem but in the end left the details up to David Packard. As Mayo said later (January 31, 1980) in a deposition to my lawyers, "We left it up to his discretion, however, armed with what we had given him . . . because he was running the Department, as a practical matter, for Mel Laird."

But at about that time McCracken, veering in the opposite direction, told Nixon that he feared a recession. Ever obliging, Laird wrote McCracken that the Defense Department stood ready to pump up the economy by spending more, if necessary.

That fall the Nixon administration decided to "get tough" — a policy proposed by Buchanan, Huston, and Kissinger and adopted by Nixon. It was the time of the "silent majority" speech and Nixon's confrontation with the Vietnam demonstrators. No one was in any mood to pay attention to the bleeding hearts and wimps who complained that my firing — on November 4 — was illegal. That firing was pulled out of the hat as a "reorganization." Nothing personal, you understand. But in explaining my removal to their supporters on the Hill, Seamans and Schedler told a different story: Fitzgerald was not a "team player." This was a personal charge having nothing to do with the supposed reduction in force. If I had had evidence of this charge at the time, I could have been reinstated.

Seamans had called Representative Gerald Ford's office and volunteered that I was fired for cause, not as the result of a RIF. He complained that at a Proxmire hearing I had "made it extremely difficult" for Assistant Secretary of the Air Force Whittaker and that he couldn't use a man who did that. (Whittaker had tried to convince the Proxmire committee that the C-5A was a great little airplane with no technical problems.) Ford's assistant wrote a memo to his boss about Seamans's complaint — a memo Ford kept covered up for many years.

As soon as the deed was done, Seamans called Bryce Harlow at the White House to let him know that I had finally been disposed of. Harlow was to rally the Nixon supporters on Capitol Hill and fend off the congressmen who might complain; their letters or petitions would do little good. Only Congressman Dickinson agreed to testify on my behalf. Senator Len Jordan, ill and retired, sent a written statement of support. Unknown to me, however, I had two secret supporters in a most unlikely place: the White House itself.

3

$$\star \quad \star \quad \star$$

"Let Him Bleed"

ONE EVENING in the fall of 1969, after I had received my notice of termination, I was at a party at the home of Jim Free of the *Birmingham News*. There I was introduced to Clark Mollenhoff, now Nixon's ombudsman. He listened to the story of my recent adventures in the Pentagon and a little later confided to my wife, "He'll be all right as long as he's telling the truth." It seemed to be an implied promise that he'd try to do something for me. (At the time I didn't know that Nixon himself was involved in my firing.) Mollenhoff's coming down on my side was not so surprising. He was an old-fashioned fiscal conservative whose political heroes were the two cheapest men in Congress: Senator John Williams of Delaware and Representative H. R. Gross, the abominable no-man from Iowa.

Mollenhoff didn't forget my case. Shortly thereafter he enlisted the help of Pat Buchanan, who was already becoming a power on the White House staff. Buchanan's roots were in the conservative, anti-Communist, Catholic middle class, which tended to see criticism of the military as a hidden thrust against our war in Southeast Asia. But these people also favored fiscal frugality in government; they didn't like crooks and wasters. What I saw in Buchanan, and a great many Republicans like him, was a transition from a belief in financial prudence as an overall principle to a belief that prudence shouldn't apply to the military. (Buchanan later crossed that bridge easily and became an ardent supporter of the biggest spender of all time, Ronald Reagan.)

Nixon had a lot of admiration for the abilities of this young, combative right-winger, who had worked for him since 1966. A fierce counterattacker against congressional probes, Buchanan was one of the movers in the new "get tough" policy. (He later routed the Watergate committee much as Oliver North routed the Iran-Contra committee.) But in my case, Buchanan made a determined effort on behalf of the truth. In fact, I might venture to suggest that he was in the same camp as Senator Proxmire and his committee.

Mollenhoff's first attempts to talk to Nixon about my case were blocked by Robert Haldeman. When Dwight Chapin tried again, Haldeman wrote him, "I'll handle. Just drop this one." So Mollenhoff enlisted Buchanan. One of Buchanan's duties was to prepare the President's Briefing Book, with sample questions and answers, before press conferences. Whenever possible, Nixon's press aides would plant questions with favorable reporters or with one who was working on a particular issue.

A presidential press conference was scheduled for December 8, 1969. On December 4 Buchanan wrote a memorandum to Nixon noting that one of the issues would probably be "Ernest Fitzgerald and the C-5A," and he wrote John Ehrlichman to ask "our position on this fellow we fired who is filing suit against the President's decision to oust him." The last six words are most revealing. The world at large did not know that the president had ousted me, but obviously it was common knowledge among the White House staff.

The questioners persisted. Buchanan wrote to Bill Baroody, Melvin Laird's assistant, saying, "We urgently need a QA on the question of Mr. Fitzgerald, the C-5A man." Mollenhoff got Bud Krogh (later famous for his role as head of the White House plumbers' unit) to write to Kissinger's assistant, Al Haig, that "it will be interpreted as if we fired Mr. Fitzgerald for telling the truth about the C-5A." The answers were, predictably, not very helpful. A Colonel Knight in Melvin Laird's office sent Mollenhoff a paper prepared by Seamans and okayed by Packard. The paper was the standard Air Force defense of my firing, and it implied that Mollenhoff should stop bothering them.

On December 5 the Pentagon sent Buchanan the sample question and answer for the upcoming press conference. They proposed that Nixon simply brush off any question about my firing by saying that he had utter confidence in Laird and Seamans and had left the decision up to them.

Buchanan, not impressed, wrote another memorandum to the president:

The Pentagon is catching hell from liberals and conservatives for firing a guy whose only crime seems to be that he was an aggressive investigator who found mistakes in the procurement of the transport which cost billions.

In PR terms we're getting a beating, and why should we?

Mollenhoff's investigation finds that the guy is a good public servant, and he has the public behind him. Why should we purge him — simply to make the bureaucrats at the Pentagon happy?

Mollenhoff's suggestion to you (with which I agree) is that the President say, if asked:

"It is true that Mr. Fitzgerald's job is being abolished, but it is not because of his performance in it; he has, to my knowledge, been a dedicated and effective public servant. After looking into it, I have decided to direct the Defense Secretary to find Mr. Fitzgerald another position, of equal pay and stature — not a make-work job — where his talents can continue to be used by this Administration."

Making the President appear to be a just man is worth ticking off the fellows out to get this guy.

Pat Buchanan was so confident he had sold his argument to Nixon that be brought the proposed Q and A to Haldeman with a slip reading, "Fitzgerald reinstated." Buchanan told my lawyers at his deposition that he recognized the handwriting on the slip as Nixon's.

But Buchanan underestimated the resources of Bryce Harlow, who was concealing a lot. In a later deposition Mollenhoff said, "[Harlow] not only told me nothing of any pre-termination communication he had had with the Air Force on the subject, but he stated expressedly that he had no prior knowledge of the termination decision and knew only what he had heard on the Hill." About three years after this conversation, the Oval Office taping system recorded Nixon saying, "Bryce was all for canning him [Fitzgerald]."

Instead of revealing any of this, Harlow told Mollenhoff that there were stories "floating around the Hill" that Fitzgerald was a "bad man in essence, and that he was someone the administration should get rid of." But, he said, if Mollenhoff could show there was nothing to such rumors, he would give Nixon the memo recommending reversal of the firing.

There is no evidence that he ever did.

Now the Pentagon decided to drop its biggest bomb on its worst gadfly. Its biggest bomb, in more ways than one, was David Packard. He called Bryce Harlow on December 6 "to register a vehement protest against any move in the White House area to require continued use of Mr. Fitzgerald." Harlow recorded this in a December 8 memo to Haldeman, adding, "He [Packard] said he would talk with you about this." That did it. Packard, the richest and one of the most prestigious of all Nixon's appointees, delivered a big bang in the administration.

My reinstatement was killed before it got off the ground.

At the press conference on December 8, Sarah McClendon delivered the expected Fitzgerald question. A veteran White House correspondent representing a string of small Texas newspapers, McClendon had been the scourge of presidents since the 1950s. Most of the other reporters considered her too aggressive, not deferential enough to our elected rulers. I thought she was terrific.

When her turn came, Sarah lectured Nixon on the injustice done me and asked if he was going to do anything about it. The assembled press corps laughed, and Nixon chuckled along with them. It was a great opportunity to defuse the issue. Instead of hauling out the pompous Pentagon script about his great confidence in Laird, etcetera, he said, "Well, Sarah, after the way you put it, I guess I'd better."

Mollenhoff, unaware that my firing had been agreed on by the Pentagon and the president months before, for years believed that it was McClendon's snapping at his heels that allowed Nixon to brush off the matter as a joke. But Mollenhoff didn't shelve the affair. The next day he got a note from Haldeman stating, "The P. [president] has asked Mayo to bring Fitzgerald into the Budget Bureau to work in non-defense areas."

When Nixon later made a deposition on all this, he correctly stated that he had been in a tug of war between the Mollenhoff-Buchanan side (apparently he never knew that Jeb Stuart Magruder concurred) and the opposition, made up of the Pentagon heavyweights and Bryce Harlow.

In retrospect, it is clear that the administration thought it was arguing over a public relations question. They completely missed the point. In the large sense, Ernest Fitzgerald was important only as a man who represented a thesis vital to the well-being of the United States of America. If any high officer had understood that the real issue was protecting the treasury against the military-industrial combine, he might have advocated replacing me with someone even tougher. The decision to fire me was bound to send a powerful signal throughout the government and the contractor community: the guard dog has been removed because he growled.

On December 17 Nixon scheduled a what-to-do-with-Fitzgerald meeting and called in Robert Mayo, James Schlesinger of the Bureau of the Budget (BoB), Ehrlichman, and (according to Ehrlichman's notes) Kissinger. The meeting log shows that the P's compromise was ratified: "Schlesinger — Put Fitzgerald in Budget on non-defense problems." Nixon's idea of a compromise — "to make the President appear to be a just man," in Buchanan's words — was meaningless. It assumed that I could be buried in the bowels of the BoB, where I could exercise my cost-cutting passions on school lunch programs and the pensions of disabled veterans.

Even the Budget Bureau had a distaste for the idea. At that time I had friends and supporters in the bureau and a record of inciting my colleagues to protect the taxpayers' interests. That would never do. Mayo, the director, and Schlesinger, his deputy, undoubtedly wanted no "maverick in their midst" any more than the Pentagon did. In a much later deposition to my lawyers, Schlesinger stated, "Given Mr. Fitzgerald's reputation as a source of information to Capitol Hill and to Senator Proxmire, specifically, I thought he would be a disruptive factor in the operations of the Bureau of the Budget." When asked where he got his impression of my reputation, the good doctor, bringing to bear all his scholarly principles of valid proof and objectivity, answered, "Well, I think that was acquired generally through the press and probably by chitchat that may have gone along." (His other source was Robert Seamans.) And naturally Schlesinger saw the danger as being "the leaks that have occurred . . . and the detrimental effect [they] might have directly on requests to the Congress regarding defense appropriations."

In the end Schlesinger prevailed upon Mayo to meet with Nixon on December 23 and plead that he had no room for me in the BoB. Nixon's small resolve crumbled. Mayo testified afterward in his deposition that the president said, "Bob, you are absolutely right that I don't think there really is a place for Mr. Fitzgerald in your organization." Packard to Seamans to Schlesinger to Mayo to Nixon — a superb infield single-play combination.

About a week later Ehrlichman told Mollenhoff the news. But Mollenhoff, knowing nothing of the high-level meeting, plunged on in his attempts to help me. While the president could easily swat a Sarah McClendon, Mollenhoff wrote to Ehrlichman, Senator Proxmire and his investigators were another order of menace, "particularly since they have allies in the liberal press and a few allies in the conservative press . . . [and] it is obvious that Senator Proxmire does not intend to drop this matter."

Proxmire didn't drop the matter but, unfortunately, he made a tactical error in pursuing it. Because my firing was on its face a violation of Title 18, Section 1505, of the U.S. Criminal Code, which makes it a serious crime to interfere with the work of a congressional committee or to retaliate against one of its witnesses, he turned the matter over to the Justice Department, along with the evidence he had gathered, and asked that the attorney general "apprehend the felons in the Pentagon" who had fired me. Ah, what an age of innocence that was! But, to be fair, neither Proxmire nor any of the rest knew that Attorney General John Mitchell would end up in prison a few years hence.

When Justice got Proxmire's request, it promptly turned the assignment over to the accused: it asked the Air Force to investigate itself. The Air Force lawyers, as was later revealed, put together a sheaf of neatly chosen evidence to show that no crime had been committed. As succinctly summarized by Air Force Assistant General Counsel Hugh Gilmore in a memo of November 25, 1969, to Colonel Simokaitis of Seamans's office, the Air Force lawyers were "assembling the necessary documentation to show that there were no violations of law."

Mollenhoff, for his part, kept the pot boiling. He was able to do so, not because the White House had such respect for an ombudsman, but simply because they feared him. Mollenhoff, an honest cop at heart, with a rare capacity for sustained outrage, had a long record of exposing waste, fraud, and corruption. And because he had a wide circle of political and media connections, the White House staff handled him gingerly. Quite a few people went through quite a few empty motions to keep him from booming. To give a hint of the general White House IQ in those days, on January 3, 1970, Haldeman wrote to his gofer, Larry Higby, asking him "to please find out the status of Fitzpatrick [sic], the guy they fired at the Defense Department." Haldeman added that "after I get this report, you should remind me that the President wants Ziegler to call in Sarah McLyndon [sic. Haldeman also referred to her as "the big broad"] and tell her what we have done with Fitzpatrick."

On January 5 Fitzpatrick or Fitzgerald, whatever his name was, packed his briefcase, wrote "time wounds all heels" on his office blackboard, climbed into his old Rambler, and drove away from the Pentagon thinking he would never return.

My more extensive parting comments appeared in the *Washington Post* the next day. Among the most incensed was Alexander Butterfield, Haldeman's deputy. He addressed his remarks to Higby on January 6. The next day Higby conveyed Butterfield's views to Haldeman in a memo:

> Let him bleed for awhile. He is one hundred percent disloyal — not without expertise in his field, but nevertheless one hundred percent idsloyal [sic]. His parting word to the administration appeared in this morning's *Washington Post* — they were, in essence, "the big dogs will be all right in this administration, but the little people never will."

That's not exactly what I said, but I wish I had. Butterfield went on to say that it would be "an admission of error" to bring me back into the government.

In his January 7 memo, Higby answered Haldeman's request to "find out the status of Fitzpatrick," relaying the two-week-old news about the meeting with Nixon and the president's decision to keep me out of the BoB.

It was time to hear from "the world's greatest newspaper," as the *Chicago Tribune* describes itself. That may be more than a little hyperbole, but the paper is very good, especially when it comes to exposing crookedness and duplicity in government. Mollenhoff and Buchanan were friends with Willard Edwards, a conservative journalist on the paper, who on December 10 had reported that the president had decided to give me a nondefense job in the BoB. When it was apparent that the double-cross was in, the *Tribune* delivered itself on a powerful editorial. As Pat Buchanan recapitulated it in the president's daily news summary:

> Despite surface indications that the Nixon administration might be different, Ernest Fitzgerald learned the truth of an old government adage — never rock the boat. Don't buck the bureaucracy. If you do, they'll get your job. Somewhere along the line, between the President's reported decision to keep Fitzgerald and the final moments of his job, the gears failed to mesh. As he cleared out his Pentagon desk, preparing to go into business as a private consultant, Fitzgerald said he had been offered no new government job. In earlier years, the Johnson and Kennedy administrations suffered from their treatment of another dedicated public servant, Otto Otepka, who also committed the sin of testifying truthfully before a congressional committee. The equally shabby treatment of Fitzgerald adds no luster to the Nixon Administration. It can only be a victory for the entrenched Pentagon bureaucrats.

The coupling of my name with that of Otto Otepka spelled big trouble for me with the liberal establishment. Otepka, a State Department security specialist in the Kennedy administration, had had custody of certain "personnel security files." Like the derogatory dirt files of General Cappucci and "Crazy Billy" Sullivan, Otepka's files contained false charges, gossip, and innuendo. When Otepka was called on to deliver his files to Senator John McClellan's investigations subcommittee, he complied. For this he was fired.

The liberals, outraged, argued that delivering the dirt files to the Senate meant that the subjects of the files suffered disgraceful exposure without any chance to confront their accusers. They missed the point: the wrong was the existence of the dirt files in the first place; Otepka was merely obeying the law and doing his duty. To be consistent, the liberals should have demanded that all government dirt files (except those that were part of an active criminal investigation) be returned to their subjects and the victims of false charges and slander be given free rein to sue their accusers for damages in a civil action. But the liberals were not consistent.

Conservatives, on the other hand, had thundered in Otepka's defense, and Nixon had promised, if elected, to make him whole. But once in office, Nixon choked. Instead of restoring Otepka to the bosom of the State Department, he gave him a luxurious and meaningless job on the impotent Subversive Activities Control Board. The *Tribune*'s parallel between Otepka and Fitzgerald was enough to pull Nixon's chain, so he marked the "treatment of Fitzgerald" passage and noted in the margin, "H [Haldeman] — I wonder if we fumbled this one — check it out again — "

So once again the staff went through the tired motions of checking out nothing. Haldeman bucked the problem to the staff secretary, who bucked it to Kissinger on January 16, who bucked it in a "Secret/Eyes Only" memo to Laird on the nineteenth.

Mollenhoff was tireless, though. He egged Edwards on to do another column titled "Fitzgerald Is Now Nixon's Otepka," and he hectored Laird to reverse the firing decision. This combination of events made the anti-Fitzgeraldians jittery; with another press conference coming in a few days, they worried that the P might backslide again and decide to restore the maverick.

Butterfield was incensed once more. On January 20 he put on his spurs, loaded his horse pistol, and delivered to Haldeman another memorandum on my disloyalty. He cited the infamous National Democratic Coalition dinner, but this time he got the name of the service in question correct: he said I'd planned to blow the whistle on the Air Force, not the Navy. Never let it be said that White House functionaries are incapable of learning. (Appendix A is Butterfield's entire screed, to give readers a sample of a certain brand of military ethics.) Butterfield sent copies of this diatribe to Ehrlichman, Kissinger, Klein, Colson, Nofziger, Magruder, and Ziegler. But he made one serious mistake: Magruder gave his copy to Senator Daniel Inouye, who later brought out the "let him bleed" memo at the Watergate hearings.

It was Magruder, ironically, who on January 21 wrote the administration's official line on the Fitzgerald matter:

> The Nixon Administration has no quarrel with the [Proxmire] subcommittee report on the C-5A program and its assertion that the prior administration did not adequately control military spending. Defense Secretary Laird had asserted that the past mistakes in the procurement of this aircraft will not be repeated.

The testimony of Mr. A. Ernest Fitzgerald on the cost overruns was no embarrassment to the Nixon Administration, for it involved actions taken under a prior administration. Conscientious efforts are being made to correct the problems pointed up by an Air Force team that included Mr. Fitzgerald. There is no reason for the Nixon Administration to retaliate against Mr. Fitzgerald, since his testimony dealt with the acts of the prior administration.

Air Force Secretary Robert Seamans has stated that there is no relationship between Mr. Fitzgerald's testimony of November, 1968 and the reorganization decisions to abolish his job in October, 1969.

This masterpiece of hypocrisy, which we later uncovered in legal discovery, was sent to Kissinger by White House staffer William Watts; in the checkoff space labeled "approve as is" were Kissinger's initials. Three days later Watts wrote a "cover-your-ass" memo for the record, noting that he'd told Magruder of Kissinger's approval.

Conveniently for my lawyers and me, Higby bundled up a lot of memorandums on the Fitzgerald problem and sent them all to presidential counsel Fred Fielding with the handwritten notation, "Eyes Only!" The whole package came to us in legal discovery some years later.

Kissinger finally disposed of his "review" of my case on February 2 with this reply to Nixon: "Jeb Magruder's report on Mr. Fitzgerald is attached at tab G. Dr. Kissinger feels no further action is necessary." Recall that Magruder's memo said there was "no reason to retaliate" against Fitzgerald and there was "no connection" between my testimony and the decision to abolish my job. And compare that with Kissinger's ultimate remark on the matter in his book *The White House Years*: "Former Air Force analyst A. Ernest Fitzgerald *who had been fired for denouncing C-5A cost overruns...*" (page 113, emphasis added). Which goes to prove, I guess, that some politicians who lie in office will tell the truth in their memoirs. I'd prefer it the other way around.

In Mel Laird's final word (a memo of February 19 to Kissinger and Haig), he noted, "Stories such as the 10 January editorial in *The Chicago Tribune* appear to emanate from other White House staff offices. It would be helpful if you could stop such stories at the source."

He meant Mollenhoff. Not surprisingly, his days as an ombudsman were numbered. The presidential log for May 25, 1970, has a handwritten note: "Had Mollenhoff in — he's quitting to go back to Des Moines Register as Bureau Chief. Good break both ways. Z [Ziegler] especially delighted."

Ron Ziegler, the White House press secretary, Nixon's flack, had good reason to be delighted. Mollenhoff had never made secret his contempt for the flack's intelligence and character. His acid test for a words-of-one-syllable explanation was, "Make it so even Ron Ziegler can understand." But what outraged Mollenhoff most were the public statements Ziegler pumped out daily with their remarkably high fraud content.

What had broken Mollenhoff's ombudsman spirit was a March 8 memo from Haldeman saying, "No member of the White House staff — and this very specifically includes you — is to have any communication with or make any statement or provide any information to any member of the press without prior consultation with Ron Ziegler."

The Nixon administration, with all its crimes, is often thought of as an anomaly, but in a great many ways, it was not much different from either its predecessors or its successors. People such as Harold Brown, James Schlesinger, and Henry Kissinger are indispensable front men and mouthpieces for the great, interlocked Pentagon-corporation complex that traffics in the greater part of our federal funds. A large part of their onstage role is to produce threats from abroad (real, half-real, or imagined) and phony economic justification for a corrupt and wasteful spending program.

These men are the Praetorian Guard commanders. But the people I offended originally were the centurions, the permanent Pentagon cadre, a powerful brotherhood. Many, though not all, of them are procurement people who go on steadily year after year, fronting for the big corporations, systematically wasting money, and in the end providing the armed forces of the United States with inferior equipment and weaponry.

On July 9, 1973, several years after I was fired, a Nixon White House lawyer, Dudley Chapman, wrote in a memorandum to his boss, Leonard Garment, that there was "a clear public impression" that I had "an independent, acerbic personality un-acceptable to the career military brass and that both Democratic and Republican appointees deferred to that view." I agree to take that as one man's comment. But it is a comment on style, not substance. What was — and is — woefully wrong is a matter of substance.

4

☆ ☆ ☆

The Cost-Plus Economy

FIRED FROM THE PENTAGON and effectively blacklisted in my former profession as an industrial engineer, I took some part-time jobs to support my family. My lawyers filed an appeal with the Civil Service Commission asking that my illegal firing be reversed so I could go back to my unfinished business in the Pentagon. Even the strongest appeal typically takes years, however, and in the meantime I had to make a living.

Senator Proxmire and Chairman Wright Patman of the Joint Economic Committee gave me some work to do for the JEC, and I was asked by the Businessmen's Educational Fund (BEF) to make some appearances and speeches under their sponsorship. The BEF was a very dignified, and expensive, kind of protest movement against the war in Southeast Asia: members were expected to contribute at least $25,000 a year to the organization.

I welcomed the chance to talk to these people about the peculiar processes of the military mind from a perspective a little different from their own. They were repulsed by the whole concept of "body counts" (the counts included women, old men, and children — some of my military friends said they knew of dead animals being counted). And, like a majority of other Americans, they were shocked by the nightly scenes of war on television.

Beyond these horrors, what worried me about the war was the evident fact that it had no goals. We were supposedly trying to protect the "idea" of an independent, noncommunist government in South Vietnam, but what specific goals we were trying to achieve and what we meant by "winning" were very uncertain.

I told my BEF friends that the body-count idea showed the military analysts' compulsion to quantify and rationalize. One hundred dead bodies here and two hundred there were just like line items in the Pentagon's accounting. Each step would be justified, and eventually they would be figured into some insane and irrelevant total. Perhaps, in the long run, we should worry most about the kind of mentality that produces such totals and believes that they prove something.

In addition, in the minds of the military and their fellows, the war created, subconsciously perhaps, a picture of an ideal society. In theory, our country would be united in a common cause, everyone would have a job, for the war economy would be booming, people (except for war widows and orphans) would be happy, and the military — once again respected — would assume its proper leadership role. The hidden elements in this equation were, of course, great waste (of life and materiel), great profiteering by a few, and the artificiality of a military-based economy. This society was draining its resources, both material and moral, and producing nothing.

My father, a skilled artisan, pattern maker, and self-taught engineer, turned to farming after his health went bad. He raised beef cattle. Once, when I recited to him the Pentagon's waste-makes-you-rich theory, he said, "I never saw a cow get fat sucking herself." He was referring to an actual phenomenon: cows that satisfy their hunger by sucking their own teats. That diminishes their urge to graze, and they produce less and less milk and begin to decline. Unless they are broken of the habit, they will die. It was a good parable.

My BEF patrons believed that once the war was behind us, we could make a healthy "conversion" back to the assumptions of a free and peaceable society. The big military contractors would beat their corporate swords into plowshares and gratefully switch from making stuff to kill people to making stuff to help us all live better. As a corollary to that, they envisioned a "peace dividend" of $20 billion to $30 billion a year that could be used for domestic needs.

What they didn't understand was that an influential part of the nation had contracted the cow's bad habit and wasn't about to give it up. My BEF friends looked forward to the end of a militarized wartime society, but I was worried about the advent of a militarized peacetime.

The shrewd old men in Congress, in whom the real power resides when they wish to use it, decided rather too late in the 1960s to end the war by their own kind of attrition. They effectively froze the Pentagon's acquisition budget, which included procurement plus research and development. As General Pete Crow told me then, the war would end when Congress decided to end it. "They'll let us know when they're serious. They'll cut off the money," he said. The mad old days when mad old Mendel Rivers could use cutthroat tactics in the House Armed Services Committee, silencing all dissent against limitless funds for the Pentagon, were gone. Congress finally got serious.

For a moment. Once the war was over, the seriousness began to evaporate. (To paraphrase Senator Aiken of Vermont in another context, Congress declared a victory and went home.) The enormous silent pressures for a military-spending economy weren't to be denied. Even in 1970 it was apparent that our bovine bad habit had become an addiction. Big business, big labor, the big universities had become war-bucks addicts. Bankers needed the contracts to bail out sick corporate clients. Communities fought for them, economists extolled them.

By now a new breed of industrialist knew that the market for killing stuff was rich and easy. Their objectives were as Professor Seymour Melman put it in his book *Profits without Production* (1983), maximization of costs and subsidy. And by and large the government purchasing market didn't worry much about quality.

In contrast, the market for better living stuff demanded, for the most part, efficient production of quality goods that real people wanted to buy at a reasonable price. This market required working hard and competing hard against the company down the street that was trying to use more efficient means to make even higher-quality goods than yours. My upright and old-fashioned BEF friends didn't understand the gap between new industry and old when they talked about the "conversion" of the economy.

By this time the big contracting corporations were in their second or third generation of management by the "new breed" of executive. These men found that the rewards lay in maximizing allowable costs and getting, under various guises, what amounted to welfare from the government. As *business* enterprises in the traditional sense, their corporations were not viable. They were massive constructions of organized inefficiency. The main thing to note about the people who ran them is that they had lost the one ruling principle of the old-era capitalists: they no longer cared about delivering the best quality at the lowest price.

There were exceptions, of course. I came to know quite a few people who felt trapped by the system. Many of them had little real work to do, but they had gotten accustomed to the large salaries, fringe benefits, and retirement prospects, and they did not believe they could earn these in a competitive business. They had lost their self-respect and had accepted the corporate immorality. To protest in any way would probably cast them up on the same desert island as Ernest Fitzgerald and Henry Durham. (Durham told the public embarrassing truths about Lockheed's mismanagement of the C-5A transport plane; as a result he was fired, and he received many threats that he would be killed, his house burned, and his teen-age daughter disfigured.)

In the late 1960s a subtle antiwar current was emanating from a not very obvious source: the Pentagon. Most people do not realize that the Department of Defense and the dominant palace guard factions of its service departments hate war. Occasional bloodlettings keep the public in the right mood, but actual war is disruptive, disconcerting, and disorganizing. A lot of strangers have to be brought into the armed services, and the pressure is on to work hard and produce results. Worst of all, a great deal of the money is spent on troops and support (the traditional Bs of logistics: boots, blankets, beans, bacon, and bullets). The Pentagon prays that war will never really happen, but it loves its main mission in life: eternally preparing for war. I once heard an Air Force general say that there didn't seem to be much military point to the war in Vietnam, "except that it's helping to buy us a new tactical air force."

In the minds of the military-industrial coalition, "conversion" didn't mean beating swords into plowshares but beating the Bs into enormously expensive weapons systems. Thus, as it became clear that the Southeast Asia war was going to end, the big defense corporations were licking their chops over the bright new prospects. This was revealed very well in Bernard Nossiter's *Washington Post* article (December 8, 1968) on the giant military-contractor conglomerate Ling Temco Vought (later LTV).

James Ling, the man who created the conglomerate, was quoted as saying, "Our future planning is based on visible contracts. One must believe in the long-term threat. . . . Defense spending has to increase in our area because there has been a failure to initiate (new weapons systems) — if we're not going to be overtaken by the Soviets."

Ling's financial vice president, Samuel Downer, described the situation to Nossiter even more vividly when he said, "The postwar world must be bolstered with military orders." He continued:

> It's basic. Its selling appeal is defense of the home. This is one of the greatest appeals the politicians have to adjusting the system. If you're the President and you need a control factor in the economy, and you need to sell this factor, you can't sell Harlem and Watts, but you can sell self-preservation, a new environment. We're going to increase

defense budgets as long as those bastards in Russia are ahead of us. The American people understand this.

Note how inexact The Threat is. Ling has us ahead of the Soviets but in danger of being overtaken. Downer has "those bastards in Russia" ahead of us. It doesn't matter, though. The main thing is to have faith in the existence of The Threat.

After being fired from the Pentagon, I served as the unpaid chairman of the National Taxpayers' Union (NTU). My close associates at NTU and I hoped to propagate the idea of a budget that would give us a strong defense for an economical expenditure without distorting the normal peacetime economy. That meant cutting Pentagon spending. I felt that the winding down of the war gave us a rare opening to send our message.

The approach we advocated involved a strange-bedfellows alliance. As the *Milwaukee Journal* reported, about a speech I made in April 1971, "Liberals who want to be effective in cutting defense spending must join fiscal conservatives who are fed up with government waste."

The voices of the Threat's guardians became particularly shrill with alarm when they realized that our seemingly unnatural coalition's message was catching on. Pro-Pentagonist columnist William S. White was one of the shrillest. In his column for April 24, 1971, he reported that the Democratic congressional leaders were "pleading" for Republican help in the effort to repel "a gathering, neo-liberal, neo-isolationist assault" on the Nixon military budget. White declared that our poor, loosely connected band, powered by only truth and ideas, had brought about the "gravest crisis" for America's national security since the 1930s. Heady stuff, that. In a way it was flattering to think that our ragtag band of yins and yangs was more powerful than Hitler, Tojo, and Mussolini in World War II, the Evil Empire in the Cold War, or the dread Viet Cong, who were even then, in the fevered fantasies of people like William S. White, threatening Denver.

The NTU did indeed give an umbrella to all sorts: conservatives, liberals, populists, and libertarians. On the board, for instance, were Robert Kephart, publisher of the ultraconservative *Human Events*, and Marcus Raskin, cofounder of the left-wing Institute for Policy Studies. We wanted to pose a strong challenge to the conventional thinking of people like William White, for we believed that the nation could have a strong defense with a minimum of waste and corruption.

*   *   *

The lessons I had been trying to teach at the Pentagon — and had taken into more public forums after I was thrown out — were, simply stated, about designing and manufacturing defense products in the most efficient way, delivering a faultless product in good time to the government, and charging no more than a fair price. In competitive private industry this was done every day in America, and in some sectors it still is. In the defense industry, such practices are more the exception than the rule.

The bad effects of defense industry practices were especially noticeable in the productivity of industrial blue-collar workers. The decline in productivity could be measured readily because we had a long history for comparison. Roughly eighty-five years ago, the industrial experts of that day developed means for measuring, more or less objectively, how much work factory mechanics and technicians should produce in a given period of time. Other industrial engineers and I were worried to see the widening gap between what industrial workers were producing now and what they should be producing.

In the early 1950s, at the beginning of my career as an industrial engineer, I'd helped install work-measurement cost-control systems in large-scale aircraft maintenance and modification. That had been a valuable lesson, and I had later applied some of those techniques to cost-cutting programs in a variety of nonmanufacturing work. Work measurement was one of the primary instruments for determining what a manufactured article should cost. Properly performed, work measurement establishes the time it "should take" a qualified worker to perform a manufacturing operation; for a complex product, the should-take times for a myriad operations must be added to arrive at an estimate. Work measurement was such a powerful cost-reduction and appraisal tool that its use was specifically outlawed by the Pentagon's cost-estimating gurus during my first tour of duty there. At first officials didn't understand what I was trying to do; when they did, they became outright hostile.

Industrial engineers call the raw should-take time for a given task or unit of product "normal time." Since no one works every minute on the job, allowances are added to the normal time for personal breaks, fatigue, unavoidable minor delays, and the like. The normal time for a job plus all the allowances is the "reasonable expectancy" of the time it should take to do the job, and that is called "standard time."

The reasonably expected amount of work to be done in one chronological hour is called a "standard hour of work." I must emphasize here that the standard hour is a measure of work *output* and has no necessary relationship to chronological time actually expended doing the job.

Old-fashioned, competitive business management tried to get as many standard hours of output as possible for labor hours expended. When a journeyman reached a certain stated level of output, he was "making standard." Often he could get extra pay for exceeding a "fair day's work" standard of output.

Although military contractors saw little sense in trying to control their costs, out of some atavistic habit they did maintain time standards sections in their industrial engineering departments. The function of these sections was to do work measurement mostly as part of a "management image" façade, but the time standards did exist and were subject to audit, verification, and adjustment if necessary.

Unfortunately, the Pentagonists viewed standard output as a limit on performance. Old-fashioned industrialists measured their improvement on how much their shops *exceeded* standard output, but the big military contractors viewed normally expected output as a goal to be approached asymptotically — only under "perfect" conditions at never-to-be-reached production quantities. The old floor for output had become the ceiling.

One aspect of the warped psychology I had to contend with at the Pentagon was that of people I called the "cost Calvinists" for their almost religious faith in one kind of predestination. The cost Calvinists believed that the future cost of a product was preordained by its past cost history, with just a couple of variable factors: the product's parameters — a change in weight or speed for a newly ordered aircraft, say — and inflation. Otherwise, once a Pentagon project was set in motion, its costs were inexorably set and were beyond the power of mere men to alter. The project manager's duty was to make sure that the defense contractor had "no funding problems," that is, plenty of money, and that no meddler would come along to impose cost controls or make major cost reductions. The Cost History god must not be angered.

This Calvinist dogma was based on numerous logical fallacies. To begin with, the historical costs were highly suspect; the contractor on a job could do many interesting and self-serving things with a cost trend line. In fact, one of my students, a production superintendent, declared that he could so manipulate the manhours per unit line by including creative labor-time charges that he could write his name with it. And labor costs were only one item. All kinds of extraneous items were added in — waste in the plant, fraud somewhere along the line, inaccuracies and "accounting adjustments" in past "actual cost" records, and so on.

The general rule was that the fair and reasonable price to pay a contractor was a figure that closely approximated the contractor's cost to make or acquire the product plus a reasonable profit. In the usual course of negotiating contracts with big firms, the government allowed contractors to include all "normal costs of doing business" in their "allowable actual cost" base. (Normal costs were not supposed to include interest, bribes, party girls, or other frills; these were all termed "unallowable.")

The contract negotiations were a kind of ritual mating dance. The contractor-creature would take three steps forward by throwing into the cost sheet some excesses, which, he knew, the auditors would catch and disallow. The government negotiator-animal would then take three countersteps forward and the contractor would take three steps back, putting him exactly where he was at the beginning and exactly where he wanted to be (he would get the excess back in the future with some tricky steps). The negotiator was happy because he could show some "savings."

Straightforward cost-plus-percentage-of-cost contracts, in which profits are calculated as a percentage of the costs incurred, were hypothetically illegal, on the theory that they invited the contractor to pile up as many costs as he could possibly get away with. In actual practice, things weren't quite so clear. Say that a company manufactures an initial order of M–12 Bibelots and charges $100 apiece, with a profit of 10 percent. In due course the government reorders at the same price. But in the meantime, the company has found a more efficient production method for making bibelots and the $50 cost of manufacture has been halved. Question: does the company put the new production methods into effect, cut staff, and thereby make a profit of $35 on each bibelot instead of $10?

Answer: don't be silly. The company either sticks with the same old costly manufacturing methods or, if its methods do change, keeps the excess people on board anyway; a dramatic cost reduction now would mean a reduction of the cost base in future contracts — and thus smaller profits. Worse, if the new "actual" (and lower) cost records were entered into the cost Calvinists' data banks, the price structure of the whole industry might be in danger. The big, protected Pentagon contractors' real product is allowable costs, the basis for calculating prospective profits; cutting these costs threatens both sales volume and profit.

Another strange phenomenon was something called, in the wonderful Pentagonese language, an "undefinitized" order. This meant that the contractor had received an order for a product or product modification whose specifications were still subject to change. The contractor was authorized to begin work, or at least start spending money, before firm prices were agreed on with the government. Now those undefinitized contract objectives were, in translation, indefinite objectives. The taxpayer can imagine some shambling jumbo corporation with $100 million to spend on indefinite purposes. When the revised contract price was finally set, the product changes sometimes cost more than the price originally estimated for the whole job. I have seen many cases where the changes actually reduced the amount of work to be done — but the contractor still charged the government a hefty sum just for making *any* changes.

Usually undefinitized change orders remained unpriced until it was reckoned that the expenditures for change were about 90 percent complete. Then would come the negotiations and the final deal, which usually gave the company all it asked for. Most of the costs incurred were labeled "good costs," the company got additional money to finish the job, and the change order profit was figured on a percentage of allowable costs. Thus, once the contractor got into the changes, the money he spent almost always produced a pure cost-plus-percentage-of-cost return — the forbidden formula — in practice.

On the government side, the program manager had at his disposal reserve funds to cover any cost increases that might occur. He was under military orders to get rid of this money — in Pentagonese, to "execute the program" by meeting his "obligations and outlays" goals. And rarely was any program manager embarrassed by having money left over.

These were the normal machinations to accommodate big contractors; small ones were sometimes held so strictly to commitments that they went into bankruptcy. Where this dodge of putting in continual change orders — "contract nourishment," in the Pentagonal idiom — might have awkward political or public relations consequences, the government sometimes simply ignored the contractual commitments and handed the big corporation whatever money it asked for. The bailout law (Public Law 85–804) used in the Lockheed case was just one example, and it set a precedent for the rescue of other failing corporate behemoths. Later the Pentagon had found an even simpler way to resolve a controversy with a contractor about cost overruns: it simply conceded.

In the early 1970s the effects of all these horrendous practices were beginning to show. The direct consequences touched our ability to supply the armed forces. The unit costs of equipment were rising so rapidly that Senator Proxmire used to make speeches about "unilateral, gold-plated disarmament." Instead of a bang for a buck, we were beginning to get a pop for many bucks.

The long-term danger that worried me was the epidemic spread of the cost-plus virus throughout the whole business community. As it had already done in the defense and space industries, so it would drive up unit costs and degrade quality in all industry, especially in corporations that must compete with the defense companies for land, labor, materials, and services.

Nixon's half-hearted price-control guidelines of 1971 gave an impetus to this trend. If a businessman could show that his costs had increased, he could raise his prices — and he was very likely to go unchallenged. Management, in industries with those administered prices, could pass on cost increases to their customers without penalty so long as the increases were industry-wide. That way no company had to worry much about its competition.

Congress was not much help in trying to halt the spread of the cost-plus virus. In fact, Congressman Chet Holifield's commission on government procurement was actually helping it by encouraging the spread of Pentagon cost-justification techniques to all contracting agencies of the federal government.

The really insidious part of the cost-plus infection, though, was what it did to managers. On the Pentagon pattern, private-sector managers prospered if they were skillful at justifying higher costs as a way to get higher prices. This was particularly true in the medical and health-care industry and contributed to the skyrocketing costs of medical treatment.

The "management sciences" academics were intrigued with the Pentagon's cost-justification procedures, especially the formula for using past "actual" costs as a basis for extrapolating future costs. Their formula for the so-called learning curve, an exponential hyperbola of the form $y = kx^{-m}$, looked so scientific and was so widely endorsed by professors of statistics, business, and economics as an inexorable law of human behavior that it had come to be accepted.

The learning curve illustrated on page 49 is said to have an 80 percent slope or improvement rate. The slope and starting point depend on the past history of manhours and costs for the same or an analogous product, cost-estimating theology, and available money. Clearly, the fatter the estimate of manhours and total cost, the easier it is to fit to the learning curve. The curve is a self-fulfilling prophecy if it is fat enough, and estimates that can be made to come true are said to be "credible." Therefore, the fatter the estimate, the more credible it is.

Actually, the learning curve hyperbola had been selected in the days before computers. When plotted on logarithmic graph paper, it was a straight line, thereby easing the computational chores of cost-justifying pencil whippers. The magic hyperbola was also indispensable

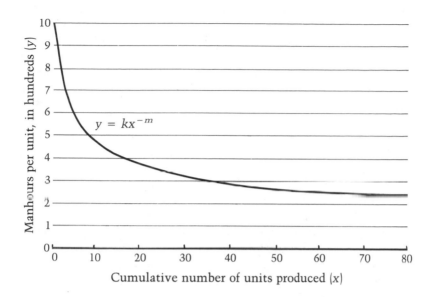

$$y = kx^{-m}$$

The learning, or improvement, curve, illustrating an 80 percent improvement rate. The number of manhours it takes to build each unit is reduced to 80 percent of the previous value each time the cumulative number of units doubles. For example, the first unit takes 1,000 hours; the second, 800 hours; the fourth, 640 hours; the eighth, 512 hours; and so on. Although it is a curve on the arithmetic scale, the learning curve is a logarithmic straight line of the form $y - kx^{-m}$, where y is manhours per unit, k is a constant, x is the cumulative number of units produced, and m is the slope exponent (.80 in the example).

to those managers who wanted to project higher costs as unavoidable. As long as contractors' reports showed that the levels and trends of manhours per unit of product were more or less on track with the learning curve, a government buying office usually wouldn't challenge them. Also, whenever a change was made in the contract, they reasoned, the curve would have to be "spliced." This meant that the "learning" would have to start over to some degree, thereby jacking up allowed costs again and compounding the already complex mathematical formulas.

In short, the whole approach was tailor-made for charlatans, while having enough pseudoscience about it to gain acceptance among well-meaning academics.

As I went around the country giving talks about military spending, I noted with increasing despair that universities were teaching cost justification instead of the hard-nosed cost-reduction and cost-control techniques I had learned as a young engineer. David Packard and his confederates were furious when I wrote, in *The High Priests of Waste*, that the leaders of the military spending complex were fiscal Typhoid Marys, carrying their bad doctrine into many parts of our national business and industrial body.

Admiral Hyman Rickover had been just about as critical as I, saying to Senator Proxmire's committee, "Many large companies are virtually unmanaged." That really didn't hurt profits, though: "Large defense contractors can let costs come out where they will and count on getting relief from the Department of Defense through changes in claims, relaxation of procurement regulations and laws, government loans, follow-on sole-source contracts, and other escape mechanisms."

Packard, it seems, didn't dare attack the admiral, who was powerful, influential, and well connected. I was none of those things, so Packard attacked me personally and viciously in his review of my book.

I resolved to fight back on strictly factual lines by making renewed efforts to show what the bad effects on our competitive private sector would be if the inefficiencies of the Pentagon-sheltered corporate giants were to spread widely. My first educational efforts were directed at the Joint Economic Committee staff. My substitute for the false gospel of "did cost = will cost" in contract pricing was the should-cost approach — what work should cost after the fat is squeezed out.

At that time my predecessor as Air Force management systems deputy, Ronald Fox, was an assistant secretary of the Army in charge of procurement. Ron, who professed to be a convert to the should-cost approach, contracted with one of my former partners, Mert Tyrrell, to help institutionalize should-cost in Army programs. They had some limited success, although they approached the giant contractors on the biggest, most political programs only gingerly.

Senator Proxmire and the JEC staff were impressed by Ron and Mert's results and by the fact that such an effort was being made at all in the Nixon administration. Proxmire arranged some hearings so that Ron could testify about how well the Army was doing in cost cutting. The unfortunate result was that the Army movers and shakers were so shaken that they moved to put a damper on should-cost. The program, nevertheless, limped along and the concept stayed alive.

At this point I decided to introduce into my congressional educational efforts a very rough rule of thumb for measuring the fat in manufacturing operations, one I'd used successfully as the head of a small but busy management consulting firm. I was often asked to survey a company to determine whether our services would pay off in reduced costs. I called these surveys gold-in-the-mine studies because they were like geologists' surveys of ore-bearing rock: without some good indication of available pay dirt, there would be no point in starting a new mine or continuing to work one that might be almost played out. I usually had to do the survey myself and with my own money, so I developed a number of simple indices of organizational effectiveness that I could rely on in recommending what needed to be done.

One of my most useful measures was the total in-house cost for a standard unit of output by the "touch labor" people. In manufacturing there are only two kinds of people: touch labor — the people who make things — and everybody else. The touch labor people are easy to evaluate and measure quantitatively, and everybody else is there to serve and support them. That is, the non–touch labor people should be focusing on efforts to help make the product better, less expensively, and faster. In the most fundamental sense, the output of the touch labor people is the output of everybody else as well. As a common-denominator measurement for labor output, I used the standard hour described earlier.

Later I found total in-house dollars of cost per standard hour of output a useful yardstick for assessing military contracts involving manufacturing, whether for production or for research and development. It was a rough measure, and I was not happy with its roughness, but given the circumstances of that time and the nature of the problem, it was the best measure available.

At that time, in the early 1970s, the government had no approved measures that were meaningful. In what became a real economic tragedy, the GAO, then headed by Comptroller General Elmer Staats, joined with the Pentagon spenders to oppose measures of the performance of military contractors. Specifically, they rejected the old-fashioned should-cost approach, recommended by the JEC, in favor of new-fangled, heavily qualitative procedural evaluations, which were misleadingly labeled "should-cost." They kept the name but changed the concept.

What the Pentagon adopted were the Air Force's old Industrial Management Assistance Surveys (IMAS) with a pro forma review of contractor work measurement systems added, and a few negotiation fillips thrown in. This process, which was predominantly qualitative and procedural, was so vague that the GAO told Proxmire they had no way of quantifying the fat that showed up in the pseudo-should-cost studies. That quantification, of course, was the point of any good should-cost scrutiny.

The pseudo-studies were also, as one might have guessed, much more expensive than the old ones. In the 1960s, four or five people could study a manufacturer's operation for four to eight weeks and typically find ways to reduce costs by about 30 percent. Under the new-look program, forty or fifty people would work for three to four months and come up with much smaller savings. (And it appeared that the initially negotiated savings were either given back to the contractor or diverted to other purposes. Certainly we could never track any should-cost savings being returned to the Treasury.)

Another reason that my dollars-per-standard-labor-hour index was useful in judging the amount of manufacturing fat was that manufacturing methods, especially within subgroupings of the industry — automotive, airframe, missile, and electronics, for example — were generally similar. The defense companies with the most diverse processes were the big so-called systems contractors, whose factories typically had three hundred to five hundred different kinds of manufacturing operations. Usually their industrial engineers had usefully accurate formulas to determine should-take times for products in each operation. Few of the operations were unique. The companies had little interest in devising methods to cut down on touch labor. After all, direct labor hours were the most defensible kinds of "allowable costs" in manufacturing. (In a completely automated factory, my dollars-per-standard-labor-hour index would have been irrelevant — but there were no completely automated plants that we knew of in defense industry.)

Contractor	Industry	Dollars per Standard Labor Hour ($/SLH) Index[1]
A	Automotive	19.53
B	Airframe	22.03
C	Missile	24.47
D	Missile	37.33
E	Missile[2]	46.54
E	Missile[3]	50.21
F	Electronics	97.70
G	Electronics	195.33

1. Figures evaluated by the government for negotiation purposes.
2. Ground support equipment.
3. Missile.

In the early 1970s ten dollars per standard labor hour was about the top cost in competitive industry. If the factory labor cost more than that, the business was in deep trouble. In contrast, observe the costs to contractors for the Army shown in the table.

I make no claim that these sample costs per SLH were scientific or even necessarily representative of the overall figures for military contractors. These were the figures we could get in Congress — and they were very troubling. Remember that competitive industry costs rarely went above ten dollars a standard labor hour, and the best showing in the table is almost twice that. The worst is almost twenty times that.

To find out some of the reasons for the discrepancies, we took a closer look at electronics manufacturer G. We found that he was having quality problems. We were told that the $195.33 included large, but not specifically identified, charges for scrapped material and for corrections to the contractor's work.

I wanted to express the rather arcane $/SLH comparisons in terms that would be meaningful to nontechnical people, especially the JEC members. I consulted some electronics manufacturers for estimates of what contractor G would have to charge if he were to make a nineteen-inch portable color TV set, which in those days sold for about $400 retail. Assuming the efficiency levels shown in G's government contracts and making other markups proportionately high, the set would cost the consumer about $8,000. And considering contractor G's lousy performance, it probably wouldn't work.

The $8,000 TV was a good example for my innocent friends in the Businessmen's Educational Fund who believed in "conversion." It also had very disturbing implications for our competitive position in world markets in the future. With work habits, efficiency, rates of pay, and management practices like those of G, our nondefense electronics industry would die a quick death.

Was I the only one who knew these secrets? Not at all. A great many people in government and in industry had both experience and a sure hand in dealing with cost bloat and poor quality. And military contracting offered dramatic opportunities for cost cutting.

Even if the feared and despised should-cost approach was unacceptable, other cost-cutting remedies could be used. For instance, Admiral Rickover testified before the JEC that only 11 percent of Pentagon procurement (including research and development) could be described as competitive. By that he meant advertised solicitations to all comers and sealed bids. The other 89 percent came through negotiated contracts that were the result of varying degrees of procurement looseness. Even limited bid competitions in the past ("cost rivalry," as I called it) had produced dramatic reductions in what the Pentagon expected to pay or had paid. The JEC gathered some statistics on sole-source contracts that were later subjected to cost rivalry: reductions in unit costs ranged from 16 to 80 percent.

There was another way to inject a little competition into the insulated world of the big defense corporations. Many of them carried on their operations in government-owned facilities. Lockheed, for instance, used Air Force Plant 6 to complete work on the C-5A. Because of the company's disastrous record, I suggested we hold a competition for the operation of Plant 6. David Packard rejected the idea, but later, when it was too late, he agreed that it could have been done.

Admiral Rickover had advocated the same treatment for shipbuilders that used their sole-source position to hold the Navy up for reimbursement for overruns. The Army had its GOCO plants — government-owned, contractor-operated ammunition plants, tank arsenals, and the like — and frequently changed contractor-tenants, which demonstrated the feasibility of changing contractors through cost-saving competition. (Though many of the changes, I suspect, were made for political rather than competitive reasons.)

Some successful examples of competition could be found, even in the Nixon administration. A notable one was the "fly-off," or competition between prototypes, that produced the F-16 fighter plane (and I give David Packard a measure of credit for this success). Most of the good work was done in the early 1970s by a maverick group within the Pentagon known as the "Fighter Mafia," led by Air Force colonels John Boyd and Everest Riccioni and an analyst named Pierre Sprey from the office of the secretary of defense. The F-16 was a momentary triumph for the spirit of competition and cost regulation, giving us a good product at a bearable price — at least until contract nourishment set in.

5

☆ ☆ ☆

Kangaroo Court

MY LONG-DELAYED CIVIL SERVICE COMMISSION hearing over reinstatement finally got under way in May 1971. The Air Force, the office of the secretary of defense, and the Civil Service Commission had stalled and stonewalled on producing evidence and witnesses. We never did get what we needed for a fair trial. It was like one of those 1930s courtroom dramas in which a judge is in cahoots with the Bad Guys, a noble young lawyer battles the local Establishment, a booming witness turns up with important evidence but is barred from the courtroom by the judge, and a nervous plaintiff (or was I the defendant, as the government seemed to think?) begins to wonder if God is really on the side of the righteous. But this was happening in real life.

I was much blessed in having not one but several dedicated volunteer lawyers who believed firmly in the slightly-out-of-fashion principle of fighting for the truth. Most of the legal work was being done by John Bodner, Jr., and his partner John Bruce of Howrey and Simon, and by Bill Sollee of Ivins, Philips, and Barker. Ralph Temple, legal director of the Washington ACLU, also helped out when he could. They had no compensation to look forward to and plenty of trouble, yet they were more devoted to me and my cause than if I were a multimillionaire who could pay top fees. Quite a few times, the lawyers and their support people — paralegals and secretaries — literally stayed up all night to do research and prepare documents. I'll never cease to be amazed at their generosity and commitment.

I had a different kind of long-lasting amazement for the administrative law judge, or, to be exact, the civil service hearing examiner, Herman Staiman. My first impression of him came at the outset of my hearing when he made it clear that he would be the absolute master of what evidence went into the record; under these rules, if he denied us certain evidence that evidence was forever lost to our cause. In addition he ruled that the hearing would take place in secret, behind locked doors, with only the principals, their lawyers, and himself present.

The latter ruling was meant to keep Clark Mollenhoff safely out — not an easy thing to do. When the hearings opened, Clark demanded to be allowed to enter. From inside the hearing room we could hear the Boomer's stentorian outrage, gradually diminishing as he was led away by the guards.

Mollenhoff's chief intention was to see Robert Hampton, chairman of the Civil Service Commission, and to get an explanation of why such a blatantly unconstitutional hearing was taking place. What we didn't know at the time was that Hampton had had a quiet handshake with Air Force Secretary Robert Seamans.

After a few days it was clear what we were up against. Staiman placed the entire burden of proof on me and my lawyers and restricted discovery of evidence to essentially whatever the Air Force chose to present. He limited executive branch witnesses to those officials the Air Force certified as knowledgeable and denied us the power to subpoena witnesses or records. Finally he stated that we must prove malicious intent, or what was "in Seamans's mind" when he terminated me.

Staiman's behavior on the bench was unjudicial, to say the least. He gave hand and eye signals to the opposition's witnesses and made one outrageous ruling after another. My lawyers protested it all, and the protests went into the eventual court record, but that was no substitute for an open hearing that would allow the public and the press to see what was happening.

The corpulent, indolent Staiman, secure in his arbitrary arrogance, was justified in his attitude for all practical purposes; he represented the combined forces of the Air Force, the Department of Defense, the Civil Service Commission, the Justice Department, and the all-powerful Nixon White House. Isolated against this awesome array was a somewhat countrified, mostly unemployed engineer represented by volunteer lawyers. But these weren't your run-of-the-mill volunteers going through the motions to fulfill a quota of public-interest hours. My guys were out to win for me and for the principles at stake.

After putting up with this treatment for a few days, Bodner and Sollee filed an interlocutory appeal with the U.S. Federal District Court in the District of Columbia requesting that presiding judge William Bryant order the Civil Service Commission to respect my constitutional right to an open hearing. In my experience, the so-called Justice Department, charged with representing the United States in court, always excuses and defends official wrongdoers in cases like mine. True to the pattern, when the hearing before Judge Bryant opened, the Justice Department lawyer began by reading civil service and Justice Department regulations to justify their holding closed, star-chamber hearings.

Judge Bryant interrupted. "I'm not interested in all that gobbledygook," he said. "Just tell me how justice is done."

It was a new concept for the lawyer, one that seemed to baffle him. (More than one Justice Department lawyer has since explained to me that their job is not to see justice done but to enforce the law.) The government men had run up against a fair-minded judge and a team of tough lawyers.

Judge Bryant ruled that "this closed hearing is unconstitutional," noting that both the Sixth Amendment and Federal Rule of Civil Procedure 77(B) required an open court. As for the Air Force's plea that the closed session was necessary to protect *my* privacy, he said, "This consideration is obviously of no validity when it is the appellant-employee who wants the open hearing."

President Nixon and the Air Force appealed the decision to the Court of Appeals, which upheld Judge Bryant. They considered carrying it to the Supreme Court but in the end backed down.

My civil service hearing before Staiman was resumed on January 26, 1973. The first witness was General Joseph Cappucci of the Office of Special Investigations (OSI). His preposterous testimony was that four secret informers (T-1, T-2, T-3, and T 4) had more or less wandered in off the street with allegations about me that he had felt compelled to investigate.

He then had to admit under questioning that he had tampered with the file on me by retaining the derogatory (false) allegations while destroying other field reports that demonstrated their falsity. He admitted that even after he had determined that the charges against me were not true, he had kept on circulating the dirt file containing them. At this point Staiman shut down this line of inquiry. He would not let us call the secret information even after we had determined that T-1 was my former assistant, Whitey Driessnack. (A closer look at all this would obviously have been painful for the Pentagon and, as it later developed, the White House.)

When Secretary Seamans came to the witness stand, Bodner first asked him if he had had any discussions or meetings with anyone from the White House before he fired me.

Seamans refused to answer.

Staiman then put the question in a slightly different way: "Did you consult with anyone in the White House or on the White House staff before you made your decision to dismiss Mr. Fitzgerald?"

"In answer to that question," Seamans said, "let me say — if I may go back, Mr. Staiman, that I did not."

Apparently realizing that he had lied under oath, Seamans then tried to waffle. All he could say for sure was that he had not discussed my firing with anyone in industry or Congress. Beyond that, he said, he wouldn't answer unless advised to do so by his counsel or Secretary of Defense Elliot Richardson.

After a recess the government's lawyer, Colonel Claude Teagarden, came back and invoked the doctrine of executive privilege.

On the second day of his testimony, Seamans, emboldened by the success of his executive privilege stonewall, was using it every time a question threatened to produce something embarrassing or incriminating. At this point we got one of those lucky breaks without which few citizens can prevail against the federal government. I always tried to have a spectator or two present, even if there were no reporters. We found that the hearing examiner's conduct was vastly improved when a stranger was watching him. Clark Mollenhoff, who had come to hear Cappucci's testimony, had been called away on another assignment. So one of my neighbors, Phil Ryther, was sitting in.

Phil was a former high official in the Federal Aviation Administration (FAA). He had written some unwelcome warnings about unsafe practices by the charter airlines; the FAA, in consequence, had been in the process of railroading him out when his case came to Mollenhoff's attention. At about that time two fatal charter flight crashes occurred, as if to prove Phil's point; he was then able to negotiate early retirement. What he remembered particularly about Mollenhoff was his hatred for the royalist doctrine of executive privilege.

When he heard Seamans invoke executive privilege yet again, Phil left the hearing room, went to a pay phone, and called the Boomer. Luckily, Mollenhoff got the call just before he left for the presidential press conference described in Chapter 1.

At the White House Mollenhoff rose and boomed the question: had Nixon approved of Seamans's invocation of executive privilege? Or had Seamans simply used it on his own initiative? Nixon was taken by surprise — the question hadn't been in the briefing book. (Years later we learned in discovery that Seamans and Colonel Teagarden had consulted on executive privilege with John Dean the day before. Dean wrote a memorandum for the president, but it didn't reach him until after the press conference.)

As I noted in Chapter 1, Nixon fudged on executive privilege by promising a "precise statement" in writing, but then blurted out the truth about his approval of my ouster.

Later in the Oval Office came the postmortem scene revealed by the tapes. Nixon was not exactly pleased with the unauthorized invocation of the sacred doctrine:

NIXON: Well, anyway, I backed it up —

EHRLICHMAN: Yeah.

NIXON: — which I shouldn't.

EHRLICHMAN: Yeah, well that's fine and we're —

NIXON: Seamans claimed it.

EHRLICHMAN: We're covering your tracks.

NIXON: I didn't want to have any indication of somebody down the line having used privilege, uh, without —

EHRLICHMAN: Okay, it's okay. We're coverin' his tracks. Uh, Seamans was wrong, he had no right to invoke it, but you backed him up and we can put it, we can put it together in such a way that everything's okay, and, uh, don't worry about it.

Nixon ruminated on this, and in a later conversation picked up on the theme again:

NIXON: But I had to back up the son of a bitch Seamans.

EHRLICHMAN: Here's what we've done. Just so you can get a feel of it. You know the procedure is if a cabinet officer wants to invoke executive privilege, he refers it to the attorney general —

NIXON: Yeah.

EHRLICHMAN: — and it eventually comes to you if it's, if it's meritorious. So I —

NIXON: I invoke.

EHRLICHMAN: That's right and so what, what we're saying is, by the language Seamans used, he was beginning the process. Here it goes on. Meanwhile, he has referred this to the attorney general. The attorney general's going to look at this and make a decision as to whether he should answer the question or not. And you were aware of this fact and you acquiesced in the procedure being started. He made no final ruling.

That taken care of, all that remained was Nixon's embarrassing admission that he'd fire me. But there was always an easy way to solve such problems: have Ziegler go out and lie about it.

At the press conference the next day, February 1, Ziegler did just that: "We can find no record . . . of the matter ever being brought to the president's attention. . . . [It] was a matter dealt with solely by the Air Force." Seamans echoed this fiction in a press conference he called a week after Nixon's.

John Bodner's next bold move in the civil service hearing was to request that President Nixon testify. Remember that this was before the crumbling of the Watergate cover-up; Nixon was at the height of his power. To call the most powerful man in the world to testify at a bureaucratic hearing into the firing of a middle-level functionary was lese majesty of an outrageous kind. It was as if some puny colonies in the New World had called George III to account for his actions in 1776. Even my friends thought Bodner was presumptuous. I thought he was magnificent.

In a written plea to Staiman, Bodner eloquently laid out the reasons for calling Nixon; if it was impossible for the president to appear himself, Bodner said, there was a Jeffersonian precedent for his testifying by deposition in a court case. Richard Nixon was served a copy of Bodner's letter, but he ignored it, as had the awed Staiman. Our requests to put on the stand all four T's (the secret informers), Melvin Laird, David Packard, OSI Training Director Michael Ross, and John Dean were also denied.

Aside from Nixon, the most controversial witness we requested was Clark Mollenhoff, who at this time was still struggling with conflicting loyalties. He had been a counselor to the president and he was not yet convinced that Nixon was a crook. He wanted to testify, but first he wanted to give Nixon a chance to remedy the injustice.

When Mollenhoff approached Ziegler with a request to talk with the president, nothing happened, so he wrote a long letter to Nixon on February 13. In it he said that what troubled him most was the testimony of General Cappucci, which revealed the secret informers, the destruction of exonerating material, and the circulation of the dirt file. Mollenhoff spoke of "an enormous wrong," a suspected "malicious conspiracy," and "an irreparable injury" to me.

According to evidence we later discovered in the White House tapes, Nixon, seemingly ready to make amends, conferred with Dean on February 28. Dean had met with Mollenhoff the night before to persuade him to turn over some of his documentation and a summary of the testimony he wanted to give. On February 28 Mollenhoff sent a three-page letter with attachments.

He had fallen into a clever trap quite worthy of John Dean and Richard Nixon: they immediately turned the letter and attachments over to the Air Force lawyers. To squelch Mollenhoff, White House lawyers Fred Fielding and Joe Adams, who were running interference for the malefactors, permitted the Air Force to draft a legal ban on testimony by Mollenhoff on the grounds of executive privilege.

Needless to say, the Boomer didn't buy it. Ignoring the legalistic obstacles, he simply appeared at my hearing and demanded to testify. The most restrained and dignified account of the scene appeared in the *New York Times* of March 22, 1973:

> Mr. Mollenhoff was at the hearing room this morning in a noisy, animated and unscheduled appearance.
>
> He called the proceedings a "kangaroo court" and said that he was ready to testify. "Every effort is being made to keep the facts from being put on the line," he said.
>
> Mr. Staiman said that he was interrupting the hearing.
>
> "If the truth is an interference, then I am interfering," Mr. Mollenhoff said.
>
> "If you don't stop your interruptions, I'll have to ask you to leave the room," Mr. Staiman said.
>
> Mr. Mollenhoff left a short time later.... "It is the most peculiar effort to extend executive privilege to someone who doesn't want it" [he said].

Actually, that is a pale and muted description of the raucous encounter between the big Boomer and the puffy Staiman. Everybody in the neighborhood of the hearing room became well informed about the wrath of a freeborn citizen with powerful lungs who was just trying to do his duty.

When Mollenhoff discovered that Dean and Nixon had passed on the material he had given them in confidence, while withholding it from me and my lawyers, he erupted again. He bundled up documents he had saved from his White House days, along with copies of his letters to Dean and Nixon, and sent them to me.

Righteous indignation was not his only motive, however. Beneath the public Boomer was a man with a warm and considerate nature, and his compelling reason came from there. In his cover letter to me, he said:

> The tragic death of Kenneth Cook and the memory of his last visits to my office leave me with no alternative. I do not want to be in the position in your case of asking myself later if I might have done more to correct an injustice, and know the answer I would have to give myself if I remained silent.

I knew how Clark felt because I too had been strongly affected by Kenneth Cook's death. Cook had been an Air Force weapons analyst, a mathematician and physicist with a fine record for evaluations of advanced weapons systems. His downfall came when he made an accurate and damning study of plans for some useless and very expensive secret weapons that his Air Force superiors favored. Under pressure from them, he refused to alter his analysis. So against Ken Cook the military used the cruelest kind of KGB tactics: they declared him mentally incompetent. Two civilian psychiatrists who examined him contradicted the allegation, and even the Air Force's own top psychiatrist found him nothing more than a "perfectionist" who was "relatively inflexible" in defending his views. I had some personal knowledge of the idiotic proposals Cook had examined, and he would have had to be insane to approve them.

I had learned about the Cook case when I was a consultant to Congressman Jerry Waldie's civil service subcommittee. We were told that the Air Force was indeed permitted to declare someone mentally incompetent without getting a psychiatrist's opinion! All it took were statements by three people equal or superior in rank to the victim. Or the local military sawbones on his own could declare a government employee mentally incompetent. (After the Cook case and other outrages, the rules were changed: a psychiatrist had to make the finding.)

After he was fired, Kenneth Cook found it almost impossible to get a job. The ACLU gave him some legal help, but the legal bases for his mistreatment were unclear. Most judges supported the idea that there was no recourse beyond a review by the Civil Service Commission, that pliant creature of the executive branch.

Cook tried hard through legal and political means to get the decision reversed, but politicians and officials alike were indifferent or hostile. He did valuable volunteer work for public-interest groups and members of Congress, helping to debunk the antiballistic missile proposals.

Eventually his slim resources ran out. When he fell behind in paying his property taxes, his home in New Mexico was auctioned off, in spite of public outcry. The sale brought him a check for fifty-seven cents. I saw him the day that happened, and when he showed me the ridiculous check, that strong man broke down and cried. He was never the same afterward. He went through the motions of fighting his case, but despair and poverty began to crush him. He ate only one meal a day. Having no bus fare, he trudged miles between his rented room in Virginia and the congressional or executive branch offices he haunted.

Though I was only partly employed myself, I bought him lunch whenever I could. Clark Mollenhoff did even more. Cook stopped at Mollenhoff's downtown office frequently, and Clark would take time out to buy him a meal and drive him to his next destination.

One January day in 1973, sick, ragged, and weak, Kenneth dropped dead in a department store across the street from Mollenhoff's office. He was just fifty-nine. Aside from a few old clothes and books found in his room, his entire estate consisted of the seven dollars and thirty-two cents in his pocket.

From Ken Cook's sad story, I learned not to be obsessive about injustice. I would fight hard, but I wouldn't let the fight consume me. I learned to close "the case" off in a separate compartment of my mind. Above all, I learned that you can't fight long without friends and allies. And I had some of the best. My skillful lawyers, along with men such as Mollenhoff, Proxmire, and Dickinson, were beginning to turn the tide in my civil service case. And when we finally beat down the absurd attempt to apply executive privilege to him, the Boomer in full basso profundo at last came into court.

On April 2, 1973, a long *New York Times* editorial described Mollenhoff's testimony. After noting that he "cut sharply through the double talk and obfuscation with which the White House and the Air Force spokesmen have muddied the case," the *Times* asked:

> Do the military believe that the protection of official extravagance, inefficiency, and collusion with the contractors is vital to national security? If that is prevailing doctrine, then Congress and the American people might as well resign themselves to giving the Pentagon a blank check. . . . It is particularly disconcerting that so many members of that cast have played important roles in a succession of alarming episodes — from Watergate to I.T.T. to Fitzgerald. All these episodes have in common the arrogant use of executive power, the aggrandizement of special interests, and the deception of the American people.

In the April 4, 1973, issue of the *Washington Post*, columnist Nicholas von Hoffman had a colorful description of the Mollenhoff intervention:

> The Big Boomer had fought his way to the witness stand and was letting fly: a good public servant is getting the axe because of the conspiracy in the Air Force . . . the scoundrels in the Air Force are trying to frame Mr. Fitzgerald . . . the brutality of the military bureaucracy.

Mollenhoff, he added, was a "loudly honest man," and the hearing "had the polite, slightly nasty decorum of an ecclesiastical trial's certainty of foregone conclusion, of a priori judgment." Von Hoffman continued his Inquisition metaphor:

> Each time the Big Boomer would let go with another epithet, Colonel Teagarden, the Air Force's lawyer, would coil backward and, like a prosecutorial abbot, turn his head away and smile the corners of his mouth downward in sweet disdain. He and the government had tried to keep the heretical Mollenhoff from testifying, but he was there, bellowing reproofs at them, so they tried to make him out as a maniac with a crazy hair inside irritating his gut.

By this time the government's case had begun to wither. Air Force Assistant Secretary Spencer Schedler appeared on the stand with a severe loss of memory. He couldn't recall his conversations just prior to his testimony to Proxmire's committee. Under sharp examination by my lawyers, though, he was forced to admit that he had not told the truth before the committee. Like Seamans, he kept refusing to answer on the grounds of executive privilege. Forced into a corner by Bill Sollee, he had to concede that he had violated the federal criminal statute against corporations lending employees to political campaigns and continuing to pay them as if they were doing their regular jobs. (As I noted earlier, Schedler had worked on the 1968 Spiro Agnew campaign — he was on the payroll of the Sinclair Oil Company at the time.)

It may have been coincidence, but Schedler was gone from the Air Force a couple of months after his embarrassing testimony, and Seamans left a couple of weeks after that. Was the Air Force quicker to correct public relations mistakes than billion-dollar procurement bungles?

The government's case had turned into an evidential disaster. Seamans had invoked executive privilege fifty-four times, and his assistants had used it repeatedly. Factually and morally we had won, but after three and a half years of the Civil Service Commission's brand of legality, I had the sinking feeling that my effort to be reinstated was doomed. Every indication was that Examiner Staiman was under orders to let the Air Force off the hook.

I didn't realize how much the tide of events in the larger world was running in our favor that spring and summer. Richard Nixon's Watergate stonewall was beginning to collapse and, unbeknownst to us, John Dean was spilling his guts to the staff of Senator Ervin's committee.

The Watergate inquiry produced some small glimmers of light on my case. Dean told Ervin's committee in public testimony that Nixon had asked him to look into my case but that he had been fired before he had done much investigation. His assistant, David Wilson, however, had "a rather extensive file" on me. Senator Inouye wanted to call Wilson as a witness and to dig more deeply into the case, but Ervin overruled him. On June 29, 1973, Bodner requested that file.

Wilson, the file revealed, had tried to reconstruct the circumstances of my firing. There was plenty of documentary evidence that Seamans had consulted frequently with White House people (especially Bryce Harlow) about firing me. As for executive privilege, the Justice Department had told Wilson that Seamans had invoked it improperly, quite without authorization.

If there is any lesson from Watergate and from my case that the American people should remember, it is that executive privilege is usually the hideout of scoundrels. I think Nixon himself summed it up with remarkable clarity when he told Ehrlichman, "You should have the most god-awful gobbledygook answer prepared. Just put it out on executive privilege. Something that will allow us to do everything we want."

After Dean and Wilson left the White House in early 1973, Fred Fielding and Dudley Chapman picked up the Fitzgerald case. On July 9 Chapman delivered a report to Leonard Garment. The uncensored portion that we have gives a straightforward account of my Proxmire committee testimony, an admission of Nixon's hand in my firing, and the remarks about my "acerbic personality" quoted in Chapter 3.

The Chapman Report, as it was known, seems to have been widely circulated in the White House. It produced this reply to Garment from Pat Buchanan:

> Fitzgerald has gone through enough, the CSC hearing is doing us no good whatsoever; there is a good measure of justice in Fitzgerald's complaint, and the president would be well served by a speedy and just, if not charitable, resolution of the matter. . . .
>
> Perhaps we should get together quietly with Fitzgerald and his attorney and find a resolution satisfactory to him — and not damaging to the president's interests.

Nothing came of this, although the suggestion was taken up with Melvin Laird, as Buchanan requested. The wrongdoing had been proved over and over again, and it was clear to everybody who knew anything about the case that the administration was guilty. Why, then, did they persist?

I believe that the reasons went far beyond my individual case. I believe that the president himself might have made amends (or so Buchanan told one of my lawyers). But the major principle at stake was that of *omertà*. The military spending complex simply had to banish the man who broke silence, the maverick who couldn't be trusted to lie. Let him back in and there goes the neighborhood. If my ordeal demonstrated a second lesson to the country, that, I hope, would be it.

In the meantime, in another part of the forest, a different dark force, generally known as the Internal Revenue Service, was at work. On the Watergate stand John Dean revealed how the Nixon White House plotted to use the IRS Special Service Staff to "screw" Nixon's enemies. The infamous White House draft memorandum of August 16, 1971, "Dealing with Our Political Enemies," laid out the objectives:

This memorandum addresses the matter of how we can maximize the fact of our incumbency in dealing with persons known to be active in their opposition to our Administration. Stated a bit more bluntly — how we can use the available federal machinery to screw our political enemies.

It went on to say that the tough guys on the staff (Colson, Dent, Flannigan, and Buchanan) should select the victims. The favored agency to do the screwing was the IRS, but — and this would have come as news to the National Taxpayers Union — the Nixon hit men considered the IRS too fair and objective. The undated (probably summer 1971) "I.R.S. Talking Paper" describes it:

The I.R.S. is a monstrous bureaucracy, which is dominated and controlled by Democrats. The I.R.S. bureaucracy has been unresponsive and insensitive to both the White House and the Treasury in many areas.

In brief, the lack of key Republican bureaucrats at high levels precludes the initiation of policies which would be proper and politically advantageous. Practically every effort to proceed in sensitive areas has been met with resistance, delay, and the threat of derogatory exposure. New plans were laid:

(A) *To accomplish:* Make I.R.S. politically responsive. Democrat administrations have discreetly used I.R.S. most effectively. We have been unable.

(B) *The Problem:* Lack of guts and effort. The Republican appointees appear afraid and unwilling to do anything that could be politically helpful.

For example:

— We have been unable to crack down on the multitude of tax exempt foundations that feed left wing political causes.

— We have been unable to obtain information in the possession of I.R.S. regarding our political enemies.

— We have been unable to stimulate audits of persons who should be audited.

— We have been unsuccessful in placing RN supporters in the I.R.S. bureaucracy.

The agreed-on solution was to lay down the (illegal) law to IRS chief Johnnie Walters. From now on he was to cooperate with White House hatchetman Fred Malek to "make personnel changes to make I.R.S. responsive to President" and was to take on discreet political action and investigations himself.

Along with all the other good stuff he revealed about the exploitation of the IRS, Dean disclosed the "enemies list." But Dean never made clear (in public, at least) what was to be done to the enemies. It took a later and much lower-key investigation by the Congressional Joint Committee on Internal Revenue Taxation to smoke out the actual operation of the IRS hit squad, the Special Service Staff.

It may be that some of the well-known Establishment figures on the enemies list were set upon by this hit squad, but I saw no evidence of it in my glimpse of the operation. The squad did make an effort to nab me.

The first entry in the Special Service Staff dossier on me was a clipping, an October 10, 1971, column by Clark Mollenhoff asking why my Civil Service Commission hearing was still being held behind locked doors. From that point on the staff collected information on my legal adventures. Years later John Bodner, whose name appeared in most of the news stories about me, told me he had been audited nearly every year after he took my case.

When the IRS learned that one of my vehicles for opposing wasteful military spending was my chairmanship of the National Taxpayers Union, they sicced the FBI on the NTU. And they targeted NTU's executive director, Jim Davidson, and our adviser, Bob Kephart.

As for me, the Special Service Staff for quite some time made the mistake of targeting *Edward* Fitzgerald instead of Ernest. (I often wondered what the IRS and the FBI did to poor Ed. Perhaps they went after him for not reporting the royalties from his translation of *The Rubaiyat of Omar Khayyam.*)

I must admit that the Staff was bureaucratically neat. They divided the enemies to be screwed into separate groups. Since there didn't seem to be a "whistle blowers" file for me, I was lumped with the NTU, Davidson, and Kephart as "Affiliation: War Tax Resister." My dossier contained several government memorandums explaining what war tax resistance was and who practiced it: Quakers, pacifists, and a group that included Bradford Lyttle, Allen Ginsberg, Pete Seeger, and Kenneth Love. But we of the NTU were in an even more dangerous subsection of tax resisters — *all*-tax resisters. As the file notes, the NTU "opposes all taxes, not just those for war."

The Staff was also watching my assistance to Representative Waldie, who was trying to squeeze some fat out of the federal employees' excessively high Blue Cross–Blue Shield Insurance premiums. Doubtless a subversive activity. An anonymous source denounced me as "a troublesome pinch penny." There was some truth to that.

But then came a most embarrassing entry in my file: "Current transcripts reflect taxpayer has filed and paid income tax for period 1971. *Overpayment* of $1,835.46 has been applied to the 1972 taxable period" (emphasis added). How could I pose as a dangerous radical with that on my record? Would my bolshie friends at NTU ever speak to me again if they knew? Thanks to my supercautious accountant (my wife, Nell) and my ultraconservative tax preparer, I was in the clear. The IRS hit squad persisted with repeated "desk audits," investigations, and close surveillance of my activities, but they lost heart about the time my civil service hearing was declared open. (After Nixon's overwhelming victory in November 1972, the White House dropped its attempts to block Judge Bryant's June ruling that my hearing should be open.) At that point the file peters out.

On August 1, 1973, the team of Nixon and the military irretrievably lost the phony civil service case against me. Again the Watergate investigation produced the evidence, and Senator Inouye brought it out. During Robert Haldeman's appearance on the stand, Inouye introduced the "let him bleed for awhile" memo from Colonel Butterfield to Haldeman. Though Haldeman's lawyer protested, Senator Ervin ruled the line of questioning relevant because it touched the issue of the loyalty owed by staffers to the president even when he and his associates were engaged in illegal activity. It was a key issue in the whole Watergate affair, especially after Butterfield's disclosure of the Oval Office taping system on July 16, 1973.

Haldeman waffled, stalled, and dissembled about White House involvement in my firing. He did not reveal what we later learned, that the Butterfield memo had been the result of a what-to-do-with-Fitzgerald meeting among top White House plotters in January 1970. But Haldeman also — probably inadvertently — did us a favor by suggesting clearly that Butterfield's attitude toward me sprang from his loyalty to the brotherhood of Air Force officers. It gave off a strong whiff of conspiracy.

After the disclosure of the Butterfield memo, civilians in the White House and the Pentagon began to show a desire to settle with me. The welter of staff memos we later acquired through legal discovery told the tale. It was suggested to Leonard Garment that the president let bygones be bygones. Peacemaker Mollenhoff met with Laird, now a special assistant to Nixon, and urged that I be reinstated. Laird seemed favorable; even Schlesinger, Laird's successor at Defense, weighed in for a resolution. His assistant, Marty Hoffman, called the White House and offered to help make peace. Apparently this brought a strong negative reaction from the diehards, and Hoffman next proposed that I be stowed away at the Department of Health, Education, and Welfare (HEW).

The civilians could propose, but increasingly the military were disposing. Al Haig, now a four-star general, had succeeded Haldeman and was fast becoming the real master of the White House staff. As students of the Nixon era will recall, Haig had been Kissinger's assistant at the beginning of the administration and had installed the illegal wiretaps for Kissinger; it's no surprise that he opposed any concession in my case.

One of Bill Sollee's sources was a secretary in the White House who was secretly sympathetic to us. Notes she gave Sollee showed that even Air Force General Counsel Jack Stempler leaned toward a settlement, sensing that he was about to lose the civil service decision. Even so, Stempler (who didn't know me at all) insisted that I was "unable to work with anyone." The White House civilian staff, now a rather different group from that of the Haldeman-Ehrlichman days of arrogance, wouldn't accept that. What scared them was the real possibility that Seamans's lies about my leaking classified documents could bring on a libel suit.

Our White House sources also told us that the staff feared a criminal action against Seamans because it was a crime to retaliate against an employee on the basis of his testimony before Congress or to obstruct a congressional committee. A White House summary memorandum commenting on my lawyers' closing CSC brief noted that the publicity surrounding my case could even hurt the administration's chances of getting what it wanted in the new defense budget. "It makes . . . sense to enlist Fitzgerald's skills in correcting the things he criticizes to the extent that they exist."

That was a naive view. The civilians in the White House simply had no idea how gluttonous and fat the military beast was. The military, on the other hand, had a good idea of the scale of the stealing that was going on. At that point it seemed to be a standoff. Then, suddenly, everything began to change.

On September 18, 1973, I was working on a writing project in my office at home when Bill Sollee called and said, "You got your job back." The Civil Service Commission had ruled that I'd been improperly fired and must be restored to duty with back pay. Senator Proxmire's office phoned with his one-word reaction, "Hallelujah!"

I was euphoric. I had won what I considered the patriotic battle, and I had also won a very personal battle. The firing and the years of financial insecurity had been stressful ones for my family. Most of my time had been taken up with legal questions; my part-time earnings in 1973, for example, had been just $6,000. The oldest of my three children was just starting college. The promise of back pay and a steady income was a godsend. Too good to be true?

Of course. As soon as I saw Staiman's written decision, I had a great sinking feeling. He admitted that my firing had been illegal, but he attributed the firing to the Air Force's unhappiness about *publicity* surrounding my loss of tenure following my C-5A testimony. No witness had ever even suggested this cause and effect. It was a phony verdict meant to stave off the possibility of a criminal prosecution.

Although he restored my job, Staiman denied me everything else. The derogatory information would not be expunged from my file. I was awarded no damages, costs, or attorneys' fees for our enormous expenses in fighting United States government injustice.

Bodner argued powerfully against the decision, citing the testimony of General Cappucci, which — against interest — showed the falsity of the Air Force case. But the Civil Service Commission, having dared as much as it wanted to, left the rest up to the Air Force.

The details of my reinstatement were now split between the civilian secretariat of the Air Force and the military Air Staff, which controlled everything except the question of whether to appeal the CSC ruling. The new secretary of the Air Force, John McLucas, decided to stall on that question until the last minute. Finally, on October 3, the Air Force announced it would not appeal. The main burden of the rear-guard battle fell on the Air Staff, which had determined to oppose me at every point and to make me and my lawyers expend time and money on every niggling detail of my return to duty.

I was mortally tired of this unequal fight. I had come to view the opposition as incredibly powerful, corrupt, and dishonest. I could think of few eras in American history when one organization so dominated its province as to be above criticism and above the law. There was the period of the big city bosses — Tammany and Boss Tweed in New York, for example — and the time when the Capone gang made the Chicago area virtually a warlord's fiefdom. And there was the era when the robber barons controlled a large part of the American economy. But heretofore in our history we had always made the military answerable to civilian laws and direction.

I have laid out the many small details of my case to illustrate a new development in our history that most Americans are scarcely aware of. In other banana republics the military comes to power with a sudden coup and the installation of a junta. Here it is different. Power in America is not a matter of controlling the police forces and the media. America runs on money. And the military has quietly come to vast economic power by taking vast amounts of the federal income for itself.

I decided to try to enlist the support of Senator Harry Byrd, Jr., of Virginia. I had long been an admirer of the tightwad instincts of the Byrd dynasty, which had dominated Virginia politics since the New Deal days. They had kept the state debt-free up to the time I moved there. The elder Senator Byrd, Harry, Sr., had fought some good battles. He had exposed the government stockpiling of tons of feathers (yes, *feathers*), and he had pointed to its stockpiling of spruce lumber for the construction of aircraft when spruce had not been used in airplanes for forty years. Senator Harry Byrd, Jr., with some of the same tightwad ideas, had played a big part in defeating the subsidy for the supersonic transport.

When I called on him, Senator Byrd promised to help. This led to a meeting with Jack Marsh, an assistant secretary of defense, and then Marty Hoffman and Hugh Witt of Schlesinger's staff. Hoffman and Witt had put their heads together, and they had a terrific deal for me. I'd work in a part of the Pentagon where I'd be separated from my "enemies" in the Air Force. I'd be assigned to a Department of Defense commission to study the standardization of small hardware parts.

Did they mean nuts and bolts, I asked.

They stammered a bit and finally said, "Well, yes."

Hugh Witt became agitated. He said, "I know what you're going to do. You're going out to tell everybody that we tried to put you in deep freeze by assigning to you a commission to study nuts and bolts."

"Well," I said, "isn't that what you're doing?"

They began to argue that the commission would study more than nuts and bolts (screws and washers?) and that it was an important subject.

I agreed as to the importance, but I pointed out that professional organizations such as the American Society of Mechanical Engineers and others had already done the job.

In the end they asked with embarrassment that I not tell anyone about their proposal. Until this writing, I have kept their secret.

Meanwhile, with the Air Force stalling on appeal and the secretary of defense dithering, President Nixon expressed the "hope," in a September 19 memo from Garment via Nixon assistant Jerry Warren to Ziegler, that the Air Force would not fight the CSC decision. The *hope?* Nixon was commander in chief of the armed forces.

On October 17, 1973, I was summoned to the Pentagon for a most interesting interview with William Woodruff, the new assistant secretary of the Air Force for financial management. I had plenty of reason to be dubious about this man, who had been an assistant to Senator Richard Russell of Georgia at the time of my testimony on the C-5A — which was assembled in Georgia by Russell's constituents. Woodruff was also an old crony of General Pete Crow — they had worked together to minimize my C-5A testimony — and Crow, now assistant vice chief of staff of the Air Force, was top bird in the Air Force military bureaucracy.

Despite our past differences, I planned to start off on a positive note with Bill Woodruff. I asked him what goals he aimed for in his new job. If they were good, I told him, I wanted to help achieve them.

"What do you mean?" he asked. "Goals?"

"What do you hope to achieve?"

He dithered for a minute. Finally he said that he wanted "three years of good service."

Translation from the bureaucratese: retirement with a higher pension at the end of three years. Government retirement pay is based on the three highest-paid years of one's career. He was now making more than he'd ever made as a staff assistant in Congress.

Another of his goals, it developed, was to deny me my old job. I was astonished. I pointed out that the CSC ruling required the Air Force to return me to that job "as though the adverse action had never taken place."

Woodruff began to lecture me sternly. "I cannot erase the stigma on you," he said. I was "under a cloud." There were "a lot of people who do not consider you a good employee." He added that he could make it possible for me to do a good job and "erase those clouds."

I had been under the misapprehension that I, at great expense of time, energy, money, and stomach lining, had *won* a decision.

He said that I would have to prove myself before I would be allowed to do anything with major weapons systems. "Surely you don't think I would let you look at the B-1 bomber?" he asked.

"Why not?" I said. "From what I hear, it's as fat as a goose."

Not exactly the most diplomatic thing to say. Woodruff noted that Pete Crow and the Air Force military comptroller, General Joe deLuca, would have to approve before I could go back to my old job. I'd also been demoted: I was now to report to Woodruff's deputy, Thomas Moran.

I decided to see whether I could work something out amicably with Moran. When I asked him what *his* goals were, Moran, a senior apparatchik overdue for retirement, said with refreshing honesty, "My goals are just to answer the mail."

I finally got an audience with the great man himself. Secretary McLucas seemed passive and completely detached. Almost dreamily, he let me know that he was "deferring to the staff," and if I didn't like it, I could appeal to the Civil Service Commission.

I didn't like it, and my lawyers did appeal, but we did not learn until later in legal discovery that the Air Force had already colluded with the

Civil Service Commission to approve my assignment to a minimal job. Given what the Air Force had on CSC Chairman Hampton (Seamans had involved him in the secret plot against me back in 1969), only minimal pressure was needed.

The lesser job assignment put me in a dilemma. If I refused McLucas's order to report for duty in the make-work job, I could be fired for not following orders. If I accepted it, I had lost my long fight against wasteful spending. If I tried again in the CSC court, I would probably lose. I decided to accept a narrow foothold in the Pentagon and see what I could make of it.

On December 10, 1973, I reported to Woodruff's office, where he had gathered as witnesses eight or ten weenies from the military staff and the Air Force legal corps.

I had a little surprise for them. I had learned enough about the bureaucratic labyrinth to know that with the reduction-in-force pretense demolished, the action to fire me had to be cancelled retroactively. I told Woodruff and the assembled weenies that I was reporting for duty in my old job.

At first Woodruff was nonplussed, but the weenie lawyers came to his rescue. My old job no longer existed, they said. I had, indeed, been restored to it at 12:01 A.M. that very morning. However, at 12:02 I had been transferred to the new, lesser job. If I wanted to make an appeal, it would have to be about the 12:02 transfer. Of course they denied that the new job was a lesser one.

I imagined a scene that could take place only in the world's greatest bureaucracy: Air Force apparatchiks stealing in the dark of the night to the Pentagon. At exactly 12:01, "Rubber stamps ready, men!" Unheard-of speed in stamping and processing the documents that restored me to my old job. Then at 12:02, with an efficiency never seen in these parts before, processing the transfer papers.

Henry Durham described the end of his career at Lockheed thus:

When it became known that I might go outside with the problem, Mr. Paul Frech, the director of manufacturing, was sent to Chattanooga to see me. [Our] conversation was predictably short. The first thing he said was, "Do you know what happened to Ernie Fitzgerald, who went to Washington with some Lockheed problems?" When I said I didn't, Frech said, "He's now chief shit-house inspector for the Civil Service Commission and will never be able to get a good job as long as he lives" [Erwin Kroll, "The Education of Henry Durham," reprinted from *The Progressive*, 1972].

6

☆ ☆ ☆

Dr. Doom's
Dollar Model

I RETURNED TO THE PENTAGON on December 10, 1973, with a gloomy feeling that when nobody was looking, the Pentagon had become an independent entity outside the laws of the United States. What should have been a solid legal victory for me had produced no more than a minor, grudging concession. And the extent of petty vindictiveness was hard to believe. Although the Civil Service Commission had ruled that I had a right to my back pay, the Air Force refused to give it to me. It took several months of legal fighting to get a partial settlement. Both John Bodner and Bill Sollee stuck by me in the continuing legal fight with the Air Force and the CSC.

Bodner was so outraged by their perfidy that he agreed to draw up a damage suit against those who had retaliated against me. I was sick of appeals and legal processes, but I decided to carry on the fight. The complaint was against Alexander Butterfield and several high-level Pentagon officials; though we did not know at the time about the roles of Richard Nixon, Bryce Harlow, Harold Brown, Robert Hampton, and others in the conspiracy, John put in a John Doe clause on the chance that others had been involved.

At first it looked as if John and I were taking on the whole federal establishment on our own, but on February 20, 1974, we received a letter from Ralph Temple of the ACLU saying that both the local ACLU and the powerful national organization "would become fully associated" with us. This meant that the national ACLU would pay the expenses of the litigation and provide some staff assistance. It seemed

74

like a gift from the gods. With those problems in the best of hands, I could concentrate on my much-circumscribed job and look for some ways to save money in the swollen military budget.

After the Saturday Night Massacre and the firing of Special Prosecutor Archibald Cox in October 1973, the Nixon presidency had seemed doomed. For me there was one significant quote that other people seemed to have missed in all the commotion. When Attorney General Richardson refused to fire Cox, Alexander Haig ordered Deputy Attorney General William Ruckelshaus to do the job, reportedly in these words: "Your commander in chief has given you an order."

This was more than the usual Al Haig bluster; it was a general's symptomatic misconstruction of the Constitution. The president is commander in chief of the armed forces, not of the entire nation. With respect to the rest of us, our elected leader's primary function is "to take care that the laws be faithfully executed." But the military mind was formed with the Macedonian phalanx of hoplites, where unquestioning obedience was the key to victory. When a commander gives an order, legality is irrelevant.

The Pentagon, from my worm's eye view, had the ethic of the phalanx, though it had no Alexander. The military men knew by heart every bureaucratic detail, every arcane regulation for what many considered the only legitimate function of government: the common defense, or at least expenditure for defense. They were the only ones with the right vision for the nation. They knew what would make the United States both secure and prosperous: military discipline and military spending.

In many ways James Schlesinger was the ideal person to con America into a defense spending boom after the disillusionment of the Asian wars. He was plausible, intelligent, energetic, and completely uncowed by facts. These talents made him a good propagandist and a favorite of Richard Nixon, who promoted him to higher and higher jobs. As soon as he became secretary of defense, Schlesinger pushed for huge, unprecedented peacetime increases in the military budget. Schlesinger's other great qualification for his new post was that he was really good at scaring the daylights out of the American people. He always saw the Russians or their missiles coming over the horizon in such hordes that the underground circle of cynics in the Pentagon named him "Dr. Doom."

Before his defense appointment Schlesinger had been director of the CIA, where he had brought to prominence an unusual method for assessing the military expenditures of the Soviet Union. This shaggy creature was called the Dollar Model. Using this model, we no longer had to ferret out how many rubles the Soviets were spending on their military establishment; we would just estimate the *size* of that establishment. Then we (or the private contractors) would estimate what it would cost us in dollars to reproduce that establishment here. In other words, what would it cost the United States to buy for dollars every ship, radar, missile, uniform, tank, plane, and artillery piece now owned by the USSR? And, furthermore, what would it cost us to maintain that establishment under American, not Russian, conditions for the coming year (as if we were paying upkeep on our new purchase)? With the Dollar Model, every price-boosting blunder in a California aerospace plant, every slick bookkeeping dodge by a contractor in Detroit was added to the "cost" of running the Soviet military machine. Each time the C-5A overran its estimate, the Dollar Model price of its approximate counterpart, the Soviet AN-22, increased proportionately.

Estimating the Soviet military payroll was an even more incredible exercise. The Red Army draftees are issued new footrags (reportedly — not socks) and a few rubles per month; American soldiers' pay is princely by comparison. The Dollar Model attributed American pay to the huge Soviet armed forces and included all military personnel doing essentially civilian duties, for example, as border guards or internal security duty.

And lo! The estimated Soviet expenditures doubled before our eyes. They got no more bang for a ruble, but they "spent" a lot more rubles. *That* sure as hell increased The Threat. As LTV Aerospace Vice President Samuel Downer had told reporter Bernard Nossiter in 1968, "We're going to increase Defense budgets as long as those bastards in Russia are ahead of us. The American people understand this" (*Washington Post*, December 8, 1968).

Schlesinger's promotion to secretary of defense gave him a wonderful opportunity to cash in on the misconception he had helped create. He was very good at his scam. He cultivated a deliberate, seemingly thoughtful manner of speech, often fumbling with his pipe, which conveyed an impression of profundity. And he had a disarming habit of punctuating his absurd rationalizations for big spending with flashes of candor that helped earn him a reputation for independent thinking and credibility.

Although I did not admire the man, I respected his shrewd sales ability. So I was encouraged when I came across this passage in his book *The Political Economy of National Security:* "We could, without substantial difficulty, double the amount of the military protection we are receiving even without doubling the military expenditures." With this heartening thought, I tried that much harder every time Schlesinger dropped a hint about some area where he would support cost savings.

At the time I returned to the Pentagon, Schlesinger was making a public noise about the "teeth to tail" ratio of our armed forces — meaning that the animal had not enough to bite with and a very large rear. Schlesinger seemed to be saying that he wanted more incisors and less derrière. Okay, I thought, I can help with that.

As deputy for productivity management, I had no real authority, but I could initiate modest projects of my own, so long as I stayed away from big weapons buying. I decided to use my little productivity job as a lever to improve the operations of the Air Force Logistics Command (AFLC). This huge, industry-like organization employed more than 80,000 people, with an overstaffed headquarters in Dayton, Ohio, five large Air Logistic Centers (ALCs) scattered around the country, and one smaller installation. The centers supplied, maintained, and modified weapons systems — planes, missiles, and support equipment. Their operations included practically everything done by the big aerospace and missile manufacturers. Although an increasing share of this work was being let out to private contractors, the AFLC still carried on a great deal of activity. I reasoned that if we could make our ALCs models of low-cost, high-quality organization, we could use that as a lever to get the big contractors to improve their performance. Or we could let the ALCs compete with them. There were already large areas of potential direct competition.

Since the time in the 1950s when I had been associated with the AFLC (then called Air Material Command), their use of industrial engineering methods had gone downhill. But a few true believers were left from that era, and they had kept the old cost-control procedures alive. They saw to it that the performance of the maintenance shops was measured by comparing the standard-hour value of work produced directly to the chronological hours spent on that work.

Perhaps out of sentimentality, in that should-cost represented the kind of industrial management that had once made the United States the greatest manufacturer in the world, I was determined to preserve this endangered species in the ALCs. As far as I knew, the rest of the aerospace industry wasn't using should-cost. The private contractors had a stake in adding as much as they could onto the should-take time, usually by multiplying it by a large factor, supposedly to account for the learning curve. For instance, if Aerospace Factory X had a job that should take 100 manhours to perform, they would typically allow ten times the should-take time, or 1,000 hours for the first item made, 800 for the second, 640 for the fourth, and so on (the 80 percent improvement curve).

This system allowed the contractor to set up an inflated level of "actual hours," and this fraudulent measure would then be applied to future jobs. Repeated cycles of this process "justified" an ever-increasing upward spiral of allowed costs.

Although the AFLC had kept, in theory at least, the old cost-control methods, their shops were not highly efficient. They didn't have the big contractors' incentive to maximize allowable costs, but they didn't have much incentive to excel. Their workloads, and therefore their jobs, rested on political considerations more than competition.

I was pleasantly surprised, though, to find that AFLC used my old in-house dollars per standard-labor-hour produced to compare one ALC with another. In 1974 the ALCs' costs were in the $12–$14 range for a standard labor hour. Those standards were too fat. And certain charges, such as depreciation and headquarters' expenses, were not included. But overall the ALC cost for good work (at least as good as that of the private contractors) was under $20 per hour, a fraction of what the contractors were charging the Pentagon.

I'd often been accused of trying to make the Air Force look bad. Here was a chance to make the Air Force look good. I was eager to bring these facts to notice and to build on them in hopes of stimulating better performance across the board. I wanted to use the AFLC as a model for improvement that could be applied to the operations of big contractors when I got back to working on them. I had an ally in Colin Parfitt, an assistant to one of Woodruff's other deputies. An experienced certified public accountant, Colin was too honest and competent to have much chance for notable success in the Air Force.

We did have a few problems. The stickiest one was that in the process of making the Air Force look relatively good, I would make the pet contractors look bad. But I thought I might be able to keep that hidden until the program got under way. The second problem was that I'd inherited some garbage called the productivity program, which was designed quite literally to be useless for budgetary work and so even more useless for cost control and cost reduction.

One wonderful part of this program was a practice called "unbundling." The AFLC measured the productivity of the civilian workers who purchased supplies by comparing the number of manhours they worked with the number of purchase orders they issued in that period. It was easy to look a lot more productive if one large purchase order was unbundled (or divided) into a host of smaller ones. End result? The mythical productivity was increased, but no more real work was accomplished. And with all the extra paperwork, the costs went up.

The situation was even worse if a boss decided that the purchase orders should be carried through in less time. Since the place was run on a cost-plus philosophy and everybody was under pressure to spend the large sums available in the budget, all control vanished. It is easy to get purchase orders out faster if nobody questions the unit cost of what you are buying: don't dicker over prices, don't waste time getting competitive bids, just spend the money.

Early in 1974 I first pointed out that their "productivity" program actually made overall costs rise. Oddly enough, nobody in the Air Force disagreed with me, but nobody changed the system, either.

There was a perfectly good measurement for productivity in the maintenance work AFLC carried out, but the Command forbade its use in the productivity program. Instead, they used a gobbledygook "market basket" measurement so bad that even the people who concocted it admitted it was invalid.

Even with the backing of the old-time true believers, I couldn't seem to persuade AFLC to adopt a meaningful productivity program. They reared back in horror at the mention of standard hours or should-take times: on March 8 General George Rhodes, chief of staff of the AFLC, wrote me:

> We do not believe a work measurement system indicator, such as the Labor Cost Trends [AFLC's work-measurement-based performance indicator] or any similar comparison of standard (earned) to actual or standard-to-payroll hours should be used as a substitute for even the most invalid productivity measurement system indicator.

I took this absurd paradox to my bosses, Bill Woodruff and Thomas Moran, but all they wanted to know was whether Schlesinger's office was happy with the invalid yardsticks. When I said that Schlesinger's people didn't care one way or the other, they said that we were answering the mail, so why worry?

About this time, there arose a monster called ALS, or Advanced Logistics System, which was so foolish that the AFLC fell in love with it. Part of it was a cost-justification scheme called Project Max (after Max Kennedy, its unfortunate instigator); it seems to have been lifted pretty much intact from Boeing's Wichita, Kansas, division. ALS was an attempt to shift the emphasis at AFLC from what work should cost to what it did cost and to engender and justify ever-higher labor costs, just as the big contractors did. The big spenders in the AFLC and Schlesinger's office wanted to get rid of one of the vestiges of sanity left, the ALCs' work measurement system, and bring in the hairy monster. Because the monster was very costly to feed — the mere administrative expense was huge — we had good grounds to oppose it. It was simply

too complicated to work. But the AFLC cherished its pet and allowed it
to eat money for years, even though Congress kept canceling it. Colin
Parfitt and I more or less fought the big spenders to a draw at the AFLC.
Project Max didn't go anywhere, but neither did our improvement
program. However, the work we did and the allies we made put us in a
good position later to effectively apply our analytical approaches to the
big contractors.

I didn't realize at the time that Schlesinger was unalterably opposed
to what I and my kind were trying to do. I had little evidence that he
was working to increase the military budget, but I began to see that the
mood in Washington favored that course.

As the hated Southeast Asia war drew to a close, the military were
trying to change their reputation for lavishly supplied but ineffective
warfare. By 1974 some military thinkers were beginning to counsel a
new public relations line. Dr. Theodore Kahn, a retired colonel, writing
in *The Retired Officer* magazine for January 1974, advised:

> By defending our country's war role in public forums and in the media,
> the military inevitably drew upon itself some of the blame for the
> existence of this policy. Any justification by military officers of
> political decisions made by our elected civilian leadership will make
> the military vulnerable as a scapegoat if, later, these decisions prove to
> be unpopular.

With the waning of the war in Southeast Asia, Congress was eager to
get back to the old pork-barrel politics, a natural instinct stimulated by
the fact that the country seemed to be entering a recession. As *Time* put
it on June 4, 1974, "The mood on Capitol Hill was shaped by the
economic slowdown." In response, Congress saw to it that the aerospace
industry began to boom again. From midyear 1973 to midyear 1974 its
employment rose from 946,000 to 962,000. Wage rates, too, took off,
from $4.91 per hour to $5.36 on average. As has so often been the case
in our economic history, defense contract pay and prices were a leading
indicator of inflation ahead.

The newspapers often describe this kind of action as "heating up the
economy." On that theory, Schlesinger was trying for a barn-burner. On
August 13, 1974, he called his top assistants together and, as this
Memorandum for the Record puts it:

> Secretary Schlesinger urged the Services to expedite the obligation and
> expenditure of funds to minimize the impact of inflation on defense
> Purchasing Power. In this connection, the Comptroller's office will
> regularly measure the progress of obligations and expenditure for each
> Service and ensure appropriate visibility.

Then there was Israel. In the opening days of the 1973 Yom Kippur war, Israeli forces had suffered unexpected and shocking losses. Americans had enormous respect and admiration for the nation of Israel, and a majority in this country were willing to sacrifice to ensure her safety. The Pentagonians played brilliantly upon this sympathy, putting out the party line in speech after speech: a dollar for the Pentagon is twenty-five cents for Israel.

After living with his predecessor's budgets through fiscal 1975, Schlesinger broke through with big increases in military acquisition in the fiscal 1976 budget and set in motion the post-Vietnam spending spree that continues to this day. From the standpoint of Schlesinger and his big-spender constituency, this was a historically successful breakthrough. They melted the de facto freeze on acquisition spending that had temporarily arrested the growth of the military spending coalition's political and economic strength. More ominously for our future national solvency and our liberties, they set in motion explosive growth in military acquisition spending as a major war was *ending*, a political feat never before accomplished in our country. The chart, which uses DoD figures, tells the story.

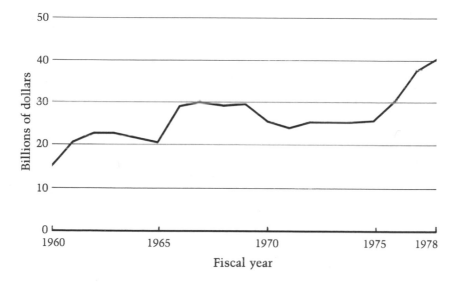

The Defense Department's total obligational authority for acquisition (research and development plus procurement), 1960–1978. Source: Office of the Assistant Secretary of Defense (Comptroller), "National Defense Budget Estimates for FY 1988/1989," May 1987.

Schlesinger, repudiating his published opinion, now announced that cutting fat out of the military budget without hurting the muscle was a "charming illusion." On January 15, 1975, he previewed his 1976 budget with a ringing "guns before butter" statement. (It is instructive to remember that this idea was first enunciated by Air Minister Hermann Goering in 1936 when he said, "Guns will make us powerful; butter will only make us fat.") Schlesinger said: "It is part of the system that we make sacrifices of consumption or domestic investment activity in order to maintain an appropriate level of defense."

Contrast Schlesinger's outlook with the classic American ideas in Dwight David Eisenhower's famous Cross of Iron speech of April 16, 1953:

> Every gun that is fired, every warship launched, every rocket fired signifies in the final sense a *theft* from those who hunger and are not fed, those who are cold and are not clothed. This world in arms is not spending money alone. It is spending the sweat of its laborers, the genius of its scientists, the hopes of its children. . . . We pay for a single fighter plane with a half million bushels of wheat [by 1987, the price was twenty million bushels]. We pay for a single destroyer with new homes that could have housed more than eight thousand people. . . . This is not a way of life at all, in any true sense. Under the cloud of threatening war, it is humanity hanging from a cross of iron.

Because I had escaped the sad fate of Kenneth Cook and had "won" a decision, many potential whistle blowers, or closet patriots, began to bring their problems to me. Everybody had a horror story to disclose, from defective equipment to dubious-quality drug supplies to cases of big-scale theft. I could only tell them that it was easy enough to exercise their First Amendment rights, but that for doing so the government would probably ruin them.

In the past, during the worst of my troubles, I had discussed my situation with Ralph Nader. He had been kind and helpful, but except for occasional forays into the field, he would not tackle Pentagon abuses. He told me that the mess was so huge that it could easily consume all his time and effort. Now that I was back in a Pentagon job, I began spending some spare time with Nader's whistle blower project, which was headed by Peter Petkus, with the assistance of an energetic young woman named Felice "Fritzy" Cohen. They were anxious to do what they could, within their limitations, to offer legal defense in legitimate cases. My association with the project was well within the bounds of the government employees' Code of Ethics, yet it exposed me to considerable carping from my bosses.

My contacts with Nader's group and with congressional staff investigators infuriated the Pentagonists. And as relations with my bosses grew chillier, I began to have some curious experiences. Sometimes I still fell into my old habit of working late at the Pentagon. A couple of nights when I left the almost-deserted parking lot, a nondescript sedan with a government-issue look would pull in behind my car and follow me closely along the circuitous route to my home in suburban Virginia. Two men with short haircuts sat in the front seat; they made no secret of the fact that they were following me. I kept this to myself because I didn't want to sound paranoid. But I remembered the remark of an investigator on Capitol Hill, "If you're in my business in Washington and you're not paranoid, you're crazy."

At this time Senator Frank Church was conducting a sweeping investigation of bribe giving abroad by American corporations, especially Lockheed and Northrop. Because of my familiarity with Lockheed, Church's investigators questioned me several times. For a while it seemed that Church might succeed in exposing a lot of this corruption, but as the scandal grew larger, the opposition grew stiffer. The investigators' success was their undoing. Henry Kissinger, now secretary of state, was a particularly vigorous and effective opponent.

At one point the staff was zeroing in on a tip that some Lockheed equipment was being exported, via third countries, to the Soviet bloc, an early instance of the illegal "technology transfer" that was to become such a heated issue in 1979. But, according to the Church committee staffers, some Republican senators put heavy pressure on Church to kill that line of inquiry for "national security reasons." Quite suddenly during the spring of 1975, much of the steam seemed to go out of the Church committee investigations, cooled by these complaints. To all of us close to the inquiry, Lockheed's millions of dollars spent abroad in "agent commissions" smelled of bribes and kickbacks. But the curtain of official secrecy was a stout one.

Some of Lockheed's imitators in the art of political manipulation were pretty amateurish; the worst and unluckiest of these was the Northrop Corporation. Whereas Lockheed had been king of the hill among Pentagon contractors for most of a generation, Northrop was still trying to become one of the big boys. It had scored a coup in persuading the Navy to buy its new F-18 fighter plane in apparent defiance of a congressional order that the Pentagon buy versions of the same "lightweight, low-cost" fighter for both the Air Force and the Navy. Northrop's F-17 had lost out to General Dynamics' F-16 as the plane chosen for both the Air Force and NATO, so Northrop simply made some changes in the F-17, renumbered it F-18, teamed up with McDonnell-Douglas, and sold the loser to the Navy. That, of course, quieted any urges for competitive excellence that the aircraft manufacturers may have had aroused by the fly-off.

Northrop's product mainstay had been the F-5 Freedom Fighter and its derivative, the T-38 training plane. The F-5 never quite made it with the U.S. military, but it had been a big seller overseas. Why foreign governments loved the F-5 so much was seen as something of a mystery, but disclosures of laundering money for illegal political contributions and even more direct baksheesh (a Persian word much honored in the Middle East) cleared the picture considerably.

Northrop probably would have gotten away with its clumsy black-bag operations if it hadn't been for Watergate: the special prosecutor's office found that the company had made an illegal contribution of $150,000 to Nixon's 1972 campaign. If there had been any criminal indictments, Northrop would have been in boiling water. One Northrop executive had the bad judgment to show back-dated documents to federal investigators (and had to confess the deception), while others told inaccurate stories about the timing of their commitments to make political contributions. Some top Northrop officials pleaded guilty and accepted tiny fines — two for $5,000 and one for $1,000. It was clear that the fix was in.

Most of the focus of the Church committee investigation was on overseas bribes, but my friends and I were more interested in laundered money coming back into this country for domestic hokey-pokey. We all were familiar with the Mexican laundry where the cash for Nixon had its past washed away, but a lot of other cleaning establishments might have been uncovered if the House Banking and Currency Committee's subpoena powers had not been cut off in the summer of 1972, just when Representative Wright Patman's men were hot on the trail.

One *blanchisserie* was operated out of Paris by a man named William A. Savy. In the course of twelve years, Northrop paid him about $1,150,000; he returned $376,000 in cash to Northrop vice president James Allen, who distributed it for "political contributions and other purposes."

Some of the money Savy returned went to a Washington lawyer named Frank J. DeFrancis, who was reported to have disbursed it to a "retired general." The "general" turned out to be a former Marine major, John Blandford (who held the rank of major general in the reserve), and who was best known as chief counsel and head honcho on the House Armed Services Committee in the days of Chairman Mendel Rivers.

DeFrancis was fortunate enough to have a fifteen-year contract with Northrop paying him more than $100,000 a year for services that Northrop's executive committee could not identify. And he helped Northrop set up a Swiss corporation whose purpose was to distribute gifts of cash or stock to those who proved "helpful to Northrop."

Northrop cried foul at the congressional investigation because, its officials said, they were only doing what Lockheed always did. Protestations notwithstanding, Northrop's board of directors, aided by its auditors, Ernst and Ernst, set up an executive committee to investigate the charges.

In fact, Northrop's contracts covering DeFrancis and the Swiss deal were copied from contracts Lockheed had with Dr. Hubert Weisbrod, a Swiss lawyer. Weisbrod ran an operation for Northrop from 1968 to 1973, receiving $750,000 in fees — charged to U.S. taxpayers when Northrop added the sum to its Pentagon bill as "indirect support costs." Under examination, Northrop could not identify any services rendered by the Swiss lawyer, but Northrop's chairman, Thomas Jones, said that Weisbrod helped the company sell aircraft to European governments. Weisbrod himself said he was a "trustee" and that his services consisted of endorsing checks from Northrop for deposit in his clients' Swiss bank accounts. He would not say who his clients were.

Naturally, all these leads tantalized Wright Patman's investigators. One of them, a bright, engaging young Texan named Robert Riggs, on the staff of the Joint Committee on Defense Production, had had a good introduction to the weaknesses of politicians when he served as an aide in the Texas legislature. Robert was one of the promising young investigators I tried to help. Riggs was certain that at least some of the loose hundreds of millions of dollars that had gone for foreign washing and bribes must have floated back to our shores for the fun and profit of native politicians. When the Northrop executive committee's report to the board of directors stiffly admitted: "It is reasonably clear that officials of the Executive Branch agencies have received corporate hospitality under circumstances in which the official involved could have been subject to disciplinary action or public embarrassment for breach of his agency's Standards of Conflict Regulations," Riggs's nostrils widened at the familiar whiff of corruption on the breeze.

"What kind of hospitality?" he asked me. "Do the contractors hire whores for the generals?"

I explained to him that things were not quite so crude as that. I'd seen some expenditures charged off as fees for "public stenographers," but the usual way was to bring together the right mix of friendly women and impressionable brass.

Riggs clung to the belief that the instincts of influential Washingtonians were no different from those of some of the good old boys in Austin. He said that few people really cared that some foreigner was bribed — it might be necessary just to get his order. And the news about laundries didn't excite the taxpayers much, either. But they really felt stung when they read about their dollars being spent on bimbos. That was a good attention-getter for more serious venality and more serious money.

So began what Robert Riggs called "the great whore hunt." I couldn't help him, but I did introduce him to Dick Bast, a Washington private investigator who had once represented a prostitute who was having contractual difficulties with her defense industry employer. Dick was very helpful.

At about this time in 1975, Ernst and Ernst filed a report with the SEC revealing that during the period 1971–1973, Northrop had entertained 123 military personnel, 21 Defense Department officials, 11 congressmen, 85 congressional staff members, 119 Northrop employees, and 49 unknowns at the corporation's hunting lodge near Easton, Maryland, on the Eastern Shore of the Chesapeake Bay.

Ronald Reagan and other politicians had had free trips in the corporate jet; Senator Howard Cannon, then chairman of the Senate Armed Forces Committee on Tactical Airpower, an approving body for Northrop's F-18, had almost a shuttle service from Las Vegas to a resort in the West Indies. (Cannon's less publicized job was as chairman of the Senate Ethics Committee.)

Though the accountants' report was too late to prevent the Northrop follies, it did reflect great credit on Ernst and Ernst, the only CPA firm involved in the bribery mess that produced anything like 530 pages of penance. Most of the heavy matters in the report were not followed up, but the hunting lodge was. When Senator Church's Foreign Relations Committee held hearings on the matter in May 1975, Senator Richard Clark demanded the names of the Pentagon officials Northrop had entertained. He didn't ask for names of congressmen and their staffers who had been at the lodge.

Riggs should have caught the significance of that omission, but he didn't. Instead, he plunged with enthusiasm into the business of hunting the hunters. He talked with prostitutes who had worked for contractors and found that most of these ladies didn't know the names of their Pentagonal johns but might recognize them if they saw them.

This sent Riggs scurrying around for pictures of officers and officials, past and present.

It was a war of nerves on both sides. The generals were mightily upset by a newspaper report that a large defense contractor had hired two prostitutes to entertain a gathering of forty or fifty high-ranking Pentagon officials at an Eastern Shore hunting lodge. An Air Force major came into my office, sat down, and read the account. After he'd finished, he remarked, "Forty generals? Two whores? Those guys aren't combat-ready."

My secret sympathizers in the Pentagon, who were always coming up with helpful suggestions, proposed that we keep track of the whore-to-general ratio as a management indicator. They prepared phony letterhead memorandums speculating whether the Russians were ahead of us in this important statistic and, if so, wondering what it would cost to catch up. Could we economize by setting up civil service classifications for call girls? Should we avoid discrimination in hiring? What about seniority?

Riggs's inquiries eventually became too widespread and too pointed to remain secret. One Sunday afternoon in September 1975, he went to the Eastern Shore to interview a duck plucker named Lawrence Gay. Riggs wanted Gay's list of clients, their hunting license numbers, and the record of their kills — all of which Gay was required to keep for the federal migratory waterfowl regulators. In the middle of the conversation, Gay was called away to the telephone. When he came back, he asked Riggs to return in the evening for the lists. Riggs agreed; but when he visited the house again, Gay had vanished for good.

Riggs's inquiries into other aspects of contractor entertainment began to shake the Pentagon tree. He managed to get a look at a section (suppressed by the Pentagon) of a Defense Contract Audit Agency (DCAA) report that disclosed lavish Northrop selling parties given by Mrs. Anna Chennault (widow of the Flying Tigers hero, General Claire Chennault) and subsidized by the Pentagon. Mrs. Chennault, a favorite of right-wing circles, the China lobby, and several Asian dictators, was known in Washington as the Dragon Lady.

Riggs told his colleagues on Capitol Hill about the report and got the cooperation of Bill Broydrick, a staff assistant to Congressman Les Aspin. Broydrick, who was just about as brash and energetic as Riggs, managed to get a copy of the DCAA Northrop report from an Air Force officer who was playing both sides. The newspapers began printing disclosures from the report, and drop by drop, the young mavericks kept the water torture going.

The first revelation was about Anna Chennault's entertainments. On the Northrop payroll since 1971, she had been hospitable to a great many of the top brass and top politicians who had something to say about military contracts. But when I saw her guest lists, I knew my friends and I were in big trouble. Prominent among the names was that of the House minority leader, Gerald Ford. We were in equal trouble with the Democrats. Another of her prominent guests was Tommy "the Cork" Corcoran, who, since his days as one of FDR's brain trusters, had been a kind of legend in the party. Now he had become Anna's friend, lawyer, and protector — and he was using his famous charm to bring her together with senior Democrats.

Corcoran's visits to the Hill, as Riggs described them, were pure theater. He would begin by invoking the sainted name of Roosevelt and recall all that he and FDR had been through together during the New Deal and World War II. Next he would recount how the dying Claire Chennault had called him to his bedside and with his last breath had pleaded, "Cork, take care of my little girl."

"He shed real tears," Riggs said. "Tears as big as horse turds."

Anna needed about as much protection as a full-grown barracuda, but Tommy the Cork's masterful lobbying did manage to weaken congressional support for Riggs's inquiries.

Then the Pentagonists landed a hard blow on Riggs's political kneecap. Displaying brilliant tactics not learned at West Point, they released a list of the *congressional* recipients of Northrop entertainment — to devastating effect. It was bad enough that key representatives and senators were on the list, especially members of the Armed Services and Military Appropriations committees. Even more painful was to find there practically the whole of the congressional staff establishment — men from the Senate Appropriations, Foreign Relations, and Armed Forces committees, and from the House Armed Services subcommittee; the secretary of the Senate; Barry Goldwater's administrative assistant; John Blandford; and William Woodruff, once counsel to the Senate Military Appropriations subcommittee and, in 1975, my boss at the Pentagon.

Only people who have worked on the Hill can appreciate the gravity of offending this powerful group. They run the day-by-day affairs of the Congress; they are courted by both contractors and the military. If they choose to belong to one of the armed services reserves, that service sees to it that they rise in rank. The unwritten rule in this powerful brotherhood is decorum. When some rich corporation is entertaining, it's all right to eat, drink, and screw as much as you can — but it must be done discreetly.

Having won the round with Congress, the Pentagonians went after another vulnerable target — me. I had just reached an agreement with Secretary McLucas about settlement of the legal dispute over my demotion and exclusion from the big weapons projects, when suddenly that agreement was reversed. In a conversation with Robert Riggs, I learned that the Defense Investigative Service (DIS) had targeted me as the source of the leak of the DCAA's Northrop report. They knew I was not guilty, but that didn't matter. At a press conference on October 20, 1975, Dr. Doom himself denounced the leak as "a criminal act."

As though I needed a reminder that I was in trouble, I was again tailed a few nights later. When I left the nearly deserted Pentagon parking lot, a nondescript sedan followed me closely. I slowed up, then put on speed, then slowed again as I headed out the George Washington Parkway toward my home in McLean. The sedan stayed right behind me.

I began to get alarmed as I left the parkway and turned into narrow, winding, hilly Kirby Road. Where the road twisted down between high banks toward Pimmit Run, I steered my old Rambler toward the center line. The sedan had to drop back, but I could hear its engine roar as we approached the bridge. Apparently my new fellow travelers didn't realize that the bridge was extremely narrow. When the driver tried to pull up beside me, he had to slam on his brakes to avoid hitting the rail or going into the creek. I drove as fast as I could to get out of that deserted place. When they caught up, I was turning into my street.

I stopped the car, ran into my house, and grabbed my 30-06 rifle. I ran out into the yard again and crouched behind a large tree, working the bolt as noisily as I could. The rifle was empty. I didn't even have any ammunition in the house. My hands shook, but I pointed the rifle at the car. The men lit cigarettes and seemed to be talking it over. I didn't know what I would do if they got out of the car. Finally, they started up and drove away.

The DIS was still trying to frame me for the release of the DCAA report. One evening when I was at Riggs's Capitol Hill apartment, his wife took a phone call for him. She said, "Robert, a man just called and said your car is ready, then hung up." It was a prearranged signal. We left the apartment immediately and walked to the Immigration building a few blocks away. As we entered, a pay phone in a booth in the lobby began to ring. Riggs answered, took some notes, and hung up.

"That's one scared spook," he said, "but he's hanging in." He went on to tell me that the DIS investigators had been trying to interview my trusted secretary, Ann Hayduck, without my knowing about it. Ann was a serious-minded, extremely competent secretary who was nearing retirement. She had loyally resisted the investigators, refusing to be interviewed anywhere but in our office. Riggs's source said that the DIS would get her to talk sooner or later and suggested I wait until afterward to ask Ann about it.

Soon after, I had to go to Alabama to visit my mother, who was seriously ill. In my absence, Riggs found out, the DIS people did interview Ann. When I learned of this, I asked her into my office, closed the door, and suggested she tell me about the interview.

She said that both the DIS men and my office mate, Colin Parfitt, who had helped set up the interview, had told her not to say anything to me. She had agreed not to volunteer anything but had said she wouldn't lie to me if I asked about the episode.

The DIS men, James E. Kartis and Daniel O. Payne, soon found out that I had no access to the Northrop audit report, which Parfitt, who reviewed audits for the Air Force Secretariat, kept in his safe. Both Ann and Parfitt testified to that. But the DIS interviewers were not easily discouraged. They grilled Ann for two hours about my contacts with congressmen, congressional staffers, and the press. Ann said she really lost her temper when they began asking "embarrassing personal questions" about me. She told them they ought to be ashamed of themselves doing this while they could have been investigating people who were taking bribes.

When I confronted Parfitt, he unhappily admitted all Ann had said about his role. Thereafter, he was a staunch supporter of mine.

I asked my boss, Arnold Bueter, to help me get the files on the DIS frame, but he refused. Bill Kinkaid, Riggs's boss in the bureaucracy, also refused. But Riggs, Broydrick, Peter Stockton, and Ron Tammen of Senator Proxmire's office helped me all they could. Broydrick even defused the whole issue of secrecy and the leak of the DCAA audit report by announcing that he had distributed 509 copies of it. That called Schlesinger's bluff; of course, the Pentagon did not prosecute anybody.

As for the DIS investigation of me, Pentagon officials lied briskly when asked about it. Jack Stempler denied any knowledge of it. Terrence McCleary, the DoD comptroller who oversaw the DIS, said my name couldn't even be found in the records, and his deputy, D. O. Cooke, said the file couldn't be released to me because it contained only material affecting the privacy rights of others. Eventually I got enough excerpts from the files to prove that all these officials were lying.

Robert Riggs won another small skirmish in the great hunting lodge affair. On February 3, 1976, when Deputy Secretary of Defense William Clements testified before Proxmire's Joint Committee on Defense Production, he said that the press had blown the whole thing out of proportion. He thought these "highly placed flag officers" couldn't be "impugned over a duck hunt." And, furthermore, nine months of investigation by the DIS had turned up no new names on the Northrop guest list.

That was funny, Proxmire said, because Robert Riggs had turned up fifty-five new names in one afternoon of research on the Eastern Shore. Riggs had gotten the names of purchasers of hunting licenses and duck stamps from the local sporting goods stores and had found a lot of familiar Pentagonal names.

But that was the end of it. The investigation fizzled out, Riggs was fired, and the Joint Committee was later abolished. In Washington you can get away with anything as long as you have the high moguls of Congress as accessories before and after the fact.

Luckily for me, President Ford fired James Schlesinger about then. The voters were beginning to look on the military with a skeptical eye, so the legislators had made small, public-relations cuts in Schlesinger's ballooning budget.

But Dr. Doom wanted it all. He could have praised congressional leaders for helping, though not quite enough, to close his invented spending gap with the Soviet Union. But instead he began to scold Congress for its "deep, savage, and arbitrary" cuts. Ironically, it was Congressman George Mahon of Texas, chairman of the House Appropriations Committee, who bore the brunt of Schlesinger's fury. Mahon was as stout a friend of the Pentagon as ever escorted a multibillion-dollar budget through Congress. Ford, as a former high mogul of that body, knew the rules of the game: Schlesinger had to go. His uses as a Pentagon front man were over.

In the last year or so of the Ford administration, the national security apparat tried hard to regain the luster lost after the retreat from Vietnam and after Watergate. The first solution that occurs to such minds is to shut people up. It wasn't their own sins that had given them a bad name, but people who talked in public about those sins. What we needed was a lot more secrecy. Congress began to cooperate with the administration in an agreement to limit probes. Incriminating material on hand was not released publicly. The courts produced a number of decisions that upheld aspects of official secrecy.

Then the White House, that leakiest of all vessels, cynically mounted a campaign against Congress for its looseness in handling secrets — mostly secrets that had to do with government wrongdoing. At one point Ford even had the effrontery to suggest assigning the FBI the job of plugging congressional leaks.

Ford issued an order giving himself broad new powers. As the *Washington Post* described it on February 19, 1976, "President Ford's new charter for the US intelligence community legitimizes domestic spying and other activities that had been considered legally and politically questionable." In the same issue, an article by Walter Pincus noted that CIA and NSA employees already had to sign secrecy oaths but that the new order extended the rule "throughout the executive branch and on former government employees and outside government contractors." CIA Director George Bush was put in charge of enforcing the order.

The administration was trying to make an issue of "unauthorized disclosures," and Pincus quoted White House Counsel Philip H. Buchen, who said the new procedures would "give the administration a real threat over people who can't be controlled by discipline." The logic was not self-evident. If a government employee broke a law by making "unauthorized disclosures," he could be punished under that law. But legal processes were apparently too chancy for this administration. It wanted something quicker, dirtier, and easier to use on selected targets. Much like the gag rule Colonel Robert Pursley had proposed in 1969 to end "the Fitzgerald kind of thing."

Fortunately, Ford and Bush left office before they could carry out the secrecy order. But the creature, alive somewhere in the basement of the White House, would rise again to haunt us.

7

☆ ☆ ☆

"I Will Never Lie to You"

RICHARD THE WICKED, succeeded by Gerald the Banal, was followed by a man who would have us believe he was Jimmy the Good. Former Georgia Governor Carter captured the Democratic Party nomination while advancing some unorthodox ideas about the nation's future course. Speaking to the Democratic platform committee on June 16, 1976, he said:

> Without endangering the defense of our nation or commitments to allies, we can reduce *present* defense expenditures by about five to seven billion annually [emphasis added]. We must be hard-headed in the development of new weapons systems to ensure that they will comport with our foreign policy objectives. Exotic weapons which serve no real function do not contribute to the defense of this country. The B-1 bomber is an example of a proposed system which should not be funded and would be wasteful of taxpayers' dollars. We have an admiral for every seventeen ships. The Chief of Naval Operations has more captains and commanders on his own personal staff than serve in all the ships at sea.
>
> The Pentagon bureaucracy is wasteful and bloated. We have more generals and admirals today than we had during World War II, commanding a much smaller fighting force. We can thin our troops in Asia and close some unnecessary bases abroad.

My cynicism about the eternal hypocrisy of politicians began to soften; here was a candidate giving ironclad, specific promises and saying, "I will never lie to you." At that time we were only fourteen days away from the end of fiscal year 1976, during which the Pentagon had spent just under $88 billion. And DoD was asking for a huge increase for FY 77. I thought there could be an interesting confrontation between the five-sided brass and a president who had spoken those bold words to his platform committee. I began to hope Jimmy Carter would win.

My friends believed that Carter would listen to the sound of the blowing whistles and would come down hard on waste and corruption. Then Jimmy Carter told us so directly and personally. On October 23, he came to Alexandria, Virginia — very near my home — and gave a speech, saying in part:

> As I've traveled across the country, I have heard thousands and thousands of Americans say they don't believe the federal government can be made to work again. This pessimism about government is so widespread that many people have lost faith in the very idea of public service. The word "bureaucrat" has become a pejorative word, almost an insult.
>
> It wasn't always like this and it doesn't have to be anymore. The federal government can be well managed. It can be efficient. It can be responsive. It can once again be a source of pride to the public and the public servant.
>
> I want to talk today about what government reorganization will mean to the thousands of federal public servants. I share the public's disillusion with its government — and I know that you do, too. But the backlash should not be directed against government employees who want to do a good job, but against the barriers that hold them back.
>
> If I become president, I intend to work with career civil servants, with Congress, with leaders of business and labor, with academics, and with many other groups to devise a reorganization that will eliminate waste and inefficiency and overlapping and confusion in the federal government and make our government truly efficient once again.

Going on in this vein, Carter arrived at a promised four-point program, with the final point directed at my case:

> Fourth, I intend to seek strong legislation to protect our federal employees from harassment and dismissal if they find out and report waste and dishonesty by their superiors or others. The Fitzgerald case, where a dedicated civil servant was fired from the Defense Department for reporting cost overruns, must never be repeated.

How often does a candidate solicit somebody's vote by singling him out by name and promising to right the wrongs he suffered? I couldn't help being optimistic. These were words I'd been hoping to hear for years.

That fall I was invited to become a board member of the Fund for Constitutional Government, an organization founded and financially supported by Stewart Mott. I'd become friendly with Mott when I was working with the Businessmen's Educational Fund and had found him sympathetic to my cause. The FCG was willing to expose governmental waste, and it was not a political lobbying organization, so the Air Force general counsel permitted me to join its board.

While I was at a board meeting at the Mott family home in Bermuda, I received a telephone call from two Carter recruiters who had tracked me down. For about an hour they spoke enthusiastically about my joining the new administration as a political appointee to help clean up the mess in the Pentagon. The FCG's president, Charles "Chuck" Morgan, Jr., an ardent Carter supporter, also recommended me to the recruiters. When I returned home, I found waiting for me some forms from the Carter-Mondale Policy Planning Group. I filled them out and sent them in.

Time passed. The transition team, an uninspiring collection of functionaries, began nosing around the Pentagon. Then I began to hear disquieting rumors that Jimmy Carter was meeting with the old Johnson-era national security apparatchiks: Harold Brown, Cyrus Vance, and others. I got a little worried and began to make phone calls. But I was reassured when Mitzi Wertheim, of the transition team, said the new administration still wanted my services. She asked me to write a paper describing my approach to reforming the Pentagon.

In response I wrote a piece titled "Motivating the Pentagon Bureaucracy to Reduce the Unit Cost of Defense," in which I argued that defense debates usually had the fallacy of either/or built into them: we must *either* allocate more and more money to the military *or* suffer an unacceptable loss of defense capability. The obvious third alternative was to vastly improve our management of defense. I pointed out that whenever we had a promising effort to follow the third alternative, somebody like James Schlesinger would announce that cutting fat without cutting muscle was "an enchanting illusion."

Only after I'd forwarded the paper to Mitzi Wertheim did I discover that Schlesinger and Harold Brown were leading candidates for the office of secretary of defense. Bad news for the taxpayer, bad news for me. I went to see Chuck Morgan. He'd heard the same stories, but he was more sanguine. His close friend Hamilton Jordan had let it be known that he'd refuse to serve in the new administration if the Johnson-era political hacks were going to be restored to high posts.

As I watched the Pentagon clipping service day by day, I began to see reports on an irresponsible, alarmist organization called the Committee on the Present Danger. The ringleaders of the group were James Schlesinger, David Packard, and Lane Kirkland, who was then secretary-treasurer of the AFL–CIO and a member of the transition team. Their pitch was: "Our country is in a period of danger, and the danger is increasing. Unless decisive attempts are taken to alert the nation and to change the course of its policy [translation: to speed up Pentagon spending even faster], our economic and military capacity will become inadequate to assure peace with security." It was the old bugle call with a new title.

Carter was listening; the sound of the whistle had faded away and he was listening to the brassy notes of the big bucks. Schlesinger "deeply impressed Mr. Carter during the briefing he gave the President-Elect after his return from a visit to China," reported the *Christian Science Monitor* on November 29, 1976. Outgoing Defense Secretary Donald Rumsfeld told a CBS "Face the Nation" audience that carrying out Carter's pledge to cut $5 billion to $7 billion of fat "would inject a fundamental instability in the world."

By mid-December I had heard nothing from the Carter camp. Some of my friends sent them copies of an interview with me *Rolling Stone* had published, in which I'd cited some significant figures about one-year unit-cost increases of 20 percent to 109 percent. There were no replies other than the usual form letters.

A few days before Christmas, Jimmy Carter announced that he would appoint Harold Brown secretary of defense. It was a great setback. Joseph Kraft, in the December 23 *Washington Post*, bade Rumsfeld goodbye with these words, "[He has acted as] a transmission belt, passing on the requests of the Services to the Congress and the White House without interference. Under this loose rein, each Service has reverted to type, ignoring strategic and foreign-policy requirements in favor of doing its own thing."

Significantly, the *Washington Star*'s headline on Brown's first announcements was: "For Openers, Brown Sounds Like Rumsfeld." Brown said in an interview, "I am concerned about . . . the upward trend of Soviet defense expenditures in constant rubles and the downward trend of American defense expenditures in constant dollars." Jimmy Carter's campaign promises began to evaporate like dew under the August sun in Plains.

On December 30, when a reporter for the *Philadelphia Inquirer* asked Carter if he would keep his economy pledge, he replied with seventeen words when one would have sufficed: "If I don't, I will be very disappointed in the performance of the secretary of defense." Then, according to the *Inquirer*, Brown said, "I don't see a reduction in military spending from present levels." The newspaper took the question to Carter's press spokesman, Jody Powell, who said he had "no memory" of Carter's ever promising a $5 to $7 billion dollar cut.

In view of such contradictions, some of the press were sharpening their tone. The *Washington Star* on December 30 carried an editorial headlined "The $5 Billion Misunderstanding." About Carter it said: "He seemed aware that a dangerously high level of cynicism is abroad in the land about the capacity of government to keep its promises . . . [and he] was the first presidential candidate of recent memory who found it useful to pledge that he would not lie to the voters. Did he?"

And Charles Mohr in the *New York Times* the same day found that Carter had changed from the indicative to the conditional in talking about budgets: "There would be a net reduction in any . . . given year's defense budget of five to seven billion, which is brought about because of the changes I've described [better management and reduction of waste]. And if we can achieve a reduction of threats to our national security, we might achieve substantial reductions in defense expenditures in years to come." Later in the story Mohr reported that Carter and Mondale would soon meet to find means to stimulate a "still sluggish economy."

In a baton-passing operation, the outgoing Ford administration leaked (read: planted) some helpful Red Menace stories. "New C.I.A. Estimate Finds Soviet Seeks Superiority in Arms" was the headline on a *New York Times* story on December 26. One of the chief sources was the retiring chief of Air Force intelligence, General George Keegan, who was quoted as saying he'd become "convinced that the Soviet Union was preparing for an offensive war against the United States." But according to the *Nation* (January 8, 1977) the ghost behind the report was George Bush, outgoing director of central intelligence.

Defense industry executives rushed in to add their weight. Robert Anderson, president of Rockwell International (principal contractor for the controversial B-1 bomber) said in the pages of *Business Week*, "I have a strong feeling that the Russians are pulling ahead." Raytheon's D. Brainerd Holmes called the Soviets "the U.S. defense industry's greatest ally."

There were a few grumbles. Senator Proxmire called upon Jimmy Carter to restore me to my full duties and to honor his economy pledge, and Senator Howard Metzenbaum joined in. But in the end they both voted to confirm Harold Brown.

Early in 1977 the Pentagon money machine was getting up to full speed. The FY 78 budget submitted by President Carter requested cash outlays of approximately $112 billion, which was about $29 billion above the reduced level promised by candidate Carter on June 16, 1976. To answer your question, *Washington Star*, yes, Jimmy Carter had been lying.

Under Brown the pressure mounted to obligate and spend. The notes of the DoD financial managers' meeting of February 22, 1977, reports Assistant Secretary (Comptroller) Fred Wacker's words: "Mr. Wacker stated that recent reports indicate that FY 1977 execution is lagging behind plan to date, both in terms of obligations and outlays, and urged the FM's to investigate the significance of this information." Translation from the bureaucratese: you guys aren't spending the money fast enough. Quit stalling!

White House instructions for this speed-up came in the form of a directive titled "The Economic Stimulas [sic] Program." My sarcastic friends said that the spelling showed the educational level of Carter's South Georgia brigade, but I knew that its spirit came straight from Wall Street.

By May 2, 1978, Fred Wacker was almost hysterically telling the financial managers to get out there and spend. He told the meeting of that date: "There is no cap on expenditures and . . . the DoD is certainly not restricted from exceeding the established target. Any unexpended balance should be analyzed to determine cause."

Apologist historians of the Carter era have said that the administration discovered the need to step up spending only after the Soviet Union's brutal invasion of Afghanistan, but as I have shown, that is nonsense. The apologist school's theory is that Jimmy the Good tried to live up to his campaign promises but was sneakily undermined by Harold Brown. This derived from the mistaken notion that Brown resented Carter's June 30 announcement that he was canceling the B-1 bomber program. It is much more likely that Brown, though disappointed, accepted that Carter had to make this ritual sacrifice because of his campaign promise. The B-1 had become an important symbol.

The fight to kill funding for the B-1 bomber was, in mid-1977, a conspicuous but misleading success. It was led by a loose grouping of organizations (including my old outfit, the NTU) called the Coalition to Stop the B-1. Pentagon propaganda held that almost every state in the union stood to get contract dollars from the B-1. The coalition countered by pointing out that the cost to the taxpayers of most of those states was far greater than the income. This rarely used device was one that our similar coalition had used earlier to kill the supersonic transport plane subsidy.

My own skepticism about the B-1 was based on its chilling similarity, especially from a technical point of view, to the F-111 fighter-bomber fiasco. All of us who distrusted the campaign to sell the B-1 to the public were relieved at the president's decision. What we did not realize but might have suspected was that the defense budget quietly included $442 million for research and development money that was intended for a B-1 research model. An alliance of Air Force military and Carter office holders thereafter managed to inject other funds — suitably disguised by misleading labels — into Rockwell International's ongoing effort to advance the B-1. (An illuminating account of this appears in Nick Kotz's *Wild Blue Yonder: Money, Politics and the B-1 Bomber.*)

In the meantime backing by the "new priorities" supporters for Carter's promised military budget cutting had begun to melt away. They were heavily influenced by the leaders of the big labor unions, who were worried about employment. The principal new priorities lobby, the Coalition for a New Foreign and Military Policy, even advocated "slow growth in the military budget" in its winter/spring 1977 legislative program.

Prosperity, fear of Soviet strength, jobs — add to that the Israeli factor. Congressman Les Aspin noted them all in a speech to a meeting of Pentagon suppliers reported in the December 6 issue of the *Philadelphia Bulletin.* He said that the 1973 Yom Kippur war had convinced Israel that America must be ready with quick and massive resupply in any future emergency. "The Israeli lobby in Congress is no longer in favor of cutting the defense budget," Aspin observed.

Carter's own frugality urge had shrunk, then vanished. By December 17, 1977, in a speech in Fayetteville, North Carolina, he was actually bragging about a military spending increase: "Under President Ford and under me, the contribution for defense efforts has gone up in real dollars . . . in other words, we have compensated for the inflation rate and then added on top of that an additional amount to increase our defense standing — quite a reversal of what had been done in the past." Then in January 1978, Jimmy Carter proposed to Congress a military budget increase of $56 billion over the next five years, putting the 1983 figure at $172.7 billion.

Partisans of Carter have latterly tried to attribute the new splurge to insubordinate and clandestine activities by Brown. Former Carter insiders told this fairy tale to Nick Kotz, who recounted in *Wild Blue Yonder* (p. 196):

> Carter spoke angrily about Secretary Brown, who now increasingly sided with the military in favor of larger defense forces. "Harold's been a horse's ass on defense budgets," Carter told his aides. "He's caused me more work and took a hard line and never yielded."

This conflict of views was never apparent at my level of the Pentagon. Everything pointed to a pact between a free-spending president and a free-spending secretary.

As every recent administration has discovered, extravagance with money can be embarrassing when there is a free flow of information in government. Every candidate for the presidency over the past sixteen years has followed the pattern of campaign speeches denouncing wasteful spending. Often, as in the above-cited Carter examples, they condemn the concealment of such waste and promised a new era of economy and candor.

Then, almost without knowing how it happened, they fall victim to one of the most powerful forces in American society — what Eisenhower long ago called "the military-industrial complex" and what we have come to know, in our own time, as a machine that eats presidents and well-meaning defense secretaries alive. To keep the giant-scale boondoggling hidden as much as possible, the politicians must resort to suppression.

On January 24, 1977, Senator James Abourezk, chairman of the Senate Small Business Subcommittee, invited me to testify on our options for airlifting military cargo. More specifically, which method was the most cost-effective — the Military Airlift Command's own operation, large supplemental air carriers, or smaller supplemental carriers? I was a logical person to ask about such matters because as management systems deputy in the Air Force secretary's office, I had done extensive work on the subject. But the request immediately set off a warning buzzer in the Pentagon.

Brigadier General Robert Tanguy was instructed to tell Senator Abourezk that the Air Force preferred to send another spokesman, someone who, needless to say, knew nothing about airlift productivity trends. I could, the general conceded, testify as a private citizen, but nothing I said was to be taken as "the Air Force position" if it didn't jibe with the official spokesman's words.

This daft ruling set off a memorandum skirmish between me and my bosses, who finally agreed to let me testify "unimpeded." However, anything I said could later be declared unofficial if it was deemed contrary to the Air Force position. (That same rule, when placed on me earlier by the Ford administration, was described by Representative Parrin Mitchell as "the height or depth of asininity.")

Abourezk wrote Carter an angry letter, reminding him that he'd campaigned on the promise of open government and a tolerance of criticism but "in this case . . . the Air Force seems to be violating your principles blatantly." Much later he received a reply from the White House saying, in essence, "Thank you for your interest in aviation."

On March 2, 1977, the American Federation of Government Employees gave me their "whistle blowers' award" and the title "Mr. Integrity."

I took advantage of their hospitality by making a speech in which I combined candidate Jimmy Carter's proposals for budget balancing and remotivating government employees with my own suggestions from the paper I had sent Mitzi Wertheim the previous fall. All in all, it was a tough talk to address to the leaders of a government union. I told them that integrity started with the understanding that there is no such thing as government money. It is all taxpayers' money. I asked them (along with the rest of us) to shape up and cut out waste. I said that meant they would have to live with lower budgets and help achieve lower costs. I gave some examples of the trials and tribulations good stewards have to suffer, but I reminded them that we were employed by the taxpayers to do an honest job. It was up to us to believe candidate Carter's commitments and to take things into our own hands to follow through.

The average American, brainwashed to believe that all merit-system federal employees are mediocre hacks with very little interest in their work, would assume that such an audience was hostile to my message. But let the *Federal Times*, a federal employees' newspaper, describe the reaction:

> Suddenly, Fitzgerald was part of the audience. He needed to explain no more. The frustration he apotheosized [*sic*] was written on almost every face in the audience.
>
> Hands were shooting up. Stories about waste, mismanagement, corruption, and cover-ups began pouring out from all sides. Complaints went uninvestigated, complainants were punished, documents destroyed. . . .
>
> It seemed an endless orgy of accusations in southern lilts, midwestern drawls, and Bronx accents. . . . There were many Fitzgeralds now, countless numbers, and all of them felt that the big shots who commit crimes go scot free, while the little guys, honoring their Code of Ethics, get slammed for revealing wrongdoing.

Carried away by all this, I went too far. I promised my audience that, as a supergrade (one of the three highest civil service categories) in the office of the secretary of the Air Force, I'd try to follow up on any horror stories they had documentation for or credible witnesses to prove.

In a vulgar but apt phrase from my native Alabama, I was letting "my mouth overload my ass." I began to get more horror stories than Alfred Hitchcock ever dreamed of. Embarrassed yet encouraged by this reaction, I bundled up my speech and some of the favorable press notices and sent them through channels to the president, explaining to the secretary of the Air Force — an inert figure named Stetson — that "I would like for President Carter to know how well his program can be received by the rank and file of DoD employees when it is put to them the right way." About a month later I got the package back with a note saying that it was "inappropriate" to send to the president.

I persevered in trying to get a hearing. I got an appointment with Greg Schneiders, a Carter adviser who was now a White House assistant. I gave him my package from the highly successful AFGE pitch and the material I had submitted to the Carter-Mondale recruiters the previous fall outlining my ideas for squeezing the fat out of the military budget. Schneiders was sympathetic but firm in telling me that Harold Brown was in charge of the Pentagon.

I redoubled my efforts to get an appointment with Brown to try to make common cause with him in fulfilling Jimmy Carter's campaign commitments. Senator Proxmire tried to help me get appointments both with Brown and with higher-ups in the Carter White House, but all of our attempts met with stony silence. My friends wrote letters to the president on my behalf and got back form replies from the Office of Civilian Personnel Operations at Randolph Air Force Base in Texas. Chuck Morgan, interceding for me, had conversations with Hamilton Jordan, Attorney General Griffin Bell, and other insiders. He never told me specifically what they said, but much later he did remark cryptically, "You never had a chance."

Discouraging though this was, I thought I might get somewhere with Ralph Nader's support. During the Nixon and Ford administrations, Nader had spoken out clearly to defend truth telling in government. And he had helped me personally. At an October 28, 1970, conference of government administrators in Washington he had deplored "the concept of heroism in civil service that called for employees to sacrifice their careers if they dared point out threats to the public purse or safety. . . . Blowing the whistle is a cardinal safeguard of public interest, and we're not going to let you be heroes." He went on to say that whistle blowers weren't the problem, it was the government employees who lied or covered up facts who were. He wanted punishment for those officials who practiced "bureaucratic unaccountability." His talk drew a standing ovation that lasted several minutes.

Nader and his organization did a lot of useful work in outlining what was wrong with the federal government's civil service system. He and his associate Peter Petkus published a good book on the subject called *Blowing the Whistle*, and another Nader associate, Robert Vaughn, wrote a superb paper called "The Spoiled System" denouncing the regression of the supposed merit system for government employees to a de facto political spoils system.

Nader's group had acted effectively when Nixon tried to put the top three levels of the federal merit system under his political control, a power grab meant to smother dissent and communication with Congress and the press. When Carter came into office and Peter Petkus was given a White House staff appointment, my friends and I took it as a very good sign.

We had another organizational ally in Chuck Morgan's Fund for Constitutional Government. The FCG had helped subsidize an important Nixon-era exposé by public-interest lawyers William Dobrovir and Joe Gebhart. Their "Blueprint for Civil Service Reform" was both an attack on Nixon's violations of the federal merit system and a proposal for greater public accountability. Stewart Mott, the FCG's founder; Chuck Morgan, its president; and other board members had strong ties to the Carter administration. Board chairman Ted Jacobs, who had been Nader's second in command, knew many of the ex-Nader people now in government. *New Republic* editor Ken Bodie, labor lawyer Joe Rauh, and Georgetown University Professor John Kramer had close relationships with Carter officialdom. This was the liberal Establishment. These people, I was sure, would use their muscle to support a superb civil service reform.

Thus I simply refused to believe Inderjit "Indy" Badhwar when he telephoned me in December 1977. Indy, a native of the Punjab, was one of the best reporters I ever knew. Writing for the *Federal Times*, a funny little weekly (which was, nevertheless, a very good paper) he uncovered scandals of national proportions. Indy and his colleague Sheila Hershow kept a very good scrutiny on the federal bureaucracy. Badhwar said that unimpeachable sources in the government had told him that Carter's and Nader's people were cooking up a new civil service "reform" even worse than the swindle Richard Nixon had tried to sell, which had been hooted down by Congress. Indy said that the new plan would strip government employees of any real protection against arbitrary action by political appointees.

Nonsense, I said. This was exactly the opposite of Carter's campaign promises. Furthermore, there was no way Ralph Nader would ever involve himself in such blatant dishonesty. I told Indy we'd go to see Nader and get his personal denial.

I had an unexpectedly hard time getting in touch with Nader, but finally, through intermediaries, I got an appointment in early January 1978. When Indy and I arrived, Nader was somewhere else. We were taken in to see Alan Morrison, Nader's lawyer; Andrew Feinstein, the organization's civil service lobbyist; and Robert Vaughn. Morrison coldly said that Nader was unavailable — what did we want?

Indy recounted the stories he had heard about the proposed reform. To my total shock and confusion, Morrison essentially confirmed

Indy's story. He said it was true they were going to "trade off" some government employee rights for certain advantages he wouldn't name. It was "too hard" to fire government employees; the system needed an easier way to get rid of people.

Indy and I said that the government had never had much difficulty getting rid of whistle blowers or dissidents, and we cited cases. And if that was so, it shouldn't be too difficult to get rid of those who were bad or incompetent. Indy cited the statistics; a lot of people had been fired in recent years. No argument made a dent. And whenever I tried to see Nader, it was clear that he didn't want to meet with me on this issue. Obviously the deal had been cut.

Indy and I went next to that true-blue public interest organization, the Fund for Constitutional Government. For them I prepared a little test memorandum, which was in essence the FCG-sponsored "Blueprint for Civil Service Reform" with the title removed. It showed the parallels between the Carter and Nixon proposals, and it contained a very slightly modified statement of the Blueprint's proposals. We gave this paper to Chuck Morgan and Anne Zill, Stewart Mott's Washington representative.

The reaction was even worse than we'd had from the Nader people. They rejected the paper out of hand. Morgan said that when a government employee was accused of wrongdoing or inefficiency, he should have to prove his innocence. All other workers except some union members had to, didn't they? He relented a little and allowed a couple of exceptions: when an employee was being accused on the basis of some allegation prohibited by civil service rules or when the employee could claim a whistle blower defense. Otherwise, Morgan insisted, a person was guilty until proven innocent.

Now I was not talking to a Nixon Watergate shyster or a French *avocat*. I was arguing with one of the finest civil rights lawyers in the country. He had successfully defended Cassius Clay (later Mohammed Ali) when the boxer refused to be drafted into the Army with the reasonable explanation, "I ain't got nothing against them Viet Cong." As an ACLU lawyer, Chuck had fought for the one man/one vote rule that helped give Southern blacks their electoral rights. His record in defense of the downtrodden and unjustly accused did him great honor. What was the reason for his turnaround in this matter?

I think it was simply that the Carter people felt that government employees no longer needed elaborate protection of their rights. The FCG's Ted Jacobs argued that the Carter election had made the FCG charter "to expose government corruption" obsolete.

When the FCG board wanted to talk about the new utopia in a series of *quo vadis* meetings, I insisted that we include a discussion of civil service reform. The White House considered the FCG important enough to send Simon Lazarus, its chief civil service reform lobbyist and former Nader lieutenant, to explain the proposal. Lazarus made no bones about the fact that Carter was adopting the discredited Nixon plan to politicize the top three civil service grades (GS 16, 17, and 18), but with an added nasty twist. Nixon would have offered three-year contracts to the supergrades; Carter offered no contracts. These employees could be dismissed for "incompatibility"; in fact, they would be political appointees. At first, Lazarus said that the number of such employees would not exceed 10 percent, but after questioning, this percentage became a bit slippery. As former merit system jobs were filled by political appointees, those appointees could "burrow in" and become career employees, thereby freeing up slots for new politicals. Lazarus finally admitted that Carter intended to replace the whole merit system, in time, with politically appointed henchmen.

According to the minutes of that FCG meeting, Lazarus said that the Carter plan, as Chuck Morgan had suggested, was to place "the burden of proof in disciplinary proceedings ultimately upon the employee in question." For all practical purposes, Carter could then get rid of anybody in the civil service.

Lazarus explained that some people were already earmarked for dismissal under the new plan, and he named one of them. Assuming that the person named was a notorious incompetent, I offered to explain the present system's mechanisms for firing incompetents.

No, said Lazarus, the employee wasn't incompetent.

What was the reason for removal, then?

Well, the administration wanted to get rid of him because "he talked to the press and said the wrong things to Congress."

That was the story of my life, and I was outraged. So were Badhwar and Frank Silby, assistant to Representative John Moss. But this roomful of noble and eminent liberals couldn't see anything wrong with dismissing a person for exercising his rights under the First Amendment and for carrying out his responsibilities under the government Code of Ethics.

I wanted to offer evidence against the Carter plan, but Chairman Ted Jacobs repeatedly ruled me out of order. I was reduced to writing letters to my own board of directors, posing questions that were never answered. How would an employee defend himself against a charge of "disaffection"? This charge, which even had a code number in the Air Force Office of Special Investigations, was not an act but a state of mind. How did someone on trial prove that he was full of affection and not disaffection? In the end the board approved Chuck Morgan's formula of putting the burden of proof on the accused.

If Sy Lazarus had been frank and consistent with us, Jimmy Carter was just the opposite. First, he argued that it was almost impossible to get rid of unwanted government employees. Then he argued that he wanted new legislation to protect whistle blowers from being fired. But he never seemed to consider that the people who were firing whistle blowers were his own appointees, and all he had to do was tell them to stop.

He lied specifically as well as in general. When he presented his Civil Service Reform Program on March 2, 1978, he said, "Last year, out of about two million [federal] employees, only 226 people lost their jobs for incompetence or inefficiency."

When I heard that, I dug out and circulated a very recent brief from the Air Force inspector general. One section titled "It's Impossible to Fire a Civilian!" read:

> How often have you heard that? Do YOU believe it? Well, don't — it's a myth. The facts are that in fiscal year 1977, 1,230 Air Force civilians were separated for cause. This included directed separations for suitability reasons, resignations in lieu of adverse actions, separations for inefficiency, termination during trial or probation period, and removals for misconduct. The figures for calendar year 1974, 1975, and 1976 and 1,823, 1,495, and 1,433 respectively.

Ken Blaylock, the only leader of a major employee union to support the Carter plan, tried to bail the president out of his embarrassing lie by saying the 226 was a typographical error, that it should have been 22,600. But the White House continued to use 226, then switched to a new figure of 1,157 employees fired in the previous year.

I then went to the source — John Scholzen, chief information specialist in the Civil Service Commission. He explained that his statistics were for fiscal years but that he'd been asked for figures for calendar year 1976. Another source of confusion was that many people who quit government service did so to avoid being fired. But it was impossible to single those out of the 212,000 people who had resigned.

The CSC figures showed something quite the opposite of a static, entrenched work force whose members could not be fired. I knew that literally thousands of government employees — usually the most talented — had quit because of dissatisfaction or disgust with political machinations. Surly secretaries and slow workers are problems in any organization, but these weren't the people committing the expensive atrocities. Most government workers will take career risks to achieve cost reduction or improvement in service if they are convinced that is what their bosses really want. It is when these efforts begin to threaten certain special interests that politicians begin to get scared. In this case, I began to wonder what had scared Jimmy Carter and his retinue so badly.

Civil service statistics showed a rate of turnover that would alarm most private businessmen: 26 percent in one year excluding deaths, 30 percent including deaths. But the problem with the system was that it protected political hacks and drones while it punished or ejected people who had a sincere wish to contribute to the public interest.

Raymond Jacobson, Carter's Civil Service Commission executive director, was quoted in the July/August 1977 edition of the *Washington Monthly* as saying, "Any unproductive employee can be fired if his supervisor has balls." But the paradox was that the productive ones seemed to get fired and the politically submissive stayed on, no matter how unproductive.

The Carter people simply could not understand that what they were doing was a reversion to the political spoils system of the nineteenth century. Beyond that, they didn't see that they were preparing the way for a Republican stranglehold on the bureaucracy in future years when the Republicans would make the appointments.

I was a lonely protester against Carter's plan. Most congressmen seemed ardently in favor, and a big majority of the public-interest organizations had fallen into line. Ralph Nader, that brilliant but unpredictable man, testifying before the House Post Office and Civil Service Committee on behalf of the reform, attacked "political intrusion into the career service" that led to civil servants "performing political dirty work of whatever administration was in power . . . as the fast track to advancement. This eagerness to please has led to violation of criminal laws." What was Nader's solution to this corrupting process? He proposed to make employees he'd described as all too responsive to political influences even *more* responsive to them. He said:

What is a democratic election for the President of the United States all about in the first place? What good is an election of a president replacing another administration if the president cannot bring in an adequate number of people who share his views and his programs and the issues that were debated during the election and won as a result of the November election?

Ulysses S. Grant or Boss Tweed couldn't have said it better.
Nader and his associates conceded that federal employees would lose

certain rights of protection against political strong-arm tactics, but they'd be rewarded with a special office to which whistle blowers could, supposedly, bring complaints. There would be a kind of chaplain called the Special Counsel. In effect, our citizens' employees could no longer protect their rights under the Constitution and laws such as Title 5, Section 7211, of the U.S. Code. These rights were passed on to a third party.

The Carter Reform Act — or, as many people I knew called it, the Carter Deform Act — was a reckless reversal of governmental progress since 1883, and promised some dire developments. The Nader followers, my friends at the FCG, and many other well-meaning liberals seemed to think that political corruption had been abolished by the election of Jimmy the Good. How many other times have liberals woven the ropes for their own hanging?

The Carter Act moved relentlessly through Congress, undergoing quite a few changes on the way. The features that supposedly promised greater efficiency in the civil service were amended until they became meaningless. I testified several times, noting that instead of making it easier to get rid of the deadwood, the act would make it easier for the deadwood to get rid of everybody else. No one was listening.

The climax of the president's attempt to sell his reform came on the evening of August 3, 1978, when he spoke in Fairfax, Virginia, in a high school auditorium:

> The essence of what we proposed also includes the protection of the rights of those who are part of the civil service system, and we are also very interested in seeing the so-called whistleblowers, those who see defects in our government, violations of law, gross waste, protected when they point out these deficiencies leading to correction of errors in our government.

After laying out his proposal for the special counsel's office, he reached the heights of hypocrisy:

> Let me give you a notable example from past history, perhaps the most famous person who has suffered. And that's Ernest Fitzgerald, who, through his own insistence, pointed out an example of great waste in the federal government. Under the present merit system, he has, through his own analysis, been punished because of that whistleblowing experience. That would not be possible under the proposed legislation. He would be protected and could not be punished, could not be silenced, in fact may very well have been rewarded.

The president seemed to be looking right at me as he uttered this astonishing deception. Fred Small, the president of a government worker's union local in Air Force headquarters, shouted back at Carter, "Here's Fitzgerald, Jimmy. Reward him!"

In truth, Carter needed no new laws to protect me. All he had to do was to pick up the telephone, call the Pentagon, and say, "Harold, stop putting Fitzgerald down. Let him go back to work."

Not long after the Fairfax speech, TV producers Judith and Harry Moses, a husband-and-wife team, came to me with a fascinating proposal they were preparing, which documented Carter's close ties with Lockheed. As governor of Georgia, the state where the C-5A was built, he had tried to protect the company during the height of the 1960s scandals. The *Marietta Daily Journal* of April 9, 1972, reported his defense:

> "A company like Lockheed which has the ability and courage to plan and design a new concept in aircraft like the C-5A must be expected to run into certain cost overruns as they must make constant modifications in the aircraft while it is being produced," Carter said.
>
> "The Defense Department understands this and allows for it. It has come into the public light so often only because certain politicians, including Sen. William Proxmire (D-Wis.) want to create a political issue with it.
>
> "The cost overruns are predictable and easy to understand in a program like that of the C-5A," the Governor said.

The Moseses had evidence to show that Jimmy Carter, while governor of Georgia, was Lockheed's best-known traveling salesman. One evidence of that was a note the Moseses obtained from Carter's gubernatorial records. On April 8, 1972, Lockheed took Carter on a fifteen-day selling tour of South America. On his return Carter wrote to Lockheed-Georgia's vice president, R. D. Roche:

> Dear Bob,
> One of the finest experiences of my life was being with you on the trip to Central and South America. In addition to the remarkable performance, luxury, and convenience of the Jet Star, the opportunity to learn more about Lockheed was extremely important to me. . . . I have carried this message of admiration to our national leaders in the State Department, Defense Department, and the Congress and will continue to do so. . . . I want to help in an active way. . . . The first step now in addition to my public and private promotional efforts should be for me to visit Lockheed and know at first hand the problems and opportunities of your company.
> Your friend,
> Jimmy Carter

This unpaid lobbyist for Lockheed clearly resented the Proxmire hearings and must have heard a good deal of bad language about me from his Lockheed friends. To gain votes in civil-servant-populated northern Virginia, he'd said, "The Fitzgerald case, where a dedicated civil servant was fired from the Defense Department for reporting cost overruns, must never be repeated." And then he produced a "civil service reform" bill that would make my GS-17 job (and the jobs of all upper-echelon government employees) political rather than professional. He was, in fact, trying to make it easy to get rid of whistle blowers and closet patriots. This was the man who said to all of us, "I will never lie to you."

Jimmy Carter's Civil Service Deform Act passed the Senate by a vote of 87 to 1 and by an almost equally large margin in the House of Representatives.

Carter's faithless repudiation of his own promises were a grievous blow to me personally. Moreover, the weakness of character that produced the debacle of the Carter presidency set in motion some of our later national calamities and set the stage for others. Clark Mollenhoff's summing up in his book *The President Who Failed* was prescient:

> The greatest tragedy of all was that President Carter's performance created an unreasoned national craving for a strong and forceful leader — any strong leader. Carter's weakness set the political stage for a bold, strong leader who might be too bold, too strong, too ruthless and too authoritarian to tolerate opposition and more skillful in the exercise of the authoritarian tools of secrecy and political retribution that Jimmy Carter and Richard Nixon used quite clumsily.

Jimmy Carter may have been too bumbling and weak to become our man on horseback, but he was plenty strong enough to saddle the horse, to help hoist the new, elected ruler into the saddle, then give the steed of state a slap on the rump to send our new leader on his way.

8

☆ ☆ ☆

The King's
Lawyers

DURING MY FOUR YEARS of exile from the Pentagon, I had spent a good deal of time trudging along First Street on Capitol Hill, a route that took me past the Supreme Court building. I seldom passed without reading the words "Equal Justice under Law," carved on the portico above the beautiful Greek columns. I was forty-three when the Air Force fired me, but I was still naive enough to believe in those words. Someday, I thought, my case would work its way through all the contrived delays and obfuscations we'd met in the lower courts and be heard in the pure air of the temple of justice behind the Greek columns.

My only experience with the federal courts had been in appearances before Judge Bryant, whose well-reasoned opinions I did not always agree with but always respected. At that time I didn't completely accept the cynical ideas of my friend and part-time employer, Congressman Jerry Waldie, who used to point out that a lawyer's success was judged by the size of his fees, that the legal processes were dominated by the rich and powerful who could pay big fees, and that most legislators and all federal judges are lawyers. Ergo . . . I had good reason not to agree because, although neither rich nor powerful, I had some of the best attorneys I knew of representing my case at no small expense of time and money to themselves.

After quite a bit of experience with the federal courts, I learned that the American people have no legal advocate to represent them at the federal level. The Roman Republic provided tribunes; the Scandinavian system of justice has its ombudsman; most of our states have attorneys general elected by (and removable by) the people. But the United States attorney general is the top lawyer — not for the people but for the president who appoints him. And he has a large and powerful department prepared to battle any opponents the administration might have.

After I returned to the Pentagon in 1974, my lawyers filed two big lawsuits on my behalf, along with several minor ones. The first maintained that the Pentagon had arbitrarily demoted me on my return. The second was a personal damage suit for $3.5 million against those who had conspired in my illegal firing and the refusal to make me "whole again" afterward.

Named in that complaint were Melvin Laird, Robert Seamans, General Duward L. "Pete" Crow, Air Force Chief of Staff John P. McConnell, Colonel Hans "Whitey" Driessnack, General Joseph Cappucci, Spencer Schedler, Colonel James Pewitt, and Alexander Butterfield.

United States District Judge Gerhard Gesell was not sympathetic. In his 1977 ruling he declared that by waiting until 1974 to file suit, I had "slept on my rights" and the statute of limitations had run out. We countered by saying that during that time I had been pursuing legal remedies through the quasijudicial civil service process and interlocutory appeals to the federal courts.

We argued that vital evidence had been concealed. Judge Gesell denied us discovery on the grounds that we were engaged in a "mere fishing expedition." Although we had learned about Whitey Driessnack's role in my firing less than a year before filing suit, Judge Gesell let him off the hook with the others, saying, "It would be anomalous and unjust to allow [Fitzgerald] to begin an action against lesser fry merely because their identity and participation were earlier unknown." He ended up by granting the Justice Department's motion for dismissal of the suit.

The U.S. Court of Appeals overturned the dismissal as it pertained to the White House staff but upheld it in reference to the Pentagon people. We were left with Alexander Butterfield and persons unknown. The prospect of making the legal discovery process work was a daunting one. Far from standing aside to smile as the sins of the Republican past were brought to view, Carter's administration, with Griffin Bell as attorney general, leaped to Butterfield's defense. Justice Department lawyers represented him, and as we gradually discovered the names of the other conspirators, including Richard Nixon, the same legal aid was furnished them. (Nixon finally dumped his Justice attorneys when their incompetence became a danger to him.)

To obtain the information we needed, we had to search the Nixon papers, which were then in the National Archives, so we got subpoenas for this purpose. We assumed that the archivists were professionals, who in answer to a court order would do a professional job of finding the documents we requested. Not so. We ran head-on into the chief lawyer for the archivist, Steven Garfinkel, who proved to be a master stonewaller, evader, and escape artist. The man would haunt me for years.

Garfinkel took his legal advice from Justice Department lawyer Rebecca Ross — who was counsel for Butterfield, the defendant! He managed to frustrate the legal discovery process all the way until September 1979, when he was still being deposed and still stonewalling. This was simply one minor example of the official obstructionism that Carter's people seemed to have learned from the Nixonian masters of the art.

Take the case of the crafty Colonel Jack C. Dixon, chief of the Air Force military judge advocate general's litigation division. On March 8, 1974 (before Judge Gesell dismissed the suit), he wrote a legal memorandum that included a number of affidavits from our proposed Air Force defendants. When we eventually had a chance to compare the original affidavits with the published versions, we found that the government lawyers had tidied up the truth to make their case stronger.

Judge Gesell's role was a dubious one at times. We tried to have Pete Crow reintroduced as a defendant, partly because his two affidavits had been especially contradictory and partly because he'd had a strong hand in denying my bid for reinstatement in my original job. We wanted to look at his documents. But Gesell, through his law clerk, secretly got in touch with the opposition's Justice Department lawyers to ask if Crow had indeed failed to produce some pertinent documents. Now, this is known in law as *ex parte*, or one-sided, communication, and it is highly improper.

The Justice Department lawyers said the general had told all, which Crow affirmed, of course, and Gesell granted a summary judgment dismissing Crow from the case. John Bodner reacted by charging Crow with perjury and asking the judge to recuse (disqualify) himself from the case. Of course, Gesell ignored the request.

One of the affidavit rewrites did cause a stir in Congress and led to some investigation. It was that of then-Colonel Whitey Driessnack (aka Secret Informant T-1), who was being nominated for promotion to brigadier general. Senator Proxmire thought Driessnack's questionable role in my case ought to be looked into. His request went from senator to senator — to Hughes to Chairman John Stennis of the Armed Services Committee, and finally to Senator Howard Cannon, a major general in the Air Force Reserve. Cannon simply asked Driessnack if all these unpleasant allegations were true.

Driessnack delivered another affidavit along the lines of the doctored one the government lawyers had purveyed in the court proceedings. In it he said, "Beyond my role as an O.S.I. interviewee, I played no part in the Fitzgerald investigation. I had no knowledge of any events in this connection beyond my own interview." These statements were not true, as his original affidavit later showed.

At the time we didn't know that Driessnack's original, presumably candid, affidavit said:

> I was aware that two other sources, not defendants in this action, were also interviewed by the OSI. They were John Badin and Eugene Kirschbaum, the men I had named during my OSI interview as the persons most knowledgeable about the PTC-AFFC contract. In fact, about a month after my own interview, John Badin came to me and told me that an OSI agent named Sullivan was waiting to interview him. . . . He said that Sullivan had indicated that I had given his name as a possible source in an inquiry into the PTC-AFFC contract. He asked me what this was about and asked me whether I knew Sullivan and could confirm that he was from OSI. I drove Badin over to the OSI office, briefly relating the story of my own interview as we went, and, once there, I introduced Sullivan to Badin, thereby identifying Sullivan as the man who had interviewed me, and left.

(The PTC-AFFC contract refers to an early attempt by the Air Force OSI to frame me by falsely alleging that I'd been involved in the letting of an Air Force contract to Performance Technology Corporation, a firm I had once headed.)

Driessnack's false public statements seriously obstructed our efforts to learn the truth about the scurrilous OSI frame-up attempt. Even after we established that Driessnack was secret informer T-1 for the OSI, we still did not know who the other secret informers were, or what they had said. Had we been given access to the original Driessnack affidavit, we would have known that Eugene Kirschbaum and John Badin were two of the secret informers. We would have learned early on that Badin and Kirschbaum had completely contradicted Driessnack and others regarding any possibility of my having a conflict of interest concerning PTC.

The Senate confirmed Driessnack and gave him his brigadier general's star, and in due course he got his second star, becoming a major general. But the case of Informant T-1 lingered on through two more investigations.

Complicated as all this was, the further history of Fitzgerald v. The Conspiracy is even more tangled and confused. It is a history of missing evidence, cover-ups, conflicts of interest, and plain old-fashioned lying. A good characterization is found in Senator Proxmire's speech

(*Congressional Record*, April 8, 1974): "I can only conclude on the basis of the record in the Fitzgerald case that the Justice Department has, wittingly or unwittingly, become a party to a coverup of criminal behavior on a rather massive scale."

In another corner of Washington, Driessnack came under scrutiny as an outgrowth of an investigation of criminal conspiracy and corruption in the C-5A affair. In early April 1978, Special Agent Robert Golden of the FBI asked me to meet with him about this. I agreed reluctantly. Golden and his immediate FBI superiors wanted to pursue this investigation. I tried to dissuade him, pointing out that high government officials were involved and that Justice was defending some of the people who had made conflicting statements or had covered up material facts. To make the point, I showed him the two Driessnack affidavits (by this time, we had a copy of the original), but I said I did not wish to bring a charge. I felt that the investigation was doomed to go nowhere.

Golden was not a man to give up easily. Several weeks later he called me and proposed that I file a complaint against Driessnack in order to keep the FBI's investigation alive. No, I replied. Whitey Driessnack was, in Judge Gesell's words, one of "the lesser fry."

But the FBI men had their own agenda. On May 23, 1978, Golden's boss, the special agent in charge of the Washington Field Office (WFO), sent a letterhead memorandum to FBI Director William Webster on the subject: "Hans H. Driessnack, Major General, United States Air Force, PERJURY." The key paragraphs were:

> It is the opinion of the WFO that by DRIESSNACK altering his unsigned affidavit into its present form of 4/18/74, and the fact that both DRIESSNACK and CROW's affidavits appear to be similar, it does give the appearance that DRIESSNACK discussed these matters with General CROW prior to submitting the final form of his affidavit dated 4/18/74. If this is the case, WFO feels that DRIESSNACK perjured himself.
>
> Special Agent Golden discussed this with Assistant U.S. Attorney DONALD E. CAMPBELL, Major Crimes, *Washington, D.C.*, and he advised the facts warrant that a preliminary investigation be instituted at this time.

Golden proceeded with energy and apparently gathered additional compelling evidence; on June 9, Director Webster telexed the WFO authorizing it to conduct the investigation on the authority of the U.S. attorney's office. Just three days later Jimmy Carter nominated Whitey Driessnack for promotion to lieutenant general. Strange things began to happen thereafter.

The strangest of them are probably lost to history because of the destruction of documents, but thanks to my former colleague Pete Stockton, I learned most of the facts that follow. Pete was then working for Representative John Dingell and later, in 1980 and 1981, for chairmen Dennis DeConcini and Orrin Hatch of the Senate Judiciary Subcommittee. At the time these two senators were the only members of Congress interested in investigating what had happened to me.

The first curious event, which Stockton learned about from a June 15 telex from the WFO to FBI headquarters, was that the FBI sent a copy of the May 23 letterhead memorandum to the military judge advocate general of the Air Force. This, Stockton commented, was like a lawyer sending his initial thoughts and preliminary notes to the opposition's lawyer.

The next day the FBI interviewed Driessnack, who explained that government lawyers had altered his original affidavit but failed to explain why he'd then signed the doctored version. He added that the issue was moot because Gesell had dismissed the case in December — a misstatement that was to have consequences later on. He denied that he had initiated the derogatory OSI file on me.

On the same day, June 16, the FBI interviewed General Cappucci, who muddled things even more by contradicting his previous testimony about the origin of the Air Force moves against me. This time he said Whitey Driessnack had come up with the PTC conflict-of-interest charge against me, and that had inspired the chief of staff, General McConnell, to initiate the investigation. (Cappucci's testimony before the Civil Service Commission is described in Chapter 5.) This blew away the whole rickety false structure the Air Force had presented to the commission hearings.

Suddenly, but perhaps not surprisingly (considering the gross conflicts of interest), the U.S. attorney for Washington, D.C., Earl Silbert, called from California and ordered a halt to the FBI investigation until he returned. Silbert was on record in numerous court documents as opposing me and defending, among others, Driessnack and Cappucci. (Watergate Trivia Quiz buffs will also recognize him as the prosecutor who wanted to put the burglars in jail and let the matter go at that — getting to the bottom of the case but making sure he didn't get to the top.)

On June 19, Silbert's assistant, Donald Campbell, closed out the FBI investigation and declined, on the basis of Judge Gesell's earlier ruling, to prosecute Driessnack or anyone else. Pete Stockton relayed a quote from Golden to the effect that Campbell and the bureau were "under tremendous political pressure to close the investigation." One of Golden's superiors had told him, "You can't prosecute a general." As for the flimsy excuse that Gesell had dismissed my suit naming Pete Crow,

Stockton pointed out that Driessnack had not been a party to the suit at that time, nor had the credibility of his affidavit been questioned in the dismissed suit.

Stockton interviewed Driessnack on June 20 and, though nothing new developed, there was one interesting threat. Driessnack was accompanied by the Air Force general counsel, Peter B. Hamilton, who had held a position in the DoD under Melvin Laird; he had helped defend Laird against my suit. Hamilton warned Stockton not "to reopen old wounds" because "there is evidence of conflict of interest on Fitzgerald's part." Again the attack by allegation and vague innuendo — never substantiated but often repeated. When I tried to clear my name, I always felt as if I were trying to shovel smoke.

The FBI may have been shut up, but it hadn't given up. Stockton and *Federal Times* reporter Sheila Hershow reported that some people at the Bureau were willing to do a comprehensive investigation of the wrongdoing surrounding my case if the administration would agree. There was no sign of that, however, until Jack Anderson's syndicated column put a firecracker under the Justice Department on June 26. The result was that Donald Campbell suddenly discovered the Air Force OSI reports that Anderson mentioned, became aware of additional witnesses to the affidavit rigging and other shenanigans (three attorneys who had played a part in my lawsuits), and reopened the investigation.

On June 30 Campbell and FBI Special Agent John D. Stapleton interviewed erstwhile opposition lawyers Bruce Clark, a former captain in the Air Force judge advocate general's department, and John Kelson, formerly of the Justice Department's main office in Washington. Clark admitted that there were discrepancies between the first and final Crow and Driessnack affidavits and that the problem of the possible conflicts had been "cured" in the final drafts. Kelson also said that Justice had been so concerned about preserving secrecy about my accusers — T-1 through T-4 — that "any information relative to their identity . . . would have been deleted from any affidavit submitted in this matter." Stockton later commented on Stapleton's report to the FBI: "Clark and the other lawyers were the linchpins in the cover-up of the government conspiracy against Fitzgerald."

Did these rather strong indications of legal impropriety worry the Carter administration? Not at all. After Campbell interviewed Whitey Driessnack again, his report on the talk mysteriously disappeared from Justice Department files. The department was anxious to give the whole affair last rites, but the journalists kept breathing life into it.

Little by little the suppressed facts were coming out. Sheila Hershow's July 3 *Federal Times* article laid out some of the more striking ones. It cast a lot more doubt on Driessnack's testimony, which was contradicted by five people: civilian official Eugene Kirschbaum (Informant T-2), General Crow, General Cappucci, OSI agent Vincent Sullivan, and Driessnack's own assistant, Lieutenant Colonel John Badin (Informant T-3). But the most important conflict was that although Driessnack had known perfectly well about Informants T-2 and T-3, he had sworn under oath, "I had no knowledge of any events in this connection beyond my interview."

Whitey Driessnack was no more or no less guilty than several of the others, but because he was being promoted to lieutenant general, he became the focus of attention. On July 5, Senator Proxmire requested that Justice investigate "perjury or other criminal violations by Driessnack or others."

Apparently Senator Stennis also asked for a report, and on July 7 U.S. Attorney Silbert replied, beginning his letter with a falsehood: "In April of this year, a complaint was made by a Mr. A. Ernest Fitzgerald to the FBI that General Driessnack had perjured himself in the affidavit of April 18, 1974, submitted in the civil service matter of *A. Ernest Fitzgerald* v. *Robert C. Seamans, Jr. et al.*"

I had never made such a charge. I was not then concerned with Whitey's statements to the court, which I had reason to think were prejudiced, but with his statements to the Senate. Perjury is a very hard thing to prove, whereas false statements in general, obstruction of justice, and conspiracy to perform illegal acts are easier to substantiate.

While asserting that what Driessnack said in his public affidavit was not intended "to mislead or make a false statement," Silbert did corroborate the history of the affidavit: that its first innocent draft had been passed to the Justice Department, and thereafter the government lawyers "cured" it. Silbert, of course, found no evidence of wrongdoing. And that explanation was good enough for Stennis.

But not good enough for senators Proxmire and Patrick Leahy. Proxmire asked for a delay in the confirmation of Driessnack's promotion, and Leahy threatened a debate and a roll-call vote. Leahy also wrote Stennis to say that he thought people who took reprisals against whistle blowers shouldn't be rewarded by promotion. Proxmire's letter to Justice was referred to the Public Integrity Section (PIS) of the Justice Department.

Then the old legerdemain worked again. On the basis of Silbert's letter to Stennis, Campbell closed the investigation on July 11. On July 19 Lee Redick of the PIS drafted a letter informing Proxmire of this. Interestingly, the PIS had made no attempt to conduct an independent investigation (as Stockton's later inquiries proved) but had simply accepted Silbert's vanishing trick. No questioning of those involved, no look at possible conflicts of interest, not even a review of Silbert's file. Assistant Attorney General Philip Heymann notified Proxmire in a letter that paralleled Silbert's to Stennis. That was an example of the Department of Justice under Griffin Bell.

Senator Proxmire put all his correspondence and documents into the *Congressional Record*; Senator Leahy now focused his efforts on trying to get me a more suitable job.

In all this close-out activity, one new note crept in. Heymann's superficial dismissal of the matter produced a falsification we had never seen flatly stated in writing. He said, "[General] Tuebner raised the conflict of interest charge against Fitzgerald." How many times does a lie have to be disproved before the Department of Justice will give up on it? The "conflict of interest charge" had to do with the Air Force contract with PTC, my former company. As I wrote in a report to the people who had helped me, Eugene Kirschbaum had several times stated that he alone was responsible for that contract and that I had nothing to do with it. Legal discovery had produced a handwritten note from Driessnack to Captain Bruce Clark saying, "I think you will discover that I was my own worst enemy — I evidently drafted the Secretarial approval for this contract myself in Feb. 1967." I also noted that the Justice Department nowhere acknowledged that Cappucci's intensive, nationwide investigation had cleared me of all charges. But the department could neither forget a lie nor remember the truth when it came to my case.

By August 22, 1978, my senatorial supporters had accepted the close-out. Senator Leahy made a kind of valedictory Senate floor speech saying that the administration had at last agreed to "find an appropriate position for Fitzgerald ... a challenging job which will call for his special talents for protecting against the wasteful expenditure of tax dollars." He went on to say, "Those responsible for the reprisals will not be forgotten and ... they will have to contend with one angry ... U.S. Senator if they or anyone else takes similar action in the future." Leahy said he would make a trade — he'd vote to confirm Driessnack's promotion if the Pentagon would give me a responsible job.

One more striking example of Justice misbehavior was yet to come. When Pete Stockton ended his consultantship with senators DeConcini and Hatch and went back to work for Congressman Dingell, Jim Phillips and Barbara Newman of Hatch's staff took over. They produced a good deal of damning evidence against the government lawyers and their clients, but the most crucial was a flagrant case of tampering.

This involved paragraph seven of the May 23 FBI memorandum about Driessnack, which said, "If this is the case, WFO feels DRIESSNACK perjured himself." The copy of the memorandum I'd obtained carried that crucial paragraph. In the photocopy that Director Webster sent to Senator Hatch, it had been scissored out, the pieces stuck back together, and the falsified document copied. (The two versions of this memorandum are reproduced in Appendix B.) In the next paragraph a blacked-out name — revealed as Golden's in the complete copy — had beside it the notation of the FBI censor, "b7c." (The indecipherable handwriting was that of Pete Stockton.)

This was a clear violation of Title 18, Section 2071, of the United States Criminal Code, which forbids alteration or mutilation of official records, but it seems to have raised no eyebrows.

As for Special Agent Golden, he gave me some interesting background on his part of the case (which I relayed in an August 24 report to the Senate). He said he'd been under extreme pressure from Justice officials not to proceed with the case, which was considered a "hot potato." It was revived temporarily only because of the Jack Anderson piece and pressure from Stockton.

In a later conversation with me and Indy Badhwar (who was then working for Jack Anderson), Golden gave a more detailed account of the rough handling he'd undergone. His superiors were particularly anxious to prevent him from testifying before Senator Hatch's committee even if he were subpoenaed. (Remember, these were not the bad old days of Richard Nixon and Watergate stonewalling; these were the forthright new days of Jimmy Carter.)

Golden told us he'd been really "worked over" by "Shaheen's outfit." Mike Shaheen was a high Justice Department official who had jurisdiction over the Public Integrity Section, among others. Trying to cast Golden as a scapegoat, "they went after me," he said. "Everybody from the U.S. attorney to the special agent in charge of the Washington Field Office." Donald Campbell and Carl Rauh were the henchmen, and Jack Keeney, of the Justice Department's Criminal Division, and Tom Henderson, head of PIS, were "calling the shots."

In the meantime my new lawyers at Hogan and Hartson, principally Peter Raven-Hansen and Kurt von Kann, were energetically pursuing the concealed evidence bearing on my damage suit. At last my persistent lawyers had obtained through discovery the Nixon White House tapes quoted in Chapter 1. Judge Gesell sealed them, but he did allow us to add Nixon and Bryce Harlow to the list of defendants on September 8.

With Nixon as the target, the suit now had a better chance of making progress. Judge Gesell, who was clearly displeased at the prospect of trying a gaggle of Pentagon bureaucrats, seemed to relish the thought of bringing Nixon into his court before a jury of twelve good and true.

During this time we were also trying to get the White House to live up to its promise to Senator Leahy to put me in a more significant and useful Pentagon job. Ron Tammen, Dan Grady, and David Julyan, all Senate staffers, along with Anne Zill and other FCG members, kept the heat on. They needed to. The Carter White House had a hard time remembering such promises. Peter Raven-Hansen, Barrett Prettyman, and I finally met with Arnie Miller, the White House personnel chief, on March 20, 1979. Miller said he was treating my case as if it were a civil rights or discrimination case and he'd offer me "the next available job" on a take-it-or-leave-it basis.

As a result I was first sent over to the National Transportation Safety Board; when nothing came of that, I was told to call my old friend Susan King, then head of the Consumer Product Safety Commission. Susan was incredulous that anyone with my cost-cutting background should be sent to her. "Our whole budget is about $20 million a year," she said. "You spend more than that on the coffee spilled every morning at the Pentagon." As for technical problems, she said that the pressing issue at the moment was insecurely fastened button eyes on teddy bears, which children might chew off and choke on.

I told the White House that I did not belittle the problems of loose teddy-bear eyes, but I had no expertise in the matter. And besides, Susan had no need for me at CPSC.

Nothing more was heard from the White House until Richard Nixon, of all people, raised the issue of getting me a job. In his deposition to my lawyers, Nixon shrewdly avoided criticizing me, noted his own "attempts" to give me a federal job, and offered "to intercede privately — on a very private basis, off-the-record basis, with President Carter, and — so that his people can assess Mr. Fitzgerald's qualifications and perhaps find him a position which would be even better and more responsible than he had before."

Just what the White House didn't want. By the time I learned about Nixon's remarks, it was 1980; Carter's people were frantically wooing the military spenders and wanted no association with cost cutters. Once the Republicans nominated Reagan, the spenders had no more to fear. (It was a bit like the scene when the rich Roman Didius Julianus went to the Praetorian Guard camp and outbid his rival Sulpicianus in an auction for the imperial throne.)

In August 1979 I was put through eight long days of deposition by

Nixon's lawyers and, thanks to excellent preparation by my lawyers, I could not be tripped up. The defendants in my suit now numbered three — Nixon, Harlow, and Butterfield — and Nixon was deposed twice, once in October and again in February 1980.

When the Oval Office tape recordings with Nixon's own voice were produced in 1978, his lawyers tried a wonderfully Nixonian trick. They said he hadn't been talking about me but about Gordon Rule, the Navy's chief critic of procurement. Nixon was clearly a little uneasy about this ploy. He probably realized that retaliation against *two* government employees was not an appealing tale to put before a District of Columbia jury. And he surely realized that the context plainly fixed me as the subject of his remarks. The second Oval Office tape we discovered ruled out Rule. On it Nixon said "Bryce [Harlow] was all for canning him, wasn't he?" But Harlow hadn't been in the White House in 1970–1973, when Gordon Rule had been most noisy in trying to keep the Navy honest. And Rule was never fired, simply transferred out of harm's way.

In the February deposition Nixon abandoned any pretense of mistaken identity. The questioning went this way:

> VON KANN: And the next point that you made, that he complained about cost overruns, that's about Fitzgerald?
>
> NIXON: That's correct.
>
> VON KANN: And "cutting up superiors" is about Fitzgerald?
>
> NIXON: That's correct.
>
> VON KANN: And "not taking orders" is about Fitzgerald?
>
> NIXON: That's correct.

Such admissions, along with the thought of having to face a D.C. jury, began to produce hints at a settlement from Nixon's lawyers.

At this point I ought to have been in the driver's seat, but I wasn't. The ACLU, which had been supporting my case since 1974, cooled off considerably, and only the intervention of my faithful supporter Ralph Temple kept our lawsuit from breaking down.

It so happened that at that time the ACLU was backing another suit against Nixon — and Henry Kissinger. Morton Halperin had sued them for bugging his telephones while he was working for Kissinger in the Nixon White House in the early 1970s. He had already won, in U.S. District Court, a judgment of five dollars: one dollar for himself, one for his wife, and one for each of his children. As the spring wore on, there was a lot of speculation as to whether the Supreme Court would take the Halperin case and, if so, what that would do to my case. Nixon, having appointed four of the nine justices, had a good chance of winning Halperin's suit against him and perhaps even getting himself declared immune from damages in private lawsuits. If that happened, my case against Nixon was lost.

Judge Gesell set a trial date of June 4, 1980, for my lawsuit against Nixon and his co-conspirators. I began to hint broadly that Halperin and the ACLU would be most considerate to forgo their five-dollar suit so that we could proceed to trial in the District of Columbia Federal Court. My case seemed so strong on every count that even the Nixon appointees on the Supreme Court would have to rule in my favor when it finally went to them.

Along with that, Nixon and the others named faced a very real threat. At a pretrial conference Judge Gesell said that if the jury awarded me $10 million in punitive damages against Butterfield, one of the "smaller fry," he would not set it aside. After this statement, settlement negotiations began in earnest.

As usual, I was in a predicament. On one hand my lawyers — Raven-Hansen, Prettyman, and von Kann — were eager to go to trial. But the attitude of the national office of the ACLU to my case fell somewhere between indifference and hostility. After twelve years of this fight I was exhausted, and my family had surely felt the strain. I couldn't afford the financial and psychic costs of the trial and the inevitable, endless appeals. We decided to settle.

Nixon was willing, but the Carter people at Justice were still vindictive toward me. In order to bleed me and my supporters a little more, they refused to settle on behalf of Harlow and Butterfield. Accordingly my lawyers reached an "agreement to specify damages" with Nixon. That meant Nixon would make an immediate payment of $100,000, then a second payment of $42,000, and finally $28,000 when the case actually came to trial. The sums were subject to adjustment if the Justice Department decided to settle. It wasn't a good compromise, but it was the best we could do.

On June 20, 1980, the Supreme Court agreed to hear the Halperin case, and Judge Gesell suspended our proceedings pending the outcome of *Kissinger v. Halperin*, which would decide the issue of absolute immunity. Nixon's attorneys and mine notified the court that the size of the payments to me would depend on the disposition of the Halperin case and the outcome of my District Court case. In another development the Justice Department requested that the Supreme Court hear my case against Butterfield and Harlow; my lawyers opposed this in a brief to the court.

On June 22, 1981, the Supreme Court handed down its verdict in the Halperin case by punting on the second down. Justice Rehnquist had recused himself on the grounds that he had been a Justice Department official at the time of the wiretapping. His action meant that the Halperin case could proceed in the lower courts, and mine would go to the Supreme Court. The department then moved to delay Halperin's case until mine was settled.

This put the shoe on the other foot. Halperin had stood in my way and now I was standing in his. As a result I was under tremendous pressure by the ACLU and others to drop my lawsuit so that Halperin could proceed. I was told that it was my patriotic duty to drop it.

By this time my circumstances had worsened. My legal team was breaking up, with Peter Raven-Hansen going to teach law at George Washington University and Kurt von Kann moving to Los Angeles. Ralph Temple had left the local ACLU, which was threatening not to pay my future expenses, an estimated $192,000. I offered to withdraw but only if Mort Halperin really intended to take Nixon to trial.

"If, on the other hand," I said, "Halperin and the national ACLU simply want me out of the way so that they can apply pressure on Nixon for a financial settlement, I want my past out-of-pocket expenses reimbursed out of their settlement monies." With that statement, everyone got very emotional. I had apparently revealed the secret agenda of the ACLU and Halperin. Sally Determan, an ACLU supporter and the "public interest" partner at Hogan and Hartson, had a temper fit when she heard of my remark and withdrew the firm from my case.

So for the moment, I was, figuratively, sitting alone on the steps of the Supreme Court beneath "Equal Justice under Law" with a ton and a half of legal records and no lawyer.

Barrett Prettyman and Peter Raven-Hansen came to my rescue, Barrett by recruiting John Noland, a senior partner in Steptoe and Johnson, and Peter by preparing a superb summary of the enormous mass of paper the case had generated and by reviewing our brief.

Then came the great shock. The Halperin faction of the ACLU joined Nixon's side in my case! Halperin's ACLU lawyer, Mark H. Lynch, along with Nader lawyers Alan D. Morrison and John Cary Sims, filed a motion to intervene in the Supreme Court case *Richard Nixon v. A. Ernest Fitzgerald*, stating they would make arguments "adverse to Fitzgerald's interests," that "the Halperins agree with Nixon" that the Appellate Court should have heard my case before trial, and that that court might find "that absolute immunity [for Nixon] is appropriate in *Fitzgerald*."

Here was the voice of liberalism speaking loud and clear, but with a forked tongue. According to their view, bugging Halperin's telephone was a stark violation of constitutional rights, but firing me for trying to save funds belonging to the United States and for using my First Amendment rights didn't count.

The new legal coalition of Richard Nixon, Halperin, the American Civil Liberties Union, and Ralph Nader might seem hilarious to outsiders, but it was painful for me. They alleged that my case presented "a far more attenuated Constitutional claim and one for which absolute rather than qualified immunity might be appropriate."

Then they offered the court a precedent for deciding against me. According to *Bush v. Lucas* (647 F.2d 573, 5th Cir., 1981), they said, civil service employees "who are fired in alleged retaliation for exercise of their First Amendment rights have no cause for action under First Amendment." Further, they told the Supreme Court that lower courts had held that "criticism of public employees of their superiors is not protected by the First Amendment."

It was a work worthy of Joseph McCarthy and Richard Nixon in their finest days, and the Nader and ACLU lawyers, having previously been involved in my case, knew it was untrue. John Noland, by patient argument, was finally able to counter this accumulation of fraud, but the damage had been done.

Rehnquist and his friends on the court must have smiled to see the liberals going on record against free speech. And Rehnquist, who as Richard Nixon's assistant attorney general had denounced whistle blowers, did not recuse himself this time.

And what had happened to the friends and supporters of free speech and whistle blowing? The only senator who dared put his name to a friend-of-the-court brief was Orrin Hatch. The only members of the House who would agree to be counted on my side were John Dingell, Robert Dornan, Barney Frank, Albert Gore, Jr., Toby Moffett, and Patricia Schroeder.

Predictably, we lost against Nixon and the American Civil Liberties Union. The only consolation was an excellent dissenting opinion by Justice Byron White.

Although the Supreme Court did rule that we could pursue the case against Harlow and Butterfield, the decision in favor of Nixon set a baneful precedent for Bill Bush's case. Bush, a brilliant and prophetic NASA engineer, had predicted that NASA's misguided policies would lead to some great disaster (as they did in the 1986 Challenger tragedy). When his case came up on appeal, the court took the advice of the Nader-ACLU lawyers and voted 9–0 against him. The court ruled that unless Congress made specific provisions to the contrary, the only way government employees could lodge a legal complaint against their bureaucratic or political superiors was through a Civil Service review. And I knew what that system of justice was like.

Jimmy Carter's civil service "reform" and *Bush* inspired a whole new set of repressive rules which, taken together, reduced a government employee's workplace rights to something equivalent to those of a slave in the ante-bellum South or of an Indian in the nineteenth century. Slaves had certain rights on paper; their only problem was that they couldn't go to court to have them upheld. Without a remedy, rights are meaningless.

My fortunes revived when John Bodner won a resounding victory in my job dispute. On March 31, 1982, Judge William Bryant, after rapping the Civil Service Commission's knuckles for failing to recognize that I hadn't been restored to equivalent status, ruled that the Air Force must do just that within thirty days. He also noted the Air Force's "improper withholding of documents" showing that the midnight farce I described at the end of Chapter 5 had been planned.

Bodner and I negotiated a settlement that included my return to areas of responsibility I'd had fourteen years previously, direct access to needed information, and authorization to travel to examine Air Force facilities and contractors all over the country. I was also guaranteed necessary authority.

The Air Force paid John Bodner $200,000 for part of my legal expenses. John wanted to give away the whole sum and pay the ACLU nothing, but I and others persuaded him to give the ACLU $60,000. I was promptly rewarded by more hostility from the ACLU. Leslie Harris, the local ACLU's new director, was against participating in my case against Harlow and Butterfield. As a result I had to settle for a modest amount in order to get on with my job.

Fourteen years of enormous legal effort and expense had more or less fizzled out. I felt particularly bad for the lawyers who had tried so valiantly to help me. And I felt morally bruised from all the dishonesty and hypocrisy I'd run up against.

I did have a moment of pleasure when I found out that some of the Air Force civilian lawyers who'd worked against me had been disgusted at Secretary Seamans's concealment of important evidence. (As he admitted in his deposition of September 18, 1979, he'd sent the most incriminating evidence against himself and Harold Brown to his brother at Peabody and Arnold in Boston, where it was stowed away in a safe-deposit box.) Because of that, the lawyers had wanted to suggest that I could keep Seamans as a defendant in the case. It didn't happen that way, but I was uplifted a little to see a refreshing spark of fair play in the dismal night of the federal legal system.

9

☆ ☆ ☆

Reagan's Big
Spender Saloon

THE TWELVE YEARS from 1976 to 1988 should go down in history as a time
when presidents Carter and Reagan each killed the conscience of his
party. The Jimmy Carter debacle seduced, corrupted, and destroyed the
ethical authority of the liberal Establishment. Ronald Reagan did the
same to conservatives who stood for fiscal responsibility and control
over the national debt.

When I went back to work for the Air Force, at the end of 1973, I had
to resign my chairmanship of the National Taxpayers Union (NTU),
which was a lobbying organization. Jim Davidson took over and did an
excellent job; by 1980 he had increased the membership to over
100,000. I kept in touch by reading the NTU newspaper, *Dollars and
Sense,* and by talking frequently with people on the Washington staff.

As I noted earlier, NTU's view was that mere tax resistance or tax
reduction could not restrain government spending. As the federal
deficits kept climbing, NTU decided to back a constitutional amendment requiring a balanced budget. The spenders couldn't waste money
if they didn't have it; they'd have to go to the taxpayers for any funds
beyond the budget total.

Among our friends were many honest politicians who supported cost
cutting. Occasionally they would break the pledge and fall off the
wagon, but we forgave them. When they came back from a spending
binge, they often sobered up and began to avoid the strong stuff even
more diligently. But I thought we'd learned from experience that even
the best of them would belly up to the bar at the Big Spender Saloon

now and then. This new bunch of Republicans *might* mean what they say about fiscal sobriety, but then again . . .

When candidate Ronald Reagan also came out in favor of a balanced budget, the NTU felt dizzy with success. I'd always been against tying the NTU to any politican or to either party. So I was horrified to see this comment in the December-January (1981) issue of *Dollars and Sense:*

> Whoopie! NTU is a non-partisan organization, but we could not help letting out a cheer at the election results that brought defeat to so many big spenders and opponents of a constitutional amendment to balance the budget. . . .
> *We have the greatest opportunity we've ever had to really win some great victories which will change the direction of life in this country.*

But, as Dr. Johnson said about second marriages, it was the triumph of hope over experience. Ronald Reagan spoke just like a fiscal-responsibility preacher, and he didn't have a red nose, shaky hands, or a whiskey voice. How was the innocent NTU to know that he would become the worst spending toper of all time? The NTU formed the Committee to Back the President and started to raise funds to "get behind President Reagan and help him get his proposals through Congress."

Everything *sounded* very hopeful. In that same issue of *Dollars and Sense,* David Stockman, soon to be director of the Office of Management and Budget (OMB) had an article titled "Avoiding an Economic Dunkirk." In it he cautioned that Reagan's proposed tax cuts must be "accompanied by a credible and severe program to curtail FY 81–82 outlays, future spending authority, and overall spending authority." Another wonderful temperance lecture from another plausible preacher.

David Stockman later confessed, explained, and rationalized his yielding to the spender's demon rum and his eventual slide to the gutter in his 1986 book, *The Triumph of Politics.* He recounted how Jimmy Carter in the campaign of 1980 matched Ronald Reagan's proposals for raising the military budget, promise for promise. By election time each was on record in favor of a 5 percent increase in "real growth" (growth over and above expected inflation), compounded annually, in the bill from the Pentagon.

In 1972 I had been called crazy for predicting that by 1980 the military budget would be $141 billion. In 1980 Carter actually topped that by an additional billion. When Stockman came in as OMB director, he increased Carter's $142 billion to $222 billion annually. The $80 billion increase, or "budget plug," as Stockman called it, was an arbitrary figure. It had been conjured up by Deputy Secretary of Defense

Frank Carlucci, columnist George Will, and Stockman. He was haunted by a memory of "the grim footage of the charred remains of U.S. servicemen being desecrated by the Iranian mullahs at the site known as Desert One." That last note is a marvelous example of American simple-mindedness about the whole matter of money and defense. It was stupidity that put the American servicemen into the debacle of the Iranian rescue mission, and no amount of money could cure it.

Now Stockman and his friends were pulling deep on the bottle of popskull. The 5 percent real growth of military spending went up to 7 percent a year — and, Stockman says, he inadvertently applied the 7 percent to the grandiose base of $222 billion rather than the Carter base of $142 billion! If Carter had generals who couldn't organize a rescue mission, Reagan had managers of the budget who couldn't do honest arithmetic. When Reagan blessed Stockman's crazy budget figures, they became Revealed Truth for a delighted Pentagon. Anything less than the sacred number, it was said, would make us easy prey for the Evil Empire.

Stockman sobered up a little the morning after. (According to one OMB staffer, Stockman was a very quick study and had a great capacity for detail.) In 1981 he began to encourage the staff to bring him ideas about how to squeeze some fat out of the Pentagon.

President Reagan invited Defense Secretary Caspar Weinberger to a meeting to discuss Stockman's package of proposals. After the OMB director made his pitch, the secretary of defense followed with a plea for continuous increases in defense spending. Why? Well, the Russians are coming, said Weinberger.

Stockman returned to his office completely dejected. He called his staff together and told them that Reagan had said, "Dave, two bars can't overrule four stars. Your job is to help Cap get the money he needs." (The mention of captain's bars versus general's stars referred to Captain Reagan's rank at discharge. He spent his part of World War II at Burbank, California, where he helped produce army training films.)

Added to the administration warning about the Evil Empire was the old, discredited argument that military spending makes us rich. The key to the Reagan Recovery Plan was escalation of spending, especially in the acquisition accounts (R & D and Procurement). The FY 83 budget for acquisition was about $104 billion, more than four times the figure at the end of the Vietnam budget freeze in FY 75.

During the height of election fever, *Newsweek* (October 27, 1980) had taken a poll of popular opinion about defense. To the question "Do you think the U.S. has been falling behind the Soviet Union in power and influence in recent years?" 68 percent said yes, 27 percent said no, and

5 percent didn't know. And to the question "Which is the nation's most serious defense problem: that not enough money is spent for defense or that what is spent is not used efficiently?" 15 percent said "not enough money," 72 percent said "not used efficiently," and 13 percent didn't know. It was a pretty good indication that some 72 percent of Americans were thinking more clearly than their president. Unfortunately, no politician with leadership stature was making an issue out of it.

Ronald Reagan was acting like the man in the Big Spender Saloon who steps up to the bar and yells, "Drinks are on me! Everybody in the house!" The thirsty military spenders almost knocked each other down in the stampede. The horror stories of that era are still surfacing almost a decade later. And, of course, the binge was charged to the taxpayers.

As the new administration settled into the bad old habits, I began to be overwhelmed with calls from closet patriots, mostly government employees but also a few who worked for defense contractors. Most of the closet patriots, I should explain, were "cheap hawks" — people who believed we could have a strong defense without bankrupting the country.

They wanted to bring to light some of the abuses they saw daily, but they were afraid of reprisals. Jimmy Carter had effectively hamstrung honest people of this kind with his civil service deform act. It was now clear that the "whistle blower protection" was nothing more than a sting operation to trap dissidents and destroy them. No one wanted to become another Ernie Fitzgerald, Henry Durham, or even Anthony Morris, who blew the whistle on the swine flu vaccine debacle and was fired for being right.

Two bright young staffers at NTU, David Keating and Dina Rasor, came to me and said they wanted to start a special project within NTU to monitor the military's extravagance and mismanagement. I'd been much impressed with their work on military spending issues; they were good at translating seemingly incomprehensible masses of expenditure facts and figures into terms a taxpayer could understand, and even better, they were in no way antimilitary. I saw their project as a good way to put the closet patriots' horror stories to good use. Dina was a careful investigator who wouldn't take my unsupported word for anything. She badgered me for verifying documents and reliable witnesses. As her project — now named the Project on Military Procurement, or PMP — grew, it seemed clear that it should be moved to another organizational home. The NTU tolerated it but didn't encourage it to become any bigger.

The National Taxpayers Legal Fund (NTLF) seemed an ideal place. Jim Davidson and I had set up the NTLF partly for educational work and

partly to provide legal defense for taxpayers who were unjustly perse-
cuted by the IRS. When I went back to the Pentagon, I swapped jobs
with Davidson and took over chairmanship of the NTLF, which was not
a lobbying organization.

When the PMP moved to NTLF, Jule Herbert, an NTU official went
along. That was significant because Herbert had some very generous
funders, principally the wealthy libertarian brothers Charles and George
Koch. PMP was an immediate success in its new home. The closet
patriots liked the conservative aura of the NTLF.

Journalists, more and more intrigued by the Pentagon spectacle,
began to come to PMP for reliable information. One unusual thing
about PMP was that it refused to receive classified documents. Washington journalism thrives on exploitation (usually unselective) of secret
government documents; famous columnists and by-liners have built
reputations on it. Readers, presumably, are impressed to read the
forbidden insider stuff. In my experience, however, most of these
journalists are pipelines for an agency or bureau or service that decides
to leak a nominal secret to make a point or get some political advantage.

Just as PMP was becoming effective, a strange thing happened. It was
attacked by a majority of the NTLF board of directors. The NTLF had a
powerhouse board with former senator Eugene McCarthy as president,
Ed Crane (who seemed to represent Charles and George Koch in
Washington), some people Ed recommended, Jule Herbert, and Anne
Zill, a director of FCG and Steward Mott's agent in Washington. I was
so smug about this group that I didn't pay attention to what was
happening.

What I didn't realize was that our big-business financial backers
would be happy with PMP only as long as its disclosures just embarrassed big government. When PMP began to get enough clout to
generate proposals in Congress for genuine change, the businessmen got
scared.

About a year after the PMP move, the project sponsored a conference
of cheap hawks, whistle blowers, closet patriots, congressional staff
members, and media people concerning practical, near-term remedies
for the military spending disaster. Although the conference was successful, Ed Crane stomped out in a rage and shortly afterward wrote to
the NTLF board complaining that "the Project on Military Procurement
is attempting to increase the *efficiency* of our fighting machine. From
my perspective, it is already grossly *too efficient*." He also said that
Eugene McCarthy believed it was "more important to cut the Pentagon's lean than its fat."

I cite this small battle to point up a very important motivation in the

position Ed Crane outlined. The "progressive" big businessmen, foundation people, labor unions, and Establishment liberals, using the same
argument as Crane, didn't want to make the military spending machine
more efficient; they would back a proposal to start disarming the
United States because they knew such an idea would not go anywhere.
Secretly they were happy with the benefits they received from big
spending.

In the campaign of 1972 George McGovern's backers, too, had been
primarily interested in cutting the size of military operating forces
rather than in trying to economize. They simply could not grasp the
idea that peacetime military spending has little to do with foreign
policy or the world situation, that it is largely driven by domestic
politics. Nor could they see that they were dealing with a military that
projected its grandiose plans far into the future. Once Congress approved
the modest start of a weapons system, that system was going to cost us
many billions in the years to come. A little thing like the end of a war
would not affect the self-perpetuating build-up.

My conversations with the McGovern people had ended when I got
this sad little message from them: labor was against the economizing
ideas, which would cost McGovern "the Lockheed vote." In the end it
was easy for the Nixon strategists to obliterate McGovern's effort on
this issue. One television commercial showed a game board set up with
toy soldiers, ships, planes, etc. A hand, presumably McGovern's,
appeared and swept half the pieces off the board.

The PMP did find another home under the roof of the Fund for
Constitutional Government, thanks to its benefactor, Stewart Mott.
And Dina Rasor's good work continued.

I had another educational adventure in the early Reagan years. I first
heard of an astonishing new proposal when a friend sent me a copy of an
editorial from the Memphis *Commercial Appeal.* Reagan had just fired
the fifteen Carter-appointed inspectors general, the "watchdogs" who
were supposed to sniff out waste and corruption in the various executive
branch departments. The administration announced that it was looking
for people who were more than just watchdogs, who were "meaner than
a junkyard dog." The *Commercial Appeal* suggested that Reagan
"might look up Fitzgerald and do right by him. Who knows, Fitzgerald
might even know a dozen or so other honest people in the federal
government who would like to have jobs as inspectors general too." I'd
never thought of myself as mean, but I guess some people may have had
that impression.

That proposal seems to have started something. Soon afterward I had
a call from Tom Scarret, a Washington correspondent for the Newhouse

newspaper chain, who told me there was some meaningful support for having me replace the retiring Elmer Staats as comptroller general and head of the General Accounting Office. Senators Hatch and Proxmire backed the idea, as did the NTU.

A friend of mine set up an appointment with Representative Jack Kemp, the conservative supply-sider who was supposed to have convinced Reagan that budget deficits didn't matter very much. Kemp told me that his philosophy didn't in any way condone waste. He took my resumé and subsequently wrote to Reagan, saying, "I would like to give my highest recommendation to Mr. A. Ernest Fitzgerald who would make an excellent Comptroller General of the United States." He suggested that Reagan have a talk with me.

Next I had a letter from Congressman Jack Brooks, chairman of the House Committee on Government Operations, and Senator William Roth, chairman of the Senate Committee on Governmental Affairs, saying that I'd been nominated for the job and asking for extensive personal history information. This seemed to be a sign that I was under serious consideration. Under a relatively new law, a bipartisan, bicameral committee of Congress had to recommend nominees to the president.

But when the word got out, the familiar alliance of big military spenders and White House staff hit the panic button. I got the news from Clark Mollenhoff, that ever-hopeful Republican, who had his usual excellent contacts at the White House, that some of the staff were calling me a "communist dupe." My position, of course, was that the people who threw away vast sums of public money and condoned deficient armaments were the real agents of the Evil Empire. Even a Reagan true believer ought to be bright enough to realize that.

What were my credentials for dupism? Clark said the only charge anybody could think of was that I'd once been on the board of SANE, "a citizens' organization for a sane world," which had backed the limited nuclear test ban treaty in the 1960s and was opposed to nuclear weapons testing, the arms race, and the Cold War. As NTU chairman, I'd joined SANE partly to further our outreach program and partly to try to convince SANE that it was futile to think of converting such dedicated boondoggle corporations as Lockheed to civilian enterprise. When my missionary effort failed, I resigned.

My detractors suggested, through Mollenhoff, that I do public penance for having had any connection with SANE. I said that was unacceptable.

When I looked back through the record of my SANE activity, I found that the only aspect of SANE I'd been officially involved in did have something to do with the Russians. On September 14, 1973, backed by

strong feelings among the membership, board members Edward Con-
don, Seymour Melman, and A. Ernest Fitzgerald had sent a letter to
Soviet Ambassador Anatoly Dobrynin:

> We are disturbed by the Soviet government's chilling persecution of
> such dissidents as Andrei Sakharov, Alexander Solzhenitsyn, and many
> other individuals we have considered our counterparts in the Soviet
> Union. . . .
>
> When Soviet scientists and intellectuals are threatened, jailed, or
> exiled, we see the spokesmen for détente with humanist values under
> attack.
>
> When your dissidents are attacked by your government, we are
> concerned about the kind of peaceful coexistence your government has
> in mind.

The letter went on to point out that the Soviet Union, secure and
powerful, hardly had to get jittery over a "handful of unconventional
thinkers." Furthermore, the Soviets and Americans seemed to be
"entering a phase of cooperation." We took a few more hard shots at the
Soviets for cracking down on their whistle blowers and ended with a
stand against any governmental repression of intellectual freedom.

Reading this over in 1981, I wondered long and hard why the Reagan
White House could be upset about me. I recalled that in 1973 Nixon was
getting so cozy with the Evil Empire that no public-interest organization
in the country had been able to persuade him to protest the treatment
of Sakharov and Solzhenitsyn. Then I saw a telling sentence in our
letter, praising Sakharov for his brave declaration titled "Progress,
Co-existence, and Intellectual Freedom." We had written, "Dr. Sakharov's study marks him as a principal spokesman in the Soviet Union
for *antimilitarism* [emphasis added] and the worldwide fulfillment of
the Declaration of the Rights of Man." Was it because we had praised
Sakharov's antimilitarism that I was now under suspicion at the White
House? Could it be anything that absurd?

I remembered the day we had delivered the letter. Sanford Gottlieb,
executive director of SANE, and I decided to hand carry it in hopes of
seeing Ambassador Dobrynin himself. As we walked toward the en-
trance of the Soviet Embassy on Sixteenth Street in Washington, an
assortment of police cruisers with flashing lights converged on us.
There were District of Columbia police cars, Executive Protective
Service cars, and other unidentified vehicles. Out jumped a number of
young men in dark business suits. Some began taking pictures of us,
others seemed to have hearing aids in their ears and to be talking into
their sleeves. None tried to stop us, however, so Sandy and I went to the

front gate and rang for admittance. We were met by a man of about thirty who could have been a clone of those outside. He had the same clothes, the same expression, the same manner. Behind him were more clones in dark business suits, wearing hearing aids and talking into their sleeves. We didn't see Dobrynin.

Another indiscretion, as Mollenhoff discovered, was my former chairmanship of the National Taxpayer's Union. My candidacy for the comptroller general's job was all but doomed. I took the whole story to the staff of Republican Congressman Dornan of California, known to his detractors as "Mad Dog Bob." Dornan, arguably the most right-wing congressman in the last quarter of this century, to my surprise saw nothing wrong with my activities. He wrote a letter to Reagan, saying:

> In my judgment, America's print and broadcast media will judge the Reagan Administration's efforts to control "runaway government" largely by what happens to Ernie Fitzgerald, the man who made the term "whistleblower" an honorable part of our political vocabulary. . . . I strongly recommend Ernie Fitzgerald for . . . appointment as Comptroller General. . . .
>
> Capitol Hill opponents of your proposed spending cuts would be more charitable to your efforts if they saw a Comptroller General with impeccable "bona fides" who could make government programs run better for less money. This is especially helpful, Mr. President, in the critical area of defense, where budget requests have been increased while other programs have been trimmed.

The man eventually appointed comptroller general was Charles Bowsher, Jr., who had served as assistant finance manager in Reagan's 1980 presidential campaign. He was a partner in the Big Eight certified public accounting company of Arthur Andersen and Company, whose clients included General Dynamics Corporation, maker of the infamous TFX, the F-111 fighter-bomber I'd had so much trouble with.

After a while Reagan's "morning in America" began to look like the end of a lot of weary days I had seen before. The administration brought out the two old, dishonest maxims of their predecessors and paraded them as if they were something new: big military spending will make the armed forces strong and will make the country rich. Defense Secretary Weinberger and his deputy, Frank Carlucci, were the talking heads for these slogans.

In the Winter 1983 issue of *Directors and Boards*, Carlucci had an article titled "An Economic Defense of the Defense Budget." He began by saying, "The current defense program is carefully designed to redress a decade of neglect of our armed forces and restore the military equilibrium necessary for deterrence." Decade of neglect? The defense budget had gone from about $78 billion to over $136 billion in those ten years. What was the man talking about?

Carlucci's first economic argument — also known as the self-milking cow argument — was that only 70 percent of our industrial capacity was in use and unemployment was over 10 percent. Defense spending would help us cure this and attain a bigger GNP. Nothing new here.

The second one was the old spin-off argument: defense spending is a stimulus to industry modernization. If there were any truth to that, we would have been six times more state-of-the-art than Japan because, as a percentage of the gross national product, we spent six times as much as they did on defense.

The third point was that the defense industry was the largest trainer of skilled manpower. But Carlucci didn't explain that defense industry "training" was far and away the most expensive in the world. And most of it was of little use in a competitive commercial economy. Further, the slipshod methods used in Pentagon contracts tended to train industrial workers to be professional goldbricks.

The most incredible notion of all those expressed by Carlucci was that defense spending was a cure for our international balance-of-trade deficit. If this were true, our trade surplus would have been far bigger than Japan's or West Germany's. But it wasn't.

I had hoped — naively, in retrospect — that the Reagan team would keep its promise for a balanced budget and improved stewardship of the Pentagon. An early sign of that, I thought, was the appointment of Verne Orr as secretary of the Air Force. Some first-rate closet patriots reported that Orr was appalled by the things we had been troubled about and that he intended to make some real improvements. Their optimism only showed that the closet patriots could be as innocent about the ways of bureaucracy as I. We forgot that Verne Orr was surrounded by the larcenous officers of the Praetorian Guard.

When I was finally restored to an approximation of my original Air Force job in June 1982, I decided to test the thesis that Orr was a "good guy." I planned to send him as much useful information as I could and watch how he used it.

Some of Orr's detractors carped that he was unqualified because he'd been "only a car dealer." But he also had an excellent business background, was versed in investment analysis, and had a good sense of politics. He was a rich man and personally secure enough to be above temptations for petty advantage. Best of all, he had a close, long-standing relationship with Ronald Reagan. Orr was a member of the Lincoln Club, an organization of archconservative California businessmen that had given Nixon his start in politics and had backed Reagan. Orr had been a political appointee in Sacramento during Reagan's governorship and had worked in the 1980 presidential campaign. This added up to a lot of clout with the president and I hoped that I could influence him in the direction of cost reduction and control.

My immediate boss, the assistant secretary for financial management, was a young, aggressive man named Russell Hale, who had been a staff member of the House Armed Services Committee. Although he didn't approve of my return to the acquisition business, he took the forced settlement in good enough grace. But he absolutely refused to allow me to report on weapons systems to Congress. He wanted the reports to be handled by a political appointee, not a career man, and certainly not a maverick. I didn't like this arrangement, but we compromised on an agreement that I'd take over the reports to Congress in December 1984, when Hale said he planned to leave his job. I was in a mood to cooperate and get on with the work.

I was given two experienced and well-qualified assistants in Colin Parfitt and Duane Packard, a Ph.D. economist. Colin had been loyal to me in my deepest difficulties, and his current boss was trying to fire him. And Packard's boss was trying to fire him. Hale had solved all his personnel problems by collecting the possible dissidents in one group.

To keep an eye on us, Hale added both a military and a political keeper, although we had no secrets to keep. In fact we wanted our political superiors to know what we were doing. Our political keeper was a young White House appointee, a Mormon named Jim Ririe. He'd been a cost accountant at a plant making plastic garbage bags, a cost-competitive business. Our military keeper was a bright Air Force colonel named Dick Ensign.

I took my olive branch to General Thomas Marsh, in charge of the Air Force Systems Command (AFSC), and explained that I planned to survey the performance measurement systems in our acquisitions programs, especially those for cost control and cost reduction. What programs would he like to have reviewed?

Marsh said one he had in mind was the Imaging Infrared (IIR) Maverick missile in process at the Hughes Aircraft Company plants in Canoga Park, California and Tucson, Arizona. This missile was descended from the older Electro-Optical (EO), or television-guided Maverick, which had been something of a dud. The infrared detector on the IIR Maverick made it possible — in theory, at least — to hit a target in dim light or at night.

Both Mavericks, the Air Force's primary weapons of their kind, were supposed to be magic bullets against invading Russian tanks in Europe. The pilot of a close-support fighter would come in, point his plane in the general direction of the target, look at the TV-type monitor in his cockpit to pinpoint the target, lock the Maverick onto it, let fly, and then pull out. Even if the tank tried to evade, it would, in theory, get hit, sort of like those electronic games in the arcade.

Verne Orr had been reading the newspapers, which said that the new Maverick was vastly overrunning its cost and not performing very well. General Marsh wanted to learn at least as much about what was wrong as the reporters seemed to know.

At my request Marsh assigned the AFSC comptroller, Brigadier General Wilma Vaught, and Lieutenant Colonel Stan Kagan to work with us. General Vaught was an old acquaintance of mine, and Kagan turned out to be a very competent, intelligent officer. He'd learned the business while assigned to the ballistic missile system division of the AFSC, and he was now in charge of applying the systems for measuring contractor performance that my colleagues and I had developed in the 1960s.

We traveled by executive jet to Wright-Patterson AFB in Dayton, where the Maverick buying office was located. There we had our first stroke of luck. Nobody had thought to warn them we were coming. By even better luck, all the generals of the Aeronautical Systems Division (a buying division of AFSC) were away at a conference. So we were able to go directly to the analysts who got the performance reports from the contractors, evaluated them, and recommended action.

They were delighted to see us, and I was delighted to hear that my old performance measurement project was alive and well. Within fifteen minutes, the analysts and I had gone through the various levels of reports and gotten to the missile's technical trouble. The cost overruns were displayed. In fact, the performance measurement reports had been signaling grave trouble for over two years. But no matter how telling these analyses were and how scathing the accompanying comments from the analysts, management had done nothing. The military managers tolerated such reports, it seemed, simply for the sake of image.

There was a good side to that, however. Since the reports were never acted on, management felt no need to falsify them. These technicians had continued to operate in their own little 1960s world of relative accuracy and integrity.

That visit was so encouraging that I decided to go to Air Force Plant 44 in Tucson, where Hughes was building the Maverick. Our whole group, except for Duane Packard, was excited by the prospect of doing some worthwhile work with the backing, we thought, of the secretary, the assistant secretary, and the commanding general of the AFSC. As we discussed our plans enthusiastically on the plane ride back from Dayton, Packard became more and more silent. The morning after we got back, he went to the personnel office, filled out his retirement papers, and left before noon.

Packard, an economist, knew something we didn't. He was tuned in to the Reagan game plan of prosperity through unprecedented military spending, and he had seen the real meaning behind the situation in Dayton.

I still believed there must be some truth to Reagan's loudly announced budget-balancing plans. Besides, I believed that the administration hawks must be deeply worried that their chief air-to-ground antitank missile didn't work, and it cost so much that quantities would be severely limited in any budget Congress was likely to pass.

In Tucson the Air Force plant representative, Lt .Col. Grant Hird, said he had instructions to give us whatever we needed. From Robert McDonald, the civilian contracting officer, I got the spare-parts pricing formula for the IIR Maverick. As was customary, the Air Force had negotiated markups based on whatever Hughes paid for that material plus Hughes's bill for labor, priced out in standard direct manhours, that is, the should-take times Hughes's engineers had determined were appropriate for fabricating, assembling, and testing the Maverick.

For starters, I saw that the should-take hours had been multiplied by a factor of fifteen to twenty. To that bloated figure, fattened by very high rates of pay, were added unbelievable further markups for "support labor and overhead." McDonald and the Hird staff assured me that what I was looking at reflected the actual costs.

I wondered. Then I remembered the case of Mr. Gillette, who, it was said, learned that he could get rich not by selling razors but by selling the spare parts, the blades. The company sometimes gave away the razors because only Gillette blades would fit them. I wondered if Hughes, on somewhat the same pattern, had found an accounting gimmick to pass excessive costs on to their bills for spare parts. But Hughes was not doing a Gillette; their overpricing of spare parts was a general reflection of all the overpricing on their Maverick work.

At the time I'm writing about, big military contractors priced spare parts by contractual arrangements called Basic Ordering Agreements, or BOAs. This was a handy means of setting prices for frequent orders for spare parts that were available only from one source without having to negotiate the price of each part separately. The markups on the standard labor and material for spare parts orders would reflect the factory inefficiencies, labor rates, and overhead add-ons that were being accepted for the big stuff at the time the parts were ordered. Spare parts pricing piggybacked on the inefficiencies tolerated and the markups negotiated for the "major end items" — airplanes, missiles, and so on. The parts prices would reflect the overpricing of the whole assembly.

On the labor side, BOA inefficiency markups on the standard or should-take times to make and test the parts were usually the same as those being used on other work in the shops involved. Then previously approved rates of pay and overhead markups were applied to standard times plus the inefficiency markups to arrive at the "actual costs" of labor. This was passed through to the government after a percentage was added for profit.

As I've described, materials and parts were generally treated as pass-through costs, too. Sole-source suppliers had a positive incentive to be as sloppy as possible in their buying, at least until they negotiated firm prices with the government.

To illustrate how this disincentive works, let's say we're buying a simple, familiar item such as a hammer. (Strictly speaking, hammers and other tools are not spare parts but "support equipment," a distinction I will explore later.) Say the military needs a hammer for its work on a weapon system. If the military is experiencing difficulty "executing the program" (spending the money), instead of ordering a hammer from supply, or, if supply is out, from a local hardware store, it gives the weapon system contractor a contract to "work the problem." In due course the system contractor's large engineering staff determines that, sure enough, the maintenance mechanics need a hand-held device to generate impacts at certain points. They ask a subcontractor, preferably another "established" contractor who knows the ropes, to give a quote on a multidirectional manually operated variable impact generator.

Then, if the subcontractor submits a quote of, say, $200 for the impact generator, the systems contractor adds his usual overhead markup for the purchasing department, let's say 25 percent, "justifying" a cost of $250. (The systems contractor can also add a slug of "engineering" and "program management" costs, both direct and overhead if he wants to, but for simplicity we'll assume he doesn't.) Then, because we are dealing with space-age capitalism, the profit is figured as a *percentage of estimated costs*. Let's be cheap and add only 10 percent, or $25 in this case, bringing the price of the hammer to $275.

A typical auditor will probably check that a document exists to show that the subcontractor actually bid $200 to supply the impact generator and that the markups are in line with those generally deemed acceptable and "reasonable."

Once this transaction is approved (or goes through automatically under BOA formula pricing), the system contractor can buy a hammer for $10 from the local hardware store, deliver it, and collect $275, pocketing a neat gross profit of $265. If the transaction is later detected, the contractor may be accused of "defective pricing" because he did not spend as much as he said he would for the hammer. He might have to give back some of the money, which wouldn't be all that important; but if news of the transaction leaks and generates a horror story, that becomes *very* important for it might ruin the racket. Usually the contractors just go through the wealth-sharing motions, and everybody who counts stays happy.

Wealth sharing for favored subcontractors was so attractive that cartel members who were not due for a prime contract in the rotating award system often were quite happy to take their turn as subcontractor to the winning lodge brother. It made for nice, gentlemanly bid rigging.

At the time of my visit to Tucson in May 1982, Hughes had already manufactured 20,000 of the EO Mavericks. Many of the parts on the new IIR model were identical or very similar to those on the EO; the major innovation was the "seeker head." Hughes had also built 93 "equivalent units" of missiles of the new design. (An equivalent unit was simply 262 standard hours of mixed production on the missile, because that was the should-take time to build a complete missile. This concept, useful for accounting, was a roughly accurate way of measuring manufacturing performance at given periods.)

When I checked the figures, I found that Hughes was spending 17.2 actual hours of factory labor to produce one standard hour of work on the IIR Maverick. Unfortunately, that was the relatively good news. The bad news was that when all the markups were added (except for certain costs such as those for the original design), the Air Force was paying Hughes $3,405 for one standard hour of work.

The worst news was that Hughes was turning out a terrible product. The quality experts in the Air Force Plant Representative Office (AFPRO) denied that, but during our factory tour, I saw some extraordinarily sloppy quality control. I didn't have time to verify the details during that visit, but I stored the memory away.

Next I took my group to Albuquerque to visit AFSC's Contract Management Division (CMD), the headquarters for all our AFPROs. There I met a civilian industrial engineer named Ompal "Om" Chauhan, who turned out to be a jewel in this business. Om had been born in Rajasthan and, after service in the Indian Army, had married an American, put himself through engineering college here, and become an American citizen. I was delighted with his quick intelligence and energy. I was also pleased that he had a good vantage point for looking at all twenty-five contractor plants where we had Air Force detachments. Even better, Om liked cost cutting. He wanted the big contractors to conform to a work measurement system that had been instituted, I believe, around 1972 by a CMD engineer named Pat Haugh but never employed.

Om was able to take the rough figures I'd gathered in Tucson and refine them, as shown in the chart. The "standard hours" line shows the measurement of should-take time, or standard work content as determined by Hughes engineers, which varied a little as the Maverick design changed. The "actual hours" line shows what really happened — the actual manhours spent in production. The variance, of course, is the disparity between the should-take time and the actual time spent. And the ominous shaded area is waste caused by bad work, that is, time taken up by work the Hughes inspectors found unacceptable. Even this, Om said, had its phony aspect. A lot of work was done and redone before it ever got to the inspectors, but *that* wasted time wasn't counted as rework time.

For people who find stories in charts, Om's chart told some remark-

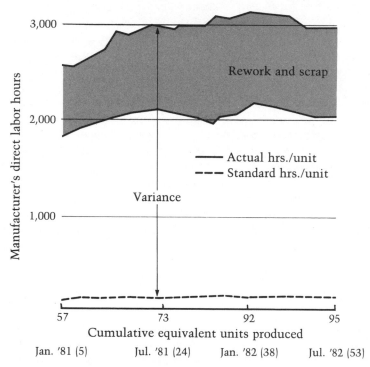

Variance between standard hours and actual hours in manufacture of the IIR Maverick missile by Hughes Aircraft. Source: Air Force Contract Management Division.

able tales. One has to do with the learning curve. The theorists say that improvement should be steady and rapid after the first unit is made. Say Hughes spent 3,000 labor hours on the first. According to theory, the next should be made in 80 percent of that time (for the typical 80 percent improvement curve), or 2,400 hours. The fourth unit ought to be finished in 80 percent of the time the second one took, or 1,920 hours; the eighth unit at 80 percent of the fourth, or 1,536, and so on. By the time Hughes had made 64 units, they should have been down to a manufacturing time of 790 hours per unit.

But look at the chart: Hughes was actually taking *more* hours on each successive unit. This was not a slow learner, it was a reverse learner. Except for Om Chauhan, the CMD people saw nothing wrong with that. They seemed to think it was somehow preordained. As for the quality control people, they shrugged their shoulders at the shocking amount of time spent on rework and scrap. It struck me that Hughes hadn't learned how to make a missile efficiently, but it had learned the great self-serving lesson: how to get away with fiscal murder.

When I brought these findings to Russ Hale, he said he was concerned and that certainly some improvement should be made, but we shouldn't appear to be picking on Hughes. He suggested we apply Om Chauhan's chart to some other, similar tactical missiles we were buying. I then discussed this with General Marsh, who listened nervously and agreed but said he'd get the information himself. He said he had good people and he didn't want me "mucking about in his plants."

By this time Jim Ririe, our political keeper, had been converted to the economy cause. Jim, Colin, and I worked out a scheme to evaluate and challenge the excessive costs of our big contractors, using Om Chauhan's yardstick to measure factory labor hours. We were going to put such things as engineering hours, rates of pay, material costs, and overhead ("costs elements" in accountants' language) to the test.

Then an interesting new problem began to develop. George Spanton, a man I'd known as a Navy auditor some years back, was now in charge of a Defense Contract Audit Agency (DCAA) group at Pratt and Whitney's plant in West Palm Beach, Florida. George had had the bad manners to challenge excessive travel and improper entertainment expenses that the company was passing on to the government, and he'd balked at the big pay raises Pratt and Whitney executives were handing out to themselves and their employees. In the course of eleven months in the previous year Pratt and Whitney had granted themselves a total pay raise of 23 percent.

The Pentagon's system for evaluating pay raises was wonderfully loony; our contract negotiators would accept any raises that didn't deviate greatly from a trend line established by past raises. So the bigger the boosts in the past, the bigger the boosts the company could get away with today. George wanted to compare Pratt and Whitney's pay scales with those in other, cost-competitive industries and with those of government employees. He proposed that the company's pay hikes split the difference between the percentages allowed government employees and the percentages Pratt and Whitney wanted.

George's injection of sanity wasn't unjust to Pratt and Whitney. The company could reward themselves just as they wished out of their ample profits. All George was concerned about was the company's habit of rewarding its people directly out of the U.S. Treasury. Spanton's proposal would deny Pratt and Whitney a $150 million raid on the Treasury over the next three years. That pinched.

When I called on the CMD in Albuquerque, I asked for Spanton's pay audits, a request that made everybody very nervous. They said Spanton's reports were meaningless, and when the produced them, I found that somebody had scrawled on the cover page, "This report was withdrawn by DCAA!" — which was not true. DCAA had only changed some of the explanatory language, not the substantive findings. Finally, the CMD people argued that Spanton's recommendations would kill the spirit of free enterprise in West Palm Beach.

When Jim Ririe saw the Spanton report, he told us that on April 15, 1982, Verne Orr had written a letter to Russ Hale along the lines of George's report. Orr had said that the zooming pay rates were "absolutely ludicrous" and had told Hale to put a stop to the permissive Air Force practices that allowed it.

That was Orr's hot potato. Nobody had wanted to touch it or even acknowledge that it existed. But our group was delighted to find a firm policy directive from the secretary that matched Spanton's independent field audit. Orr seemed pleased that somebody was getting into the problem. He told me he wanted the Air Force to be just as firm about holding the line on executive and white-collar pay as on hourly wages. That was a good sign; that summer of 1982 for the first time I was very hopeful that we could put a few controls on the giant jackpot machine.

Seeming proof that Verne Orr was on the right side came when he addressed a luncheon meeting of the *Washington Times* editorial board. He praised my work highly and said that my rehabilitation was a symbol of the Reagan administration's desire for economy and efficiency. I was happy for the good words and pleased that Orr had chosen this forum to praise me. Clark Mollenhoff, who had taken a summer leave from his professorship at Washington and Lee University to report on the Pentagon for the *Times,* was there. The newspaper — nicknamed the "Moonie Times" because it was owned by the Reverend Sun Yung Moon — was trying desperately to establish journalistic respectability and had brought Clark in to help. The paper had strong right-wing connections with the administration and, according to the editors, it was the first paper Reagan read every weekday morning.

But now the Air Force buying alliance was getting ready to shaft George Spanton. His DCAA bosses decided, quite illegally, to block his access to key records he needed for his work and to transfer him to California. They wanted to frustrate him to the point that he would decide to retire. When I spoke to Russ Hale and to Willard Mitchell, his principal deputy, Mitchell warned me not to carry on a campaign to help Spanton "directly." Being a good bureaucrat, I obeyed — and carried on the campaign indirectly.

Clark Mollenhoff, with the help of Greg Rushford, eventually wrote more than a hundred stories about the Spanton case. His stories goaded the Office of Special Counsel (OSC) into action. The OSC was the "chaplain" that was supposed to protect government employees' rights under Jimmy Carter's grotesque whistle blower protection scheme. It did get some of Spanton's bosses removed from their jobs, but the victory was temporary. The OSC presented a flawed case — deliberately, I thought — and was reversed on appeal. Meanwhile George, stymied in his reform efforts, retired. Both the reforms and the reformer were lost to the taxpayers.

Things seemed to be going well for me personally, so I turned to help Om Chauhan get his work measurement scheme accepted. For ten years the engineers in CMD and the army had labored patiently to perfect a Military Standard for contractors, who would be required to measure work by that standard. These engineering time standards would give us a better handle on cost control, on tracking progress, and on pricing. But each time the engineers had come up with a blueprint for the standard, the contractor-military opposition had conjured up an objection.

I decided to put an end to this nonsense by calling a big Pentagon conference and inviting representatives from Weinberger's office, all the services, the Defense Logistics Agency (DLA), and anybody else who cared to attend. Om Chauhan and his boss, Colonel Jack Bryan, came. A coven of Air Force procurement types turned up. The DLA sent some knowledgeable people, and the defense secretary's office sent some brass. Ed Kindinger and Al Addlefinger, two able technicians representing the Army Management Engineering Training Agency, were even tougher than I in pushing for the standard.

I had announced that the conference would last until we had an agreement on the final form of military specification for work measurement. We reached an agreement in less than four hours, which enabled Chauhan and Bryan to go back to the AFSC with a Military Standard ready to be published. We expected approval and distribution within a few weeks.

Summer turned to fall, and nothing happened. There were no evident signs of trouble between my bosses and me. Orr and Hale seemed ready to let our work proceed. My promotion to GS-18, the highest grade in the old civil service merit system, came through, and the written justification was gratifyingly flowery.

But still nothing was happening on any of our improvement fronts. The generals hadn't produced the factory cost performance figures we'd requested months before. And people who had once seemed to understand what we wanted were suddenly uncomprehending. Colin Parfitt observed that the British Army once had a court-martial offense officially called "dumb insolence," — or pretending stubbornly not to understand. I had a vision of long lines of U.S. generals, colonels, and admirals waiting to be tried on the charge. It would decimate the Pentagon.

At about this time the AFSC and DoD people who opposed the Military Standard work measurement got together, and soon Richard Stimson, of Weinberger's office, forbade publication of the Military Standard until "industry objections" were met. Clearly we had to think of another way to skin the cat.

On the Orr-Spanton initiative on pay raises, the situation was even worse. The generals were not only ignoring Secretary Orr's direct order to stop paying for huge raises for contractors (so much for military discipline) but were lobbying against it on Capitol Hill. Congressional staffers told me that General Bernie Weiss and a troop of procurement officers were drumming up congressional opposition. We reported this and other evidence of obstruction to Russ Hale, but still nothing happened.

Thomas Amlie, who had replaced Duane Packard, was a fine asset to our group. Along with four engineering degrees, including a Ph.D., he had an outstanding record as a designer of guided missiles. Tom had started his career as an assistant to William McLean, director of the Navy's China Lake lab, at that time the best weapons laboratory in the world. McLean was largely responsible for the highly successful Sidewinder air-to-air missile. When Tom succeeded McLean as director, he developed some new weapons and worked out some refinements for the Sidewinder. But — the oft-told tale again — Tom had a habit of telling the truth, and that was something the admirals wouldn't stand for.

Tom recalled that while McLean was developing the Sidewinder with a total of about 125 people (including secretaries), Hughes was developing the Air Force Falcon missile with about 4,000 people on the job. The only difference in results was that the Falcon failed and the Sidewinder worked.

As Tom, Colin, and I discussed our problems, we suddenly realized that the people we had to persuade didn't have a single day's manufacturing experience among them. Not one of them had ever designed anything. Hale was an Annapolis graduate who had had an Air Force commission, a job with IBM, and a congressional staff post before coming to the Pentagon. Verne Orr, ex-car dealer, was an astute politician. Frank Carlucci was a professional bureaucrat. Caspar Weinberger was a lawyer who had held some government posts. Education! We needed to educate our technologically illiterate bosses.

Not a bad idea, but I wasn't sure how we'd do it. These men were too busy and preoccupied to hold still for a tutorial. We hit on the idea of showing, in graphic form, how some old, familiar products we had been buying for years had shown dramatic price boosts that no inflation indices or product improvements could explain.

A good example was the C-5B, which was vastly more expensive than its disreputable older brother the C-5A, my nemesis. The chart shows the price differences, using the learning-curve prices negotiated for each model. The C-5A prices, originally negotiated in 1965, were renegotiated in 1970 to reflect inflation and alterations in the design. The prices shown are for the aircraft alone; the four huge engines were separate.

On the C-5A, all of the great cost overruns I had testified to had occurred or been exceeded. Even the diehard partisans of the old did-cost/will-cost estimates had to admit that we had ended up with "polluted actuals" for C-5A costs. But that great accumulation of waste and "polluted actuals" became the basis of costs for the C-5B! And further, the Pentagon added in new inflation figures that were higher than the actual rate of inflation.

But that was not the end of this series of absurdities. The big excuse for contracting for the B series after the disasters of the A model was that everything would be cheaper. The salesmen argued that Lockheed had learned its lessons with the C-5A. The new model was to be built

in much the same way; in fact, after some changes, it was simpler to
build. Ninety-five percent of the tooling was the same for the two
planes. I was told that 55 percent of the C-5A was still in production
because of spare parts orders and the $1.5 billion wing replacement
program.

Thus Lockheed wouldn't have to invent the wheel all over again.
They could start at the point of greatest efficiency on the learning curve.
Correct? Not at all. Lockheed had to start out by spending $305,900,000
per airplane because, presumably, it didn't remember how to build
them.

As Dina Rasor recounted in her book, *The Pentagon Underground*,
the Air Force people who flew transports shuddered at the idea of
buying a new-model tin balloon. But they were under heavy pressure to
go along. Even some of the brass were opposed to the C-5B. Whitey
Driessnack, now assistant vice-chief of the Air Force, told me he
thought the proposed price was outrageous. He said that the first C-5B

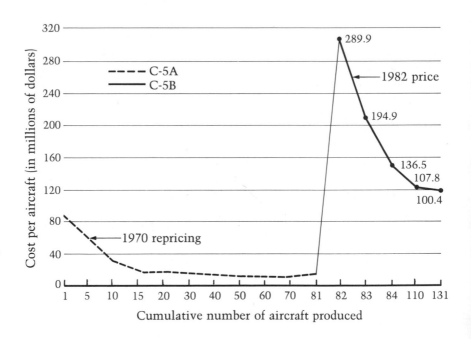

Unit prices negotiated for Lockheed's C-5A and C-5B aircraft, not including
engines. Source: Air Force Plant Representatives Office, Air Force Plant 6,
Marietta, Georgia.

should be considered the eighty-second C-5A, to avoid the fat part of the learning curve. I had an idea that this horror story might be a good place to begin the education of my bosses. But to my surprise, I discovered that Verne Orr and Russ Hale were pushing for the purchase of the C-5B.

I tried another angle. I went back to my old favorite yardstick of dollar cost per standard hour of output. By 1982 the most "reasonable" of the big military contractors was charging $95 per standard hour. Most of the others charged between $150 and $300. Hughes, of course, was the all-time champion hog at this county fair with a feed bill of $3,405 per standard hour.

How could we illustrate the difference between reasonable costs in commercial enterprises and those in military contracting? It occurred to me to go back to a comparison I had made in 1973 and ask, what if Hughes Aircraft were making nineteen-inch television sets (which now cost about $360 dollars retail) instead of Maverick missiles? In 1973, using the rates and markups of the most expensive military electronics contractor, I had estimated that the military would have paid $8,000 for a TV set retailing for $400. By 1982 I couldn't find any companies making TV sets in the United States, which made the estimate more difficult. But going back to my 1973 calculations and inserting Hughes's known markups, I figured that the lowest estimate would be just over $100,000! Tom Amlie added a footnote to that: we knew that the $100,000 Hughes set wouldn't work very well or last very long because Hughes didn't know how to solder. In the best Pentagon tradition, I reduced this to tabular form, as shown here.

Military contractors' in-house costs in dollars per standard hour of output.		
	1973	**1982**
Lowest	$19	$95
Highest	$195	$3,405
Cost of 19-inch TV set	$8,000	$100,000+

We made other estimates and guesstimates of what consumer products might cost if made by military contractors, but the lessons didn't get across. Our bosses were certainly competent at extracting money from Congress and spending it on schedule, but they weren't very good at assimilating our teachings.

Finally we hit on another teaching tool: spare parts. Scarcely a taxpayer in the country has ever gone out to buy a C-5A transport or a Maverick missile for their back yard. These complex systems of expensive hardware are beyond most people's comprehension. But some of the spare parts are very similar to items we all buy in the hardware store. If we could teach our bosses that the prices being charged for spare parts were outrageous, we might be able to explain that this only reflected the outrageous overpricing of the complex mechanisms to which they belonged.

Our small team thought we saw a way to make a telling case about spare parts, even though it wasn't a new topic. Whenever an economy-minded politician wanted to make a speech, he would dip into the spare parts barrel and come up with a simple tin widget that the Army had bought for $500. The military spenders soon discovered how to handle that line. A $500 widget? Well, we deal with hundreds of thousands of parts manufacturers, and there might have been a slip-up on this one tin widget. But give us a chance. If Congress will appropriate an adequate sum for new computers, additional auditors, and perhaps a reshuffle of administrators, we will, sooner or later, get to the bottom of this. In the end the little flurry over the tin widget would be forgotten. And no one ever got to the root causes of overpricing. The Pentagon seldom seriously questioned markups and almost never questioned whether contractors were spending money wisely or wastefully.

The spending craze in the late years of Carter and the early years of Reagan had produced so much money that the Pentagon steam shovel was having a hard time getting rid of it. The ever-willing contractors pitched in and jacked unit prices sky high — so high and so fast, in fact, that even the Pentagon machine couldn't keep up. And among the greediest of the price-jackers was Pratt and Whitney.

This company had negotiated contracts that allowed charges higher than the pricing formulas applied at the time of purchase or even after the parts had been delivered. As usual, the formulas were so flexible that Pratt and Whitney could raise pay rates or boost charges for overhead or for inefficiency almost at will. And, as I noted, they charged more and faster than the money machine could spew it out.

This loose arrangement and the resulting price increases were brought to light at our Oklahoma City ALC, a buying division that had the great advantage of an exceptionally energetic detachment of "competition advocates" from the Small Business Administration (SBA), headed by

Frank Miller. This group kept a sharp watch for hardware and services that could be furnished more cheaply by a small business than by the big contractors. Miller tried to institute competitive bidding wherever possible. The SBA had similar teams elsewhere, but none approached the effectiveness of Frank Miller's three-person operation. It was worth a squadron of auditors and a gaggle of inspectors general. The SBA operation not only saved the taxpayers a lot of money, it made the Air Force buying officers quite a bit more prudent in letting contracts.

Because of the shocking, unanticipated price increases, the Oklahoma ALC complained bitterly in writing about Pratt and Whitney. On July 12, 1982, Robert Hancock, the civilian deputy chief of buying, signed a memorandum to his bosses citing thirty-four examples of Pratt and Whitney spare parts for which quoted prices had rocketed up 300 percent in one year. Then Hancock committed an unforgivable sin: he criticized a big contractor. The memo said, "Pratt & Whitney has never had to control prices and it will be difficult for them to learn."

The Project on Military Procurement got the Hancock memo from a closet patriot. When they released it, the memo got a big play in the newspapers. Congressmen were upset; the Pentagon established review teams. It was the scandal of the week. But nobody except our group wanted to go to the root of the evil, which was the markup factors Pratt and Whitney and their suppliers used to justify higher prices.

The Fitzgerald-Parfitt-Amlie team decided on a new tactic. If we could relieve the Reagan Pentagon management from some bad-publicity pain, we might be able to make some genuine improvements and at the same time change their attitudes for the better.

I made the pitch to Russ Hale, saying that the generals were still dragging their feet on the improvement projects we'd advanced. While keeping up the pressure on them, we should shift our emphasis to the immediate problem of spare parts. Russ's face gladdened with a big smile. "Done deal!" he said.

He was relieved to be rid, for the moment, of the problem of the generals stonewalling against my access to information on the really big, embarrassing military programs. Spare parts seemed a relatively innocuous trail to let me go off on. It didn't occur to him that eventually we'd tie the overpricing of parts to the overpricing of everything.

When Colin Parfitt returned from a visit to Pratt and Whitney's main plant at East Hartford, Connecticut, in early October 1982, he reported that he'd found the managers cooperative but the Air Force Plant Representative hostile. And he confirmed that Pratt and Whitney's spare parts price markups were the same as those for complete engines.

The financial people at the plant had gathered samples of their complicated cost-accounting worksheets for Parfitt, showing how all this was done. But Colonel J. M. Syslo, the resident Air Force man, objected, saying that the papers would have to be sent to us through his chain of command. Colin thought this a little bizarre, but he decided not to make an issue of it. After all, how long could it take to forward a few papers through channels?

Thus began another strange, but typical, tale of the Pentagon's Fabian tactics. (Quintus Fabius was a Roman general who wore Hannibal's army out by opposing it with endless marches, countermarches, and skirmishes. It is rumored that he has been awarded posthumous four-star rank at the Pentagon.)

After a week or so Colin made some follow-up calls. He was told that the papers had to be mailed from Hartford to the Contract Management Division in Albuquerque, where they would undergo "staffing" and "coordination." After these arcane operations, the papers would be reviewed at AFSC headquarters at Andrews Air Force Base in Maryland. After more "review" there, they would be sent to the Pentagon.

In the meantime the Air Force military had set up a special blue-ribbon commission (what else?) to study the spare parts problem. It was headed by retired Air Force general Alton Slay, who had been commander of the AFSC and thus had monitored the price markup factoring systems he would now be reviewing. A conflict of interest? Slay was also on a retainer as consultant to United Technologies, Pratt and Whitney's parent company! Another conflict of interest? That never entered the Pentagonians' heads. Or did it? Clearly, a big preemptive strike was about to be launched. The bombers were on the runways, armed and ready. The generals were climbing into the cockpits.

To forestall the Slay commission, I personally got into the hunt for the Pratt and Whitney papers. After about three weeks, we got the papers pried loose from Albuquerque and sent to Andrews AFB. There, we were told, they would have to be further "staffed" and "coordinated," then sent to Air Force headquarters for more staffing and coordination before going to Colin.

When I tried to take the matter up with Russ Hale, he was suddenly very busy. Mitchell, his deputy, promised to look into the matter, but nothing happened. So I got General Bernie Weiss of the AFSC on the phone. Where were the papers? Weiss was "personally reviewing the package." What on earth was there to review? They were simply Pratt and Whitney's accounting records, and no amount of staffing, coordination, or review would change them. Weiss said he would expedite the matter.

Again, nothing happened. The climactic scene occurs at five o'clock, the afternoon before Thanksgiving 1982. After trying for an hour to extract the papers from the AFSC, I go to Russ Hale's office. He has left for the weekend, but Peggy Johnson, his secretary, is still there. I express my irritation, bafflement, and misfortune. Peggy, sympathetic and quick thinking, says she will call the AFSC commander's office and say that Assistant Secretary Hale's office is sending a car to pick up the report. She explains that anybody who is anybody has probably already left the AFSC office.

Peggy is extremely good on the phone, pulling rank on the minor bureaucrat at the other end of the line and telling him "the Secretary" must have the report before Monday. The bureaucrat finally disgorges the fact that General Weiss has taken the papers home with him, presumably to staff and coordinate in front of his own fireplace.

Very businesslike and brisk, Peggy asks for the general's home address. We'll send a car around to pick up the papers, she says. The bureaucrat stalls, but he is weakening. Something in his brain is sending a faint electrical signal that the Secretary's office might complain if he doesn't cooperate. He chokes out General Bernie Weiss's address.

Peggy calls the car pool and dispatches a car. And about an hour later, the papers arrive.

Thanks to Peggy Johnson, we were able to complete the Parfitt Report, which showed beyond doubt that the amount of fat in Pratt and Whitney spare parts was exactly proportional to the fat in Pratt and Whitney engines. Colin also made good recommendations for correction.

What was the Air Force management's reaction to the report? They did not howl and denounce us, they didn't take steps to abolish Colin's job, they didn't put the security boys on us to get proof that we were Reds (so far as we know). They simply behaved as if the report didn't exist.

We made dozens of copies of the Parfitt report and distributed them as widely as possible in the Pentagon. No one ever disputed Parfitt's findings; everybody who was willing to talk about it agreed that Colin was correct. What the Parfitt Report delineated so plainly had, of course, been a commonplace to me and my associates for a long time. But now our bosses also realized that this gross overpricing, not just on stray widgets but across the board, was still a pretty well-kept secret. It wouldn't do to draw attention to it.

I pressed Russ Hale's principal deputy, Willard Mitchell, for a discussion. Even if he wouldn't talk about the substance, he ought to be willing to comment on the recommendations for savings. At last, in a somewhat confused way, he said, "We're adopting the Slay recommendations." He was not sure what those were, but he promised to get me a copy of the Slay report.

When I saw the list of the Slay commission members, I realized that the general was not the only one burdened by a conflict of interest. As employees of the big contractors who flourished on overpricing practices, the commission members would be unlikely to cut their own throats in public by producing a realistic report. The general had solved that problem by not mentioning the affiliations that tainted the commissioners.

Slay solved the bigger problem — the shortfall between the money the Pentagon said it required and the appropriated sum — by recommending more money for the Air Force budget, beginning with an additional $4 billion dollars a year for spare parts.

He also recommended new procedures at the AFLC. That wasn't the real problem, but it gave the AFLC bureaucracy a wonderful excuse to revive the old, discredited Advanced Logistics System (ALS) under a new name. As I noted earlier, the ALS was a parent scheme for Project Max, a plan that could make our ALC maintenance operations as bad as those of the big contractors. Year after year Colin and I had to keep shooting down the descendants of Project Max.

On New Year's Eve 1982, Colonel Ensign returned Russ Hale's copy of the Parfitt Report with the penned notation, "No longer required by us. Dick Ensign."

Pratt and Whitney had not, however, been allowed to fade into the shadows. Clark Mollenhoff and Greg Rushford's investigations had been followed up by columnist Jack Anderson. And now, in early 1983, Pratt and Whitney was going to be featured on ABC's "20/20" show.

The ABC producer was my old friend and neighbor Charlie Thompson, a tough, experienced reporter. As he began to delve into the subject, he found case after case of chiseling the government. One of the most sensitive incidents he turned up was Pratt and Whitney's gift of $67,500 to an Oklahoma City art club. A little research revealed that one of the club's directors was Mrs. Jay Edwards, the wife of the commanding general of the Oklahoma City ALC. This officer had solicited Pratt and Whitney for the gift, and the company had charged the expenditure to an account for government reimbursement.

Another discovery of Thompson's was further confirmation, by an Air Force review team, of the memo Robert Hancock had written from Oklahoma City in July 1982. Pratt and Whitney had indeed enjoyed profits on the spare parts Hancock had listed far beyond what *any* pricing system — even the lenient did-cost/will-cost — would allow. As soon as Charlie started asking questions about the Hancock memo, the Air Force hastily set up a "senior review group" to arbitrarily overrule the Hancock findings.

That didn't stop Charlie Thompson. He compiled his own report. He talked to the working-level people in the Oklahoma City ALC and verified Hancock's figures. We helped him all we could. But we touched an even more sensitive nerve when he found that parts manufactured by the ALC were far cheaper than the same parts bought from Pratt and Whitney. It violated the firmest notions of both presidents Carter and Reagan that lazy, overpaid, incompetent government workers could manufacture quality products at a fraction of the cost charged by big private corporations. But it was true.

In the course of all this, Charlie had to talk to Air Force flacks a good deal and listen to a lot of lying. He took to tape recording some of the talks. Then, in a later session, he would produce the facts that showed up the lies. This made the officer flacks a little crazy, and one of them yelled at him, "Gentlemen don't tape each other." No, Charlie answered, gentlemen don't tape each other because real gentlemen don't lie.

The "20/20" program on March 10, 1983, was a brilliant and devastating exposé, the best of its kind to date. Charlie's principal correspondent on camera dramatized the story with interviews, commentary, and examples. He even used the tried-and-true demonstration of holding up a series of rather ordinary-looking spare parts with quite extraordinary price tags on them. Some of the prices would have been right for an expensive automobile.

General Jay Edwards, when interviewed about Pratt and Whitney's munificent interest in his wife's art club, could only mumble that he didn't know the government was paying for it. George Spanton, on camera, gave an admirably restrained and cool-headed account of his difficulties with Pratt and Whitney management. (His bosses rewarded him the next day by ordering him transferred a second time. Both transfers were blocked by the public controversy they provoked.)

That night the television in the president's living room was tuned to "20/20" and Reagan was upset at what he saw and heard. He later told Senator Charles Grassley (as reported in Rasor's *The Pentagon Underground*) that the next morning he telephoned Weinberger to ask what was going on in the spare parts business.

Weinberger summoned our friendly political keeper, Jim Ririe, and asked him to explain about spare parts. Ririe gave him the straight truth: the parts were highly overpriced, and a great many other military purchases were correspondingly overpriced.

The world has not learned what Weinberger reported back to Reagan, but Grassley told both Dina and me that the president "was satisfied with their response that ABC had sensationalized the situation to make it appear worse than it was."

That was certainly the concerted response of the Air Force and the Pratt and Whitney flacks, who immediately disclaimed everything in the "20/20" inquiry — except for one small admission: they agreed that a certain rivet had been overpriced. We did, however, get the reassuring news from Orr's assistants that this barrage had been sent up without the knowledge or consent of Verne Orr.

We decided to press ahead with the spare parts educational program and to find some villains other than Pratt and Whitney. After all, they only charged $150 to $300 for a standard hour of work, sweatshop rates in comparison to what Hughes got away with. Our problem now was that we weren't getting very much officially transmitted information from the Air Force military. So we hit on a shortcut.

After our earlier revelations about Hughes Aircraft, "Whitey" Driessnack had joined us in persuading Orr to "declare war on high costs." One of the practical steps was setting up an office with a hotline to take reports of egregious waste. We'd heard nothing from that office, so I asked Tom to find out what calls they'd had. (Colin Parfitt was seriously ill, and Tom Amlie had taken over his duties.)

He came back with two prize horror stories, both involving Boeing Aircraft Company's work on the Airborne Warning and Control System (AWACS) airplane. The first one was about a spacer, a flat, metal washer with a big hole, each of which cost the government $693.44. The second story was about a plastic stool cap. The navigator on an AWACS plane has a small stool, much like a kitchen stool. To keep it from scarring the deck, the stool has a plastic cap, actually more of a plug, in the end of each hollow leg. When these caps wore out, they were replaced as spare parts. For the new order Boeing was asking $1,118.26 apiece.

Tom took this information to Verne Orr, who said he considered these prices outrageous and thought the taxpayers ought to know about them. It came to pass that the taxpayers did: NBC news told the story a few days later. The evening news program ordered an identical spacer made in a machine shop (which is an expensive way to duplicate a normally mass-produced item) for a cost of $5.00. When the program aired, it featured Verne Orr denouncing the excessive prices, and it showed the two spare parts. The stool cap became a sort of media symbol for Pentagon arrogance.

The Air Force military contracting people swallowed hard, then sent a young captain around to explain to us about the stool cap. (Colin, Tom, and I were still being treated with a modicum of deference.) The Air Force pricers, the young man said, hadn't "specifically" justified the $1,118.26 current Boeing price tag but had done a thorough "cost analysis" a couple of years before, when the last stool cap was purchased from Boeing. He gave us the cost-justification figures shown in the table. The young captain wasn't really joking; he was deadly serious. He actually believed that if Boeing said they had spent 49.56 hours manufacturing that simple piece of nylon, well, the government should pay them what they asked.

But how about the "inspection labor hours"? Did the captain honestly believe that an inspector could spend a whole work day — 8.01 hours — staring at one of these stool caps?

In the loyal spirit of the Light Brigade (theirs not to reason why), he said, "Well, the figures were all audited."

And how about the big jump in price from the older figure of $916.55 to the present $1,118.26?

There had been a lot of inflation in the past few years, the poor lad explained.

The *Washington Post*, while not accepting the sophistry represented

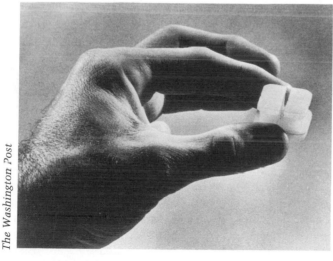

The plastic stool cap for the Boeing AWACS airplane.

Boeing's bill
for three plastic stool caps.[a]

1. Direct labor cost		
Production labor hours	49.56 @ $12.35	$612.07
T&PP labor hours	2.86 @ $13.10	37.42
Tool labor hours	6.28 @ $12.80	80.38
Inspection labor hours	8.01 @ $12.93	103.57
Subtotal	**66.71**	**$833.49**
2. Indirect costs		
Fringe benefits	41.5% of $833.49	$354.23
Manufacturer's overhead	66.71 hrs @ $15.33	1,376.83
Subtotal		**$1,376.83**
3. Material costs		
Product material	$.26 x 3	$.78
Distributed material		53.52
Tool material		19.09
Subtotal		**$73.39**
4. Sum of 1, 2, and 3		$2,283.71
5. Direct charges: 43% of 4		$9.79
6. State and local taxes for 66.71 hours		$97.40
7. **Total cost**		**$2,390.90**
8. Profit fee @ 15%		$358.65
Total charge for 3 caps		**$2,749.65**
9. $2,749.65/3		$916.55
		(cost of 1 cap)

a. Arithmetical errors are Boeing's.

in the chart, nevertheless ran a story that was "balanced" enough to comfort Boeing, whose flacks quoted it ever after as a rebuttal to the horror stories.

I don't know how permanently beneficial these exposés were, but I did see a healthy effect, limited and short-term though it was. Taxpayers put the heat on their elected representatives and they, in turn, tried to brake the administration. Without the spare parts scandal, the Reagan spenders probably would have done even more damage to the country.

What the scandal exposure didn't do was change the Pentagon buyers' basic philosophy. They stuck doggedly to their "actual costs are good costs" philosophy, however fat the "actuals" might be. They never learned that any piece of goods sold to the government ought to be priced at what it *should* cost to make or acquire economically and efficiently, plus a moderate, decent profit. Only a handful of congressmen and a few reporters ever understood that principle.

Mid-1983 was a critical time in the Reagan administration, a testing point for its philosophy of massive spending. Were the neo-Keynesians right in their belief that a great infusion of money would correct a downward trend in the economy?

The results seemed to support their viewpoint. Of course there were horror stories, and of course the waste was enormous, but weren't those acceptable corollaries to the stimulation? The flood of new government contracts did put an end to the statistical symptoms of the 1982 recession. On January 22, 1983, a *Washington Post* headline claimed, "Inflation Falls to 3.9 Percent for '82; Orders Surge for Durable Goods." The heart of the story was:

> Commerce said orders for durable goods rose $8.5 billion, or 12 percent, to a level of $79.1 billion. Orders for defense goods, including ships and aircraft parts, rose $6.9 billion, up a huge 135 percent since November.
>
> Outside the defense area, orders rose a more modest $1.6 billion, or 2.4 percent. However, analysts noted the gains were spread across a wide range of industries, probably indicating a recovery is imminent.

Note that "defense goods" accounted directly for 81 percent of the increase in orders for durable goods. This, in turn, provided money for the contractors to meet payrolls and buy materials and so influenced the "modest" upturn in the private sector.

But the economy was winning a small battle while losing the war. The looming problem was that the federal government was running up a net deficit of $207.7 billion for the year — nearly *three times* the deficit Jimmy Carter had accepted in his vain effort to buy the 1980 election. The rather artificial good news in the *Washington Post* story disguised some very bad news for the decades to come.

Sitting before his TV set and watching the "20/20" program, Ronald Reagan could not grasp the connection between Pentagonal squandering and all the dire things about the national debt he had told us so often.

But some of the press, some of the public, and some members of Congress could.

Those who were awake in America were becoming even more concerned that the deluges of money were producing weapons systems that didn't work. Throwing dollars at technical problems solved nothing. It was an interesting example of an uncomprehended analogy. The Reagan team had announced that this same flaw in logic — trying to solve a problem by mere funding — had resulted in the failure of the War on Poverty. But here was a parallel they didn't wish to see. The Project on Military Procurement and its friends produced ample evidence about weapons that did not work. Many of these stories are summarized in the Fund for Constitutional Government's 1983 book, *More Bucks, Less Bang*. Most of this book was an anthology of overpriced weapons that didn't work as advertised. Some of them appeared to be more dangerous to the people who would operate them than to potential enemies. The book was well received among our friends on Capitol Hill. Several of its recommendations became congressional proposals for reform.

Congress went home for the 1983 summer recess in an uncertain, surly mood. Members were pleased with the big economic rush provided by the Pentagon's intravenous injection, but they were also embarrassed by the publicized signs of foolish prodigality. The home folks had learned about spare parts. They had also learned about generals who arranged for the taxpayers to subsidize neighborhood art clubs, and who knows what else? If "defense" money could be converted to such purposes, what were the limits of such conversions? Bribes? Robert Riggs's whores? Or even more sordid and dangerous horrors? Some congressmen were worried about the Pentagon excesses. Others thought the excesses were okay, business as usual, but were worried about the embarrassments brought on by the media.

Toward the end of the recess the Pentagon was rescued by an unlikely angel: the Evil Empire itself. On September 1, 1983, a Soviet fighter plane shot down Korean Airlines' Flight 007 after it had intruded a long way into militarily sensitive Soviet airspace.

By strange coincidence, Tom Amlie and I, just the day before, had been discussing how the military spending coalition needed some international atrocity to revive their failing fortunes. We'd talked about the Germans' torpedoing of the British liner *Lusitania* in 1915, which had changed Americans' attitudes about entering World War I. As soon as we heard about the Flight 007 disaster, Tom and I looked at each other and said in unison, *"Lusitania!"*

Tom was incredulous that such a thing could happen by accident. He had been familiar with civil and military aviation, particularly the electronic aspects, for most of his life, and he had served as a top technical expert in the Federal Aviation Administration. All this experience told him that if a scheduled flight had strayed so far from its path, all manner of alarms and warnings would have alerted the flight crew, the American monitoring agencies, and, by hotline, the Soviet government. He showed me navigation charts of the area with heavy black lines and a dire notice: "WARNING: AIRCRAFT INTRUDING INTO THIS AREA SUBJECT TO BEING FIRED UPON WITHOUT WARNING." Highly sensitive Soviet military installations were located in the forbidden area.

When Tom started asking questions, his first source told him that Flight 007 was on an intelligence mission and had been fitted out as a "spy plane" at Andrews AFB a couple of weeks before its fatal flight. Not at all convincing, Tom thought. There would be no reason to bring the plane to Andrews to be fitted out for an NSA monitoring or intrusion mission.

Tom passed the story on to Jim Ririe, who took it to his "rabbi," his sponsor at the White House, Fred Fischer.

Jim was taken to see Judge William Clark, the president's national security adviser. Clark's reaction to the story was firm and immediate: "That's Soviet disinformation." At that time the administration was professing to know nothing whatever about the cause of the tragedy.

Tom, still puzzled, wondered why the government hadn't immediately tried to involve the skilled investigators from the National Transportation Safety Board (NTSB) to the scene of the disaster. At the FAA Tom had developed great respect for their analytic and investigative skills. Ordinarily, Tom said, a tragedy involving an American-made aircraft, carrying U.S. citizens on a flight originating in the United States and for which we searched in international waters, would have attracted intense attention from both FAA regulators and the NTSB. Instead, these agencies seemed incurious and detached.

Whatever investigations of the incident the government carried on in secret, no great effort was made publicly to identify and eliminate the causes of the "navigation error," a chilling air safety problem. Reagan and his spokesmen properly denounced the Soviet Union for criminal recklessness and, on September 5, four days after the shootdown, the *Los Angeles Times* reported that Reagan told congressional leaders he had "definite proof that they intentionally shot down that unarmed civilian airplane." In an address to the nation the next day, he was quoted as saying, "There is no way a pilot could mistake this for anything other than a civilian airliner," and again referred to "incontrovertible evidence." Amid the hysteria, no one demanded to see that evidence.

If Reagan's remarks were as reported, he was lying to the leaders of

Congress. After more than four years of evasions, the State Department finally agreed to a request by Chairman Lee Hamilton of the House Intelligence Committee to declassify information on the president's deception, which Hamilton had known about for more than a year. On January 12, 1988, Hamilton released the long-concealed, damning passages from a U.S. intelligence report on Flight on 007: "We had concluded by the second day that the Soviets thought they were pursuing a US reconnaissance plane through most, if not all, of the overflight."

The administration's most cynical internal exploitation of the 007 disaster, however, was National Security Decision Directive (NSDD) 102, "US Response to Soviet Destruction of KAL Airliner." The unclassified version of this document (see Appendix C), does not say anything about measures taken to investigate the tragedy or to prevent future ones. It simply crows over the propaganda victory and exhorts its select readers to exploit the incident further.

At this writing we don't know whether the KAL 007 was a U.S. government operation *before* the atrocity of its downing, but it surely was afterward. It was a secret propaganda operation of Reagan and his National Security Council. By secret edict the president mobilized the most powerful executive agencies to propagandize the taxpayers with their own money. And it worked like a charm. The shootdown was the magic potion needed to cure the dyspepsia of Congress and the country. The honorable members trooped back to Capitol Hill asking, "How much can we vote for the Pentagon?" The answer came back: "A lot more than you were ready to." And Congress proceeded to vote a huge increase in the already bloated military budget.

Logic, logic! Why did no congressman press for more information than they had from the media and from Reagan's offhand remarks? Why did nobody see that there wasn't the slightest connection between protecting civilian airliners and giving the Pentagon vast new sums?

The whole affair was a setback for our truth-in-spending movement. After my civil service restoration, our political bosses, at least, had treated us gingerly. With the 007 victory, however, the opposition grew bolder. Om Chauhan was harassed by his bosses and denounced as "a Fitzgerald man." Others who had cooperated with us — George Spanton among them, even though he was on his way out of government — got the same treatment.

Several inquiries were made into Spanton's charges about Pratt and Whitney and overspending generally, including a federal grand jury investigation. The Pentagon was essentially offering one defense:

sloppiness. It dismissed the charges of wrongdoing by saying that government overseers had broad discretion in what they allowed Pratt and Whitney to do. The overseers' acquiescence or inattention wasn't illegal; it was just part of the way things were done.

A tug of war developed between the South Florida U.S. attorney and the FBI, according to Spanton, who was working closely with the FBI. The U.S. attorney didn't want to prosecute because of "acquiescence" by government officials in the wrongdoing George had charged. No matter, the FBI argued, an inside job doesn't make ripoffs legal. Certain Pratt and Whitney officials and Air Force officers appeared vulnerable.

The Air Force rushed its best military minds into the breach. The USAF inspector general appointed Brigadier General Raymond C. Preston, Jr., to investigate. General Preston and his fellow officers selected the Air Force Plant Representative in the West Palm Beach plant, Colonel John E. Roberts, to be the chief witness. Here is his astonishing sworn testimony given to General Preston on September 28, 1983, and recorded in the files of the inspector general's report. The syntax is the colonel's own:

> I don't want to do anything that would embarrass the Air Force, and don't take that as that somebody's going to cover something up to keep from embarrassing the Air Force, but I think we have an obligation today to the American public to, not to embarrass the Department of Defense because that has a major impact on the budget that we get, some of these things.

Translated into English, this could become a classic Pentagon statement of purpose: "the George Spantons of this world should not embarrass the Defense Department because it is the Great Slush Pump in the Sky from which all blessings flow." That would excuse breaking the law.

George Spanton said he'd once had a conversation with Roberts, and the good colonel had advised him to stop trying to cut out waste. "It's the system, George," he said. "You can't change it."

10

☆ ☆ ☆

Adventures of a Born-again Muckraker

PROVING COLONEL ROBERTS WRONG was a never-ending task. Our effort to defend the interests of the taxpayers and the country seemed to be too abstract to win official support. The industry-military conspiracy, on the other hand, knew exactly what it was after and what arguments to use in rationalizing it. I got another view of that defensive reasoning in the fall of 1982 when Richard Stimson of the defense secretary's office referred me to Gordon Urquart, a Boeing executive, for the official word.

Urquart was high contractor brass, and if anybody had the Writ, he did. He was chairman of the Manufacturing Executive Committee of the Council of Defense and Space Industry Associations (CODSIA). When I talked with him, he sounded a little like a Bourbon courtier defending the divine right of kings. He said his powerful firm and association would continue to battle the idea of should-cost standards for estimating contract costs and uphold "actuals" (past "actual" costs). The whole system, he said, "is primarily oriented to actual costs." Precisely. And that's where the worst problem lay.

Verne Orr and Russ Hale renewed their commitment to support our attack on this "actual costs are good costs" line; in fact, Hale went on record in the November 13, 1983, issue of the *New York Times* to call the actual-costs argument "crazy." He seemed firmly on the side of "the Attic Fanatics," as he called us, because of the location of our Pentagon offices and our cost-cutting zeal.

One of the important contributions to "actual" costs, of course, was labor cost. Colin Parfitt reported that in 1970 labor rates in the aerospace industry were 24 percent above the Bureau of Labor Statistics' "All Manufacturing" rates, and by 1981 the gap had widened to 38 percent. Another comparison showed aerospace rates 22 percent higher in 1970 than those for all "durable goods workers," with the gap increased to 39 percent by 1981.

That was largely for blue-collar pay. Raises for executives and middle management people were proportionately higher. The interesting secret was that engineers on the payroll often outnumbered blue-collar workers — in one big plant 50 percent of those employed were engineers; only 20 percent were blue collar. The companies were warehousing their engineering talent, holding on to technical people even when there was no work for them.

Thus, Parfitt found, executive salaries, were, on average, 130 percent above the durable goods industry average. (Except at Pratt and Whitney, which kept its figures to themselves.) That added up to a lot of overpaid people and an enormous vested interest.

One might expect the established government "audit community" to keep a sharp eye on all personnel costs, but that didn't seem to happen at the General Accounting Office or the Defense Contract Audit Agency (DCAA). The latter, instead of standing firmly behind their most courageous man, George Spanton, shrugged off responsibility for anything except blue-collar wage rates. It was beginning to be clear that feeble audit control by the government was one of the great flaws that allowed the whole scandalous system to flourish.

During my visit to the Hughes plant in Tucson, I had observed a peculiar practice among supervisors. In the "process" areas, where different kinds of parts were commingled, supervisors would assign employee time charges to various job orders on a more or less arbitrary basis. When I brought this to the attention of DCAA officials, they agreed that it was illogical but dismissed it as having a minor effect on overall costs. At our urging, however, the inspector general's office requested that the DCAA investigate. We heard nothing for more than a year.

In late 1983 Senator William Roth, chairman of the powerful Governmental Affairs Committee, was giving Pentagon procurement hell. What particularly incensed him was the famous antenna hexagon wrench, which was just a plain old allen wrench with an "'aerospace design" handle. As it turned out the only use for the special handle was as a place for the contractor's part number so that the Air Force wouldn't have to look it up before reordering more wrenches at the bargain price of $9,609 apiece. The company that actually made the wrenches charged twelve cents each. Westinghouse Electric took them on delivery and sold them to General Dynamics for $5,205 apiece. In short, the Air Force got one wrench for the price of 80,075 of them. And that was just the beginning of Roth's horror stories.

All of this pointed a stern finger at the DoD audit agencies. Roth's chief source was his investigator Chuck Woehrle, an ex-Pentagon auditor who shared our frustrations about the DCAA. On January 30, 1984, the Roth committee announced that it would hold hearings, beginning March 1, to discover just how effective or ineffective the audit agencies were.

George Spanton was among the witnesses to be called. Another one was A. Ernest Fitzgerald. From past experience, I should have caught a whiff of trouble on the wind. Russ Hale, however, seemed delighted at the news. Irritated at the stubborn noncooperation of the DCAA, he had put a bitter complaint on record. Hale made sure that I was being requested to appear in my official capacity, and he and Verne Orr assigned a team of four to help prepare the testimony.

Just about this time I learned — somewhat after the fact — that the DCAA had reported on the Hughes Aircraft labor-charging practices and, as usual, had found nothing amiss: "The reported internal control weaknesses were not found to exist."

We asked for a look at the work papers of this review, and when no one seemed able to pry them loose, Chuck Woehrle and Major Wayne Christein visited Hughes and came back with their own report. It showed that the DCAA had questioned only thirteen employees, but those thirteen had told the DCAA team about all sorts of negligence. Many workers simply estimated their work time, some signed time cards in advance, others had not worked on projects to which their labor hours were charged, and so on. This and more was in the work papers, but the official report gave Hughes a clean bill of health. This raised severe questions about the integrity of the audit agency.

Even though the defense secretary's office and the DCAA refused to provide data we needed, our team went ahead and prepared my testimony with the facts we had. After Hale had reviewed it, we sent it on to the Air Force security review, whose real function is to delete anything that might embarrass the Air Force procurement faction and their big contractors. The security review does have a side benefit for the bureaucrat; with its okay, he or she has official backing for statements pertaining to matters within his or her jurisdiction.

At the end of February, the security review officer, Lieutenant Colonel Hugh Burns, wrote a memorandum, not to me but to my legislative liaison keeper, Lieutenant Colonel Bill Thompson. "Mr. Fitzgerald will testify as a private citizen," he said. I was ordered to lead off by saying, "The views expressed in this statement are my own and do not reflect the official policy or position of the U.S. Air Force or the Department of Defense."

A rather dramatic turnabout. As I told Verne Orr, the testimony had been prepared by our whole office with the help of Senator Roth's investigator. We'd be willing to correct any factual misstatement or amend anything that conflicted with "official policy or position." For the first time since I'd known him, Orr began to crawfish. He tried to avoid the issue by saying it would be easier on everybody if I agreed.

I argued that our carefully assembled testimony would probably be denigrated by opponents as the isolated views of a lone fanatic. That point seemed to be effective, and Orr directed Colonel Burns to send a memo to concerned parties saying that my testimony was "to be processed as an official USAF witness statement." He asked for "concurrence-comment" by one o'clock on February 29, some twenty-four hours later.

One o'clock came and went, and nothing happened. After making several fruitless inquiries at the Pentagon, I went to Capitol Hill to see Chuck Woehrle and learned from him that something very fishy was going on. A group of Air Force officers had descended to lobby his nominal boss, Linc Hoewing, of the Governmental Affairs Committee staff, and Pentagon officials had been on the phone with Senator Roth that morning.

I then called Delbert "Chip" Terrill, an OSC investigator on the Spanton case, to see if he had any news. He had nothing firm but, he said, the rumors on Capitol Hill were that Pentagon officials had worked up a plot to frame me. They would force me to testify without the protection of being an official witness. Then, if I produced cost and performance information that was arguably "proprietary" to the contractors, I would be set up for possible criminal prosecution or a civil damage suit. It was a neat and vicious trap to get rid of a whistle blower.

I went back to my office. About seven that evening, I received a memo from Orr's military assistants saying that my testimony could not be cleared, for reasons that were not specified. However, Secretary Orr warmly recommended that I testify in my "private capacity," and this had been approved by Linc Hoewing. It was obvious that the fix was in.

The next morning at eight o'clock, I was waiting in Verne Orr's outer office when he came to work. I told him that I had sent a letter to Senator Roth explaining my likely nonappearance. But, I added, in the next two hours we could still make factual changes in my testimony.

Orr, looking very old and harassed, sent me to Dick Harshman, who was taking over as acting assistant secretary because Russ Hale had resigned. Harshman had before him a list of objections compiled by General Bernie Weiss's weenies, but they were so flimsy that he didn't try to defend them. "It's the DCAA thing," Harshman said. "That's the problem."

At the hearing that day, the senators were appropriately outraged that I was not present. Senator Roth told Joe Sherick, the inspector general, who was then testifying, to go back to the Pentagon and "clear this situation up" through "the highest channels."

I don't know whether the Capitol Hill rumors about criminal or civil prosecution had been cleverly planted by the Air Force opposition to head off my testimony, but their strategy had failed to deal with George Spanton and W. W. Murphy, the two DCAA auditors, whose testimony about the operations and management of the DCAA was devastating. Chairman Roth scheduled another hearing for March 7, and it looked as if something might come of all this.

I had to survive one more sneak attack. First Verne Orr put out the story that he'd encouraged me to testify even before the committee's request but that I had refused: "Mr. Fitzgerald's decision not to appear before the committee . . . was his own decision." A little later Orr changed his story for *Fortune* magazine, saying I'd never been asked to testify as a private citizen. A year and a half later, confronted with the lie while testifying before Representative Dingell's committee, he retracted and apologized graciously. I accepted the apology. I liked the old guy, despite everything.

At the immediate time he was hardly as straightforward. On March 1, 1984, he sent a deceptive letter to Roth and succeeded in conning him into dropping the whole DCAA inquiry in favor of hearing "the official views of the Department on this issue of contractor labor rates and labor distribution." In my place as witness, Orr would send none other than General Bernie Weiss.

Bernie's March 7 testimony was harmless, except to anybody who wanted to stay awake. It completely avoided the original purpose of the Roth inquiry.

By this time the congressmen had lost interest and the whole investigation died away. Joe Sherick did produce his own counterfeit report of what had happened, saying that my prepared testimony represented no more than my "personal view" and that I'd tried to make the Air Force let me "present it as the official position of the Department." He even misstated my letter to Senator Roth to try to bolster his foregone conclusion. He cleverly avoided mentioning the issue of criticizing the DCAA for, among other things, covering up their auditors' findings, which, as Harshman had noted, was the real sticking point.

Late one Saturday night in early 1983, I had received a phone call. The Midwestern voice on the other end of the line said, "Hi. My name's Chuck Grassley, and I'm a senator from Iowa. Are you the Fitzgerald who wrote *The High Priests of Waste?*"

Uh-oh, I thought. This very conservative type is going to hassle me for *that* old heresy. It must have taken the news eleven years to get to Iowa.

"Is all the stuff you wrote in that book true?" I said that it was. "Are the same kinds of things going on in the Pentagon now?" I assured him that the Pentagon was getting even more money to do the same kinds of things. "Well," Grassley said, "I'd like for you to come in and talk to me about this."

Soon after, I met with Grassley and his two very astute young assistants, Kris Kolesnik and Lisa Hovelson. Grassley quickly grasped our sometimes-arcane cost-cutting proposals and it wasn't long before all of them became enthusiastic supporters of the Attic Fanatics movement.

Franklin C. "Chuck" Spinney, a Pentagon colleague of ours, had made a telling study showing that the Pentagon's concealed spending plans far exceeded even the supergenerous funds it was getting from Congress. When Grassley requested a copy of the study, Spinney's superiors, true to form, refused. Grassley didn't hesitate; he went straight to the Pentagon and marched into Weinberger's office to demand that Spinney and his papers be produced. They were. (He did the same thing at the White House to get a fair hearing for George Spanton, although in this case Reagan listened and did nothing.)

"What are they trying to cover up?" Grassley asked when he heard about the fiasco of Senator Roth's hearings. Amlie, Parfitt, and I told him. The senator and his staff quickly got into the details of the horrendous overpricing of major weapons as illustrated by the examples of their overpriced parts and by our work measurement initiative. He kept pressing for more and more comparisons between actual hours worked in defense industry compared to should-take hours for that work. Like everyone else who perceived the drastic discrepancy, he was deeply concerned.

"Mr. President," he once said to Reagan, "you've done the right thing in bringing the welfare queens under control. However, you've got to realize that there are welfare queens in the Pentagon, too. They're the big contractors."

Picking up the ball that Roth had dropped, Grassley decided to schedule hearings in late June 1984 before his own Administrative Practices Subcommittee of the Senate Judiciary Committee. He invited Ompal Chauhan and me, among others, to testify.

Was I going to be the victim of mixed signals once again? On the one hand, I remembered my treatment by Verne Orr and the Air Force in the Roth fiasco, but on the other hand, Orr had come forward again and made bold public statements damning too-high costs.

In putting together materials for the Grassley hearings, I based practically everything on official documents, nearly all from the executive branch. I even made an effort to include the views of our most hostile critics.

One good example came from an angry Air Force major named Ketcham. Tom Amlie, in a visit to the Hughes Aircraft California Division, which was working on the Advance Medium Range Air-to-Air Missile (AMRAAM), had uncovered enormous hidden costs in the program. Ketcham was the commander of the Air Force watchdog unit there, and his embarrassment was acute. His January 27, 1984, memorandum to us read, in part:

> You have allowed yourselves to become little more than born-again 19th century muck-rakers, which is a disservice to the Air Force and the nation. We need to re-arm America. We need to spend our defense dollars prudently. We need whistle blowers and watch dogs to *keep internal vigil and help make needed changes from within. We don't need internal detractors to add more fuel to the pacifist anti-defense movement by going external with all their information* [emphasis added].

Knowing something about the history of "muckraking" (Major Ketcham obviously didn't — he even failed to get the century right), I was pleased to be counted with Lincoln Steffens, Samuel Hopkins Adams, and Charles Evans Hughes.

I also used my hearing statement to carry the message that not everybody in the Air Force was a scoundrel ready to pay outrageous prices for junk hardware. For example Colonel Jack Bryan, director of manufacturing operations at the System Command's Contract Management Department, wrote his boss on January 27, 1983, that he wanted to furnish me some significant cost information I had requested. "Suggest you do nothing," replied his boss, Colonel Engelbeck.

I even included one internal Systems Command memorandum that described a data analysis we had pushed through as providing "instant visibility into program costs and schedule." The memo added, "We will have some opposition from the contractors if we use this format." Yes, there still were some good guys around.

Balanced and impersonal as I tried to make it, the statement still didn't pass. Verne Orr, Undersecretary Edward Aldridge, and their flacks denounced it as "not an expression of official Air Force policy" even before they saw it. A certain Major Whittaker later tried to explain to the *Federal Times* why the Air Force refused to clear my prepared testimony. No, there weren't any specific violations of policy, he said. Administration policy, Whittaker said, was "to view things a certain way." Here goes, I thought. The Roth hearing farce all over again.

Then one midday I heard a great commotion in my outer office and my secretary, Bette Dudka, shouting, "Oh, my God!" My door opened, and before I could turn around, flashbulbs began to pop. When my eyes cleared, I saw Senator Charles Grassley surrounded by photographers and reporters who had pushed past the bewildered Pentagon door guards. Yapping at the heels of this entourage were a lot of Air Force officers, trying to tell Grassley that he couldn't do that.

Very politely and formally, Senator Grassley served me with a subpoena to appear before his committee with my prepared statement and back-up documents. When my bosses and the Air Force general counsel saw copies of the subpoena, they caved in at once. The moral was clear: Congress could overcome executive branch cover-ups when it wanted to.

Senator Grassley was in a militant mood. He and Senator Howell Heflin, the ranking Democrat on the committee, put all my documentation into the record. Even better, they gave me plenty of time to explain how "bad management has shot down more airplanes, sunk more ships, and immobilized more soldiers than all our enemies in history put together."

I had been saying such things for sixteen years, and nobody was surprised to hear it again. But Om Chauhan's was a new voice, and his presentation opened a lot of eyes. He stressed that many people in the Air Force acquisition process were neither crooked nor incompetent, and he made a plea for support for the honest, dedicated, patriotic ones.

Senator Grassley and his staff gave that support. For the first time in my experience, I encountered a staunchly conservative Republican willing to attack military acquisition waste with vigor and skill. Our previous supporters had largely been liberals. It seemed paradoxical that the Republicans, who profess to believe in free enterprise and competition, could condone a governmental process so clearly full of favoritism, inefficiency, corruption, and monopolistic practices — a process that was driving us ever deeper into debt.

In this case, though, concern for the nation's welfare cut across party lines; Kris Kolesnik was able to put together an unusual coalition in support of Grassley's cause. In the House it ranged from the extremely liberal California Democrat Mel Levine to Republican Denny Smith of Oregon, an ex–Air Force pilot who was especially concerned about the "less bang" aspects of Reagan's spending binge. What brought them together was a mixture of idealism and enlightened self-interest. They liked frugality. They hated the thought of American servicemen going into a war with bad equipment, or too little, because of Pentagon blunders. And they knew that "more bang for a buck" was still a good political stand.

Grassley had demonstrated the latter point. When I first started discussing things with him, some of my know-better friends had warned me that Grassley's star was sinking. His "family issues" seemed increasingly irrelevant to the hard-pressed Iowa farm economy. In the polls it was said he had about a 37 percent approval rating and was sinking fast. But once he started attacking military waste, he became the most popular politician in Iowa history.

The lesson, though, was lost on the national Democratic Party. With striking myopia the 1984 Mondale campaign wrote a platform plank that offered the Pentagon continued spending increases of inflation plus 5 percent.

In Denny Smith's district in Oregon, for example, the Democrats were frantic to defeat him. They had just gerrymandered his district. They found an attractive opponent, a popular state senator, and poured in campaign money from all over the country to support her. Denny Smith called for a military budget freeze; his opponent went along with inflation plus 5 percent.

Denny won.

But the American taxpayer lost. It soon became clear that the Reagan military build-up was no more than a spend-up. Despite Grassley and his allies, Congress continued to approve wild escalation in military budgets. But that escalation was buying fewer and fewer weapons: a lot more bucks and a lot less bang, and "stretchouts," which spread acquisitions over more years, were becoming commonplace. Projected unit cost increases could not be accommodated even within the huge sums Congress was giving Reagan. Pentagon budget planning starts about twenty months in advance of any fiscal year; the FY 86 plans were being made between January and May of 1984. Closet patriots on Weinberger's staff, appalled at the effects of letting unit costs get out of hand, leaked the figures shown in the table.

	More bucks: change in average unit cost (%)	Less bang: reduction in quantity (%)
Weapons procurement stretchouts for fiscal year 1986 (Oct. 1, 1985–Sept. 30, 1986), showing changes between January and May 1974.		
Program		
Army		
AH-64 helicopter	+20	−33
Patriot missile	+17	−28
Pershing II missile	+82	−72
Bradley fighting vehicle	+10	−26
DIVAD anti aircraft gun	+24	−19
M-9 ACE bulldozer	+16	−68
FAASV supply vehicle	−5	−17
Stinger missile	+26	−47
TOW missile	+12	−33
Hellfire missile	+10	−24
Air Force		
C-5B transport plane	—	−13
F-15 fighter plane	+10	−20
F-16 fighter plane	−5	−17
T-46 trainer	+27	−33
GLCM cruise missile	−3	−13
MX missile	+11	−17
Laser bombs	+1	−53
AMRAAM missile	+400	−91
IIR Maverick missile	+51	−56
Navy		
F-14A fighter plane	+12	−25
F/A-18 fighter plane	+9	−18
AV-8B fighter plane	+19	−30
P-3C patrol plane	+29	−44
CH-53E helicopter	+13	−29
Phoenix missile	−23	−12
Standard missile	+33	−73
MK-48 torpedo	+220	−15
MK-46 torpedo	−15	−67
USMC		
Hawk missile	−5	−10
Stinger missile	+32	−73
TOW missile	—	−17
M-198 cannon	−4	−52

Senator Grassley followed up with another hearing in September 1984. To this forum congresswoman Barbara Boxer brought two military whistle blowers, Sergeant Thom Jonsson and his superior, Captain Bob Greenstreet, who brought a large box of overpriced spare parts that the Military Airlift Command had acquired for the transport planes Jonsson and Greenstreet were helping to keep flying. The most memorable of these items was the $7,622 coffee pot for the C-5A. Other tidbits included a $670 passenger seat armrest.

Defense's defense, as pronounced by Undersecretary William Howard Taft IV was that the spare parts problem had already been cured by the discovery and elimination of "equal allocation of overhead costs." This was a formula by which the defense contractor supposedly allocated an equal amount of overhead, or indirect cost, to each part regardless of the part's direct cost. That is, a complicated and expensive spare part with a direct cost of $4,000 would have $1,000, say, of overhead added to its cost and be listed at $5,000; a cheap, simple part with a direct cost of $1 would also absorb $1,000 of overhead, thereby making the simple part cost $1,001. In an April 24, 1984, memorandum the DoD said this formula would no longer be used because it resulted in "distorted unit prices. Parts with very low intrinsic value appear grossly overpriced."

True or false?

False. The formula simply did not exist. Everyone who had anything to do with acquisition knew that contractors allocated their overhead as a function of the direct charges, usually as a percentage of direct dollars or sometimes as an amount per direct labor hour.

Grassley was infuriated by the equal-allocation excuse. Of Weinberger's promise to clean up spare parts procurement practices, he said, "Those who know better stamp 'B.S.' all over it."

Shortly thereafter Colin Parfitt and I were requested to appear before Senator Proxmire's Joint Economic Subcommittee to testify about the markup formulas of major contractors. After we had prepared the evidence, we were warned by the Air Force general counsel that the figures were "proprietary" and that we might make ourselves vulnerable to criminal prosecution if we revealed them. It was the same threat as before, and again it worked. It so inhibited my testimony in the hearings that I made a poor job of explaining matters.

On November 1, 1984, Richard Carver, the Republican mayor of Peoria, Illinois, replaced Russ Hale as secretary of the Air Force for financial management. The first memorandum we sent him was a request that the Air Force military chief of procurement, Lieutenant General Robert D. Russ, furnish some examples of contractors' equal allocation of overhead.

After a number of memorandums back and forth, General Russ, on January 15, 1985, confessed that there was no substance to the "equal allocation of overhead" excuse. He said, "All of the contractors over which we have cognizance use some measure of direct effort as a basis for allocating costs."

But lies are often very hard to kill. Just as I'd heaved a sigh of relief over the death of this one, it was born again in George Will's column in the *Washington Post* (February 3, 1985). Will, a medieval scholar who sometimes cites authority rather than relying on facts to "prove" his points, declared that the spare parts scandals were being exaggerated, a notion he based on an article by an academic:

> Now, in the winter issue of *The Public Interest*, — no liberal journal — [Stephen] Kelman, of Harvard's Kennedy School of Government, argues that the horror stories about "waste" are almost always gross exaggerations. The [Grace] Commission specialized in such stories as: the Pentagon has been buying screws, available in a hardware store for three cents, for $91.00 each.
>
> Make your blood boil? Simmer down.
>
> Pentagon acquisitions rules stipulate that "overhead" expenses be allocated to each shipment as some fixed proportion of the value of the product. If the value is $5 million, the corporation might be entitled to add, say, 20 percent ($1 million) for overhead. Overhead includes cost above materials, machines, and labor — cost of everything from legal departments to company headquarters.
>
> The Pentagon orders many kinds of spare parts simultaneously. As an approved accounting convenience, many contractors allocate overhead on an "item" rather than "value" basis. Kelman illustrates this with an example of a $20 million order for 10,000 parts, some of which have a direct cost of $25,000 each, and others 4 cents each.
>
> Instead of apportioning the $1 million overhead such that the $25,000 part gets a lot and the 4-cent part a little, the computer printout will allocate $100 to each part. This produces a charge to the government of $25,100 for the expensive part and $100.04 for the cheap one.

This drivel was so astonishing that I made a point of reading the *Public Interest* article to see if Kelman was really saying that. He was. He concluded that the whole misconception was based on an "accounting quirk" and that "although this produces horror stories, nothing horrible has happened."

I called Professor Kelman that Sunday morning to find out the source of his information. Did he have any specific, factual examples?

Well, no, he said. As a civilian, he "was not allowed to see actual cost figures."

Where, then, did he get the ideas for his article?

Kelman had called Bill Kaufman (a noted "defense intellectual") for referral to someone "whose judgment you trust" who could give "a dispassionate explanation" of the spare parts horror stories.

But, I asked, did judgment or passion have anything to do with the issue? Wasn't it purely a question of facts?

Kelman waffled a bit, then admitted, "Maybe so." At any rate, Kaufman had referred him to somebody whose name he didn't now remember — possibly the minority staff director of the Senate Armed Services Committee. This authority had referred him to a Claude Messamore at the Pentagon. Messamore had given him the material for the article.

When I looked him up in the Pentagon phone book, Lieutenant Colonel C. E. Messamore turned out to be one of General Bernie Weiss's men in the Directorate of Contracting and Manufacturing Policy in the Air Staff. I called him.

Yes, he said, he was the source of Kelman's information.

But, I asked, how could he have given the professor such misinformation? I reminded him that the Air Staff, after many memos, had finally admitted that there was nothing to the "equal allocation" fable.

The colonel admitted that "equal allocation has not been a major problem." But, he said, there had been some examples. Air Force generals Dewey Lowe and Jim Dever had settled on a policy of "line item integrity" in pricing to make sure there were no pricing "distortions."

Had the generals dealt with the *levels* of spare parts prices? That, said Messamore, wasn't in their charter because it had to do with "productivity."

In short, Messamore was talking about a cosmetic treatment for overpricing, which was the root cause of the spare parts scandals.

We held a meeting with General Weiss, Colonel Messamore, and others, to which they were asked to bring some "equal allocation" examples. They produced nothing in the way of documentation, but a Major Mahler did assert that the infamous $435 hammer that the Navy had bought from the Gould Corporation's electronics division was a "true case." We could check that one out.

The hammer history (actually, there were two, a claw hammer for $435 and a hand sledge for $436) began when the walloping prices of these and other items in an order so shocked a Navy enlisted man that he went to Representative Berkley Bedell with the story.

Bedell, who had been a manufacturer himself, was baffled to see the price tags on the hammers, the figure of $652 for an ordinary tool box, and the $10,168.56 for the very ordinary tools that went inside. He went to a hardware store and bought all of these items — of equal or better quality — for $100.38.

The Navy's Bernie Weiss counterpart was a rear admiral named Joseph S. Sansone, Jr., who sent an explanation to Bedell's Small Business Committee hearings in October, 1983: "In Gould's proposal each item received an equal share of the non-hands-on support labor requirements, regardless of the value of the line item, which, when fully loaded with overhead and profit, amounted to approximately an additional $385.00 per line item."

Had we finally run an elusive "equal allocation" fox to earth? Colin Parfitt and I gave it a simple sanity test. We took the box and its tools and applied Sansone's "equal allocation." The table on page 178 shows the results. Sansone's excuse failed the sanity test. After the alleged "equal allocation" of $385 per item was removed, a $7.66 hammer still cost $50. After removing the equal-allocation markup from the Phillips screwdriver set, the cost would be *negative* $126.44. Confronted with this and other factual refutations of their fairy tale, Sansone's lackeys stammered to Colin Parfitt that the allocations were equal except when they were unequal.

Despite the total discrediting of this Pentagon fabrication, apologists have continued to trot out the same argument. Doubtless in the future other writers as gullible as George Will and Professor Kelman will front for the Pentagon again. The January 1987 *Washington Monthly*, in fact, got suckered with an article by James Fairhall titled "The Case for the $435 Hammer," in which the old myth got a new showing.

By this time, it was clear to anyone who wanted to know that equal allocation wasn't the basis of the trouble — but what was? Were the defense manufacturers outright thieves? Or was there an unspoken excuse for these gross overcharges? When Bedell and his committee were totally stonewalled by Caspar Weinberger, the House Judiciary Committee picked up the matter and assigned it to investigator Ginny Sloan. She came up with an answer.

When she queried GAO executive Clark Adams, he explained that the apparent overpricing was the result of "full absorption accounting." Colin Parfitt, in a follow-up conversation, asked Adams how an accounting system, "full absorption or otherwise," could explain and justify the horror-story prices.

Adams finally answered, "Well, yes . . . I did say that . . . government is dedicated to full-cost absorption . . . because it is the basis of our prices."

Parfitt commented in a memo for the record:

The difference between what the military pays for tools and what the consumer pays.

Tool	Retail price[a]	Contractor's billing price	Base price using "equal allocation" excuse[b]
Hammer	$7.66	$435.00	$ 50.00
Wrench, end box,			
1 set	4.99	768.00	383.00
Pliers, slip joint	3.77	430.00	45.00
Pliers, slip joint	5.97	449.00	64.00
Pliers, vise grip, 2	15.88 (@7.94)	486.00	101.00[c]
Wrench, socket set,			
3/8"	12.88	545.00	160.00
Bar extension	1.99	430.00	45.00
Bar extension	2.19	431.00	46.00
Socket, 1/2"	1.49	456.00	71.00
Screwdriver, sq.-blade,			
1 set	1.69	265.50	−119.50
Screwdriver, jeweler,			
1 set	1.97	232.00	−153.00
Screwdriver, Phillips,			
1 set	1.69	258.06	−126.44
Screwdriver, offset	2.79	225.00	−160.00
Crimping tool	3.96	729.00	344.00
Superjust wrenches	4.88	1150.00	765.00
Wrenches	1.57	234.00	−151.00
Drill set	1.69	599.00	214.00
Hex driver	3.99	469.00	84.00
Feeler gauge	4.27	436.00	51.00
Circuit tester	3.39	489.00	104.00
Tool box	11.67	652.00	267.00
Totals	100.38	10,168.56	2,083.56

a. As priced by Representative Berkley Bedell at a Washington-area hardware store.
b. Derived by subtracting Admiral Sansone's figure of $385 alleged "equal share" allocation from contractor's billing price.
c. $385 subtracted only once.

Mr. Adams meant that the prices the government pays major defense contractors are deliberately set at levels to insure total cost reimbursement, plus profits over and above that . . . regardless of the intrinsic value of goods or services.

In short, the exorbitant prices . . . are the result of incestuous partnership between DoD procurement . . . and defense contractors to increase prices to whatever level it takes to absorb the total allowable costs.

Thus, when the Pentagon paid for a hammer, it also paid for a portion of all the expenses, the waste along with the necessary, of the favored supplier: heating, electricity, repairs, paper, salaries, office equipment, insurance, cocktail parties, advertising, the salaries of nonproducing engineers, trips for the CEO and perhaps his family, and a thousand other things. In short, because that seaman needed a hammer, the government was willing to give a corporation this all-expenses-paid free ride. And then pay it a profit on top of that. It was incidental whether the hammer head broke off at the first blow.

But wait, wouldn't "line item integrity" end all this nonsense? There happened to be some pliers almost as famous and even more exorbitant than the Gould hammer. They were Channel Lock duckbill pliers whose only distinction was a small groove in the jaws for holding a round pin. The pliers were supplied to Boeing by a consortium of the aircraft engine division of General Electric and SNECMA, a French engine manufacturer. They cost about $7.50 retail. Boeing resold them to the government for $748 apiece.

After Om Chauhan cited them before Grassley's committee in late June 1984, the Air Force announced, a bit prematurely, that the price had been reduced to $90 by formal contractual action. What followed was a typical Pentagon tragicomedy of errors.

We found that the total price of all the tools in the order had been reduced from $528,536 to $433,545. A step in the right direction? Not quite. Boeing had charged an additional $28,964 to "prepare the proposal" in the first place. With the new paperwork, the proposal preparation cost went up to $30,648. And another new cost popped up, an imaginative item called "Support Equipment Management," which cost the government $93,307. Lo and behold, after all the cost cutting, Boeing was still charging the government $557,500.

Wait a minute, we said to the Air Force flacks, this is a scam. Ninety dollars is still too much for a pair of $7.50 pliers, even if they do have a notch. And what of that support equipment management shell game? They agreed to take another look.

When we checked again in February 1985, the order had indeed

Progress in pricing (definitization) of the Boeing pliers, 1984[a]

Item	Price		
	March 14	July 25	October 24
Pliers, one pair	[$748]	[$90]	[$80]
All tools, including pliers	$528,536	$433,545	$385,277
Proposal preparation	28,964	30,648	28,964
Support equipment			
management	—	93,307	143,259
Total	557,500	557,500	557,500

a. Air Force records show that the pliers were delivered on April 9, 1984.

been repriced a second time, with the results shown in the third column of the table. The pliers were now a bargain at $80 apiece, but the support equipment management bill had gone up to $143,259. The total price was exactly the same it had been at the beginning. So much for line item integrity.

A certain group of Air Force Intelligence operatives in the Pentagon who called themselves the Air Staff Closet Coalition contrived in 1984 to spring an interesting leak. My underground circles had nothing to do with this, but we were widely blamed for it. The coalition did a skillful job of leaking their case. They packaged their documentary evidence in case-study form with an excellent introduction:

> At the end of each fiscal year (Sept.), DoD invariable [sic] fails to obligate some funds that have been budgeted for specific purposes. The "fallout" funds result from various bureaucratic imperatives, including not getting the appropriate competitive bid or contractor. . . .
>
> The important point is that if certain *budgeted* funds are not obligated (as in a contract) by the end of the FY, they are by law returned to the treasury. The scramble to avoid returning . . . unobligated funds is the real story here.
>
> Here is how it works:
>
> The team proceeds on the assumption that some DoD fallout funds will always be available as the FY draws to a close. In anticipation of this, a Pentagon office (in this case the Assistant Chief of Staff of AF

Intelligence, or ASC/I) will negotiate "unofficially," in advance, a sole-source contract with a pet or crony contractor. The contract is drawn up in advance so that it may be signed on short notice when funds become available. By the time fallout funds are identified, it is too late for DoD to let competitive bids or otherwise legally obligate funds before the end of the FY. This is always so because the funds were originally budgeted for other (approved) DoD projects.

To move these funds from the fallout category and into pet contractor pockets, some cooperative agency other than DoD must "launder" the money for the prearranged contract. In this case that agency is the CIA.

The CIA is always a good choice for a number of reasons, the most important of which is that they are not subject to the same contracting restraints that apply to DoD. CIA can legally obligate funds in late September and they don't have to advertise for competitive bids. In short, CIA agrees to act as the official "sponsor." . . . The advantage for CIA is that they get to build some capital with contractors with another agency's fallout budget monies.

The advantages for the originating DoD agency are obvious:

— They can funnel funds to cronies who have retired and now make their living selling "papers" to the government.

— These unregulated fallout funds represent a large, tax-supported slush fund that encourages conflicts of interest (e.g. government officials feathering their retirement nests by throwing contract monies at future prospective employers).

The Coalition's target was Major General James C. Pfautz, then assistant chief of staff, for intelligence (ASC/I):

> The guy who is sponsoring the Pitt [University of Pittsburgh] connection is the Chief of AF Intelligence . . . He is trying to farm out "sole source" contracts [without competitive bids] to some cronies at Pitt. The chancellor, the research director, and the proposed project director are all retired AF officers. To boot, the subject "papers" don't have a thing to do with AF intelligence concerns. The atchd. is another example of government/industry incest where the "old boys" take care of each other at taxpayer expense. Or the sponsor may just think he is feathering his retirement nest by throwing money at prospective future employers. Similar largess has been lavished on Dr. Jureidini at Abbot Assoc. of Alexandria, Va.

The memorandum went on to note that the proposed contract for the University of Pittsburgh had only the vaguest of terms and that in any case Pitt had no intelligence research capabilities.

The contract that had gone to Dr. Jureidini of Abbott Associates in

Alexandria, Virginia, was for $41,000, for a paper on "the near-term events in Lebanon that impacted on USAF interests." The Closet Coalition noted that "the AF does not have any interests in Lebanon." The memorandum closed by asking why the general didn't ask his own staff of several hundred analysts, or CIA, or DIA (Defense Intelligence Agency) to produce such a paper if he really needed one.

Whereas such handouts to retired officer-teachers seemed to be no more than a small waste of money, other contracts to major defense systems contractors looked a good deal more sinister. Remember James Schlesinger's wondrous Dollar Model, described in Chapter 6, which paid (hypothetically) for the Soviet military machine in American dollars and with American contractor waste built into the equation? Now Pfautz was fueling up the old Dollar Model to once again inflate the Soviet threat and use our huge price markups to justify higher spending.

Task 12 on Pfautz's list of proposed projects, marked "CIA will fund in 1984," was titled "Development of CERs for Aircraft and Helicopters based on New Prices." CERs (Cost Estimating Relationships) were self-fulfilling did-cost/will-cost estimating formulas. In a note on Task 12, Pfautz wrote, "Based on the new production cost [American cost, that is] derived over the past several years, new CERs for aircraft and helicopters will create better [read: higher] cost estimates of Soviet military aircraft."

Paying the major systems contractors to make studies of CERs for their own products and to apply the same high costs to similar Soviet products permitted them to build in all the future waste and inefficiency they could imagine. It was like giving an alcoholic a key to the liquor store. Obviously, this was a job that demanded heavy conflicts of interests. Vought, a division of LTV, and McDonnell-Douglas, both of which made planes for the Pentagon, seemed ideal. The general tapped them. And who could better attribute their own padded inefficiencies to Soviet research, development, and production of jet engines than General Electric and Pratt and Whitney? Who knew better how to zoom the putative costs of command-control communications systems than the TRW Corporation? But the all-time prize practical joke was the project to estimate costs of the Soviets' new air-to-air and air-to-surface missiles. That was to be carried out by none other than Hughes Aircraft.

The Closet Coalition's comprehensive leak provided other interesting insights. General Pfautz — obviously a man with no ear for the language — even proposed a project he labeled "SCAM Improvement." And indeed it was. The Stonehouse Group was to "supplement current

CIA efforts to improve the computer data base and model used to make most of their estimates of Soviet defense spending. It is basically a 'Price × Quantity' approach."

Sheila Hershow, now reporting for Cable News Network (CNN), did excellent broadcast coverage. The press (the *Boston Globe, USA Today,* and *Defense Week*) had discerning reports on SCAM Improvement. Writing in the March 20, 1984, *Boston Globe,* Fred Kaplan quoted an Air Force spokesman who said, "Who else would you turn to? These guys have the technical expertise and the knowledge." But he also quoted other Air Force officials who agreed with the comment of a former CIA official that "the estimates don't mean anything." Kaplan spelled out the fallacy in the whole notion: "If a company that gets one of these [Pfautz] contracts manufactures its weapons inefficiently, then the CIA estimate will automatically assume that the Soviets produce their weapons with equal inefficiency."

The great disappointment was that Congress failed to respond to these disclosures. Perhaps, after all the years of swallowing something akin to the Dollar Model figment, it was too embarrassed.

My first close look at my new boss, Richard Carver, came when we met in early October 1984 to discuss current programs. I told him that we had a series of promising cost-reduction initiatives under way, hampered only by the military's reluctance to concur. I suggested that establishing a series of tough goals for cost reduction and quality improvement, through a program for Air Force commanders and managers, would help to get us all on the same target. Such a course was designed to put into force Secretary Orr's announced objectives.

Carver looked at me coldly and said Orr had warned him about "the Fitzgerald problem." He didn't want to explain what that "problem" was, however.

Then, on October 15, 1984, Winslow Wheeler, assistant to Senator Nancy Kassebaum, called to warn me that the administration planned to get rid of me after the November election. His source was "a high-ranking Pentagon official." A month or so later Nancy Ramsey, chair of the Fund for Constitutional Government, told me she had heard that Carver's plan for getting rid of me would get around the obstacle of my court-supervised agreement with the Air Force: he'd make such outrageous provocations that I'd get angry and retaliate. Then I could be fired.

Jim Ririe was scheduled to depart from his Air Force job on December 1, 1984, and, as I had agreed with Russ Hale in June 1982, I was to take

over the job of reporting to Congress on weapons systems. I wrote to
Carver about beginning to work closely with Ririe on the reports in
order to make a smooth transition. Carver replied ambiguously and
spoke of the "apparent agreement." It was a foretaste of his later
actions.

When Kris Kolesnik paid him a courtesy call and expressed the hope
that Carver would abide by my legal agreement with the Air Force,
Carver replied that he didn't intend to let a court order tell him how to
run his office. He quickly assigned Major Jim Wolfe to redistribute the
duties of my office to other deputies. As revealed in an office diary
Wolfe kept at the time, which Congressman John Dingell's investigators
later captured and distributed, he met with Carver and others, including

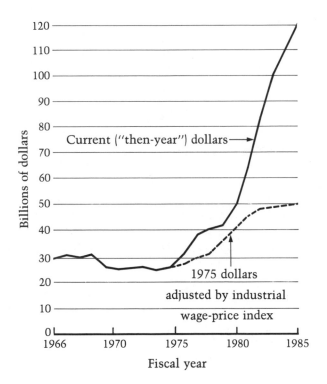

*The Defense Department budget: total obligational authority for acquisi-
tion (research and development plus procurement), 1966–1985. Source:
Office of the Assistant Secretary of Defense (Comptroller), "National
Defense Budget Estimates for FY 1988/1989," May 1987.*

Air Force General Counsel Gene Sullivan, on January 4, 1985. Sullivan felt that reassigning some of my duties to another deputy was improper because it "infringes on FMM [Fitzgerald's] position description."

Carver thereupon ordered Wolfe and Colonel Warren Nogoki to write a new work plan for me — one that would effectively put my office out of the cost reduction business. And in the end the general counsel approved the job description that began the whittling away of my responsibilities.

The timing of all this was interesting. My period of uneasy acceptance by Verne Orr and the Reagan team was over. They had identified the real enemy: it wasn't high costs, it was Fitzgerald. Reagan, who had just won a landslide victory and would never run for office again, could have ignored the pressures of big contractors and Pentagon generals. But as the chart on page 184 shows, his FY 1985 acquisition appropriations were the biggest in history. If Reagan had applied the cost controls we had shown him, he could have had an overwhelming military machine. Instead, the Reaganites were having to cut planned quantities of weapons. Even with the huge increases in available money, the military buildup couldn't be sustained.

11

☆ ☆ ☆

Poor Richard's Network

CONGRESS, STUNG AT LAST, tried to slow the Reagan Pentagon's spending orgy by means of the Freeze. It was a little more than a tut-tut, a little less than a pair of handcuffs. Someday, when the fiscal history of the nation in the twentieth century is written, there will be one page for the half-courage of Congress in the mid-1980s, which tried for a moment to stem the Republic's slide toward bankruptcy.

The Freeze was the brainchild of Senator Charles Grassley and his assistant Kris Kolesnik. Some members of Congress found it easy to put on a show of clucking over a $500 cotter pin, but many of them just walked away after the show was over. Grassley listened to us, and listened hard. He absorbed the lessons about our effort to make separate but related drives against the various elements of overcost, that is, labor, material, overhead, and so forth. He was especially concerned with our work measurement initiative for its usefulness in depicting factory incompetence, gauging management efficiency, and indicating cures.

He summarized all this in his June 25, 1986, letter to President Reagan:

> Fitzgerald and his associate, Dr. Thomas Amlie, helped me and the Senate Budget Committee that year [1983] to understand the extent of the spare parts problem and its impact on the rest of the budget. It has become clear since then that the overpriced spare parts phenomenon is a symptom of an overpricing policy in general in the defense weapons business.

Grassley also noted the costly problems of factory inefficiency and ended with this delicate expression about the Freeze — that the Senate, after a two-year fight, had set a budget in 1985 that "did not create further disincentives to efficient weapons pricing." That is, the Senate had removed some of the money that the Pentagon would have felt obligated to waste.

Senator Grassley recognized the value of true competition both as a spur to cutting costs and improving quality and as a means of limiting opportunities for bid rigging. Advertised solicitations and sealed-bid responses were used for only about 6 percent of the Pentagon's acquisition dollars. The rest was sole source, "competitive negotiations" (lodge brothers only), and "follow-on to competition" (sole source, too). Beginning in 1983, Grassley introduced a series of bills that he called "Creeping Capitalism." The first of these bills required an increase of 5 percent per year in the Pentagon's competitive procurement until true competition reached 70 percent of the total contract dollars spent.

By moderating the bureaucratic necessity to shovel out the money before the end of the year and by putting a little downward pressure on weapons prices, we hoped to rally all true hawks around the Freeze flag. After all, wasn't it better to have in the arsenal more weapons that work than to have fatter and fatter generals and defense contractors? But the race of true hawks either had been corrupted by the pork barrel or had died out. They simply didn't show up at the antiwaste rally.

A notable nonshow was Verne Orr, whose oratorical war against high costs was over: high costs had won. Verne had surrendered. Now it was entirely up to a few tightwad members of congress like Grassley. In early 1985, when he began to work on the FY 1986 budget, Grassley tried unsuccessfully to get the usual update on work-measurement information from Orr's office. The office of the secretary of defense had not been forthcoming, either.

So Grassley wrote directly to me and, working with Carver's principal deputy, Richard Harshman, and the Air Staff's chief financial lobbyist, Duff Young, we prepared to furnish the information. The three of us planned to meet with Kolesnik in Harshman's office to go over the details. At the last minute Carver got wind of the meeting and moved it to his office, where he took charge and declared that Grassley was not to get the information.

Kris wanted the denial directly from Orr; Carver said that could be arranged, but not with Kolesnik present. Carver disappeared for a few minutes and came back with an oral reply from Verne Orr: no work measurement information for Congress.

As he'd proved before with his subpoena invasion, Charles Grassley was not a timid man. He — in alliance with Representative Barbara Boxer — decided to pass a law to get the weapon systems cost data he wanted.

In due course, after some interesting congressional battles, the Grassley-Boxer bill was enacted in 1985. The law, which was known in my circles as the Richard E. Carver Memorial Cost Data Act, came as a big shock in a lot of contractors' board rooms, at lobbyists' cocktail parties, and to their Pentagon lodge brothers.

From time to time, in the early days, I'd been praised for my labors in getting a useful system of work measurement, but that was because I seemed to be a good public relations symbol. Once it was clear that I and my office wanted a real knife (work measurement) that made real slices and drew real blood, things changed.

The Troika — our name for the unholy alliance of the Air Force procurement people, the office of the secretary of defense, and the industry associations — had to put a stopper on Grassley-Boxer. They picked Maryanne Gileece, Eleanor Spector, and Richard Stimson from the secretary's office to do the infighting.

Gileece and her team didn't know much about work measurement, but they did know the right buttons to push in Congress — or so they thought. There had been a time when an authoritative letter from Gileece would have cowed the pliant Armed Services Committee. But, though the Troika didn't realize it, they were dealing with a new, tougher breed on the Hill. Tougher and more honest. Donna Martin, for one, had made a difference when she left her job as assistant to Dina Rasor at PMP to work on military issues for Representative Barbara Boxer. Donna's PMP experience had toughened her outlook and given her good insights into how the Pentagon acquisition system worked.

At this point it came down to a duel, if David's little episode with Goliath could be called a duel. The Armed Services Committee staff had seen the wild discrepancy between our documentation and what the Troika was trying to sell. So they arranged a debate in the committee's staff room to clear matters up. Goliath had the bulk: all the resources of the office of the secretary of defense, the vast research facilities of the big contractors, and plenty of tame academics. The Attic Fanatics had one pebble of truth and an old, much-battered engineer to sling it.

At the appointed time, I appeared at the Armed Services Committee forum, but Goliath didn't show up. Needless to say, my side took advantage of the chance to educate the assembly.

Meanwhile, Richard Carver was stealthily doing what couldn't be done in open debate; he used the bureaucratic mechanism to disarm us by sending us a lot of busywork assignments. He made a pact with General Larry Skantze, head of the Air Force Systems Command, to impede us. And he began to dismantle my hard-won jurisdiction awarded by the courts.

At one time I'd delegated part of my work measurement responsibilities to the AFSC, and now I wanted it back, simply because my flow of information on the subject had been narrowed to the trickle I got from closet patriots. General Robert Reed, to whom I'd sent my request, quietly got together with Carver, and the two of them decided to tell the military staff and field commands to disregard me. When this was revealed later by John Dingell's investigators, I faced Carver and asked him how he could so easily overlook my court-ordered contract.

It was simple. "Your court order only says that you can give guidance and direction," he said. "It doesn't mean that anybody has to follow it."

On September 9, 1985, Carver and I were invited to testify before Senator Proxmire's subcommittee. Without giving me any notice, Carver used the occasion to announce a sharp reduction of my authority. I had been the person in charge of work-measurement matters at the highest level in the Air Force; now I was to be no more than a staff adviser on the subject.

Even at that, there were still some painful things for the big contractors that Grassley-Boxer had made into law. The provisions for ready availability of figures and, more particularly, for comparisons of should-take hours times with actual times was a nagging headache for the acquisition community, both sellers and buyers. They regarded it with the affection of a bank robber for a closed-circuit television pointed in his direction.

Grassley-Boxer had to go. General Skantze, engines roaring, made the first bombing run at a meeting of the Aerospace Education Foundation Roundtable on August 15, 1985. As the November, 1985, *Air Force Magazine* reported:

"Sometimes it is an arcane feature of the acquisition rules that leads to misunderstanding and the loss of public confidence. For example, a statutory provision new this year — use of a 'standard work hour' in billing labor costs — seems almost certain to generate the sort of misinterpretation that has so often enraged the taxpayers."

General Skantze pronounced it [the Grassley-Boxer approach] "an enormous club with which we can be beaten continuously."

"Very few people on the Hill really understand what a standard hour is and how you arrive at it," he said. "It is the calculation made by an industrial engineer who picks out a point in the production cycle where changes have slowed down, where there's stability in a design, and where the people are trained." He says that "under these ideal circumstances (a given job) should take a number of hours."

"Used properly, the standard hour is a handy tool for estimating and pricing. Applied as an absolute yardstick at the beginning of production, though, it may be off by a factor of five or ten," General Skantze said.

"So someone will take that data, as they have over the past six months, and say that the industry is only one-third or one-tenth as efficient as it should be and that they're wasting all the taxpayers' money," Skantze said. "We're going to have a terrible problem with this because we've got to provide the data, and it will be interpreted by those people who want to use it for their own purposes."

Among Skantze's various misunderstandings, he clearly didn't comprehend that our "fair day's work" approach called for setting attainable times reflecting *current*, not ideal, conditions and methods. His eccentric address proved again that the Troika was desperate to avoid legitimate reporting: "We're going to have a terrible problem with this because we've got to provide the data."

Apparently the Troika couldn't find an independent professional industrial engineer to defend their view; at least they never came up with one. Their usual spokesman was a procurement functionary with obvious conflicts of interest, so we had no trouble busting their balloons.

In trouble, the Troika turned to high-tech conspiracy. They went to an enterprise called the American Productivity Center (APC) in Houston, Texas. That optimistic name made my heart soften — until I saw the list of advisers, sponsors, members, and sustaining members: Boeing, General Dynamics, Lockheed, Northrop, McDonnell-Douglas, Rockwell, TRW, et al., along with their Big Eight certified public accountants and the bosses of big defense-industry unions.

APC set up a "Defense Industry Productivity/Quality" computer message network, which began an attack on the hated Grassley-Boxer law. Computer conferencing is obviously the late-twentieth-century substitute for secret messages left in a hollow tree.

As might be expected in the committee culture of big business, the network had a moderator, whose stated role was to "help set the initial agenda for discussion, to guide and direct the discussion as it moves along, to make 'weaving' and 'summarizing' comments, to synthesize thoughts, to stimulate the group, and to remind them of priorities." He was Dr. Richard Stimson of the office of the secretary of defense, code name "Poor Richard," code number 2103. (Benjamin Franklin, the original Poor Richard, said in his *Almanack*, "A penny saved is twopence clear.")

As the Troika was beginning to find out, Congress had changed from the good old days of Mendel Rivers and his ilk. The House Armed Services Committee, long known as a money shop for the Pentagon, was under new management. Les Aspin, an intelligent, energetic, and ambitious congressman, had succeeded Mel Price as chairman — just in time to be faced with a snakepit of horror stories too fearsome for even the old committee to explain away.

Aspin set up a special subcommittee on procurement policy, headed by Congressman Nick Mavroules of Massachusetts. On it he put, as ad hoc members, some of the most caustic critics of Pentagon boondoggling in Congress, including Barbara Boxer. Mavroules, with consent from Grassley and Boxer, offered to mediate the dispute over their law.

Step one was public hearings in April 1986 at which Senator Grassley, Ompal Chauhan, and I were invited to testify in favor of work measurement. The opposition witnesses were some titans of industry and Assistant Secretary of Defense Jim Wade. Through Kolesnik's good offices, I'd previously had a meeting with acquisition czar Wade, and we'd actually persuaded him to agree to some of our technical positions. In the hearing he announced his modest concessions and tried to avoid the hazards of work measurement. The titans just mumbled. We scored a no-hitter against them.

The titans of industry tried again. They got Mavroules to set up a meeting in his office with Grassley, Boxer, and me in the lineup against various Daddy Warbucks types. The result was an impasse. In the spirit of fair play, Mavroules did agree to more attempts at mediation; he appointed Rudy DeLeon, one of the committee's most competent staff assistants, as mediator to try to clarify provisions the Troika representatives said they didn't understand. But it was like dealing with the old Russians; the other side wanted to get but not give. Each time Grassley and Boxer made concessions, they were faced with bigger demands from the Warbucks side.

Then, making their move in Congress to strike down Grassley-Boxer, the Troika committed some dire mistakes. To lead the fight, they picked Republican Representative Jim Courter and Senator Dan Quayle. Neither had substantive knowledge of the issue. Courter had been a member, albeit a somewhat suspect member, of the Military Reform Caucus on Capitol Hill. He had shown considerable reluctance to hurt the feelings of the big contractors. And he didn't know much about work measurement. With Quayle and Courter as point men, the Troika decided to push for a repeal of Grassley-Boxer.

Donna Martin was crushed. She had worked hard and in good faith to negotiate a compromise solution, and now she had been double-crossed by the move to repeal. But as she mournfully gave me this news on the phone, I could hear Barbara Boxer, a small woman blessed with a powerful voice, in the background. She was denouncing her opponents, swearing to fight them on the floor of the House and suggesting some rude violations of their persons.

Grassley's reaction was more measured but equally determined. In a floor speech on the double-cross, he said that industry was trying to "shut all the windows we opened last year on defense factory inefficiency, on huge defense contractor rates, and on excessive costs for defense weapons." He knew why the repeal effort had been launched: "Open windows reveal a lot of embarrassing activity." And Kris Kolesnik gave a hint of Grassley's strategy to *Aerospace Daily* when he told it, "This has the potential to hold up a conference agreement on the defense bill."

Actually, the double-cross was good news for us. Our side, with nothing to offer in the way of campaign contributions or jobs, was bound to lose in backroom "mediation" dealings. But in an open floor fight Grassley and Boxer had the better of the argument.

The traffic on Poor Richard's ironically named productivity-quality network became more urgent. Some of the addressees in the network, unsympathetic to the Warbucks cause, were keeping us informed. On July 1, 1986, Richard Engwall, a Westinghouse official, sounded the alarm:

SUBJECT: Grassley-Boxer — Shift on Work Measurement. Please find attached article in June 27, 1986 *Aerospace Daily* of Grassley, Boxer Shift on Work Measurement. Pat Sullivan, AIA [Aerospace Industries Association], has asked me to help defuse this activity. Please contact your Senator/Congressperson of your views and/or help furnish our White Paper On Work Measurement/Cost and Price Management Interrelationships as requested in my letter of June 10, 1986.

The message went on to mention the aborted compromise attempt and said that Courter's attempt to repeal Grassley-Boxer "has backfired on us." It continued:

Rep. Boxer has withdrawn any support for compromising and is planning to take the legislation back to the full house for a "repeal/no repeal vote." We need to communicate to all of our individual congresspersons of our concern for the cost and price management legislation being implemented as stands, and urge repeal. We were and still are willing to insert language similar to that submitted to James Wade, 30 January 1986. We have an apparent tough job ahead of us. I welcome your ideas and comments.

Engwall's network message also went to Pat Sullivan of AIA, to its "Productivity Committee," and to the "15-80 work group" of CODSIA, and it was helpful for us to know what these powerful lobbies were up to. We also got information from industrial engineers at various contracting companies. As a sidelight, it was fascinating to see Representative Courter, who was being educated about work management by the Sperry Corporation repeat his well-memorized lessons in his speeches. Sperry later merged into Unisys Corporation, which became a prime investigative target.

Grassley and Boxer let the industry partisans in Congress have their fun in repealing Grassley-Boxer I. Then Representative Boxer offered a measure almost identical to the one repealed except for clarifying language. Boxer's restoration was passed overwhelmingly by the House. In the next move, she and the senator used all their leverage to see that Grassley-Boxer II stayed in the Defense Authorization Bill in conference with the Senate.

During the Freeze period Congress did some good work in digging into the acquisitions mess. One who sort of sidled into the fray was Representative John Dingell, known as "the Truck." As chairman of the formidable Energy and Commerce Committee and the tough Oversight and Investigations Subcommittee, with the biggest budget and the broadest jurisdiction in Congress, except for the appropriations committees, Dingell was a very large truck indeed. If some matter of interest didn't fall into the category of either energy or commerce, it very likely fell under the jurisdiction of one of the regulatory agencies, which Dingell also oversaw.

One of those regulatory agencies was the Securities and Exchange Commission, so no eyebrows had been raised in May 1984, when Dingell asked Verne Orr to permit me and my two assistants to give the Oversight and Investigations Subcommittee some part-time help in "an SEC matter."

The matter he had in mind was the still-gestating General Dynamics scandal. Orr didn't know that, though, and he was very happy to divert the Attic Fanatics to any seemingly harmless activity. The broad story of that scandal has been amply chronicled elsewhere. But some of the lesser-known aspects still stick disagreeably in my mind.

Pete Stockton led the charge for Dingell. Soon after the start of the investigation, he confided to me that General Dynamics officials had told Dingell that if we persisted, we would hurt some people we liked and admired. That had no effect on either the congressman or Stockton, but we shortly found out what they meant.

The company officials made it very easy for us to find records of thousands of dollars' worth of gifts and favors they had bestowed on Admiral Hyman Rickover. The sharp-tongued old admiral had his faults, as we knew, but they were outweighed by his readiness to denounce ripoffs by the big contractors and the seriousness with which his pronouncements were received on Capitol Hill.

Slowly, methodically, patiently, General Dynamics wove a trap for the admiral. Rickover used to make frequent trips to the company's Electric Boat shipyard in New London, Connecticut, to check on the construction progress of "his" nuclear submarines. He was present at launches, and he went on shakedown cruises. General Dynamics saw to it that he lacked for nothing on these visits. He didn't have to bring as much as a toothbrush or an extra shirt on a shakedown cruise. At a launching, where gifts to dignitaries are the custom, there was always some expensive bauble for his wife. (Two gifts of jewelry for Mrs. Rickover were shown in the General Dynamics accounts as "10 retirement watches.")

In Rickover's case the General Dynamics accountants kept marvelous records. They might not know exactly what they were spending on multimillion-dollar submarines, but they knew to the last cent how much they had spent on Rickover's toothbrushes. They hoarded all those little expense vouchers for twenty years, but somehow managed to have almost no records at all on other high-ranking government officials. These expense vouchers were, for the most part, blank.

The discovery of the Rickover records came as a hard blow to me. For years, as I rode the shuttle bus between the Pentagon and Capitol Hill, I'd had time for a few minutes of reflection. Some of my greatest highs and lows of spirit had come then. The bus ride back after Stockton showed me the Rickover records was one of my lowest points.

Before the subcommittee hearings on General Dynamics began, Secretary of the Navy John Lehman made a desperate attempt to change the focus from the great and grave accusations against General Dynamics to Rickover's acceptance of gifts. It didn't work, and Dingell wrote Lehman a blistering letter telling him just why it wouldn't work. Without condoning the admiral's faults, Dingell refused to be sidetracked.

The investigation pressed on. Dingell and Mike Barrett, the subcommittee's staff director and counsel, drafted some good auditors and investigators from GAO. Once free of the stifling GAO hierarchy, such men as Bruce Chafin and Art Brouk did first-rate service.

They also brought in George Spanton, now retired from the DCAA but still involved in the special counsel's investigation of his ordeal.

When Chip Terrill came up with evidence that Weinberger and his assistant, Vince Puritano, were implicated in the plot against Spanton, the special counsel choked, took a wrong turn legally, and eventually lost the case in court.

The key witness in the General Dynamics investigation never appeared in court. He was P. Takis Veliotis, a former executive vice president of the company who was by then a fugitive from justice. Faced with imminent indictments on the charge that he had taken kickbacks from subcontractors, he had fled to Greece, his native land, taking along a lot of evidence about other General Dynamics executives.

Veliotis didn't understand the American system of justice — I mean the one practiced by our Justice Department. He naively thought that the department would be so eager to get incriminating evidence on the other General Dynamics suspects that they would let him plea-bargain for a reduced sentence. He didn't understand that the *last* thing the Reagan Justice Department wanted to do (especially with Ed Meese in charge, toward the end) was prosecute the highest officials of our largest defense contractor.

When he got no response from Justice, Veliotis began to leak information to Stockton and Pat Tyler, a *Washington Post* reporter. At this time Dingell was under heavy pressure not to proceed with his hearings, but when Stockton shrewdly disseminated tidbits from his hoard of evidence, the media took such an interest that Dingell was able to fend off the political pressures.

His first General Dynamics hearing, on February 28, 1985, brought out the largest and most diverse group of print and electronic media reporters I've ever seen at a military procurement scandal hearing. At one point I counted thirty television cameras in the hearing room.

Dingell's staff had done a superb job of preparation; the committee congressmen — especially three young Democrats, John Bryant of Texas, Gerry Sikorski of Minnesota, and Ron Wyden of Oregon — were raring to get started. Sikorski led off with an eloquent statement about "the charmed life of General Dynamics":

> Who else can record the largest loss in history, over five billion for tax purposes, at the same time record a two-billion-dollar profit for SEC purposes, and still pay no federal income taxes since 1972?
>
> Who else can buy in on a major defense contract, do a miserable job of managing the construction of the weapons system, overrun fixed-price contracts by one billion dollars, be willing to settle a claim against the government for one hundred and fifty million dollars, and later receive close to one billion dollars in taxpayers' money?
>
> Who else could use non-conforming steel in a submarine, foul up the

welding program, suffer a total collapse of its quality control program, make a preposterous claim against the Navy insurance process, and then obtain another government bail-out?

What small contractor could suffer the wrath of the Secretary of the Navy, go to the White House and meet with Mr. Meese, then have a pleasant meeting with the Secretary of the Navy that results in the Assistant Secretary running out to your corporate limousine like a puppy dog to assure you that the Navy will take care of you? And where else can that Assistant Secretary get hired eighteen months later as an executive vice president? Mr. Chairman, the questions continue.

Chairman of the Board David S. Lewis and Executive Vice President Gorden MacDonald could see they were in for a rough day. They had to listen to P. Takis Veliotis's tape recordings of General Dynamics executives plotting to conceal cost overruns caused by their own inefficiency so that the charges could later be attributed to changed requirements from the Navy. Dingell and other subcommittee members grilled them mercilessly on that.

They had to listen to the live testimony of their former vice president, who testified that those same overruns were indeed caused by General Dynamics' bad management and ineptitude.

They had to endure allegations that Lester Crown, a director and the son of their beloved former chairman of the board, had admitted to involvement in a bribery scheme and that he had been given a Top Secret clearance afterward. (As stated in a February 7, 1985, letter from Dingell to Weinberger, Crown had bribed certain Illinois legislators with $15 thousand of his own money — he'd then had a wholly owned subsidiary falsify its books to reimburse him.)

General Dynamics put up a rickety defense, mostly by attacking Veliotis. MacDonald and a couple of his flacks, F. Bettinger and R. Duesenberg, had tape-recorded their conversation with Pat Tyler on the proposed strategy. When MacDonald, under oath, had to admit the taping, he was forced to produce the tape. Duesenberg said to Tyler:

Pat, that guy began to steal, Veliotis, almost immediately upon coming aboard began to set up the scheme by which he stole from this company. So you know what the guy was doing, was just carrying out his sordid criminal instincts by creating Pearl Harbor files that he may hopefully, from his point of view, use sometime down the line. Because as he's stealing this money, along with his colleague, Jim Gilliland, he has to have in mind that somewhere he may be caught, and that's exactly what happened.

Luckily for General Dynamics, the Justice Department was the evaluator of many of the heavy-duty charges, so the company was able to slither out from under them. When it came to human-scale offenses that the ordinary taxpayer could judge, they were not so lucky. The expense vouchers turned up by the investigators were plentiful and outrageous. There was the $18,650 bill from the Old Warson Country Club in St. Louis, $17,000 of it for executive James Mellor's initiation fee and $1,650 for the club's "debt conversion note."

Crown, Duesenberg, Lewis, and E. J. Lefevre ran up hefty hotel bills at nice resorts. Former Navy Assistant Secretary G. A. Sawyer, who had run after the corporate limousine like a puppy dog, relaxed in equal splendor. General Larry Skantze and many others were entertained at the Annual Wallow of the Military Order of the Carabao (water buffalo). General Dynamics spent and the Pentagon paid. Out of the defense budget. (Take that, Evil Empire!)

John Dingell's favorite infamy was the expense account of General Dynamics' Dr. A. M. Lovelace and wife. Their expenses were charged to the common overhead expense pool, of which the taxpayers paid 94 percent. Dingell read aloud, "Fursten, boarding at Silver Maple Farm, $87.25." "Who is Fursten?" he asked. Fursten was a dog. When Dr. and Mrs. Lovelace took luxury trips at the taxpayers' expense, Fursten lived in canine bliss at $25.26 a day. That was more than I received in expense reimbursement when I stayed on military bases on government business trips.

Question: of the numerous sordid examples of big-time larceny and of moral and legal failure in the General Dynamics scandal, which one caught the attention of the press? Fursten, of course. The subcommittee office was overwhelmed with requests for vouchers showing his board bill. Fursten was probably the least expensive General Dynamics executive feeding at the public trough, but his case was one that people could understand.

When the case against the company had been well-displayed in all its ugly details, the Pentagon damage-control PR crew went into action. Their party line read this way: yes, General Dynamics is much to blame, but this is a unique case, an aberration. We don't know of anything else like it.

Dingell wanted to shoot this down quickly, so he called another round of hearings for April 23 and 24, 1985. At this point Weinberger announced that he was going to try to recover $244 million in excessive overhead charges from General Dynamics. Dingell was unimpressed. In his opening statement at the April 23 hearing, he said:

In announcing his actions to recover two hundred and forty-four million dollars from General Dynamics ... Secretary of Defense

Weinberger claimed that General Dynamics was an aberration. Today and tomorrow, the subcommittee will expect to hear testimony and see evidence that, far from being an aberration, the company was just one of the gang. False reports and false claims, incomplete records, and an unfortunate attitude of "catch me if you can" seem to be standard operating procedures for major defense contractors. The cost of these things to the taxpayers is, of course, immense.

Several days after the committee disclosed that the government was paying for obviously unallowable overhead expenses, including the boarding of this country's most famous dog, Fursten, Secretary Weinberger announced his get-tough policy. His first action was to require all defense contractors to submit certification, under penalty of perjury, of the propriety of overhead charges at various steps.

When major defense contractors complained, the Department of Defense general counsel advised them that the Pentagon was not really considering criminally prosecuting fraudulent certifications. They continued to complain, so a deputy undersecretary further softened the blow: the contractors would have to certify their overhead charges only at the final settlement, thus eliminating any benefit to the taxpayers of the certification requirement.

Pratt and Whitney was the star attraction at the April hearings. George Spanton, the principal witness, had worked closely with FBI Special Agent James Cavanaugh of the bureau's Miami office on the FBI's investigation of Pratt and Whitney. When Stockton went to see him, Cavanaugh was frustrated over what seemed to be Justice Department moves to ensure that Pratt and Whitney would not be prosecuted effectively. This, along with other devious behavior by the department, convinced Dingell and company that the fix, if not already in, was en route.

Spanton did his usual, calm, meticulous, and devastating job of explaining how Pratt and Whitney unloaded huge entertainment bills for their executives and Pentagon lodge brothers onto the taxpayers. Dingell and company went through the whole grand swindle. There was the $67,500 company contribution to Air Force General J. T. Edwards's wife's art club. And the $53,268 bash at the posh Breakers Hotel in Palm Beach; the $10,220 for fancy gift pen and pencil sets; $3,231 for a gathering at the King David Hotel in Jerusalem; $9,100 for Navy baseball caps (top brass got gold scrambled eggs, middle brass got silver, and the hired help plain cloth); $43,672 for an outing at the PGA Sheraton Golf Resort in Palm Beach; $7,085 just for hors d'oeuvres at the same resort; $4,596 to pay for a seminar for executive wives — the bills went on and on endlessly. Pratt and Whitney showed a touching love of hearts and flowers: $813 for corsages at the Fighter Fling Ball and $2,735 for strolling musicians at another party.

The company didn't forget charities to needy politicians who could help out. Candidates for the Florida legislature, the local sheriff, the local supervisor of elections, the Palm Beach County Commission, the county school board — all of them went away happy. And you and I paid the bill.

Spanton testified that these corporate thieves even billed the government *twice* for many of these expenses. Over the years, he said, Pratt and Whitney "duplicated two million, nine hundred thousand dollars in various general and administrative expenses." When caught, the company had paid the money back. When George asked for an investigation of this fraud, the DCAA doctored his report, trying to reduce its impact, then passed it on with his original signature.

What did the hearings accomplish? They probably ensured the success of the legislators' "constant dollar freeze" on the Pentagon, and they were the high point of congressional resistance to Reagan's profligate spending.

Enough was enough, though. The administration wasn't going to take any more of this exposure to the cold winds blowing on the Hill. It refused to let FBI Special Agent Cavanaugh testify, on the excuse that it had reopened Cavanaugh's investigation of Pratt and Whitney, which was therefore "ongoing." (Actually, no new investigation took place.)

In addition, the Air Force refused to clear my statement — about how the Pentagon's audit and investigative organizations performed in internally controversial situations — for open publication. The Air Force's final verdict was that I could testify at Dingell's hearing but that any testimony I gave about my first-hand experience wouldn't be cleared except "for security purposes." This again left me vulnerable to the private damage suits Chip Terrill had warned me about, so I did not testify.

A good thing, too. Later investigation by Dingell's staff showed that my bosses were just waiting for me to slip up. The Air Force general counsel and several subcontractors discussed how Pratt and Whitney could sue Colin Parfitt and me for releasing Pratt's formulas for pricing spare parts and engines. We didn't release the formulas, but Senator Proxmire did. The Pentagon plotters had no stomach for taking him on, however.

Other traps were set (several are outlined in Major Jim Wolfe's diary of events during the period). I managed to avoid any misstep, but once again the administration, both in my case and in Cavanaugh's, had denied Congress information and had gotten away with it.

12

☆ ☆ ☆

The Phoenix Flop
and Other Horror Stories

POOR RICHARD'S DEFENSE INDUSTRY Productivity/Quality Network was distinguished both by its breezy style and by the unintended opportunities it provided for insights into the motives of its correspondents. The messages were almost always edifying. For instance, the July 2, 1986, alert from Poor Richard (Stimson) himself:

> Here we go again! The AF [Air Force] conducted a "tear down" of a missile. They found a large number of minor discrepancies — none of them critical to operation.
> So what's the Problem? — Fitzgerald participated in the review.
> I'll make a bet that "horrer" [sic] story on quality will hit the papers soon. If you like that bit, how 'bout another bit that a congressial [sic] hearing will also be in the wind.
> It seems like AF likes to shoot themselves in the foot. If they take the position that there is a big problem, why didn't the AFPRO catch it earlier? If they take the position that there is no problem, then it's the classic cover-up with Fitzgerald blowing the whistle. Either way the industry loses.

Here we have Poor Richard, a high Defense Department official, not exactly worried about a bad missile but much concerned about bad publicity for "the industry." In this case the part of the industry he referred to (but was too delicate to name) was the Hughes Aircraft enterprise at Air Force Plant 44 in Tucson, Arizona. That plant reminded me of the traditional saying of British drill sergeants as they looked over a bunch of awkward recruits: "I don't think you'll scare the enemy, but by God, *you do scare me!*"

Poor Richard seemed sensitive to one of our group's small successes. Our efforts had contributed to the shutting down of Plant 44 because of poor-quality work. I'd kept in mind my 1982 visit and the serious problems we turned up then. With the valuable help of Ompal Chauhan, we kept trying to pierce the Blue Curtain whenever we could to track the quality problems at Hughes. In April 1983 Tom Amlie and I had made another visit, meeting privately with a civilian named Al Colt, who was deputy quality control chief at Plant 44.

Colt didn't deny or downplay any of our observations. He just shrugged. Getting a little annoyed, I told him that when I was a young quality control engineer, the Air Force had shut down my employer's plant for far less serious shortcomings than the ones in Plant 44.

"Are you suggesting I should shut Hughes down?" Colt asked incredulously.

"Damn right," I said. "Why not?"

Colt just laughed; he wouldn't say anything more.

Over the next months we kept hearing horror stories of astonishingly high costs and astonishingly bad quality. One constant source was John Long, an investigative reporter for the *Arizona Star* in Tucson. Many Hughes employees had gone to him with such stories, and urged us to meet with some of them.

In January 1984 Colin Parfitt and I made another visit to Tucson. In our long first day reviewing the plant, we found the situation as bad as or worse than it had been before. And the Air Force plant representative was downright obstructionist.

At midnight that night my telephone rang. The caller identified himself as a young Air Force officer who had been in on some of the day's meetings and had seen how the AFPRO was stonewalling. He'd agonized over making this call, but he'd finally decided he must. "What's going on out there is sabotage," he said. We were on the right track, asking the right questions, and we shouldn't give up until we got answers. He'd do what he could behind the scenes to help — but if his superiors suspected he was even sympathetic to us, his career would be finished.

John Long led us to some excellent sources, most of whom we met at his home. One of them was seriously ill and in the hospital, where John arranged for us to talk with him and his wife. From what this man said, Hughes seemed to have had a quality-control collapse (along with its cost-control collapse), and the Air Force plant representative was helping cover it up.

If Hughes had trouble building a high-tech missile, it was still very good at building a low-tech stone wall. We finally went away frustrated, with plenty of disturbing information from clandestine informants but no objective, documentary evidence with which we could make a case to the Air Force.

Tom Amlie thought he had a roundabout method. Among his very good contacts in the Navy acquisition organization was the chief of naval materiel, a four-star admiral named Steve White. Tom was convinced that White was committed to stopping the flow of shoddy equipment and weapons to the fleet. As it turned out, Admiral White needed our information more than the other way around. He had heard nothing but good reports — "happy talk" — about the Navy's Phoenix missile being produced at Hughes's Plant 44. This had raised some questions in his mind, so he asked Tom Amlie for a special out-of-channels report for his eyes only. It was so secret that it was typed with Tom's fingers only, and it went directly to White.

At the time I was trying, without success, to get Secretary Orr and Acting Assistant Secretary Dick Harshman to do something to correct the cost problems and the less well documented quality problems in Tucson. But in early June 1984 we had a breakthrough. Out of the blue, I had a telephone call from John McGee, whom I'd met through Senator Proxmire in 1969. John had been a Navy fuel inspector who had blown the whistle on some big-time fuel thieves in Southeast Asia and had gotten into serious trouble thereby. Proxmire had headed off the worst of the reprisals, but John had had to get out of the fuel inspection business. After a long time in do-nothing jobs, he had found a place in the Navy as a quality control specialist and had since worked up to a supervisory position at the Navy Fleet Missile Test Center at Point Mugu, California.

McGee was in charge of a group of Navy quality specialists who traveled around the country doing "tear-down" inspections. They would select a missile that had been accepted by the contractor's quality control system and by the Navy's contract administration organization (the counterpart of the Air Force's AFPRO). The completed missile would be disassembled under scrutiny and reinspected by John's team.

McGee told me that one of his crews had just completed the tear-down of an AIM 54-C, the latest version of the Phoenix, at the Hughes operation in Tucson. They had found thousands of deficiencies. "It was just junk," he said.

He had written a report on all this, but it was bottled up somewhere in the Navy department. The worst of it was that the AFPRO, acting on behalf of the Navy and with full knowledge of the Navy technical representative at Plant 44, was still accepting the Phoenix missiles being built for the Navy as if the tear-down had never happened. Could we, John wanted to know, get the information through to some top people?

That was where John's pressing problem and Tom's connection with Admiral White came together. Tom took a copy of John's report to White, who, without revealing that he had read it, requested a copy from his own organization. When this hit the fans in the Navy and Air Force procurement bureaucracies, the consternation was extreme. But nobody could see a way to deny the request of a four-star admiral.

White responded to the report decisively: as of June 22, 1984, the Navy would accept no more Phoenix missiles from Plant 44 until further notice. On September 10 Verne Orr wrote a memorandum to Secretary Weinberger noting the consequent events leading to a temporary shutdown at Air Force Plant 44:

> Results of the Navy review prompted the Air Force to tear down a Maverick missile in early July and the Army followed with a similar inspection of the TOW missile [Phoenix, Maverick, and TOW were the principal products at Plant 44]. The tear-down of the Maverick showed quality problems similar to the Phoenix missile. The Air Force stopped acceptance of the Maverick on August 3 and issued the 90-day cure notice which put Hughes on notice that their quality assurance program could be disapproved if satisfactory progress was not made.
>
> We now had a plant-wide problem and each program had a common discrepancy — poor workmanship caused by systemic operating problems. Hughes finally recognized this fact and, on August 9, they suspended final assembly of all three missiles . . . so as to begin a major management push to correct their poor operating procedures and practices. As part of this action, they notified their suppliers to stop shipments until Hughes's management could review the quality of the items. Subsequent to Hughes stopping production, agreement among the three services led to suspending progress payments. After notice of intent on August 21, Hughes was advised by the administrative contracting officer on August 27 of the actual 100 percent suspension. Hughes has complained that the government action was inappropriate and would result in an unwarranted detriment to our national defense. I feel continued acceptance of poor quality products is more detrimental and cannot be tolerated.

A logical man reading this might conclude that the Attic Fanatics and their friends had been vindicated — but Orr couldn't quite bring himself to say that. Politicians and bureaucrats are not notable for giving credit where it's due. Orr did write in his memo, "It is apparent that early signals from our reviews of the Hughes Tucson facility indicated that the company's manufacturing and quality assurance programs were suspect and that lack of aggressive follow-up by both Hughes' management and the Air Force Contract Management organization allowed the production and quality deficiencies to continue."

The scary part was that Hughes, though the worst of the lot we'd seen, was not alone. The "systemic operating problems" and "lack of aggressive follow-up by . . . contract management organization" applied to many other shoddy giants in the defense contracting business.

At Orr's request I wrote another report summarizing our past recommendations. This resulted in a meeting with Orr, Harshman, and Tom Cooper, assistant secretary in charge of research and procurement.

The one problem we three subordinates — Cooper, Harshman, and I — agreed on most strongly was the AFPROs; we had to stop putting job-hunting colonels in charge of AFPRO detachments in the plants. It almost always happened that they went native and began to represent the contractor rather than the government. A good example was the plant representative who had obstructed our earlier efforts at Hughes, although, to be fair, he was under orders to do that. By this time he had retired from the Air Force and had moved down the hall to his new office as a Hughes executive. He was just one of many.

Orr said yes, it was unwise, but then in a plaintive voice asked, "I've got more than six thousand colonels; where can I put them?"

We made some strong recommendations for correction, but when the time for action came, Orr allowed himself to be shunted aside by the military who recommended — of course, of course — a blue-ribbon commission. I wrote to Verne to give him an idea of what we could expect from this august body. It would:

1. Change the subject by performing a worldwide "study" of truly cosmic problems, avoiding all particulars, most especially the specific problem that led to the blue-ribbon commission in the first place.

2. Buy time by taking as long as possible to perform the worldwide study. Other issues will arise that will command the attention of people previously concerned about the collapse of quality control at Hughes, and everybody will forget about it, permitting an early return to business as usual.

3. Ensure bland results by properly selecting the blue-ribbon commissioners. Make sure the chairman, at least, has a vested interest in preserving the status quo. Make sure that the majority of the other commissioners have similar conflicts of interest.

Air Force colonels do not become generals on the strength of a great sense of humor. AFSC Commander General Larry Skantze was furious at my little satire. At a blustery meeting with Verne Orr, my bosses, and me, he said he was outraged that I'd even suggest such things. He ended his remarks by promising that we'd have a "full report" on the Hughes debacle by December 1.

So far as I know, Skantze never delivered it. What he did do was appoint the former vice commander of the Air Force Systems Command, retired Air Force Lieutenant General George Sylvester, to head the blue-ribbon commission. General Sylvester fitted neatly into point 3 of my memo. In his former position, he'd been the architect of the mess he was now supposed to look into. Nowadays he was a consultant to the acquisition community. The other commissioners were mostly ciphers, but not without conflicts of interest.

As for point 2, the commission took a very long time to do its thing, whatever that was. Actually, it was never clear when the commission finished its work. As people forgot the Hughes scandal, the commission just faded away. As for my point 1, many months later we got a clue to its performance when we saw a few skimpy Vu-Graph charts showing that the commission had toured the country having philosophical bull sessions with AFPROs and "experts." There was no evidence that it had ever faced the problem. Skantze's blue-ribbon troops had fulfilled my predictions to a T, but somehow he never got around to thanking me.

I kept itching to get back to quality control — a field where I'd enjoyed some successes early in my career. The issue was a fascinating one. John McGee and others reported that Plant 44's quality had improved somewhat but that throughout the industry the DoD was still accepting products that did not meet contractual specifications. The services either lived with defective products, repaired them themselves, or gave the erring contractors profitable repair contracts to fix their own mistakes.

Surely, I thought, the military and I would have a common viewpoint on this. Even if they cared nothing about costs, they must be concerned about malfunctioning weapons and planes. But, I am sad to say, Admiral White was the only man we ever detected among the high brass who showed the kind of concern warranted by the quality problem.

One of Richard Carver's ways of trying to neutralize the Attic Fanatics was to appoint something called the "Private Sector Cost Management Group" (Private Sector Group, for short), which was made up of businessmen and professors and, especially, people he wanted to flatter. Carver's deputy, Eric Thorson, a political appointee, was a sort of general secretary and chaperon to this group as it traveled around the country listening to briefings by the contractor companies and military bureaucrats.

One day in 1986 Carver decided that I should take part in this by briefing the group on the cost and quality problems at Hughes pre-shutdown, that is, 1982–1984. I was to speak to them in Tucson on June 20 and provide a kind of "before" picture to contrast with the brilliant "after" picture that management and the Air Force would draw, according to the word I got from Eric Thorson.

I found, however, that the good news came first: the AFPRO briefers said there was a "basically positive trend." The Phoenix C missile (AIM 54-C) now showed up with an average of only four defects per hundred inspections, whereas in June 1985 the average had been thirteen and a half.

The AFPRO briefer described the tear-down procedure, now required for all programs, and said that an IIR Maverick guidance and control system torn down earlier in the year had disclosed only three minor defects. My own information was that the tear-down had been completed just a few days earlier and that over three hundred defects had been found. He went on to say that a Phoenix tear-down was in progress. I learned that evening from my sources that it had taken place about two weeks before and had turned up 2,578 defects, some of which could have caused mission failure. The AFPRO had been informed of this but wasn't telling.

I asked some questions. The AFPRO briefers looked fearful and responded evasively. After each question the Hughes executives present would whisper among themselves. Then I would back off and soften the challenge, and they would look relieved. I was determined to stay on my best behavior and learn all I could.

Next came the Hughes dog-and-pony show. It was easy to tell the Hughes briefers from the Air Force people: their Vu-Graphs had more color and were generally better. And they were wearing much better suits.

They were full of equally good news. The first Hughes man said that Maverick production was being moved to the La Grange, Georgia, plant, with some of the work to be done in the Eufaula, Alabama, plant in Congressman Bill Dickinson's district. As he said that, the briefer looked intently at me as if to say, "So there!"

As for quality-control problems "beginning in June 1984," Hughes management had recognized them and had shut down the Tucson plant in August (no mention of our 1982, 1983, and 1984 warnings). "Now, we're doing very well," said the briefer, and declared that the Air Force had reported their defect rate the lowest — by a factor of two — of all plants the Air Force oversaw for contract management.

Ken Richardson of Hughes then said we'd probably hear something about the Navy's recent tear-down of a Phoenix C. A full report was expected within two weeks, but early findings showed that there were no final hardware problems, no new problems, and that the results overall were "rather good." Seventy-five percent of the defects had to do with solder joints. In 1982 we had found that Hughes's workers didn't know how to solder, and apparently they still didn't. The clincher was that Will Willoughby (the Navy's civilian quality control guru in Washington) and Admiral Wilkerson, commander of the Naval Air Systems Command, had said there was nothing to indicate trouble with Hughes's products. The AFPRO people present didn't comment on the Phoenix tear-down.

I skipped the scheduled social activities that evening to meet with John McGee and his ace tear-down supervisor, Fred Maloney. They produced documentary and photographic evidence to show that of the 2,578 Phoenix defects they had found, 106 were extremely serious — even more serious because they had all turned up on a single guidance and control system.

Along with the systemic problems that we had been familiar with for years, there were some new ones in accounting for the configuration status, or design documentation, of the missile and in quality control by Hughes's suppliers. In fact, a legal inquiry was being made into reports that one supplier had deliberately shipped defective products.

In my briefing to the Private Sector Group and the AFPRO people, scheduled for eight to ten-thirty the next morning, I intended to stress the importance of giving top management timely notice of the truth, the whole truth, and nothing but the truth on weapons development and production. My case study was Hughes-Tucson: the evidence-of-trouble stage, which lasted from about May 1982 to May 1984; the facing-facts stage, from June to August 1984; and the follow-up stage, from September 1984 on.

I also intended to declare that a new cover-up was taking place. To support that, I'd asked the two Navy inspectors, McGee and Maloney, to come to the meeting with their Phoenix findings, including enlarged color photographs of some of the more significant defects.

Carver and his group were openly hostile to my message, but when John and Fred joined us, the hostility turned into fear and loathing. After a quick, whispered conference, Carver and Colonel Westover, the plant representative, ordered the inspectors out of the meeting room.

Eric Thorson and I followed them into the hall. Eric apologized profusely, handing them his card and saying he was available to help if they felt any repercussions from the incident.

When I returned to the meeting, the discussion soon degenerated into personal attacks on me. While our procurement community had been doing a great job, people like me had been putting out negative reports that hurt our image and hindered improvement. Then the group further degenerated into the standard Republican-businessman Congress-bashing.

Carver returned to my case with the assertion that I had accused General Skantze of being in "the contractors' hip pocket." When I denied saying that, Carver said that the charge showed up in my writing about the way the Troika had watered down the application guidance for work measurement.

Apparently maddened by such an indictment, one of the Private Sector Group, a very large and blustery type, threatened to attack me. He was an Ohio businessman named Sy Laughter, who remarked loudly, "If we weren't on government property, I'd grab you by the scruff of the neck and kick you out of here. I'd kick your ass good." His respect for United States property was a sentiment I found very touching. Since Sy was at least six inches taller and fifty pounds heavier than I, I tried to mollify him before I was asked to leave.

After I'd returned to my quarters, Colonel Westover came to try to smooth things over. After explaining that he wanted to "work the problems" at Plant 44 himself, he began to question me. He was especially curious about one thing. In the course of defending myself against the mob in the meeting room, I'd let slip something that John and Fred had told me: every single Phoenix 54-C missile was in storage because of defective target detection devices and fuses. The Navy had been willing to pay Hughes for them, but as for putting them in the fleet — no thanks. Westover said this information was extremely "close hold." Of course it was.

Back in Washington I tried as usual to rock the boat toward corrective action. I told both Carver and Harshman that our office had a responsibility in the matter of the defective missiles. And again I predicted that both the Navy and AFPRO would get their whitewash buckets out. My recommendation was that we put back into effect my office's program called Quality Control and Cost Control at Point of Payment, which Carver had mothballed. Carver didn't remember the program. Harshman said he'd take it up with the acquisition people, which was like asking the usual suspects to help solve the crime.

Admiral Steve White, his job abolished by Secretary of the Navy John

Lehman, was long gone. That left Will Willoughby as the Navy's quality expert. When I talked with him, he assured me that he had indeed given Hughes a clean bill of health. His message to the company was, "You're all right, keep going, get better."

How could he say that, I asked, in the face of the hard evidence — photographic and documentary — that his tear-down team had discovered?

Well, he could say that because the Phoenix C field results were good. The fleet had assured him that there were no operational problems with the missile.

Of course the fleet's not having problems, I said. The fleet doesn't have any Phoenix 54-C's.

Not doing very well on these lines, Willoughby shifted to what he considered the main trouble: the quality inspection results being "blown out of proportion," the "irresponsible reporting by the press," "too many people reporting irresponsibly."

I noted that the recent Phoenix problems had not been in the press at all.

Well, there were his inspectors. He wanted them to have broad latitude to look at such things as soldering — actually, he didn't think that was a real problem — but if the adverse reports kept coming in, he'd have to put some restrictions on the inspectors. "If I have to cut them back, I will," said Willoughby.

As it turned out, the reports did keep coming, and McGee and the other Navy tear-down inspectors were ordered to stop counting defects. They could still look for defects and find them, but they had to be sorted into categories and only the categories reported.

But to go back to Poor Richard's plaintive message in 1986 that began this tale: everything he said was wrong. The Navy conducted the tear-down, not the Air Force. The Navy did, in fact, find "discrepancies" critical to the operation. Fitzgerald did not participate in the review. The tear-down did not produce a "horror story," at least not then. And finally, "the industry" did not lose.

It did not lose what it ought to have lost — its indifference to production blunders — apparently because there were no powers in the Pentagon honest enough to find and use a big stick.

In the early months of 1985, the Pentagonal spenders had been taking a battering on Capitol Hill. Back home, the folks around the country were disturbed by all the news of procurement ripoffs and kept writing their congressmen. Maybe they didn't understand what a large, complicated thing like a Maverick missile should cost, but they knew about hammers and pliers. And it was perfectly clear in Keokuk that dog boarding, big parties at luxury resorts, and strolling musicians didn't do much to fend off the Evil Empire.

In *The High Priests of Waste* in 1972, I had predicted, "Once the great majority of exploited taxpayers understand that the Pentagon is far and away the biggest protector of welfare chiselers and law-and-order violators, some of the same, hot indignation that has settled upon the hapless welfare mothers will be directed against military waste."

By 1985 Grassley had prepared his case and was ready to apply the Freeze to the Pentagon budget. To be truthful, the Freeze was not much more than a sharp frost. It was being imposed on a very high budget that had almost doubled since Reagan took office, and it was stated in "constant dollars," meaning that the budget limit was allowed to rise with inflation. There was small danger of hypothermia in the Pentagon.

The story of the figures is interesting. The administration, foreseeing a freeze attempt, first put out the story that Weinberger had proposed a "rock bottom" budget of $334 billion for FY 1986, $40 billion above the previous year's budget (all figures in this passage refer to OMB's "Total National Defense" account, which includes substantial non-DoD sums). Then there were tales that Cap Weinberger had suffered savage slashes — down to $324.8 billion before Reagan stepped in to protect the DoD.

The Senate rebels weren't hoodwinked, and Robert Dole knew it; Grassley staffers even said he was secretly sympathetic. Seeing that he was in for a fight, Dole, with the other Republican leaders, got the request down to $313.3 billion, which was about $10 billion more than the then-current budget.

In the climactic debate, reported in the May 2, 1985, *Congressional Record*, Grassley and his allies cited all the horror stories, from Fursten the executive dog to billion-dollar overruns. But meanwhile Grassley, Kolesnik, and company were doing what politicians do when they are really serious: dealing behind the scenes. They had already persuaded Dole to schedule the debate while Reagan was on his trip to the Nazi war cemetery in Bitburg, West Germany.

After a motion by Senator Goldwater to table had been defeated, Dole laughed and said, according to a reliable witness, "It's now five minutes after midnight in Bitburg, too late to place a call and have him come over." (The *Congressional Record* showed Dole saying Bonn, not Bitburg, but I like my witness's version. He said the *Record* was revised before it was printed.) With Reagan sound asleep in the Federal Republic, the Senate invoked the Freeze by voice vote.

*   *   *

The aftermath for me was another retaliation attempt by Richard Carver. To make a complicated story simple, he used my evaluation report in an attempt to get rid of me. His rating can be summarized as "Does not work and play well with others." That was so outrageous that Dingell came to the rescue with an investigation, and Orr was forced to overrule Carver.

Despite such unpleasant diversions, the Dingell detail was becoming very productive. We were completing a successful investigation of the procurement practices that were used to justify the enormously expensive "support equipment," which meant ordinary tools for the most part. Chuck Woerhle had uncovered some of this two years earlier, and Senator Roth had publicized the matter, but they had run into a stout Pentagon stone wall.

Dingell was not so easily put off. Because his oversight responsibilities included the accounting practices of publicly traded companies, his subcommittee was interested in that old fantasy, equal allocation of overhead. Colin Parfitt and I told them, first, it had never existed, and second, even its ghost was thoroughly discredited. But the members wanted to prove that for themselves. In the end this turned into one of the most enlightening investigations I'd ever worked on. The GAO was helping us, too, and after an unproductive start, they finally did an excellent job.

On September 19, 1985, Dingell wrote Caspar Weinberger a letter with a list of charges too lengthy to repeat here, but the general charge was "fraudulent intent" on the part of contractors. Taking up the "equal allocation" question, Dingell said:

> It is important for you to understand that the GAO debunked a phony idea widely spread by some Air Force generals that the $435 hammer is a result of the "equal allocation of overhead" to these parts which are of minimum intrinsic value. The 12-cent Allen wrench did not increase to $9,606 by the "equal allocation of overhead" — *General Dynamics and Westinghouse actually charged engineering time to the wrench that resulted in that kind of price.* According to an examination of the labor records, Westinghouse charged 63 hours of engineering time to develop a 3-inch piece of common wire for $14,835 — a tool officially dubbed an assembly pin when Westinghouse had been using a wooden peg for five years for the same purpose.

In short, it took seven engineers a total of sixty-three hours to design a straight, three-inch piece of wire. No, there is nothing arcane about its composition or function — it's just plain wire. Their engineering design drawing is reproduced on page 212.

Spare parts — the actual pieces of engines, missiles, or planes — were

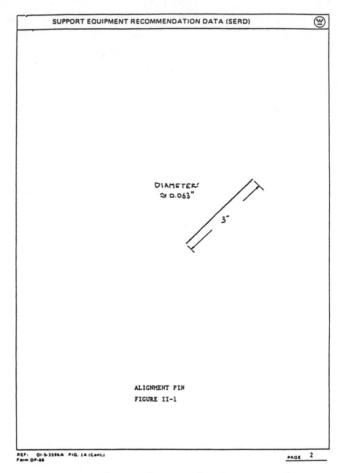

Engineering design drawing for the Westinghouse assembly pin.

priced by formula, and illustrated the degree of overpricing of the big stuff. Tools, on the other hand, were priced individually and separately after long negotiation. The tool-buying process, then, offered a good chance to understand just how Pentagon procurement rules work, because tools are bought in the same way as the big stuff.

One of the best-documented examples is a piece of F-16 support equipment called a pulley puller, which cost $8,832 (see the photo and cost chronology on page 214). Many readers will recognize that such a too, used to remove wheels, pulleys, gears, and so on, can be bought commercially for about five to fifteen dollars. If you were to buy one, you would most likely find that it had two longitudinal slots in place of the two outer holes shown on the F-16 model. In addition, the commercial model would have a selection of sizes of the two outer machine screws or bolts to be screwed into the part to be pulled off. The body of the puller would also have slots for the outer screws to accommodate varying distances between holes in different pulleys. In short, your hardware-store pulley puller would be much more versatile than the F-16 tool, which accepts only one size of machine screw.

If, instead of buying a pulley puller, you decided to make one, you'd take a steel bar of approximately the correct cross-section, cut it to the right length, drill the three holes, tap the center hole to accept a threaded jack screw, and buy two machine screws and a jack screw. Presto!

As a test we decided to have a pulley puller custom made, so Tom Amlie called Jon Williams, owner of a first-rate aerospace machine shop near Dallas, on a Friday afternoon with an "emergency" order. The pulley puller shown on page 214 arrived from Dallas at Tom's home in Bethesda, Maryland, on Sunday morning, less than forty-eight hours after the order was placed. Its corners were neatly chamfered, the whole assembly had an attractive, gold-colored protective finish, and it worked perfectly.

Jon had given the order to his foreman on Friday and was given the finished product thirty-six minutes later. Picked up at the shop, the tool would have cost $25. On this emergency basis, the total cost, including profit and air express charges, was $69.

Compare this with the Air Force record. The Air Force placed its order on September 21, 1982, nine days before the end of the fiscal year, when funds had to be obligated before they expired. It then waited seventeen months for delivery and paid $8,832 for the item. Then the Air Force found out that its pulley pullers didn't even work!

This was bad, but even worse was that this "price justification" meant that the Air Force might pay the same $8,832 apiece, or more, for any reorder. Since the F-16 tool was a "unique design," it was probably claimed to be "proprietary," so we would have to buy it from Westinghouse through negotiation rather than get competitive bids. There would probably be some inflation between the time of the original purchase and the reorder, and the Air Force buyers would raise the price to account for that. And what about the cost of redesigning the pulley puller to make it work? Would the next shipment cost $10,000 apiece? $15,000?

Chronology of the General Dynamics pulley puller.

Jan. 18, 1982	General Dynamics recommends pulley puller to the Air Force	No price given
Sept. 21, 1982	Air Force places sole-source order because of "urgency"	No price given
Nov. 17, 1982	Original price proposal	$10,630
July 12, 1983	Revised price proposal	13,717
Feb. 23, 1984	Pulley puller delivered to Air Force	No price given
Feb. 28, 1984	Second revised price proposal	9,007
Mar. 19, 1984	Price negotiated by Air Force	8,832
May 14, 1984	Price "definitized" (put in contract)	8,832

According to the report prepared for the GAO, "This item does not work as intended. The pulley puller delivered has a bolt head requiring a screwdriver rather than a wrench, which does not allow the user to get enough torque to remove the pulley."

SERD 74966, the F-16 pulley puller.

Pulley puller custom made by Jon Williams's machine shop.

Patrice Earley

The important point is that the pulley puller transaction was perfectly regular. When the participants were questioned about it, they were outraged. They had meticulously followed all the procurement rules, hadn't they? In appearance before the Dingell subcommittee on September 23, 1985, General Dynamics Vice President Frederick Wood, a former Air Force procurement officer, stoutly defended the deal.

He displayed a huge flow chart depicting sixty-five steps designed to give the tool a proper pedigree and make sure it worked as intended. The fact that it didn't work was not important — it had been certified. General Dynamics had a signed compatibility test report, witnessed by three contractor experts and a government representative, certifying that the item was "suitable for the purpose intended." Not functional, just suitable.

The big price tag didn't bother Frederick Wood, either. He explained that his duty was to observe the rules and follow the set procedures. The price was just a natural outcome of that. Here is an exchange from the subcommittee hearing:

MR. DINGELL: Do you have a duty to see to it that these things are done in the most cost-effective fashion?

MR. WOOD: I would have to say no, then. I would like to explain why, then.

MR. DINGELL: When you tell us you don't have a duty to do it in the most cost-effective fashion, I think you not only have the right, but the duty to explain why you make that statement.

MR. WOOD: I think it is incumbent upon all of us to develop a process that would result in the most cost-effective way of doing business. In many ways, the processes we use in any part of the government are not specifically designed to be the most cost-effective.

Air Force Brigadier General Ronald Yates, the F-16 systems program director when the pulley puller was bought, was even more hard-nosed on the defensive. He didn't at all like Secretary Orr's request for a refund from the company after the ripoff had become embarrassing. When the GAO interviewed him on February 26, 1985, Yates said that he couldn't see anything in the data to support a refund request. Questioned further on this by Congressman Gerry Sikorski on September 23, 1985, General Yates said, "The straightforward answer is that in fact they spent the cost incurred. We knew that."

Now recall that the Pentagon rule is that the specific negotiated price should be close to what it actually costs the contractor to make or buy the item plus a percentage of the cost as profit. That was the basis of

Yates's defense. But the Air Force waited until March 19, 1984, more than three weeks after the pulley pullers had been delivered, to negotiate the $8,832 price. This gave them good "actuals" — costs that could then be audited by the Air Force and the DCAA. The chart reflects the zany way the final figure was arrived at.

First General Dynamics and Westinghouse proposed a price of $9,007 each for the pulley pullers. Our astute Pentagon negotiators were not to be fooled that easily, though. They *knew* that the actuals, as audited by the Air Force and the DCAA, came to $5,384. Now entered a mysterious figure: $246 to "finish" each pulley puller. Finish what? The defective tools had already been delivered. The Air Force had approved them, so Westinghouse hadn't the least intention of altering them to make them usable.

Then came the previously approved markups for G & A (general and administrative expenses), the cost of money (interest), and profit. The total was now a "fair and reasonable" cost to Westinghouse of $7,009 for each little gadget. For the frosting, General Dynamics got $789 per item just for dealing with its own subcontractor plus a profit of $1,034 for each item.

At this point some inquisitive busybody might ask who really made the things in the first place, and where? The answer was not General Dynamics, and not Westinghouse, but a subcontractor machine shop. Possibly because it is harder to find a machine shop to make defective pulley pullers than one that turns out something usable, the machine shop charged the rather high price of $353. That charge is hidden under the misleading accounting label "material."

Was General Yates fazed by any of this information? Not at all. He told GAO that if the Air Force had walked down to the corner hardware store and bought *x* number of pulley pullers off the shelf for $25, they would not have saved any money. That was because the related engineering and testing costs now on the bill would be shifted to a "sustaining engineering" charge that the Air Force would eventually pay for anyway.

This is one of the wonderful effects of the "full absorption accounting principle," which allows favored big contractors to take all allowable costs of doing business and distribute them willy-nilly onto all the work going through their plants.

When the GAO audited the General Dynamics refund ordered by Verne Orr, they found that the company had recorded a separate 359 engineering hours for the Westinghouse support-tool work but had excluded them from the final price proposal. Nevertheless, those hours "are used as a basis for progress payments by the Air Force on the F-16

The GAO's breakdown of the Westinghouse pulley-puller price[a] buildup.

	Hours	Cost
Engineering	31	$1,042
Create drawings	37	1,157
Subtotal		2,199
Manufacturing	44	1,501
Subtotal		3,700
Product management	36	1,292
Subtotal	148	4,992
Material		353
Subtotal		5,345
Allocated costs		211
Subtotal		5,556
Adjustment		−172
Subtotal		5,384[b]
Estimate to complete		246
G and A		613
Cost of money		28
Profit		638
Total Westinghouse costs		7,009
General Dynamics charges		789
Subtotal		7,798
General Dynamics profit		1,034
Total negotiated price		8,832

a. Price = cost plus profits. $7,009 is cost to General Dynamics of Westinghouse subcontract. GD adds "subcontract administration" costs of $789 and profit of $1,034 to arrive at its price to the Air Force of $8,832.
b. "Costs incurred" at time of negotiation.

contracts. . . . Therefore, the Air Force could end up paying the cost for these hours even though they were excluded from the proposed and negotiated price." (As the cost breakdown chart shows, General Dynamics charged $33.61 per engineering hour. That meant an additional hidden charge of $12,065.)

What if the Air Force simply made such tools in its own shops? The

GAO reported: "Four items were locally manufactured by the Air Force and the SPO [Systems Program Office] was billed $995 for these items. In contrast, General Dynamics had proposed a total price of $41,514 for the items, or a difference of $40,515."

Having produced this eloquent illustration of how the procurement system works as to support equipment, the Dingell staff decided to go back to the spare parts conundrum, especially to the important point that each expensive part fits into a proportionately expensive whole. Stockton preferred not to use our former examples; he wanted something new and exciting.

On a Sunday afternoon late in 1985, he called me and asked, "What do you think about a $317 piss pan?" He explained that this item, properly called a toilet pan, looked something like an oversize fiberglass cafeteria tray, about twenty-nine inches long and two and a quarter inches deep. It slid under the toilet of the C-5A transport plane to catch any splash or overflow.

Reluctant though I was to have anything more to do with the C-5 turkey, I finally agreed to visit the Air Force repair depot at San Antonio with the Dingell investigators. There we found the generals and their assistants rather proud of their toilet pan — at least proud of the fact that it now cost only $286.75. They had pushed Lockheed down from the $317 demanded, they said. This time, the Air Force people had made their own estimate of what Lockheed would spend on manufacturing the pan. But we saw a flaw in the usual stack-up of costs. The cost subdivisions, or "cost elements," in the Air Force estimate were radically different from those in the Lockheed estimates I had seen.

Under questioning, the Air Force analysts admitted that they had made up the numbers. After estimating that it would take 1.92 standard hours to manufacture each article, and adding the cost of material, they had simply plugged in some finagle factors to make their estimate approximate Lockheed's cost. Nobody at the depot could see anything wrong with that.

We decided to move on to the next toilet pan stop, Air Force Plant 6, at Marietta, Georgia, where Lockheed assembled C-5s. First we had to sit through the tribal ceremony of the boiler-plate briefings. I recognized one of the briefers as an old acquaintance, Reginald Andrews, a senior, influential civilian in the AFPRO. We'd been friendly long ago, but his bosses had so condemned my C-5A activities that I'd assumed that Reg, while knowing the reality, had kept quiet in order to hold onto his job.

Now an amazing thing happened. Right in the middle of his boiler-plate briefing, Reg Andrews began telling the truth. In some detail he told us how Lockheed was ripping off the Air Force once again on C-5B prices. He spoke of his own efforts to inject some sanity into the process, principally his effort to see that Lockheed didn't build projected C-5B prices on top of cost figures that were higher than the actually expected costs. He said there was good evidence that they had made the phony boost on wages and salaries. He said the Air Force audits would prove it if we could only get a look at them.

Hearing this, the Air Force military were in disarray. Colonel Looney, the plant representative, tried hard to change the subject. Reg resisted, and so did we. In the confusion we managed to get hold of Lockheed's actual estimate sheets for the toilet pan. The company's first try added the cost of factory inefficiency in the conversion of standard hours to "actuals." With the usual markups, the price for each pan was $642.35.

But that price had some problems. Herblock's *Washington Post* cartoons had shown Caspar Weinberger with a $640 toilet seat (an earlier horror story) around his neck, an image that had made the DoD acquisition community very sensitive about anything having to do with toilets. In deference, Lockheed had reduced the tag to a "policy price" of $325. The Air Force penny pinchers had then reduced the price to the $317 "last price," and finally to the "better estimate" of $286.75.

The C-5A toilet pan.

Patrice Earley

We had all the information we needed. After making adjustments for errors and omissions by the San Antonio estimators in standard-hour content, I estimated that Lockheed had originally foreseen spending just over $300 per standard hour of output to manufacture the toilet pans.

This corresponded to about $275 per standard hour of output for the manufacture of the whole C-5B under the current contract, as estimated by the AFPRO engineers. (One of the engineers told me privately that I should add $10 or $15 per hour to that figure for costs that had been left out.) Close enough, Stockton and I decided. We might be able to stimulate some cost reduction with the notion that the cost of the C-5B was parallel to the cost of a collection of $600 toilet pans in flight.

Even though only one group of twenty-one aircraft out of the total planned purchase of fifty C-5Bs remained to be negotiated, we had to persuade the Air Force procurement people to do a should-cost study, which they started reluctantly. But first we had to break through the resistance of the Air Force auditor general, who didn't want us to see the reports Reg Andrews had referred to. Then, when it seemed that this study was headed in the usual direction — toward "finding no evidence" of fat — I decided to step in. Should-cost and other estimates were part of my jurisdiction, so I wanted to keep the verdict honest.

In July 1986, when I visited Air Force Plant 6, however, the information I wanted was denied me. It seemed that the Air Force generals had negotiated a back-room agreement with Richard Carver that "should-cost findings cannot be released until an ASD [Aeronautical Systems Division] position is determined and negotiations are complete or the FY 87 [last] option is exercised." In English that reads: after we get this thing wrapped up and signed, we'll let Fitzgerald get a look at it.

On the strength of some in-house Air Force encouragement about saving a few bucks on the despised C-5B, I'd taken on the should-cost matter by myself. Now I had to pay the price and confess failure to Stockton and Dingell's staff. It was worth eating a little crow, however, because they then managed to cut a peephole in the Blue Curtain, and I had a look at the should-cost team's results. They were nearly worthless, and I had to say as much in my critique. We also learned that even though I, the Air Force official legally in charge of such matters, had been denied information, Lockheed had been fully briefed on the team's findings.

On September 17 we had another of those clamorous debates, this time in a Lockheed auditorium, where I was confronted with dozens of

Air Force officers, Air Force civilians, and expensive consultants trying to defend their fruitless results against my critique.

Fortunately for me, John Lynskey, the Air Force deputy chief of pricing (the top civilian in that capacity) was present. He later made an accurate record of my critique and wrote a report that essentially agreed with my findings. Even more fortunately, a draft copy of that report fell into the hands of the Dingell subcommittee before any general could censor it.

The result was that Secretary Richard Carver was now in a vise, one jaw being the Lynskey report and the other being a new discovery by Stockton that Carver was on the payroll of the big investment house of Smith, Barney ("They make money the old fashioned way") while serving as Air Force assistant secretary for financial management. Being paid by the investment house and having access to much inside information — especially as to where "black," or supersecret, contract money was to be spent — Carver represented a potential scandal. Because Dingell had jurisdiction over SEC matters, this question was of concern to him.

Carver was asked to come to the Dingell staff office to explain his situation to Stockton, Mike Barrett, and others. The report to Dingell of this meeting reads:

> On Thursday, October 2, 1986, the subcommittee staff interviewed Air Force Assistant Secretary Richard E. Carver in connection with his ongoing consulting relationship with Smith, Barney. The staff's inquiry into possible conflicts of interest with respect to Mr. Carver's Smith, Barney relationship is ongoing and will be the subject of another memorandum. However, during the interview, Mr. Carver said he wanted to bring us up to date on the fiscal year 1987 C-5B procurement. . . .
>
> Mr. Carver led us to believe that the Air Force might just be on the right track to recouping for the government up to $1 billion in overpricing on the C-5B aircraft. He was full of praise for the subcommittee's work, as well as for the work of his Management Systems Deputy, A. E. Fitzgerald, in focusing the spotlight on this potential waste of money. In contrast, he was highly critical of the "deficient should cost study" recently completed by General Skantze's Air Force Systems Command (AFSC).
>
> Mr. Carver said that before the Air Force opens negotiations with Lockheed on the fiscal year 1987 C-5B — when, according to him, everything including Lockheed's return on investment and DCAA's defective pricing findings would have to be put on the table — a new "should cost" study would have to be done by someone competent to do such an analysis. . . . Throughout this discussion, we were led to

believe that Mr. Fitzgerald would be in charge of the new "should cost" study.

This was a nice example of the soft answer that turneth away wrath — or so they hoped. Neither Carver nor Pete Aldridge, now secretary of the Air Force, had the slightest intention of letting me have a close look at one of their most favored contractors. The next day Carver announced that Eric Thorson would be in charge of the new study. This did not please Dingell's staff:

> From our conversations with Mr. Thorson, it is clear that he has little, if any, experience in such matters, while Mr. Fitzgerald and his associates developed the "should cost" approach in the early 1960's. Furthermore . . . the Air Force's legal agreement with Mr. Fitzgerald specifies he is responsible "at the highest Air Force level" for such studies. Apparently Messrs. Carver and Aldridge simply ignored their legal agreement.

I was permitted to participate in the work under Thorson's supervision, and luckily Eric was a very decent person, and his military assistant, Colonel Jim George, was a highly intelligent and well-motivated officer. We also had some closet patriots on the should-cost team, as well as the powerful backing of Reg Andrews.

Dingell was a great help, too. He brought the toilet pan controversy all the way to the desk of Larry Kitchens, Lockheed's chairman of the board. Haunted by that expensive piece of cheap plastic, Kitchens finally told Dingell he would reduce the price to one dollar if that would satisfy him.

It didn't satisfy me. I used the picture of the toilet pan as a prop in numerous television and newspaper interviews to hammer home the connection between overpriced spare parts and overpriced airplanes.

Finally the ASD team had to swallow their pride and ask Reg Andrews to help them in their renegotiations with Lockheed. In the end, though we didn't get nearly what we should have, the hard work and pressure paid off. The new option price was $1.947 billion, $498 million lower than the previous price. After adjusting for savings they might have had without the should-cost study, the Air Force announced a saving of $273 million.

They had good reason for announcing the lower figure; both Dingell and Proxmire were determined that the savings be returned to the Treasury and not dissipated elsewhere. Even though Lockheed did not return any money on the previous options and managed to keep a lot of fat in the last one, the effort was still worthwhile.

That was the short-term benefit. The long-term benefit of our educational effort was that the high brass could now see very plainly the whole disastrous array of factory inefficiency, excessive rates of pay, specious "engineering" costs, insane overhead charges, and so on. The moral was that we should cut Pentagon unit acquisition prices drastically.

We had done everything we could to educate our leaders, but the question remained: were they educable?

13

☆ ☆ ☆

The Poindexter-Packard
Coup

BY 1985, THE GUERRILLA MOVEMENT in Congress aimed at exposing the
excesses of the military spending machine and trying to curb them was
in full swing. The Pentagon quickly understood the present danger and
wheeled up its big battalions for the attack. Ronald Reagan denounced
the "incessant drumbeat of negativism" he heard coming from Capitol
Hill and the press. The Air Force drafted new plans to interdict
information. FBI agent Cavanaugh's testimony had been blocked. So
had mine. But the Hill tribes were still restless.

Senator Charles Grassley of Iowa, the chief of the congressional
mujaheddin, wanted to freeze the budget. He was one of the few public
figures who had ever understood our message that the spare parts
horrors reflected similar overpricing on the big stuff. In other words, he
fully recognized that military airplanes, for instance, were collections of
vastly overpriced spare parts flying in close formation.

On the other side of the aisle, Senator Proxmire and Richard Kaufman
continued to pursue information developed at their 1984 hearings at
which Amlie, Parfitt, and I had testified, much to the disgust of the Air
Force General Counsel, who threatened us with the possibility of
criminal prosecution if we revealed big contractors' excessive costs.

The Capitol Hill Military Reform Caucus, which included Senators
David Pryor, Charles Grassley, and Nancy Kassebaum, and representatives Denny Smith, Mel Levine, Charles Bennett, and Barbara Boxer was
also harassing the reckless spenders in the Pentagon. A true coalition
from left to right, the Reform Caucus had fastened on the ultimate

defense problem: the Reagan two trillion-dollar spend-up was producing very little in the way of better or better-equipped armed forces. The Pentagonists particularly hated Barbara Boxer because she had shamed them by exhibiting the $7,662 C-5A coffeepot, her symbol of contractor greed and Pentagon profligacy.

John Dingell, a member of the "College of Cardinals" — the committee chairmen who run the show in the House — had also joined the rebels. His exposure of the General Dynamics and Pratt and Whitney scandals in the first few months of 1985 had profoundly changed the politics of questioning Pentagon procurement spending. To the dismay of the old-line congressional establishment, Dingell seemed to have invaded the jurisdiction of the House Armed Services Committee, which had always been the cheerful rich uncle of the military spenders. No more blank checks, Dingell seemed to be saying.

It was time for the Pentagon to mobilize and put down the Hill tribes. The evil rumors of waste and corruption must be buried. How does one handle such a problem? If one is Caspar Weinberger, one first sets up something with a sweetness-and-light name like "Defense Council on Integrity and Management Improvement." To avoid the danger that the group might be influenced by its own name, one appoints a reliable undersecretary of defense like William Howard Taft IV to head it.

But someone like Representative Timothy Wirth always gets the idea wrong and wants to set up a new version of the World War II Truman Commission. Truman described that painful experience, which occurred during his vice presidency, to Merle Miller, his biographer:

> Down at Curtiss-Wright at the airplane plant in Ohio, they were putting defective motors in the planes, and the generals couldn't seem to find anything wrong. So we went down, myself and a couple other senators, and we condemned more than four or five hundred of those engines. And I sent a couple of generals who'd been approving, who'd okayed those engines, to Leavenworth, and I believe they are still there. I certainly hope so.

That specter still haunted the Pentagon. Especially when Wirth's idea for a congressionally directed blue-ribbon commission began to gather support.

Representative Bill Dickinson, ranking Republican on the Armed Services Committee and Reagan's point man on military matters in the House, was worried. The Reaganites were protecting Pentagon waste, but he had supported me, and I was attacking waste. Apparently Dickinson, trying to work out a compromise between the ideas of the Taft figleaf council and the Truman junkyard-dog committee, urged

Reagan to appoint his own blue-ribbon commission. He and the other kingpins on the Armed Services Committee might have been content with the Defense Council on Blah Blah if they hadn't viewed Taft as such a dumbbell. Taft had shown no talent at either substantive reforms or convincing cosmetic actions. Recall that it was Taft who announced that he had cured the spare parts cost horrors by abolishing "equal allocation of overhead" — a method of accounting that had never existed.

Dickinson and his allies got the ball rolling on Reagan's blue-ribbon commission when Robert McFarlane, then head of the National Security Council staff, met with the president and agreed on a "bipartisan" membership. If one happened to be named Caspar Weinberger, one's reactions to this were deeply mixed. The *Washington Post*, on June 8, 1985, commented:

> The Pentagon issued a statement yesterday saying that Weinberger "fully supports the concept of a presidential commission."
>
> But senior Pentagon officials said Weinberger privately opposes the plan, feeling that it is criticism of his stewardship. He indicated his position by encouraging Deputy Defense Secretary William Howard Taft IV to hold a meeting of top Pentagon officials to work out procurement reforms. Weinberger scribbled a note in the margin of a memo from Taft that the meeting might be a "preemptive strike," according to one official.

The President's Blue-Ribbon Commission on Defense Management was established formally on July 15, 1985, by Executive Order 12526. The order immediately accomplished the first two objectives of any blue-ribbon commission: it bought time, by giving the commission nearly a year to work, and it changed the subject, by not mentioning any of the Pentagon bad smells, from overpriced spare parts and weapons systems to defective armament.

The message was clear to anybody who had ever padded a contract cost. It was also clear to *Aviation Week and Space Technology*, which reported on July 22, 1985, that "President Reagan created the commission in response to Congressional concerns that *negative publicity* about military procurement had produced a surplus of reactive, uncoordinated attempts at reform" (emphasis added).

Next came the choice of commission members. By time-honored rule, the majority had to be people strongly biased in favor of the establishment under examination and, furthermore, tainted by gross conflicts of interest. The members chosen by the administration passed this test with flying colors.

In naming David Packard as chairman, the administration couldn't have found a man better equipped with massive conflicts of interest. This multimillionaire industrialist, chairman of the board of Hewlett-Packard, a big defense contractor and a supplier to even bigger contractors, was also a member of Boeing's board of directors. And, as Nixon's deputy secretary of defense, he had managed the billion-dollar Lockheed bailout after the C-5A disaster. (Lockheed, of course, was a customer of Hewlett-Packard.) Packard held such a favored position that he wasn't required to divest himself of his stock in companies that had government contracts.

At the time of the Lockheed affair, the terms of the deal — and Packard's role in it — were not fully understood. Packard managed to make Congress and the press think he was going along quite reluctantly with the government loan guarantee. Behind the scenes, however, he was contriving to give Lockheed over a billion dollars more than the company had coming under the most permissive interpretation of their contracts. In addition, he let Lockheed off the hook when the C-5A transport failed to meet technical requirements. That, in turn, paved the way for another Lockheed bailout of $1.5 billion when the company had to make good its blunders in designing and manufacturing the plane's wings. Because of a media blackout at the time, the only near-contemporaneous account of how all this came about appeared in *The High Priests of Waste*. Apparently that fiscal atrocity was just too awful for the taxpayers to contemplate, so the big-time news people didn't cover it.

At the Pentagon Packard had greatly reduced civilian control over the military contracting community by putting "good" military officers in charge and "letting them alone." By the end of his tour, I had a much more accurate view of David Packard. He detested auditors almost as much as whistle blowers. As head of Hewlett-Packard in the 1960s, Packard had refused to allow the General Accounting Office to audit records of his company's negotiated contracts with the Pentagon. The GAO took the case to court and won, and won again on appeal. That victory may have had a bit to do with Congressman Chet Holifield's drive to halt the GAO from making direct audits of defense contractors, a drive that resulted in the neutering of the congressional watchdog.

The GAO's defense auditing role was then assigned to the Pentagon's Defense Contract Audit Agency, but as soon as Packard became deputy secretary, he set out to geld the DCAA as well. On October 9, 1970, he directed a memo on the defense contract auditor's role to the comptroller and to the Pentagon's chief buyer, both assistant secretaries. The memo said, "We should avoid actions by auditors in their advisory capacity which appear to dispute or question specific decisions of contracting officers." And, just to make sure that no bothersome questions about improper contracting got out, he added, "The escalation of possible disputes relative to specific decisions should be avoided."

When David Packard's appointment was being confirmed by the Senate in 1970, Senator Albert Gore, Sr., argued that Packard couldn't avoid conflict of interest by placing his stock in trust. Gore said:

> What of the economic impact on the value of electronics stock five, ten, fifteen, or twenty years from now, if the Department of Defense, the President, and Congress decide, upon the recommendation of the Department of Defense, to launch upon a multibillion dollar deployment of antiballistic missiles? And what of the conflict of interest involved in the possible loss of value of the stock in case a decision is made to reduce the level of weaponry, and not to deploy ballistic missiles, but to decide upon a program of disarmament?

Packard himself has been quoted as saying, "I have an almost impossible conflict of interest." It didn't bother him much, however.

He very boldly attacked would-be military reformers and cost cutters, of whom I was one of the worst in his eyes. Packard's chance to denounce me publicly came when he reviewed *The High Priests of Waste* in the October 23, 1972, issue of *Business Week*.

What excited Packard most was my suggestion that the military budget should be cut to the point that people would have to make a practice of good stewardship. What was Packard's answer? More generals, fewer cost experts. He wrote:

> With few exceptions, the military services have not assigned well-trained, competent officers to manage important programs.
> Instead, a whole host of "experts" like Fitzgerald had been brought in to tell inexperienced managers how to manage these programs. . . . I felt no need for his [Fitzgerald's] kind of expertise.

Then Packard blamed me for various management schemes, such as CWAS and "total package" contracts, that I had denounced in every possible way. When I read that, my head swam. Here was a man who, without careful editing, might accuse Hitler of being a pacifist or Yassir Arafat of being a nice guy. He saved his hardest rabbit punch for my budget-cutting proposal. He wrote, "This would, no doubt, please the doves in America and the hawks in Moscow and Peking."

The diatribe returned to Packard's familiar theme: "Get rid of all the Monday morning quarterbacks like Fitzgerald. . . . Put *officers* . . . in charge" (my emphasis). And, further, let's have no more annoying schemes like should-cost measurement for reducing contract expense.

As I noted in Chapter 7, Packard was one of the hardy band of big spenders that called themselves the Committee on the Present Danger (CPD). Some of his co-conspirators were such Establishment figures as James Schlesinger, William Casey, John Lehman, Jeane Kirkpatrick, Max Kampelman, Paul Nitze, Richard Allen, Lane Kirkland, William R. VanCleve, and, most important of all, Ronald Reagan. As cochairman of the CPD and one of its most generous financial backers, Packard exerted a weighty influence.

In all, sixty of these present-danger watchers were appointed to high jobs in the Reagan administration, dominating arms control matters and the national security apparatus. The CPD was not shy about making this public, as its book, *Alerting America*, stated: "The Committee on the Present Danger has taken control of American national security policy."

Nor was the CPD reticent about military acquisition policy. According to the book, "We *want* prices and wages in the defense sectors to rise relative to prices and wages elsewhere enough to attract the labor and capital needed for the defense effort" (emphasis in original).

Thus, through David Packard and others, the philosophy of the CPD was transferred directly to the Packard blue-ribbon commission. What elaborate rituals of deception we go through in the government of the United States. The executive branch had, in effect, set up a commission to investigate an organization, the Pentagon, that was its identical twin in outlook and had an almost interchangeable membership.

The commission staff also arrived with conflict-of-interest luggage. Air Force Colonel James Lindenfelser, a competent technical man, was best known for his public defense of the $7,622 coffee pot. Rhett B. Dawson had been chief of staff for Senator John Tower, chairman of the Senate Armed Services Committee. One senior consultant was Vincent Puritano, formerly one of Weinberger's assistant secretaries, whose notable effort in office was putting down George Spanton. Defense industry consultant Jacques Gansler, former CIA flack Captain Herbert E. Hetu, USN, retired — and so the list went, thoroughly Old Boys in this Old Boy network.

Any able bureaucrat-manipulator worth his invitation to the Inaugural Ball knows the blue-ribbon commission tactics. You have some show-biz public hearings for the media and you do your real business behind closed doors. For the sake of the media, you invite some of the critics to testify in public, but in secret sessions, forget it.

In early December 1985, David Berteau, the commission's executive secretary, talked with me about giving testimony. In the days when Dave had been an assistant to Vince Puritano, he had seemed sympathetic to our cause. I'd always considered him a straightforward man, and he hadn't changed: he said quite frankly that the open hearings were for "public show" only.

I asked him how the commission was going to get around the "Sunshine Law," which required that all hearings be public unless they concerned genuine national security matters.

He said that the DoD was "executive agent" for the commission and could grant Packard the right to secret sessions whenever he asked. He added that Packard had had a long session about this with General Larry Skantze, chief of the Air Force Systems Command and number-one opponent of the more-bang-for-the-buck underground.

As for my own testimony, Dave was perfectly candid: some of the commission members were interested in hearing me, but what I had to say would have no influence whatever on the commission. The same would be true of any other dissidents.

At this point, the president sent his military budget to Capitol Hill, where it was declared dead on arrival. Clearly the administration couldn't wait until June, when the Packard Commission report would create a diversion. The natives had ambushed the Pentagon machine and were definitely restless: reform legislation had been introduced in both houses.

The administration cleverly initiated a PR blitz by planting reports of an internal battle within the Packard Commission and leaking a few interesting documents to media people who wouldn't ask too many questions. Commission member James Woolsey, so ran the tale, had drafted a rogue report that was "contentious" and "highly unflattering" to Pentagon management, and the other members were sharply divided over it. The only trouble with this story was that Woolsey was an old-line Pentagon team player and a staunch member of the big-spender club.

Those reporters who were considered too nearsighted to recognize a trial balloon when they saw one — or too innocent to shoot it down if they did — got copies of the hundred-page Woolsey report. They dutifully filed stories but, by significant coincidence, the stories did not detail Woolsey's actual findings or recommendations.

The counterpuff was not long in coming. David Packard began to confide in the Defense Department critics, telling them that in his heart he was really in favor of their tough line but that political considerations kept him from saying it in public. He assured them they would have his behind-the-scenes support.

It was time to throw Ronald Reagan into the mock battle. On February 10, 1986, he again charged the drummers, saying that the American Taxpayer had heard "a constant drumbeat of propaganda about defense scandals and defense spending and all that is wasted." The Packard Commission was going to be the only answer "in the face of this propaganda."

Uh-oh, David Packard whispered to the media; in the face of Reagan's statement, he couldn't possibly come up with a really tough report. The president would be bound to reject it. Instead, Packard produced an "interim report," a flimsy affair of twenty-six nominal pages. (A final report appeared months later.) One full page listed the commission members; another page listed staff members; pages four, twenty-two, and twenty-six were blank; page twenty-five carried an eight-line conclusion that said nothing. The remaining twenty pages covered the subject of procurement so superficially that they were hard to take seriously. The dubious substance of the report was that Packard was in favor of "contractor self-governance," to be effected by asking contractors to "implement internal controls" over their business ethics. The Department of Defense was encouraged to "vigorously administer current ethics regulations."

Packard was especially worried that somebody might be prejudiced against contractors with a bad record; in Pentagonese, he wanted to limit suspension and debarment to unethical "ongoing conduct." He didn't want them held responsible for their past sins, just for crimes in progress. It was like arguing that crooks should be punished only while they were actually stealing, mugging, or raping.

Our defenses against collusive fraud — bribes, kickbacks, overbuying and overpricing, "material shrinkages," and the like — were already woefully weak. Now the big spenders, undaunted by known defalcations and those lurking just beneath the surface, were proposing to strip away most of the remaining safeguards.

The Packard interim report may have looked like a joke and read like a joke, but the laugh was very brief. Soon there were signs that business and the Establishment press were going to give it a lot of weight. A number of our reporter friends had been telling us for some time that it was becoming ever harder to sell their bosses stories critical of the Pentagon. After all, most of the news media lords were part of the business establishment and shared their brethren's distaste for our populist uprising. Most establishment figures seemed tired of the drumbeat of negativism, tired of hearing stories about simple spare parts that cost as much as if Tiffany's had made them out of platinum, tired of tales about costly military hardware that didn't work, and, most of all, tired of taxpayers in a state of shock. It was all very bad for business. They seized on the Packard report as an opportunity to declare a victory.

The House Armed Services Committee scheduled hearings on the report for March 5, 1986. To prepare the way, the Pentagon machine laid down a rolling barrage of flackery. Weinberger appeared on CBS's "Face the Nation" on March 2 and gave a perfect rendition of a high official forced to accept the "tough" Packard recommendations. Drama critics would have given him excellent reviews. On March 3 the *Wall Street Journal* quite seriously reported this and other aspects of the sham battle among the Pentagon titans.

The *New York Times* on March 5 contributed its bit with an editorial titled "The Packard Bombshell." It was a superb job of ignoring the disastrous recommendations that actually appeared in the report and finding comfort in reading between the lines. The *Times* said, "The commission implies" criticism of Congress for using the weapons-buying process for the "distribution of weapons contracts and jobs." There were no such words in the Packard report.

The House Armed Services subcommittee hearings opened that morning. Chairman Bill Nichols of Alabama introduced Congressman Dickinson as the man "whose idea resulted in the creation of the Packard Commission." Dickinson said how much he had been gratified by the *Times* editorial and, addressing David Packard, said that the committee's job in dealing with the defense and appropriations bills would be helped along "if we can get public sentiment behind your commission." The violins were already launching into "Hearts and Flowers."

David Packard was treated with the worshipful deference that is a billionaire's due. His commission had so successfully changed the subject that he felt it unnecessary to go into such disagreeable matters as the procurement fiascoes. It was much more uplifting to philosophize about the organization of the Joint Chiefs of Staff and matters of grand strategy.

His incidental mentions of procurement simply repeated the familiar Packard chestnuts about "contractor self-governance" and the need for "a more productive partnership between government and industry."

There were a few serious questions from some of the representatives. Congresswoman Boxer asked why the commission was against letting the DoD use investigative subpoenas when looking into alleged misdeeds by contractors.

That would discourage contractor "self-governance," Packard said.

When she asked why Packard had not endorsed a civilian procurement corps instead of a military officer-dominated one, his response was minimal and unilluminating.

Congressman John Bryant asked the toughest question of the day. Who was responsible for putting that outrageous "only the crimes in progress" clause in the commission's report?

The prime movers, said Packard, were "Bill Clark and Carla Hills." Judge William Clark, who had been NSC staff chief before Robert McFarlane, was now working as a partner in the law firm of Rogers and Wells, Lockheed's lawyers. Carla Hills was senior partner in the huge corporate law firm of Latham, Watkins and Hills, whose many defense contractor clients included Hughes Aircraft. But nobody thought to remark on Emperor Packard's new clothes. In the Reagan era, let it be remembered, such conflict-of-interest nudity seemed taken for granted.

Congressman Mel Levine, known as a reformer who might be critical of the Pentagon, was allotted just thirty seconds for questioning. Ron Wyden asked a question about unpriced contracts like the one for the $8,832 pulley puller that should have cost no more than $69. Packard answered obscurely and wouldn't make any commitments about correcting the practice.

Packard's back-up witnesses were Frank Carlucci (later secretary of defense), retired Army General Paul Gorman, retired Admiral James Holloway (a Washington lobbyist and consultant to the big brokerage house of Paine Webber Mitchell Hutchins) and retired Air Force General Brent Scowcroft. No congressman asked any of them about their possible conflicts of interest.

In the end the administration had pulled it off. Almost all of the people had been fooled at least part of the time. The commission's work was hailed on Capitol Hill; the Pentagon was ecstatic. On March 12, National Security Adviser John Poindexter wrote Weinberger a SECRET memorandum noting that this "most favorable" reaction in Congress would give "the President considerable leverage in dealing with the more radical proposals for reform that abound in both Houses." He asked for Weinberger's comments on an attached draft of a secret National Security Decision Directive (NSDD) that would "implement" the Packard program.

At nine-fifteen on the morning of March 13, I was given copies of this memo, the draft directive, a proposed presidential press release backing the Packard Commission and extending its term, and a draft of a presidential letter of endorsement to be sent to the speaker of the House and the president of the Senate. I was given just an hour and a quarter to write my comments on all this. Poindexter explained in his cover note to Weinberger that the directive was designed to strengthen the secretary's hand against the pending reform legislation and to ensure his control over any enforcement of reforms.

In short, the serious fix was in. The only reason all this was classified as secret was to hide the fact that the Packard exercise was indeed antireform. As I wrote my hasty comments, I had an ominous feeling that the big payout machine was about to win. The victory was proclaimed by the White House on April 2 with a press conference to signal acceptance of the Packard recommendations.

The final document was a National Security Decision Directive titled "Implementation of the Recommendations of the President's Commission on Defense Management." With minor changes, this was the same garbage that Poindexter had sent to Weinberger in draft form along with his SECRET memo. The directive produced a small mystery. We discovered that there were two versions of it: the official, public one, which was undated, and a classified one designated NSDD 219. When we obtained a copy of the classified version from Lieutenant Colonel Bill Byrne of the acquisition management office I found that the effective date was April 1 — April Fool's Day — 1986. On the signature page was a hand-drawn X ("his mark"?) and next to it a signature that read "Ronald Reagan." But Reagan was on the West Coast the day the paper was issued from the White House. Could it have been that the White House auto-pen was having an April Fool's joke on the country?

After Packard's triumph on March 5, the administration sent him back to the Hill for a mopping-up operation before committees in the House and Senate. As befitted a victor, he was greeted with flowers of rhetoric and exaggeration. "You are a perfect example of complete ethics in government," said Congressman Charles Bennett. "I've often cited you as that."

Congressman Dickinson quoted Packard's former military aide, Ray Furlong. "He said, in looking over your proposals, that you had the same idea then fifteen years ago and you hadn't changed your mind yet. Is that right?"

Packard answered: "That's about right."

Right. And the results of those "same idea[s] fifteen years ago" had been order-of-magnitude price increases, technical weaknesses in our big weapons systems, and a sapping of American industrial competitiveness.

Packard's afternoon at the Senate was even more of a love-in. Senator Sam Nunn, thanking Packard for his sterling effort, said, "Senator Goldwater and I stayed in touch with Mr. Packard and other members of the commission for many months of their hard work." Goldwater, more florid, said, "I have followed David Packard on this thing since the day he has gotten in town, and every time he had the answer I went to sleep with it and enjoyed sleeping with it very much." Then Goldwater went on to produce the most thunderous false prophecy of the year:

I am thinking, for example, of the B-1, at one time one of the most expensive programs we ever conceived, but under proper *uniform* management, the aircraft was being brought in under cost and ahead of time. That is what we are after [emphasis added].

At that time the catastrophic failures of the B-1 were still under wraps of secrecy. But Goldwater turned out to be right about one thing: the B-1 debacle was a splendid example of what David Packard's reforms had to offer.

The administration moved immediately to solidify its victory. On April 10, D. O. Cooke, deputy assistant secretary of defense, issued formal orders for "implementation" of the Packard Commission's recommendations. All this congressional and bureaucratic approval came, oddly enough, before the final Poindexter-Packard report was made public on July 2. When that happened, my associates and I saw full confirmation of the bad news.

The bad news wasn't so much the report's separate recommendations — we were prepared for all of those — it concerned a bigger concept: the long-established set of rules for organizational checks and balances. In a large bureaucracy it is important to have different offices and agencies check on one another's activities to inhibit collusive fraud.

In June 1988, when the news of the Pentagon scandals broke, few people seemed to realize that actions such as Packard's had invited the corruption the FBI investigation was bringing to light. When ABC's David Brinkley discussed the matter with a panel on his "This Week" program on June 26, 1988, the question heard again and again was, "How did this happen?" George Will asked, "Why, in the middle of 1988, is this suddenly erupting like Vesuvius in a meadow — as if no one had any inkling?"

Part of the answer lies in Packard's recommendations, and those of other high administration officials, in regard to cross-checking, auditing, and overseeing. "But what about the guards?" Sam Donaldson asked the two defense-contractor representatives on the panel. Was there no one responsible for preventing such abuses as collusion between corrupt officials and crooked industry consultants?

The answer, from Donald Fuqua of the Aerospace Industries Association, missed the point: he did not believe that secretaries Weinberger and Lehman were personally responsible for laxity. No one pointed out that the relaxation of independent vigilance and the crippling of cross-check authority under Reagan had led to the greatest opportunities for waste and conspiracy.

From the start the Reagan administration was opposed to such checks. In 1981 administration appointees in the GAO brought in a new procedure that was an obvious sham. Instead of offices or organizations being responsible for checks and balances individual *people* would be. Thus an inspector might report to a manufacturing manager one on one. Without the oversight function of an independent office, if the inspector and manager connived with each other, no one would know the difference. The perpetrators of this atrocity were appointees from the big eight CPA firm of Arthur Andersen and Company, advisers to the Packard Commission.

It is easy to see how this company's Packard Commission work, entitled "A Study of Government Audit and Other Government Oversight Activities Relating to Defense Contractors," might be tainted by a gross conflict of interest. Among Andersen's big contractor clients was General Dynamics, then under investigation by Congressman Dingell's committee.

Even more telling was the fact that the Andersen study faithfully paralleled the October 2, 1985, recommendations to Packard from the National Security Industrial Association (NSIA). This organization, a creature of the big contractors, was established to make known their views on "contracts, production procedures, specifications, and requirements." Its October 2 letter complained at length about "overregulation and micromanagement on the part of Congress and the DoD." In other words, the association was worried about increasing oversight. Arthur Andersen's report agreed that that was a bad thing.

NSIA said that "in recent years, the authority of the contracting officer has been whittled away" and that pushy auditors should be put back in their place. Andersen's report echoed that in slightly different words. NSIA said that Congress ought to declare a "moratorium on procurement legislation." Andersen said, "There should be a moratorium on the issuance of new procurement laws and regulations affecting defense contractors."

But one of the worst mischiefs of the Packard reforms was the insistence, fully endorsed by his CPA firm consultants, on the Pentagon's cost-justification rule. The cost-plus formula had proved to be such an easy rationalization for high prices as to make stealing seem legal. "One definition of a fair and reasonable price . . . is a price that closely approximates the seller's cost to make or acquire the part plus a reasonable profit." This, of course, was the antithesis of the honest should-cost yardstick my colleagues and I had so long advocated.

The Packard Commission asked the CPA firm of Peat, Marwick, Mitchell and Company, auditors for General Electric and other military contractors, to review the audit and control recommendations in its report. Peat, Marwick was concerned with "necessary benchmarks for establishing the composition of the 'costs' of contract performance." Their report favored proper "assignment of costs to final cost objectives, or the allocation of costs to contracts."

This meant that contractor companies should submit a clean sheet for any claims, a sheet without errors and with no illegitimate items. In other words, all the numbers had to foot and cross-foot, and any charges for bribes or whores had to be well disguised.

The Packard Commission had a habit of going to poisoned — or at least tainted — wells. There was the matter of businessmen's ethics in the contractor "self-governance" clause. Packard hired a consultant firm called the Ethics Resource Center (ERC) to write the "Conduct and Accountability" portion of his report. After conducting a survey of defense contractors, the ERC recommended that they adopt unambiguous codes of ethics. It failed to address how Sunday School lessons would impress the Hell's Angels or whether contractors who made their profits because they had no ethics would be converted by lectures to the ways of righteousness.

This performance drew the attention of the Project on Military Procurement, which looked into the background of the ERC. It reported:

> The Center has received significant amounts of money from corporations that have been found to be guilty of misconduct. Ethics Resource Center sets up programs for companies, working on such a program for General Dynamics just before working on the report for the Packard Commission. [ERC] received $30,000 from General Dynamics. GD had contacted ERC immediately after being suspended for misconduct. The Center also received money from McDonnell Douglas while that company was being investigated for misconduct, and from Clifton Precision after that division of Litton was suspended. The Center wrote, in the conclusion of its report, that many defense contract firms have taken significant action to establish, communicate, monitor, and enforce policies and procedures to ensure a high level of business conduct. In each area, actions could be improved upon.

As Juvenal asked, "But who is to guard the guards themselves?" (*sed custodiet ipsos Custodes?*). Who teaches ethics to the Ethics Resource Center?

The only newspaper I knew of that was willing to report the flaws in the Poindexter-Packard report was the *Boston Globe,* which carried Fred Kaplan's comprehensive account on July 27, 1986. Most of the press had been fully and truly conned, however. A typical headline would be: DEFENSE CONTRACTORS ASKED TO POLICE THEIR EMPLOYEES, and the story would cite contractor self-governance as a part of the Pentagon's "get-tough" policy. The bitter harvest of our laxity, capped by this self-governance policy, was to come in June 1988 with the news that fifteen large defense contractors, a number of defense consultants, and at least six Pentagon officials were targets of FBI investigations into collusive fraud.

The central purpose of all the testimony, reports, and directives, of course, was to influence the bill Congress was putting together. The Air Force launched its own lobbying effort and at the same time set up a "study" group under the rubric of the Acquisition Streamlining Panel, headed by Dan Rak, deputy to the Air Force assistant secretary in charge of acquisition, but otherwise dominated by military officers.

Meanwhile Congress was fighting a sharp behind-the-scenes battle over the Poindexter-Packard plan. Most of the big spenders pushed for the recommendations in the report — in effect, putting the military in charge. Traditionalists on the armed services committees, under severe pressure from the reformers, fought for a broad commitment to civilian control.

Who finally won the battle of Goldwater-Nichols, Public Law 99-433, on October 1, 1986? On the one hand the law provided for an Air Force inspector general who would be "selected from the general officers of the Air Force." It also required that all of his deputies be "officers of the Air Force." On the other hand, its first stated purpose was "to reorganize the Department of Defense and strengthen civilian authority." That language gave comfort to the Capitol Hill reformers and to me. We hadn't quite reckoned with the awesome duplicity power of the U.S. Air Force.

Its foresight in setting up the Acquisition Streamlining Panel, a so-called study group, was now about to pay off. Strategy? Simply ignore the Goldwater-Nichols commitment to civilian control and shift as much power as possible into the hands of the military. On November 24 the panel submitted its report for reorganizing the Air Force acquisition system. Instead of Goldwater-Nichols, the report took as its overriding authority NSDD 219. And, most ominously, the panel called its proposed plan "the New Order." It took considerable arrogance to produce that name. Adolf Hitler's "New Order in Europe" was only forty-one years in the past.

The civilian side of Air Force headquarters is the Secretariat; the military side the Air Staff. Goldwater-Nichols forbade the Secretariat from surrendering certain controls to the Air Staff. But the New Order got around that by delegating those controls to the next lower levels of military command — the Systems Command (AFSC) and the Logistics Command (AFLC). The areas delegated to AFSC and AFLC were:

Refunds. Verne Orr had used this authority to try to recover some particularly horrendous overcharges for spare parts from contractors. The generals bitterly resented this because it spotlighted their give-aways.

Progress payments. Under the old system, John Boddie, a deputy to the assistant secretary for financial management (SAF/FM), was responsible for making payments on contracts. We had started a promising scheme called "Quality Control and Cost Control at Point of Payment," meaning that if the contractor's work was done on time and up to standard, he would be paid the agreed-on price. Progress payments were supposed to depend on genuine progress.

Work standards. The military would now decide whether contractors should live up to the Military Standard for work measurement. (Assistant Secretary Carver had already taken this out of my hands in 1985.)

Authority to grant contracts in the face of protests. The right to proceed with contracts in spite of charges of irregularity was transferred from the Air Staff to the four-star purchasing commands.

Authority to approve multiyear contracts. This was transferred from the Air Staff to the AFLC and the AFSC.

The last two shifts evaded Goldwater-Nichols by quickly transferring areas of power to the four-star commands before they had to be turned over to the Secretariat.

Along with all this, the New Order gave most of the purchasing authority to a three-star general, the director of acquisition, with a staff of four hundred people. The new civilian assistant secretary for acquisition had a handful of people and a lesser role.

The New Order wasn't classified as secret, but it was considered "close hold." Nevertheless, the scheme was revealed when a closet patriot gave it to the Project for Military Procurement, which gave it to the press on February 26, 1987. This produced a small revelation of another kind: the press was quite as ignorant of modern history as the military: almost no reporter had heard of Adolf Hitler's New Order. Hitler gave the world fair warning in *Mein Kampf* of what he was up to. And our own military and their allies have given us fair warning of their uses of the *Wehrwirtschaft.*

Was the New Order takeover uncongenial to the administration appointees in the Pentagon? Not at all. Air Force Assistant Secretary Carver was agreeable; the military had promoted him to be a full colonel in the reserve. Undersecretary Aldridge had been part of a move to set Parfitt and me up for possible criminal prosecution and contractor damage suits in retaliation for our congressional testimony. And the new undersecretary of the Air Force, James McGovern, was an important figure in the New Order. As Goldwater's Armed Services

Committee staff director, he had not been notable for being tough on the military spending coalition.

I tried a number of times to arrange a meeting with McGovern or Aldridge to work out our differences, but the attempts were ignored. Representatives Dingell and Aspin wrote to Weinberger protesting the coup but were brushed off. Under their commander in chief, the military were marching resolutely toward the New Order.

14

☆ ☆ ☆

The Santa Claus Coup

ON AUGUST 2, 1776, fifty members of the Continental Congress blew the whistle on their king, George III. They signed the Declaration of Independence, asserting that George had "so abused the Laws of Nature and of Nature's God" as to justify casting off the royal authority. Count number twelve against the king was that "He has affected to render the Military independent of and superior to the civil power." That was a very real concern among the founding fathers, who relied on the warnings of history in establishing the new republic.

In the *Federalist Papers* 41, James Madison wrote:

> If one nation maintains constantly a disciplined army, ready for the service of ambition or revenge, it obliges the most pacific nations who may be within the reaches of its enterprises to take corresponding precautions. . . . The veteran legions of Rome . . . rendered her mistress of the world [but] not the less true it is that the liberties of Rome proved the final victim to her military triumphs; and that the liberties of Europe, as far as they ever existed, have . . . been the price of her military establishments. A standing force is a dangerous, at the same time that it may be a necessary, provision.

Madison went on to say that large armed forces are at the least an inconvenience, at the worst fatal to the liberties of a nation.

In the past such valuable safeguards had kept the country free of military influence in politics. When generals were elected president — Washington, Jackson, Grant, and Eisenhower — they were rewarded as retired heroes, not as men on horseback. General Douglas MacArthur's defiance of President Truman's orders and the subsequent MacArthur boomlet for the Republican nomination are about as close as we've come to a military presidency, and that was not very close.

The interesting thing about American history is that the patterns are usually different from the patterns of history in other countries. One of the big contrasts is that we do not expect to see the military coup, the man on horseback, or the military junta in charge. Our dictator will not arrive at the head of a tank column coming down Pennsylvania Avenue. But it is only too easy to overlook him in the form of a thousand unarmed, well-behaved, anonymous officers sitting at their desks in the Pentagon and, in alliance with civilian contractors, gradually taking power over a huge part of the public economy and a whole range of governmental decisions.

Dwight Eisenhower, who knew the American military subculture as well as anyone, made one of the most clear-sighted democratic statements in our recent history when he warned in 1961 against allowing "the military-industrial complex" to have "undue influence in the councils of government." This was the first definition of something we'd never quite reckoned with before: the importance of econo-military issues in national policy. The new force Eisenhower was describing had arisen from the interlocking of the national security establishment and a great war industry. (Unfortunately, although Eisenhower described the problem, he did little to solve it.)

Herbert Hoover had recognized some of its dangerous effects. The 1956 Hoover Commission report, titled "Unbusinesslike Attitudes," said:

> The performance of its national role, almost of necessity, introduces into the Defense establishment a philosophy and an attitude that are inconsistent with sound business principles as well as with economy in Government. Essentially, it is the military attitude that it is much better to have a surplus of supplies and of personnel than to have too little, because deficiencies might cause defeat. Obviously, this is true, and, obviously, also, it is unbusinesslike and wasteful. This philosophy is epitomized in the remark of a prominent flag officer:
>
> "Our military people are not hired primarily to see how little they can get along with; they are hired primarily to seek to get enough materiel to meet their responsibilities."
>
> An Assistant Secretary of Defense expressed the same view:
>
> "It is not unreasonable to expect responsible military personnel to desire sufficient manpower and materiel at any place and at any time to minimize potential risks. Cost, even though given active and sympathetic recognition, tends to assume a secondary role."

The Hoover Commission noted some improvement in the "management structure" of the Pentagon but found that the secretary of defense had little real control over the joint chiefs or the three services. The efficiency level, Hoover found, was low, especially in the use of personnel. Here the commission made an important philosophical and psychological distinction:

> The dual personnel system, with both military and civilians working side by side, involves increased costs and difficult problems of management. This is made much more difficult because the uniformed personnel are expected to function on the basis of command while the civilian personnel are expected to operate on the basis of sound management principles. These two dissimilar approaches are bound to clash.

And clash they did. Over the years, however, the military faction won almost every encounter. A few patriotic officers, it's true, tried to buck the System, but they quickly found themselves ostracized.

As the military party in the Pentagon steadily gained influence, attitudes in big business, Congress, the banking community, and major universities altered dramatically. From the post–World War II view that military spending was a necessary evil that ought to be curbed in peacetime, these powers and principalities began to view defense, or at least spending for defense, as necessary. Every one of them was profiting from it, after all. Then came the High Priests of Waste, those strange economists who reassured us that wasteful spending was not only necessary but good. It made jobs; it kept the economy humming; it subsidized the universities; the whole country just got richer and richer spending money on something we hoped we would never use.

The Hoover Commission's excellent insights went further:

> This anti-economy and unbusinesslike attitude is of fundamental importance, for it permeates the thinking of the entire establishment. Although civilian control of the armed forces is accepted as a principle of American Government, this approach of a professional soldier has influenced the thought and actions even of the responsible civilian officials. This type of influence is not easily eradicated by reorganization or other simple means. Yet every responsible step should be taken to make civilian control of the defense establishment a reality; otherwise we might end up with a military dictatorship.

Hoover's thoughtful report in 1956 and Eisenhower's thoughtful warning in 1961 came too late. By that time the alliance of suppliers and the military was becoming the single most potent force in the economy. One soldier even had the audacity to speak its guiding motto out loud.

On August 2, 1967, in a meeting at Wright-Patterson Air Force Base with me and others, Major General "Zeke" Zoeckler said that "inefficiency is national policy." Significantly, the general was in the process of defying written orders from Deputy Secretary of Defense Paul Nitze, DoD Comptroller Robert Anthony, and Assistant Secretary of the Air Force Ted Marks, all of whom wanted him to cut the fat out of the F-111 fighter bomber program of which he was director.

Zoeckler's successful insubordination was the beginning of a series of triumphs for the military. Emboldened by the indulgence of the Nixon administration, they began to come out from the dark corners of the officers' clubs and speak their piece in public. Lieutenant Colonel William Simons in the official *Air University Review* of March 1969 wrote:

> In the continuing controversy over Vietnam, it has become the vogue for those critical of U.S. involvement to challenge the policy role of the military. Charges of brainwashing the public have been leveled against that old bugaboo "the military-industrial complex." Some extremists [Eisenhower?] have demanded an end to "the Pentagon's unwarranted influence" on national policy formulation. But in this respect the current confrontation between Vietnam "doves" and "hawks" has provided only the most recent episode in a recurring controversy in American public life.

Simons went on to say that the military officers already deeply embedded in the government had developed an unfortunate tendency "to accept the political objectives stated by civilian authority as given." This was quite unacceptable to Simons: "To borrow from Clemenceau, if war is too important to be left to the generals, the maintenance of peaceful order is too complex to be left to the politicians or the political idealists."

The Declaration of Independence and the Constitution be damned, this officer implied. The military "have an obligation that goes beyond purely constitutional imperatives." He summed up, "It remains only for the military profession to use the institutional staff structure provided for it to help relieve these shortcomings in the nation's policy-making processes."

On the face of it, this might sound like a statement dear to the heart of Generalissimo Franco or the Argentine high brass of 1976–1983, but it is not quite that. Notice the language — not that of the rebel commander at the head of troops but that of the bureaucrat who sees "the institutional staff structure" as the lever of power. With this kind of thinking going unchallenged, it is no wonder that the Poindexter-

Packard coup was so easy to pull off or that the Air Force's New Order was so readily accepted.

For me, the move that came closest to home was the attempt to destroy my usefulness. On March 7, 1987, the *National Journal* carried David Morrison's full-page article titled "Extracting a Thorn, Air Force Style." The thorn, of course, was "procurement expert, A. Ernest Fitzgerald." Congressmen Dingell and Aspin thereupon wrote a letter of protest to Weinberger saying, "We fully expected the Air Force to use the Reorganization Act to take punitive action against A. Ernest Fitzgerald — which they have done with a vengeance."

When they wrote this letter, the two committee chairmen did not quite realize that the Air Force was not reorganizing in accordance with the Goldwater-Nichols bill, now law, but in accordance with its own secret agenda, the Poindexter-Packard plan. Thus they were surprised at the scope of the takeover. The statutory civilian post of my boss, the assistant secretary for financial management, was to be abolished and his oversight functions allotted to a three-star general. As I noted in Chapter 12, the new assistant secretary of the Air Force for acquisition, a civilian, would be a figurehead; his deputy, and the man with the real power, would be a three-star general, Lieutenant General Bernard Randolph.

"Obviously," the chairmen wrote, "the three-star general is under the Air Force command structure. Reducing the civilian component will mean that the Secretariat will, in effect, be depending on a three-star general to oversee the effectiveness of various commands headed by four-star generals. In other words, a three-star general is being asked to hold four-star generals accountable."

That was an anomaly, but the worst effects, the chairmen recognized, were the emasculation of civilian controls over purchase of major weapons systems and the virtual elimination of checks and balances:

> This portends the worsening of an already dismal record of financial and technical management of major acquisitions in the Air Force due to inadequate or non-existent cost and technical controls. The B-1 debacle is only one example.
>
> We would like to receive your assurance that what appears to be a virtual elimination of civilian control in the Department of the Air Force will not take place, and that instead, you will take immediate action to ensure that civilian control is reinforced in the Air Force reorganization, as well as in the reorganizations of the other military department headquarters.

In answer, Weinberger thumbed his nose. The next day, March 27, he put the New Order in place. My office was put under Lieutenant

General Claudius E. "Bud" Watts III, the military comptroller of the Air Force. Other generals assigned to the civilian Secretariat reported through the military chief of staff to their nominal civilian supervisors. The coup was as complete as the Air Force wanted, at least for the moment. Its generals now had approximately $100 billion for patronage.

Representatives Dingell and Aspin were not pleased. The March 30, 1987, *Washington Post* headlined a story, "Ill Winds for Air Force Staffing Plan," with the subhead, "House Chairmen Say Reorganization Weakens Civilian Oversight." Capitol Hill expected a joint hearing and an attempt to undo the coup. But in the end it was Chairman Bill Nichols of the House Armed Services subcommittee — openly unhappy at having to question the boodle-distributing military — who held the gavel.

He led off by saying that he wanted to "step back and let the responsible officials in the Department of Defense . . . implement the law." But, he said:

> The subcommittee is . . . caught in the middle between two very prominent chairmen . . . and the Air Force Secretary [Aldridge], who maintains that he has been faithful to the law. It is for this reason that I have invited the Secretary . . . to begin this series of hearings. I would also note that I have invited both Chairman Aspin and Chairman Dingell to participate in these hearings as they see fit.

Unfortunately, they did not see fit. And thus Nichols's deferential attitude was an influence throughout the hearings. (One evident source of interest to some subcommittee members was the rivalry between Dingell's energy and commerce investigating subcommittee — Dingell was also chairman of the full committee — and the Aspin committee.) In the course of the questioning, the focus turned to my work for Dingell. Congresswoman Beverly Byron had this exchange with Secretary Aldridge:

BYRON: You stated that there is a court order describing his job description and mandating that. In that court order, does it say — First of all, what are the hours at the Pentagon? Eight o'clock to quarter to five?

ALDRIDGE: My hours?

BYRON: No, no. Just general.

ALDRIDGE: I think there is an official order around that says eight to five, I believe.

BYRON: Eight to five, okay. Having said that the official time is eight to five, is Mr. Fitzgerald in the Pentagon from eight to five on a daily basis?

ALDRIDGE: Not at this time.

BYRON: Has Mr. Fitzgerald been subpoenaed by a subcommittee to be on Capitol Hill on a daily basis from eight to five?

ALDRIDGE: Well, Mr. Fitzgerald has — There is an agreement that Mr. Fitzgerald is part-time reporting to Congressman Dingell's staff for activities as they call for.

BYRON: So, really, he is not full-time back in what was his old job?

ALDRIDGE: At this point, he is not.

BYRON: Which is what the court order stated he should be doing? Is that correct?

ALDRIDGE: That is correct.

The point of citing this bit of testimony is to note how the Air Force managed to twist it. Major Skip Morgan, Aldridge's legislative lobbyist, summed it up this way in the resumé he sent around to Pentagon offices: "Mrs. Byron asked what percentage of Mr. Fitzgerald's time was spent on the Hill giving inside information to certain other committees of Congress."

Petty as this revenge was, Aldridge's grossly misleading testimony was worse. The "court order" said nothing about hours of work; I always averaged more than forty hours a week at my Pentagon job, apart from the committee work (ironically, I first read Aldridge's testimony while working in my Pentagon office on a beautiful Sunday morning in May); I was assigned to Dingell's committee as an Air Force duty, not as anything else. The Dingell detail was an item on my evaluation sheet so that my Air Force bosses could grade my performance on it.

But the most bizarre of Aldridge's aberrations in his testimony was this: "Mr. Fitzgerald does not have an evaluation form [a form on which principal job duties are recorded]. He refuses to fill out an evaluation form on which he can be evaluated."

This was absurd in view of all the controversy about my so-called work plan and "evaluation form" (see Chapter 11). Aldridge was clearly trying to change the subject by his false personal attacks on me. As Dingell's November 6, 1985, hearing had shown, my repeated submission of work plans had been misused by Aldridge's assistant, Richard Carver, to try to discredit me. When that was exposed, Carver was embarrassed into withdrawing his unjustifiably unfavorable evaluation. Aldridge was well aware of all this, and he also would have known that my revised evaluation form had been approved by Carver on February 23, 1987. So the useless lie takes its place in the long list of minor harassments and retributions of my Pentagon career.

With serious Air Force management problems already evident under the New Order and with the FBI's secret investigation of collusive fraud under way, Aldridge had focused his attentions and mental effort on damaging me with lies rather than looking to our weak and crumbling defenses against waste and fraud. And the Armed Services Committee let him get away with it.

Even though they didn't take part in Nichols's hearings, the Dingell staff was keeping watch on the New Order. Among the relevant documents the staff acquired was an interesting New Order organizational chart. It showed that the nominal head of the project was Dan Rak, deputy assistant secretary (acquisition management), a friend of the big contractors but a man who was passive to the point of near-inertness. An ideal front man. The real leader of the enterprise was Colonel Jim Lindenfelser, one of the Air Force's most intelligent, energetic, and capable officers. From a lowly beginning as defender of the (figuratively) gold-plated, diamond-studded C-5A coffeepot, he had risen to be one of the most effective workers on the Packard commission staff. Then, having helped to formulate the Poindexter-Packard recommendations, he returned to the Air Force to carry them out.

Another interesting name on the chart is that of Lieutenant General (retired) George Sylvester, head of the Organizations subproject in the New Order. As vice commander of the AFSC, he had presided over some of the greatest boondoggles in history and had headed the commission that finally put the lid on the Hughes Aircraft scandal.

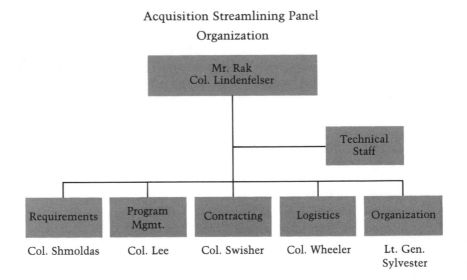

Acquisition Streamlining Panel
Organization

Organizational chart of the New Order.

At first the Nichols subcommittee found little to criticize in the New Order. However, it later relented somewhat and pushed a bill through Congress requiring the Air Force to restore a civilian to the top financial management post — in 1989. Reagan vetoed the measure, but it was passed again and finally signed by a departing Ronald Reagan.

Toward the end of May 1987, I again gave the soldiers of the New Order reason to want to gag me. Following Dingell's investigators, I went to California to inspect and review the MX missile program. We scheduled stops at Northrop's MX operations in Hawthorne and the Air Force Program Management Office at Norton AFB in San Bernardino.

When I arrived at Hawthorne, the committee staffers had already collected sensational evidence of the familiar kinds of mismanagement and corruption. Out here, we discovered, closet patriots were called "allegators" — those who allege — and enough of them had spoken to Peter Stockton to give him a picture of an incredible mess in quality control and material control. The Northrop engineers' frequent design changes had produced chaos in the factory. After materials were ordered according to design specifications, the specs would change several times before delivery. Orders for new material were placed, but old orders weren't canceled. So much unusable material was stacked up in the plant that Northrop didn't know what to do with it.

These were not ordinary spare parts. It was complicated, expensive hardware, quite a bit of it plated with gold and much of it classified. How did Northrop solve the problem? They simply threw the hardware into dumpsters and junked it. To prove this, the allegators produced eighty-three banker's boxes full of missile guidance parts, some gold-plated and classified, that had been put in the trash.

The huge volume of orders and reorders had so swamped the purchasing department that management was sending the engineers out to buy spare parts wherever they could — Radio Shack was a favorite vendor — and be reimbursed out of petty cash. This desperation measure bypassed the elaborate and expensive quality control system the Air Force paid Northrop to maintain. And Northrop's internal control systems did nothing to flag the breakdown and attendant defalcations.

Total chaos threatened when the run on petty cash grew out of proportion. The allegators told us that the lines of engineers waiting to be reimbursed got so long that the halls were clogged. Clearly out of its depth by this time, management resorted to authorizing some key employees to set themselves up in business to buy spare parts. It worked this way: the employee would take out a business license, get a mailing address (usually the check-cashing store across the street from the plant), buy parts, then reimburse himself out of a revolving fund. Each employee "company" was given a name but, generically, they were known as DBAs — "doing business as."

When word of these Rube Goldberg ways of running a company leaked out, management got scared enough to decide that the DBAs should be audited, at least nominally. That in turn scared the employee-proprietors, who thought they might end up as the fall guys. So they were eager to tell their tales to the congressional investigators.

Both Air Force and civilian managers at such plants have tactics for dealing with snoopy official visitors like us: they bore them to death. They try to use up as much time as possible with lengthy boiler-plate briefings and Vu-Graph lectures in hopes that the intruders won't have enough time left to find out where the bodies are buried.

When I arrived at the Northrop plant, Stockton and his associates, Bruce Chafin, Claudia Bevill, and Charlie Rey, were late because they were dealing with the huge bonanza of allegator evidence. We explained to the plant managers and USAF officers who met us that we were behind schedule and wouldn't they please dispense with the usual time killers?

Sorry, no, they said. At great expense and trouble, Northrop had prepared complete and extensive briefings for us, explained the group vice president and acting MX program manager, D. N. Ferguson.

To speed things up, couldn't we at least have paper copies of the Vu-Graphs? That would save us the trouble of taking notes on each graph or chart.

A very difficult request, Ferguson thought; it would have to be referred to the Air Force.

I said that I was the senior Air Force representative present and that Northrop had my permission to distribute copies of the unclassified Vu-Graphs. And while they were about it, I'd also like copies of the latest cost performance reports (CPRs) for each of the Northrop MX contracts.

Suppressed consternation. The Air Force officers present — Colonel Speed, the program manager; Colonel Hatfield, the plant representative; his aide, a captain; and some Northrop managers left the room.

We had won a point, it seemed; after they came back, Northrop handed out copies of the Vu-Graphs and the captain gave us copies of the available CPRs. But something continued to agitate the Air Force officers, who kept leaving and returning throughout the meeting.

During the ponderous and rather pointless briefings, we interrupted from time to time with questions about our specific line of inquiry, but we got no substantive answers. Northrop's lawyer suggested that we be quiet and listen to the lecture.

Would Northrop answer some questions as to the extent of their public disclosure of their contingent liabilities arising from substandard contract performance? Northrop should understand that Chairman Dingell's committee was responsible for overseeing the Securities and Exchange Commission, which requires full and timely disclosure of such contingent liabilities.

No, Northrop was not prepared to answer any such questions.

Would Mr. Ferguson then bring to the meeting Mr. J. R. Roehrig, vice president and manager of the finance department? Mr. Ferguson surely remembered that one of our advance requests was to meet with the plant's top financial person.

Mr. Ferguson seemed to be having an attack of nerves. We were throwing too much at him at once! Why couldn't we ask our questions in a more orderly manner? He would have to staff them. Finally, he turned to one of his assistants and ordered him to get "the girl" so he could prepare written questions for the staff.

Mr. Ferguson's secretary appeared and he began to dictate questions:

1. Who is Mr. Roehrig?
2. Is he here?
3. Can these people talk to him?

He then told his "girl" to type the questions and bring them to him to sign. In a few minutes she returned with the paper, which he signed. Now these important questions could be staffed.

Eventually, we got our answers:

1. Mr. Roehrig was Mr. Ferguson's vice president of finance. (We already knew that. It was printed on the organization charts.)
2. Mr. Roehrig was not in the plant. (At least not by this time.) We couldn't talk with him.
3. Mr. Roehrig was recovering from a heart attack. (Possibly brought on by the scams he was involved in?)

In the meantime, as we learned later, some serious telephoning was going on between Hawthorne and the Pentagon. General Larry Skantze checked with Lieutenant General Bernard Randolph. A few minutes later the Air Force officers came into the meeting and requested that I give back the CPRs.

I didn't fall for it. This had happened to me once before, in 1986, when an Air Force officer at Lockheed-Georgia had demanded I return some contractor documents. That time I had given in.

But the big secret that Northrop was trying to wall up in the cellar was the dummy companies, the DBAs. We had asked to speak with a Mr. Kroll and a Mr. Peterson, both of whom had firsthand knowledge about them. For about an hour and a half, in some separate office, the Northrop managers and two Air Force officers tried to persuade Mr. Kroll not to talk with us. But Mr. Kroll said he had nothing to hide; he didn't mind meeting us.

When our talk with Kroll finally took place, Mr. Rosenberg, a Northrop assistant general counsel, and Colonel Speed were there to monitor. Kroll, cautious but helpful, explained about the DBAs. He also gave us some other troubling information: that certain important red-line drawings (design drawings modified in red pencil by engineers), documents, and records may have inexplicably — and very recently — gotten lost.

The upshot of this was that Kroll, accompanied by an AFPRO captain, went off to lock up the papers and records, reinforcing the locks with a quality-control seal. Colonel Speed expressed dismayed astonishment at the DBA revelations. He seemed cooperative and promised that when we reconvened next morning at his Norton AFB headquarters, there would be no more of the nonsense we had just encountered.

But a chill wind from Washington must have swept in overnight. When we arrived at Norton, the temperature had dropped by fifty degrees. We didn't get the customary handshake from the commander, Brigadier General Barry, but we did get visitor badges and escorts. We were taken to a small amphitheater and held there. When we went to the men's room, an Air Force lieutenant came along to watch us.

After the meeting finally began, it was clear that the Air Force had determined not to surrender the way Northrop had the day before. They were determined to head off our pursuit of the gold-plated trash and the DBAs. The boiler-plate briefing was endless. The Vu-Graph papers were denied us; General Barry told us that anything we asked for would be requested in due course through channels. Remembering Colin Parfitt's remark about old-fashioned British military justice, I longed to hold a court-martial for "dumb insolence."

Since Barry told us he was acting on orders from Skantze with approval from Randolph, we asked to set up a conference call with these gentlemen. Barry thought that would be "inappropriate." So we called Skantze from phone booths. Not to much avail, however; he stonewalled stubbornly, saying he was backed up by the deputy Air Force comptroller, the Air Force vice chief of staff, and the undersecretary of the Air Force.

General Barry and his people gave a great dumb insolence performance the rest of the day. They pretended not to understand. They couldn't remember things. They quibbled. They dissembled. They changed their stories repeatedly. If we hadn't known that these were officers and gentlemen, honor-bound to tell the truth in matters affecting their country's welfare, we might have believed that we had wandered into a den of very suspicious characters.

We made little progress until we questioned Cecil Blaznik, an engineer "rented" to the Air Force from TRW Corporation. (The company had for many years rented out employees to monitor other firms for the Air Force.) Blaznik, not long before, had been involved in following up allegations in "the Hyatt case"; a Northrop employee, Brian Hyatt, had brought charges of management irregularities and systems breakdowns, including falsification of test results of the MX missile guidance system. Those charges had been declared "baseless" by Air Force General Aloysius Casey. We asked Blaznik, were they in fact baseless?

Not at all, Blaznik conceded. The charges were serious and some of them had been provable. Northrop and the Air Force had tried to correct what they could.

But how about this? — and we read the text of General Casey's repudiation of Hyatt.

Blaznik, rattled, tried to recant what he had just said. In his confusion he blurted out that fourteen folders of the original Hyatt allegations had never been shown to us. They were in the files of Air Force Major Boardman, since departed.

Blaznik was sent to search for the files, but he returned empty-handed and thoroughly subdued. It appeared he had received an *omertà* booster shot. General Barry said he didn't know what else to do. We suggested he start by calling Major Boardman to find out what had been done with the documents. General Barry did not respond.

A little later we did get a look at the district files of the Air Force Office of Special Investigations (OSI), and, of course, the evidence was not at all baseless. We proceeded to question the judge advocate general (JAG), who eventually admitted that he had written the letter closing out the OSI investigation and that Casey had signed it. The JAG tried to explain the "baseless" description by saying that he'd determined there was no basis for *criminal prosecution*. He further admitted, however, that a Mr. Fahy of the U.S. district attorney's office in Los Angeles had warned him not to talk to us about the Hyatt charges because the D.A. was considering criminal prosecution. It is almost needless to say that the Meese Justice Department didn't see anything criminal going on.

After I returned to Washington it was apparent that our quick review of the MX operation had disclosed symptoms of much larger problems, which could be serious enough to jeopardize the whole program.

Northrop was already more than two years overdue in delivering MX guidance systems, and the quality of their work was highly suspect. In fact, some of the allegators charged that the missile, a supposedly vital deterrent, was so poorly conceived and badly built that it might never work correctly.

Northrop's problem now was to find a soft landing. They and their Air Force allies had to head off our investigation with some pro forma inquiry and find a sympathetic venue in which the case could be heard. The obvious choice was the House Armed Services Committee, which held hearings to preempt Dingell. The Northrop–Air Force alliance had to take some routine abuse from irate committee members, but it was worth it. The Dingell subcommittee held its own MX hearing several months later, then turned to other Northrop problems.

I was preoccupied, however, with preparing my testimony before the Nichols Armed Services subcommittee hearing on the New Order reorganization. With Colin Parfitt's help, I laid out the evidence to show that the Big Eight certified public accounting firms had degraded the standards for internal controls in big corporations, particularly defense contractors. This applied especially to the organizational independence of financial management, quality control, industrial engineering, and the like. I traced the history of internal controls in business and noted that in the era of American industrial dominance, leading businessmen always demanded proper organizational structure as a basis for other management controls. Properly designed, such controls inhibit the sort of fraud the Pentagon and its suppliers were accused of following the FBI raids in June 1988.

From our research, I'd concluded that the firm of Arthur Andersen was a major culprit. I've noted their conflicts of interest in connection with the Packard commission and their echoing of recommendations by the National Security Industrial Association for reducing controls on defense costs. And some of their own recommendations were equally bad.

As I noted in Chapter 9, President Reagan had appointed an Arthur Andersen man, Charles Bowsher, Jr., as comptroller general of the United States and head of the General Accounting Office. Bowsher, in turn, had appointed another Andersen partner, Fred Wolfe, to direct auditing and accounting policy in the GAO.

Before these appointments the federal Office of Personnel Management had been training government auditors and comptrollers in the good, old-fashioned checklist for evaluating internal controls in both government and contractor operations. But the head of the OPM training school was soon faced with a new checklist from Wolfe, one that practically eliminated any mention of the need for organizational checks and balances.

I wanted to present my testimony in a noncontroversial way because I expected I would have to face some hostile questioning when I appeared before the subcommittee on June 4. And I was right.

Chairman Nichols (from my home state of Alabama) treated me politely, and Congresswoman Barbara Boxer, by then a full-fledged member of the committee, was fiercely protective. But whenever I'd testified before, there had been at least one committee member out for my scalp, and this time was no exception.

The first to attack me was Congressman Sam Stratton from upstate New York. Stratton is a man who can hold a grudge, and he'd held this one for seventeen years. In 1970, shortly after I was fired from the Pentagon, Congressman Dan Button had arranged a speaking engagement for me at a service club in Albany. Unbeknownst to me, Button and Stratton were election rivals because most of their two districts had been combined into one through redistricting.

After giving my then-standard speech about waste in the Pentagon, I departed and thought no more of it until I began getting attacks from Sam Stratton during testimony before his committee — allegedly for campaigning on Button's behalf.

By the time of the June 1987 hearing, he'd added a new sour note. He accused me of intervening in the 1970 congressional elections and thereby violating the Hatch Act.

As gently as possible, I tried to explain to Stratton that the Hatch Act applies to government employees and that I had not been employed by the government at the time. Unable to grasp this, he kept hammering away until his time ran out.

Then Congressman Larry Hopkins, ranking Republican on the subcommittee, took over. He began with these questions:

> The information that you gather in your position, what do you do with that information? How do you go about exploiting that to the public? or to whomever it is that you might report to? What is the series of steps that you take?

I tried to explain that my small office handled a great volume of paper, most of which went routinely through channels to Congress. Selected Acquisition Reports were a good example.

"Do you ever leak information to anybody? Do you ever hold press conferences? Do you talk to staff members here?" Hopkins wanted to know.

No, I said I hadn't held a press conference for many years. I did talk to his subcommittee staff and to members of the committee as well. I explained that my work with the Dingell committee was part of a formal assignment from the Air Force.

Congressman Hopkins then took it upon himself to lecture me about the proper jurisdictions of various congressional committees. "This is the House of Representatives Subcommittee on Investigations," he said rather redundantly, "and we are the only subcommittee that investigates waste, fraud, and abuse involving the Pentagon. I have never seen you here."

I said I hadn't been invited before.

"Why is it," he asked, "that we read or hear so much about the Energy Subcommittee [Dingell's] rather than this subcommittee involved in some sort of work; why is that?"

This question was so daft it was difficult to answer, so I explained again that the Dingell detail was just part of my job.

Congressman Bill Dickinson, the ranking Republican on the Armed Services Committee, bailed me out. Dickinson, at his most persuasive, recalled taking my side in the C-5A affair. He noted that I'd had some bad experiences with congressmen on the committee who were trying to protect the Pentagon, and he said he could understand my situation in my job. Lapsing into his thickest Alabama accent, he said it was something like a coon hunt. "You take a stick and you jab that coon and he falls out into a pack of dogs and then he has got the option: he can either whip all those dogs and walk off or not."

Dickinson added, speaking to the committee members, "Here's a resource you can use. Mr. Dingell has used him because he is available and Mr. Dingell was smart enough to call him." The dogs stopped barking after that; the subcommittee treated me very considerately during the rest of the hearing.

This agreeable outcome, however, could only cause resentment at the Pentagon. My participation in the Dingell MX investigation had inflamed the old sore spot. On the other hand, the pentagonal New Order had come out of the hearings unscathed, and this gave the military renewed confidence in their power to squelch me.

The next move was not long in coming. Suddenly, on July 2, General Claudius Watts issued a memorandum unilaterally canceling my assignment to the Dingell detail, which had, of course, been set up by agreement between Chairman Dingell and the secretary of the Air Force. The general simply repudiated the civilian agreement. And he made it stick.

General Watts's figurative thumbing of his nose at the politically powerful John Dingell was symptomatic of the ascendancy of the uniformed military. They had captured control of two vital levers of political power: distribution of Pentagonal contract patronage and checking up on how the patronage money was spent.

The military's coup was shrewdly conceived in that they seized control only of the very popular function of government distribution of military contract largess. Unpopular aspects of the system, such as kneecapping the taxpayers and small savers to pay the bills, were left to the civilians. The military acquisition people were the new Santa Clauses of our political economic system.

With Congress under control, for the moment at least, the Santa Claus coup was a stunning success. All that remained was to make sure that no more acquisition horror stories emerged to disturb the tranquillity.

15

☆ ☆ ☆

Carpet Bombing the Constitution

ASSUME YOU ARE the mastermind of a conservative administration in a faraway democratic country. Assume also that you know of a number of scandals brewing in your defense purchasing establishments as well as a potentially quite nasty scandal in your National Security Council involving illegal payments to mercenary soldiers. Your highest military officers, subverting a law passed by the legislature, have just taken power away from the civilian officers who are their legal supervisors. As you see it, your problem is to keep the country from getting upset about these unsavory affairs.

The trouble is, a number of individual employees in your own executive branch think such things are wrong. And they feel conscience-bound to bring the wrongdoing to the attention of the legislative body. That will surely cause a furor that will damage both you and your political party. What do you do to protect your interests?

Perhaps you find the answer in new and much tighter secrecy restrictions on government employees, restrictions even more severe in some respects than any your country has applied in time of war. The best way to stop the leaks, you decide, is to throttle the leakers by making everybody sign the toughest new secrecy oath your legal people can devise.

But you have to deal with troublesome private organizations that spring to the defense of individual rights under the constitution. One of the chief of these is a lawyers' union dedicated to defending unpopular causes and attacking restrictions of civil liberties. And suddenly you have the key. If you can neutralize that lawyers' union by some kind of pressure, you will have disarmed a large and influential part of the liberal Establishment. With your new regulations, you can then hunt down and get rid of dissenters without fear of a public attack.

Of course, as Sinclair Lewis phrased it in the title of one of his novels, *It Can't Happen Here*. But those who look for comparisons and analogies in everything might imagine some parallels between this fable and the situation in Washington in the fall of 1986.

On October 15 of that year, Chairman John Dingell of the House Energy and Commerce Committee sat down and wrote a long letter to President Reagan. He told the president that he'd been having trouble with his correspondence; most of the officials he had written to either refused to answer or would not answer frankly. It had crossed Chairman Dingell's mind that they could be hiding something.

Secretary Weinberger, for instance. He hadn't answered Dingell's request for a copy of National Security Decision Directive 219 (containing the Poindexter-Packard plan), but his deputy had replied, "Under policies governing the release of classified documents, requests for release should be directed to the originator of the document."

The originator, of course, was Vice Admiral John Poindexter, the national security adviser. The admiral, being busy with various secret arms shipments to the east and south, did not answer his mail. Rodney B. McDaniel of the NSC did, however, write to tell the chairman that it was "not the policy of the National Security Council to provide a copy of classified NSDD's to anyone other than the addressees." He enclosed an unclassified fact sheet on the Packard commission's recommendations for the chairman's edification.

Dingell, of course, was simply testing; he had read NSDD 219 and knew perfectly well what was in it, as he proceeded to tell the president:

> Although we do not have a copy of the Directive we requested, we have had an opportunity to examine it. We know that two documents are involved. One is a letter from Admiral Poindexter to Secretary Weinberger and the other is the Directive itself. The Poindexter letter consists of three paragraphs. One of the paragraphs, which is classified SECRET, indicates that the attached Directive is "intended to strengthen your hand vis-a-vis legislation on the Hill." The third paragraph in the document, which is classified CONFIDENTIAL, indicates the "Packard Commission got favorable reviews and this gives the President leverage in dealing with reforms on the Hill." In effect, the SECRET and CONFIDENTIAL classifications were used to conceal an agenda intended to avoid more sweeping Congressional reforms of the Defense procurement system.

Attached to Admiral Poindexter's letter is the Directive itself. Within the Directive, there is a paragraph, classified SECRET, which would effectively negate the current Packard Commission recommendations relating to accountability of defense contractors. That paragraph indicates an intention that it apply only to situations where the contractor lacks "present responsibility." It would not rely on former or ongoing contracts which are already awarded in making decisions relating to suspensions and debarments.

Dingell pointed out to the president that his assistants were violating Reagan's Executive Order 12356 by classifying documents not for national security reasons but in order to withhold information from Congress. The chairman closed by requesting criminal or administrative proceedings against the suspects and renewing his request for the Poindexter-Packard documents.

The president did not reply. He, too, was a poor correspondent.

In the meantime, Reagan's security people were stiffening controls by reviving NSDD 84, "Safeguarding National Security Information," which had been issued in early 1983. This directive gave lip service to the declassification of information "that no longer requires protection in the interest of national security," but it also contained a long list of measures to repress the free flow of information. The three most salient were: greatly increased and wider use of the polygraph, or lie detector, much wider prepublication review of any writing by anyone who ever held a compartmented security clearance, and a new secrecy oath, or "nondisclosure agreement," for people with security clearances.

To impose and monitor the complicated new secrecy oath, the directive gave responsibility to an already existing organization called ISOO — Information and Security Oversight Office. ISOO, for budgetary and housekeeping purposes, is a part of the General Services Administration, which is also responsible for the National Archives. Thus it was that Steven Garfinkel, who as general counsel for the Archives had stonewalled our subpoenas in the Carter administration, was now head of ISOO.

Garfinkel told me he got his "policy direction" from the NSC but reported directly to Reagan. He said that the NSC staffers who were drawing up the secrecy oaths were Deputy Director Robert McFarlane, Commander Paul Thompson (the attorney who later distinguished himself by finding nothing wrong in the Iran-Contra scam), Brenda Reger (a security expert whose later claim to fame was omitting to seal Oliver North's office to stop him from shredding his records), Major Robert Kimmit, and Kenneth DeGraffenreid.

When Congress had held hearings on NSDD 84, beginning in Sep-

tember 1983, the administration had downplayed its harsh new stipu-
lations. Speaking for the Pentagon, retired Army General Richard G.
Stilwell dismissed any immediate concerns about the new gag order
(Standard Form 189, or SF 189) by saying: "This requirement will be
implemented prospectively — we will not ask current employees to
sign them, unless they are processed in the future for a new level of
clearance." This displayed a shrewd insight into the congressional
mind: as long as current employees are exempt from the particular
outrage, no one will care what happens in the future.

The administration did have problems with the polygraph provision,
though. In the House Government Operations Committee hearings on
October 19, 1983, Chairman Jack Brooks demolished the NSC's position
by producing some damning evidence from the Pentagon itself. It seems
that back on December 16, 1982, Dr. John F. Beary, III, then DoD acting
assistant secretary for health affairs, had written Secretary Weinberger
a memo on the subject of polygraphs:

> 1. No machine can detect a lie. The machine can only detect stress;
> however, the stress may result from several emotional causes other
> than guilt: such as fear, surprise, or anger.
>
> 2. Even setting aside the argument that the argument is flawed, there
> are *accuracy problems.* We have only been able to locate two scientif-
> ically acceptable studies so far.... In one, the polygraph accuracy is
> 62%. In the other ... 72%. (You get 50% by tossing a coin.) The several
> studies in the scientific literature that report accuracy rates of 95% to
> 99% are flawed by inadequate experimental design and sometimes by
> conflict of interest (people doing the study who make their living from
> the polygraph).
>
> 3. The polygraph *misclassifies* innocent people as liars. In one study,
> 49% of truthful subjects were scored as deceptive. In another study,
> 55% of the innocent were misclassified.

Dr. Beary was supported by Henry E. Catto, Jr., the assistant secretary
of defense for public affairs, in a memo to Weinberger the following day:

> Cap, I believe we are headed for real trouble if the proposed changes in
> the polygraph regulation are published, and I *know* we are headed for
> trouble if they are approved....
>
> ... it is totally disingenuous to try to portray these changes as
> "updating of regulations," as a search for subversives, or as an attempt
> to speed clearances. These may all be true, but the fact is that we are
> trying to stem leaks which hurt the country (which is nothing to be
> ashamed of) and the press knows it.

Catto wrote, "The polygraph has a whiff of the jack-boot about it,"
and summarized his plea to Weinberger:

In short, I urge you to end this whole thing at once. As Dr. Beary reported in your December 16 staff meeting, the reliability of polygraphs is in question. They will scare our people. They will infuriate the press. They will hurt Cap Weinberger and, in the process, the President. Let's forget it.

By the time Dr. Beary testified before the Brooks committee, he had found work with a more honest employer at Georgetown University's School of Medicine. He reiterated his views, saying that people who ask, "How accurate is the polygraph?" are asking the wrong question; they should be asking, "Does it work at all?" He added that a stopped clock shows the right time twice a day. At those two instants, it is 100 percent accurate, even though it does not work at all. He then made this parallel:

> I have brought with me a polygraph machine today. I would like to show it to you. It has some advantages compared to the one up here on the witness table. It is inexpensive. It is very portable. It has very low maintenance costs. It has about the same range of reliability as the polygraph.
> It is a simple coin. It will be right 50% of the time in a dichotomous situation, that is, lie or nonlie.

So much for the polygraph.

The proposed censorship of writing for publication got an equally hard going-over by the committee. Publishers, publishing trade associations, journalists' associations, government unions, and the legal profession all sent impressive witnesses to condemn it. The press joined in. An excellent editorial in the *New York Times* summed up newspaper opinion:

> The secrecy madness will not shut down rumor mills or plug leaks, especially those at the highest levels. But it will deprive Americans of much information that ought to circulate freely between the public and its servants. It will especially chill discussion of national security issues.

The outcome of the hearings was that Chairman Brooks introduced a good, though seriously flawed, bill, the Federal Polygraph Limitation and Anti-Censorship Act of 1984 (HR 4681). It tamed polygraphs and censorship, but it failed to deal with the gag agreements in NSDD 84. It also exempted the CIA and the National Security Agency (NSA), the two most secretive government agencies, from meaningful restrictions. (Testifying before the House Subcommittee on Civil Service, Brooks said of the spook agencies, "We are going to exempt them. They can use thumb screws, water torture, whatever they want to do to prove their people are honest, clean, pristine Americans.") Brooks's bill went nowhere. In a compromise negotiated between the NSC apparatchiks and the congressional staffs, McFarlane gave assurances that NSDD 84 would be suspended indefinitely but it would not be rescinded.

Indeed, the new secrecy oath provision lay dormant for about two years. Then, in mid-1986, the pressures to put it into effect began quietly. Noted whistle blower Chuck Spinney was given a form to sign by his bosses in the office of the secretary of defense. If he didn't sign, he would lose his security clearance and, consequently, his job. If he signed, he could be framed for phony, contrived "security" violations. Worried about this, Spinney went to the Government Accountability Project (GAP), a public-interest law group, for advice. The GAP lawyers, lacking expertise in arcane security matters, passed the question on to an expert, attorney Allan Adler of the ACLU's national office in Washington. Adler said there was nothing wrong with the form, so Spinney held his nose and signed.

In late 1986 Lieutenant Colonel Jim Wolfe brought a copy of SF 189 to my office and asked me to sign. What was his authority for this? I asked. Jim had a couple of letters from a captain and a major in Air Force security, which said that Air Force members should be "encouraged" to sign the secrecy oath. Now, "members" is a term of art for uniformed members of the Air Force; civilians are "employees." So the terms didn't apply to me, and in any case, I hardly felt encouraged to surrender my rights.

I heard no more about this matter until several months after the Santa Claus coup. Then, on May 13, 1987, Captain David Price, General Watts's assistant, came to my office with a copy of SF 189 and an ultimatum: "Sign this or your security clearance will be taken away." Price also brought a pamphlet (DoD 5200.1-R/AFR 205-1) that made the same threat and, worse, went on to say, "Reluctance to sign an NdA [nondisclosure agreement] will be considered a lack of personal commitment to protect classified information."

I've already lost, I thought. I'm reluctant, and therefore I'm untrustworthy. By this logic, I may even be an espionage suspect. All it would take to expose me is a good Thought Policeman.

When I read the rest of the truly daft regulations, I knew I was in even more trouble. It said that the government could decide, retroactively, to classify information that was already public. Furthermore, the hapless signer of the oath might be held accountable for "indirect" leaks. That is, if I gave a congressman an unclassified government document, and a security officer discovered that the document contained something he considered sensitive information (or that he just wanted to cover up), he could declare that the paper was now classified SECRET. And if the congressman had already given it to a reporter, the government could indict *me* on a criminal charge!

I was in a box. If I didn't sign, I'd lose my security clearance and be fired. If I did sign, my official ill-wishers could frame me and send me to prison. Thinking I must have missed something, that there ought to be some reasonable solution, I called Steven Garfinkel and put the question to him.

Garfinkel is no man to try to sweeten the pill. He said that the whole point of the oath was to "simplify going after leakers."

Signing the oath would mean that I couldn't any longer communicate with Congressman Dingell's staff without getting the approval of third-party "authorities." Despite repeated questions, verbal and written, the Air Force wouldn't even identify who those omnipotent authorities were. I could almost hear the ghost of Mel Laird's assistant, Colonel Bob Pursley, saying, "Such a paper would be of great value if he were to jump the fence again." Meaning: "Then we could cut him off at the knees." Other voices from the past came back with the same message: Gerald Ford's CIA chief George Bush, Jimmy Carter, Nixon's Alexander Butterfield.

Paragraph 7 of SF 189 read, "I understand that *all information* [not just classified information] to which I *may* obtain access by signing this agreement is now and will *forever* remain the property of the United States Government" (emphasis added). Garfinkel made it clear that "the United States Government" did not include Congress or the judiciary of the United States. A nice distinction.

I called Peter Stockton and told him about this incredible conversation. The upshot was that two days later, on May 15, Stockton, Bruce Chafin of Dingell's committee, and I questioned Garfinkel at length. He was even more weird in person than he had been on the phone.

The Air Force regulation supplementing the gag agreement said that "the SF 189 did not impose any obligation beyond those set by law." If we had a law, we asked, why did we need SF 189?

It was just to "simplify going after someone," Garfinkel said. The White House was very angry over leaks. Garfinkel asked a rhetorical question, "What always upsets people at the White House?" And he found the answer: "Leaks!" (Not illegal leaks, or leaks of classified information, or leaks that might endanger national security. Just any leaks.)

Standard Form 189 spoke of classified information as something "that is either classified or classifiable." What did "classifiable" mean? we asked.

"Arguably, it could be anything," Garfinkel said. Well, he added, information that would be universally understood to need classification even though not so marked.

But the DoD pamphlet on SF 189 had a much broader construction. "Classifiable" material, it seemed, could be classified long after it was published on the front page of the *New York Times* — just in order to stick it to the person who'd originally released it. I read Garfinkel a passage from the pamphlet:

> Question 8B: Can a signer of the SF 189 be held liable under the provision for releasing information from publicly available sources which became classified after these sources were published, but the sources were never sanitized or destroyed?
>
> Answer: Liability would depend on the circumstances of the case. In the case cited (i.e., Snepp v. United States), it is unclear whether the signer had any knowledge that the information from publicly available sources became classified after the sources were published. Therefore, ISOO cannot make a blanket ruling on such limited information.

Another important point: why didn't the word "classifiable" appear in the secrecy agreement to be signed by contractors' employees, SF 189A?

That, Garfinkel said, was because the Defense Investigative Service (DIS) had wanted to simplify the form. If the word were put in, DIS had advised him, "industry will come back screaming."

Would Mr. Garfinkel remove the offensive "classifiable," which "could be anything" and make the government employee form at least as fair as the industry employee form?

Not a chance.

Another discrepancy: SF 189 said government employees who signed were accountable for "all information," but contractor employees were accountable for "classified information" alone.

A discrepancy, Garfinkel agreed. But he didn't want to try to correct it.

What did "indirect unauthorized disclosure" mean?

Garfinkel didn't know. Maybe it would mean leaving classified material lying around for just anybody to pick up. There are "probably a million" examples, he said.

Garfinkel thought the prosecution was beautifully simple. "No common law, no statutes — just show the form to the judge and say the agreement has been violated — you don't have to argue principles."

But surely the accused must have some recourse, some protection against selective, arbitrary, and capricious application of the secrecy rules?

Garfinkel couldn't think of any.

Then what about existing contracts? The stiff new secrecy rules seemed to be a retroactive change in the employment contracts of government workers.

Yes, he said, that was the effect. But it was within the president's inherent powers and his authority as commander in chief.

We pointed out that the president was C in C of the armed forces, not of the nation; furthermore, it was the responsibility of Congress "to make rules for the government and regulation of the land and naval forces."

Another dubious aspect was that the new rules went beyond the DoD and the contractors and applied to most executive agencies and government corporations as well. What about the Department of Energy, Commerce, SEC, and TVA (all part of the Dingell committee's oversight) — would their employees also be muzzled by the gag agreement?

No problem, Garfinkel said. DoE employees and others throughout the government were signing voluntarily.

Knowing that if they didn't sign voluntarily, they'd lose their clearance and their jobs? That, in Henry Catto's phrase, had the "whiff of the jack-boot about it." We went on to press Garfinkel about the statement that "reluctance" to sign raised questions about a person's trustworthiness and loyalty.

He didn't at all care for this provision, he said, but he had no intention of getting it corrected.

After the interview, Stockton said incredulously, "My God! Reagan's carpet bombing the Constitution just to simplify going after a few leakers. Mostly you."

I protested that I didn't "leak" in the accepted sense of the word. I told embarrassing truths in public when I knew that embarrassment was the only way to right wrongs. About the carpet bombing, I agreed.

Drawing on the interview with Garfinkel, we wrote a long report for Dingell, who passed it on to Chairman William Ford of the House Post Office and Civil Service Committee. Ford assigned it to subcommittee chairman Gerry Sikorski, who began to look into SF 189 vigorously.

Perhaps the most startling of Garfinkel's answers was his claim that Mort Halperin, director of the Washington office of the ACLU, had reviewed and approved SF 189 before it was issued.

I called Anne Zill, president of the Fund for Constitutional Government, whose offices were in the same building as the ACLU, and she talked with Halperin directly. When she asked him if he had approved the secrecy oath, he would say only, "Anne, it could have been much worse." He said this was not the right time to go up against the Reagan administration.

At the May 19 meeting of the FCG's board of directors, Anne Zill reported on this, and I reported on my interview with Garfinkel. Louis Clark, director of the Government Accountability Project (GAP), and Tom Devine, its legal director, were particularly interested in the issue. Tom said he would oppose SF 189 in practice and in his forthcoming testimony on constitutional rights for government employees before Senator David Pryor's subcommittee.

I felt that it was crucial to get the ACLU to repudiate SF 189. For better or worse, most liberal members of Congress accepted the ACLU as *the* authority on First Amendment questions; they would endorse what it endorsed.

Timing was becoming critical. So far, I'd received nothing but oral threats from low-ranking officers for not signing. But let a general officer put the threat in writing and it was a different game. Once a general's pride, prestige, and arrogance were on the line, the administration couldn't back down. Air Force procedures required giving thirty days' notice in writing of its intent to revoke the security clearance of someone who refused to sign the secrecy oath.

Our first soundings of the ACLU brought the reaction that the new requirements, although undesirable, were quite legal; old curmudgeon Fitzgerald was just being obstinate. So on June 12, 1987, I called Allan Adler of the ACLU. He was mildly sympathetic. Only mildly. He said he agreed that the Air Force interpretation of SF 189 requirements was unduly harsh he'd talk to Garfinkel about that — but that the ACLU, after initial opposition, had okayed the "contract," as he kept calling SF 189. He also thought the government intended to require only new hires to sign.

We then got into a complicated discussion of the legal justification for SF 189. Adler said the president's right to make employees sign a secrecy oath derived from his own executive order and from case law.

I pointed out that there was no mention of the new gag rule in the then-current Executive Order, EO 12356, and that NSDD 84, which the government claimed as its legal basis, spoke of *an* agreement only. There was no mention of a "contract" and, in any case, a contract was invalid if one party to it signed under duress.

Irrelevant, said Adler. The executive could impose an "adhesion contract" and dictate its terms.

But surely the president couldn't attach illegal or unconstitutional provisions to his contract or agreement?

Wrong, he said. There are no established limits on what the president may attach to such contracts in the national security area.

It was quite interesting to find the ACLU in bed with Robert Bork. Adler's position recalled Bork's argument at the American Bar Association's 1979 workshop on law, intelligence, and national security. Bork suggested that it was irrelevant to argue that extralegal violations of an individual's rights for "national security" reasons were unconstitutional. "The question is," he said, "in the circumstances, given the exigencies of the situation and so forth, is there a constitutional right?" Answering himself, he said, "Constitutional rights vary enormously according to the circumstance, according to government need, according to safety, according to all sorts of things."

In other words, if the government has the need to perpetrate some unconstitutional outrage, it may do so. Robert Bork and the ACLU, in the SF 189 case, would sanction it.

Adler went on to lecture me on the importance of working with the "right people" on the Hill if I wanted anything done. Dingell wasn't one of them; Nunn, Stokes, Boren, and Aspin were.

He ended the conversation with a little tutorial on the case of Frank Snepp, reading a "dictum" by Harold Koontz and Cyril O'Donnell, people I'd never heard of, to the effect that the executive could do whatever it wanted in national security matters, and giving me a list of congressional hearings that would show me the error of my ways.

I thereupon got copies of those hearing transcripts and spent a weekend reading them. One witness who struck me as especially well informed and articulate was Jack Landau, then executive director of the Reporters' Committee for Freedom of the Press. He had testified with reason and vigor against NSDD 84 before Jack Brooks's subcommittee on October 18, 1983. But in the course of four and a half months, something strange seemed to have happened to him. When he appeared before Pat Schroeder's subcommittee on February 29, 1984, he was meek and noncontroversial.

When I called Landau to find out the reason, he explained that he and practically all of the working press had wanted to repudiate NSDD 84 once and for all, but they had run up against the power of the ACLU. He said Mort Halperin had "gotten to" the important media editors and persuaded them to live with NSDD 84. Halperin had done the Reagan administration's work for it. "I couldn't take on Mort," Landau said bitterly. "I hope he's happy with what he has."

Meanwhile, Tom Devine and Judge Joe Kennedy of GAP and Dina

Rasor of PMP had been talking with Allan Adler to find out why he had swallowed the Reagan administration line. These were the points Dina derived from Adler's apologia:

1. Fitzgerald had signed one security agreement; why make a fuss about the new one? It had been carefully worked out by the Reagan security experts.
2. The fact that the contractors' secrecy agreement differed from the employees' was explained by their being derived from two different executive orders.
3. We were working with the "wrong people." We should be working with the intelligence committees.
4. The ACLU Washington office had initially been in a "big fight" with the administration over NSDD 84 but had been forced to give in.

This was such a collection of surmises and misinformation that I had to answer it point by point.

1. I'd never signed any secrecy oath. Why was Adler pushing such a falsehood?
2. The inequality of the two gag rules was created because, as Garfinkel had put it, "industry would come back screaming" about the harsher version. Further, no one had argued that either gag agreement was required specifically by an executive order, much less by statute. Garfinkel and other authorities insisted that the legal basis was NSDD 84.
3. The House Intelligence Committee had never held hearings on NSDD 84 or SF 189. But one Senate committee (Governmental Affairs, which has jurisdiction over civil service matters) and two House committees (Government Operations and the Post Office and Civil Service's Subcommittee on Civil Service) had.
4. The ACLU's "big fight" wasn't apparent in the records. Halperin had appeared before Congresswoman Schroeder's committee in February 1984, but only to oppose prepublication review of writings by government officials. Even that opposition was much qualified: he didn't want the words of senior officials reviewed and "censored" by junior bureaucrats. For instance, he wanted the wisdom of Harold Brown's writing in an op ed piece to be undefiled by government scissors. Anything else would be a "serious threat to the First Amendment." He failed to mention any concern for the First Amendment rights of junior officials or whistle blowers.

Pursuing this attempt to look into the mind of the ACLU, I looked at Halperin's 1977 book, *Top Secret: National Security and the Right to Know*. There he wrote (page 65):

> In addition to legislative categories for mandatory disclosures, Congress should designate certain kinds of information as presumptively secret, because they are not in general important for public debate, while their release could have detrimental effects on national security.

"Presumptively secret" sounded a lot like Reagan's ineffable "classifiable information." Perhaps the Reagan team had stolen the idea and changed the name. Halperin's list of such mysteries included:

1. Weapons systems: Details of advanced weapons systems design and operational characteristics.
2. Details of plans for military operations.
3. Intelligence methods: Codes, technology, and spies.

The first category was the scary one. If it had been in place and rigidly enforced under the *ex post facto* "classifiable" lunacy, the Pentagon underground would never have been able to disclose dangerous deficiencies in some of our advanced weapons systems. We'd be faced, hypothetically, with having to go to war with faulty planes and missiles that didn't work, with nobody the wiser. And Halperin's rules could have me in prison, along with Dina Rasor and a lot of other good people.

Halperin's other rule was that senior officials know best: "presumptively secret" information can be released "if responsible officials are satisfied that there is a strong need for the information for public debate on a major issue" (p. 65). This is a corollary to his congressional testimony: *all* senior officials believe that "everything is classified unless they decide it ought not to be classified."

It is hard to imagine the Reagan administration taking its cue from an ACLU lawyer, but the Defense Department regulation of April 28, 1987 (DoD 5200.1-R) echoed Halperin's ideas:

> Classified information may be made available to individuals or agencies outside the Executive Branch provided that such information is necessary to the performance of a function from which the government will derive a benefit or advantage, and that such release is not prohibited by the originating department or agency.

From all this I decided that Ken Lawrence had been right. Lawrence, a civil rights activist, in the fall of 1981 wrote a sixteen-page memorandum to "people concerned about the decline of civil liberties in the U.S." Titled "Subject: Morton Halperin, Jerry Berman, the American

Civil Liberties Union and the Campaign for Political Rights," the memo claimed that:

> When ACLU representatives are convinced that the political climate is such that the legislatures and the courts won't respect constitutionally guaranteed rights, they seek to strike the best possible compromise, sacrificing some rights (or the rights of some) in order, as they see it, to preserve others, rather than to take a "purist" position, which many of them ridicule.

Hardly the views of an Alexander Hamilton, a Clarence Darrow, or a Martin Luther King. Would any of them have made a quiet deal — okayed the contract, as Adler put it — on civil rights with Ronald Reagan?

D-day for the Air Force assault on Fitzgerald came on July 2, 1987, at five o'clock in the afternoon. Lieutenant General Claudius E. Watts III sent two of his men to my office to deliver two messages. The first, as I mentioned at the end of Chapter 14, canceled my assignment to assist Congressman Dingell and his committee. The second revoked my security clearance on thirty days' notice and, practically speaking, removed me from my job.

The timing of the delivery was intended to be devilish shrewd. It was just minutes before the beginning of a three-day Fourth of July weekend, after which was scheduled the biggest media event in years: the public testimony of Lieutenant Colonel Oliver North in the Iran-Contra hearings.

The attempt to bury me silently might have worked if it hadn't been for the dedicated young people at the Project on Military Procurement. Friday, July 3, was a holiday in Washington, but Dina Rasor, John Riley, and Danielle Brian-Bland hand-delivered press packets on the Pentagon's plans to "get rid of that son of a bitch Fitzgerald," as Nixon had said so long before, to media offices all over town.

Because of the holiday, most of the reporters on duty were junior people. Veteran reporters might have dismissed this as just another Fitzgerald-in-trouble tale, but to the younger ones it seemed a significant story on a deadly dull news day. As a result, Associated Press and United Press International put excellent stories on the wire to appear in just about every Sunday paper in the country. The *New York Times* and the *Washington Post* interviewed me by telephone and wrote their own stories. The *Cleveland Plain Dealer* carried its hard-hitting story with a banner headline on the front page. Once again the Pentagonists had outsmarted themselves.

In response to questions raised by Representative Barbara Boxer, Reagan's national security adviser, Frank Carlucci, wrote a letter (September 21, 1987) summarizing the history of "the current controversy over Standard Form 189," as he put it. Carlucci first noted that the controversy "began when Air Force Employee A. Ernest Fitzgerald was first asked to execute the non-disclosure agreement in January 1987." The meeting with Garfinkel, and the subsequent letters from members of Congress to the White House, the Office of Personnel, and the ISOO, questioned the legality of certain things in SF 189. Carlucci continued:

> These letters were also released to the news media, which commenced a series of news articles, stories, op-ed pieces, and editorials on the nondisclosure agreement, almost all of which contained serious errors of fact. This media attention, in turn, led to constituent correspondence to other members of Congress, more congressional inquiries, more media attention, etc. Within a couple of months, the situation had snowballed into a major controversy. Fueling the controversy have been a number of misrepresentations and misunderstandings about the SF 189 that have appeared repeatedly in both the media accounts and congressional pronouncements.

Carlucci did not back up his charges of "serious errors of fact" or "misrepresentations," nor were any ever revealed, but otherwise his account was a fairly accurate summary.

The ACLU continued to play a dubious role. *Newsday* reporter Marie Coco, working on a story about SF 189, killed it when Allan Adler told her (according to Dan Sweeney of GAP, who had been working with Coco) that the form was "underhanded and odious but legal." By July 7, when he talked with Dina Rasor, Adler was hedging a little more. He said that no First Amendment rights were involved in SF 189 and that no citizen had any right to a security clearance, but since I already had one, I had certain procedural rights that had to be observed before it could be taken away.

On July 8 I had an interesting conversation with Kirk Robertson, assistant to Senator David Pryor. He said that the senator wanted to help us, but he warned me that the ACLU seemed to be running a *sub rosa* lobby against us. Someone from ACLU had called Pryor's office to argue that SF 189 was not illegal.

That same day Russ Hemenway, chairman of FCG, called to report a sign of moderation at the ACLU: Halperin had said that GAP and the ACLU were negotiating the term "classifiable" with ISOO, and he thought they'd get a compromise that would persuade me to sign SF 189. Another note of some interest was Kris Kolesnik's discovery that

Garfinkel's supporting cast in approving the standard form had been Ed Meese's assistant attorney general, Richard Willard; Andy Feinstein of Pat Schroeder's staff — and Allan Adler.

In the meantime, the ACLU was gradually feeling the pressure. Marion Edey of the FCG board rallied some of its financial supporters to our side and persuaded Ralph Nader to make calls to Halperin and Feinstein. The GAP lawyers negotiated with the ACLU for two weeks. The result was a July 16 memorandum from Adler, which contained some fairly tough dissection of SF 189. That was a short-term tactical benefit for us, but what drew my attention in the memo was a fascinating constitutional issue. Adler wrote:

> The ACLU finds no inherent constitutional barrier to an Executive Order requirement that government employees and other individuals, as a condition of being granted access to classified information, must sign an agreement which (a) imposes an obligation not to disclose such information without authorization and (b) is legally enforceable in a civil action for breach of contract.

Here the ACLU seemed to be taking Robert Bork's advice that the government can do anything not expressly forbidden in the Constitution. My friends and I argued that the government can do only those things expressly authorized in the Constitution. Was the ACLU really willing to set aside the Ninth and Tenth Amendments?

Another salient constitutional point at issue was that of "unauthorized disclosure," especially in regard to giving information to Congress. Heretofore all members of Congress had been considered "authorized" to receive information, classified or not, from executive branch employees. By reason of their election, members of Congress are presumed "trustworthy" and therefore have "security clearances" and access ("need to know," as determined by the aforementioned nameless "authorities") to classified information *in accordance with the rules of the House and of the Senate,* which restrict distribution of some classified information within Congress.

By default, many members of Congress had acquiesced in the executive's control of "classified" information (under Reagan, almost everything important or embarrassing). The Reaganites were seeking to make formal the substitution of executive branch rules for congressional rules governing access by members of Congress. The Reagan team was trying to keep Congress in the dark by imposing its own rules under which "authorization" meant specific approval by the executive branch of each specific communication to Congress.

Steven Garfinkel underlined this in a *Boston Globe* interview on

September 13, 1987: "Garfinkel maintained . . . that legislators must demonstrate a 'need to know' before receiving classifiable information. 'No worker may provide classifiable ["it could be anything"] information to Congress without first receiving the approval of the agency he works for,' Garfinkel said."

The ambiguous behavior of the ACLU aroused the interest of civil rights activist Mae Churchill, and in August she wrote Ira Glasser, the ACLU's national executive director, with some questions. (Churchill later packaged her exchanges with Glasser and distributed the package as widely as possible to First Amendment defenders.) Did the positions of the Washington office reflect those of the national board? Did the national board approve them? Did individual affiliates have any voice in such policy decisions? How did the Washington staff arrive at the positions it took in dealing with the administration and as "spokesman for the ACLU"? Then, the most pointed question of all: "Why has government secrecy been given tacit approval in ACLU's name?"

She was defining the second major issue that had arisen out of the controversy over SF 189: was an institution known as a dedicated protector of civil and individual rights being compromised by a few men playing an insider game?

On October 19 Glasser belatedly replied with a Machiavellian answer. He did not deal with the queries about policy formulation or accountability, nor did he venture a reply to the question about tacit approval of government secrecy. What he did do was paint a highly imaginary picture of a fearless ACLU springing early into battle with the administration over the secrecy agreement. Consider this:

> We raised substantial objections from the outset both with respect to pre-publication review requirements and with respect to the overbroad definition of "classifiable" information, citing, in our July 16 memorandum, the potential for "overreaching *ex post facto* interpretations which would illegally and, we believe, unconstitutionally broaden the government's authority under this agreement to reach disclosure of *unclassified* information and other communications that are not prohibited by law [emphasis added].
>
> The memorandum goes on to oppose SF 189 and urge its rescission. Our letter of July 28 to Stephen Garfinkel responding to ISOO's draft rule, which purported to address the concerns in our July 16 memorandum, repeats those concerns and opposes the draft rule as insufficient. The letter concludes by urging ISOO not to proceed with the promulgation of the draft rule.

"From the outset"? SF 189 had been around since 1983, but the first detectable evidence of any ACLU objection (save for Halperin's narrow dispute of the prepublication review) came in Adler's memorandum of July 16, 1987. By then, of course, there was all that accumulated evidence that the Washington ACLU had "okayed the contract."

Glasser then mixed fiction with sarcasm. His letter to Churchill went on:

> Even if, from your distant outpost in Pacific Palisades, you are unaware of *the firm and steady opposition of the ACLU to the singularly oppressive qualities of SF 189*, it seems to me impossible to fairly read our memorandum of July 16 and the follow-up letter of July 28 and nonetheless conclude that the ACLU "raised no substantial objections" [emphasis added].

Having been in no "distant outpost" but in the Pentagon attic in the middle of the storm, I had plenty of reason to believe that the "firm and steady opposition" had been very late and unsteady. In fact, there was good reason to think that the ACLU was still privately content with SF 189. In late July Adler had told Tom Devine that the SF 189 storm was all just because "Ernie doesn't like secrecy agreements. Ernie wants to attack secrecy agreements and the administration." He added that the only real problems with the agreement were vagueness in the term "classifiable" and conflicts with provisions of the whistle blower law.

By then Adler was a step behind the administration, which had admitted some errors. In a series of changes published in the *Federal Register* during July, it had backed down on the notion of holding employees accountable for "all materials" and had narrowed that to "classified materials." And it had dropped the ambiguous provision holding employees accountable for information that "may have" come into their possession.

Nevertheless, in October the Reagan team pushed its security fixation to the point of absurdity. Representative Jack Brooks had requested some information from the Department of Energy in order to carry out the oversight functions of his committee. James Herrington, the DoE secretary, then had the foolhardiness to send a functionary to Brooks with an SF 189 that was to be signed before he would hand over the information.

The administration had chosen the wrong man to push its bad idea on: Brooks's blast was majestic. He wrote that this act "deeply offends the basic constitutional framework of the separation of powers," and that "such a contract is incompatible with the First Amendment to the Constitution, regardless of who is asked to sign it."

When Representative Gerry Sikorski's subcommittee held its hearing in mid-October, I testified. No representative of the ACLU was invited to appear, but Allan Adler was present and busy in the corridors explaining to reporters or anyone else who would listen that SF 189 was not all that bad. During one break he tried to trap me in the presence of some Air Force judge advocate general (JAG) officers — military lawyers — and challenge me to say whether I'd support any sort of secrecy at all. Then, as the JAG officers scribbled away, he made his own case for secrecy. The ACLU was still bringing up the rear in this fight against "the singularly repressive qualities of SF 189."

In my difficulties I had a lot of generous and heartwarming support. Senator Grassley and Kris Kolesnik went to see Howard Baker on my behalf; senators Proxmire and Pryor offered support; and representatives Sikorski, Boxer, and Aspin demanded an explanation from National Security Adviser Carlucci. When the military prepared to drop the axe on me, John Bodner requested and got a hearing before Judge Bryant to argue that the administration hadn't provided the substantive answers (which they were required to provide) to our constitutional and legal questions about the gag order. The Pentagon then extended my deadline for signing by two weeks.

Just a few days earlier the National Federation of Federal Employees (NFFE) had filed a suit challenging the gag agreement in the U.S. District Court. The NFFE suit was assigned to Judge Oliver Gasch, who had a reputation for more or less blind support of the federal national security apparatchiks. Sensing an opportunity to escape from John Bodner and constitutionalist Judge Bryant, the administration decided to stage the whole legal fight in the much more favorable climate of Judge Gasch's court.

In the meantime the American Federation of Government Employees (AFGE) had filed a similar suit in which an Air Force cryptologist named Louis Braase was a central figure. Braase had an unblemished record of thirty-two years of government service. A highly regarded teacher in the field of cryptology, he had held a Top Secret clearance for most of his career.

His only crime was that he had stood up for his constitutional rights against the gag agreement. The colonel he worked for, saying that in his position Braase had no constitutional rights, suspended him from his duties and sent him home. When public and congressional pressure forced the Air Force to back down and allow Lou to go back to work at the Air Force base, he was restricted to nonsecure areas and given routine clerical work.

A man of high character and exemplary record, Braase was ideal for a test case. My handicap was that my reputation had been scarred (the stab wounds were largely in the back) by successive generations of politicians and brass. And unlike me, Braase had never suffered the animus of the ACLU or Ralph Nader's lawyers. That made it possible for a redeemed Nader to make the *beau geste* and send one of his bright young lawyers, Patti Goldman, to represent the congressmen who had joined the legal fight. Ralph's return to the fold restored my faith in the perfectability of man. The Halperin-led ACLU sat on its hands, though.

The next move was led by Senator Grassley, who got Congress to attach to a spending resolution for fiscal 1988 a provision forbidding the executive branch to implement the new secrecy agreements for the first ten months of 1988 and allowing federal employees to communicate directly with Congress.

When the suits were heard in Judge Oliver Gasch's court, the executive branch argued that the president has "plenary" responsibilities and power in the national security area ("plenary" in this context means "absolute" or "unqualified"). The administration also brought as a witness an Air Force general working for the CIA, who said flatly that the intelligence community would not abide by the provision outlawing the gag agreement in the Continuing Resolution (the omnibus substitute for appropriations laws) passed by Congress and signed by the president.

In a judicial opinion laden with scary implications, Judge Gasch, on May 27, 1988, ruled against the congressmen's suit. He agreed with the contention that the president has "plenary powers" over national security matters, and he placed no bounds on the domain of national security. He cited NSDD 84 and "sovereign prerogative" in ruling that any nondisclosure agreement for federal employees was not subject to existing laws. And he found "particularly offensive" Congress's assertion of its right to receive information directly from government employees despite the constitutional right protected by Title 5, Section 7211, of the U.S. Code (the law passed in reaction to Teddy Roosevelt's gag order).

Thus the administration and its judicial ally had done everything in its power to prevent citizens who work for the government from transmitting any embarrassing information about abuses of trust to their elected representatives in Congress.

How had the great security campaign evolved in the Reagan years, and to what purpose? Early in the administration, Assistant Attorney General Richard Willard, had headed a commission on "leaks" that had, in part, concluded:

The unauthorized disclosure of classified information has been specifically prohibited by a series of Executive Orders dating back at least to

1951. Such disclosures also violate numerous more general standards of conduct for government employees based on statutes and regulations. It is clear that any government employee may also be discharged or otherwise disciplined for making unauthorized disclosures of classified information. Moreover, in virtually all cases the unauthorized disclosure of classified information potentially violates one or more federal criminal statutes.

Furthermore, Willard said, laws already on the books could be used to "protect" against the news media: "These laws could also be used to prosecute a journalist who knowingly receives and publishes classified documents or information." The report did not really deal with the problem of disclosures to Congress.

There was one rather startling and iconoclastic admission. The commission found that "some of the most embarrassing leaks do not involve classified information at all."

In sum, the commission felt that protection of classified information and violations of security could be easily treated under existing law. Even Air Force Regulation 205-1, which put SF 189 into effect, argued, though insincerely, that "SF 189 does not impose any obligations beyond those set by law."

Then what was the source of this drive for a new and troublesome secrecy requirement, overlaid on a perfectly effective body of law? The evidence offered by Stephen Garfinkel, certainly an authoritative source, suggests that the idea was to have a handy instrument for summary punishment on the vaguest of charges. Recall that the White House was worried not about security leaks specifically, but about leaks in general, including "indirect release" of "classifiable" information.

As John Dingell wrote in his letter of May 18, 1987, to Congressman Ford, Garfinkel said that SF 189 would "simplify going after someone." How? In our interview he explained: "No common law, no statutes — just show the form to the judge and say the agreement has been violated. You don't have to argue principles."

In other words, no due process.

In France, under the old monarchy, there was a legal instrument called a penal *lettre de cachet*. By the king's order, any subject could be seized and, with no opportunity for defense, sentenced to imprisonment or transportation. The king seldom knew anything about the issuance of such letters; they were signed by a secretary of state, and they served as a swift and secret way to get rid of the government's enemies or dangerous writers. It took a revolution to abolish them. To repeat Stephen Garfinkel's formulation, "No common law, no statutes. Just show the form to the judge and say the agreement has been violated."

16

☆ ☆ ☆

Operation Ill Wind

THE PRO-ECONOMY WARRIORS on Capitol Hill seemed to have run out of energy and spirit by early 1988. They were beginning to lose battles to the counterattacking big spenders. And the freedom fighters in the Pentagon underground were so thoroughly demoralized that many buried their weapons for use at some more favorable time. Those of us in the public Resistance found ourselves isolated and powerless. In an election year, when no campaigning politician wants to be attacked as weak on defense, our prospects looked poor. At that time, we had no inkling of the "ill wind" to come that might — just possibly — blow the nation a great deal of good.

In the meantime our cause was suffering a heavy cannonade in studies by noted professors at great universities, "defense intellectuals," and experts at prominent think tanks — all, apparently, rented out to the defense establishment. Washington does not produce much in the way of ideas, but it does consume them. The city has nothing like a Harvard or a Stanford, but it has a thousand columnists and reporters who must turn out copy containing some kind of thought content every day. A Rand Corporation study, a Harvard report, or an article in *Foreign Affairs* is quickly appropriated, simplified, and popularized for tomorrow's newspaper or next week's magazine article. Thus an arm of the government that can rent a think tank or eminent professor can produce scholarly justifications for practices that might cause lifted eyebrows at a meeting of Mafia dons. The previously cited case of misinformation that traveled from the Defense Department to Professor Kelman to columnist George Will is a good example of propaganda that became "scholarship" that became punditry.

One practice that needed justification was a wonderful Pentagon handout of $5.634 billion — that limit imposed by Congress for 1988 — to subsidize about one hundred favored contractors. (As a rule, the bigger the contractor, the bigger the grant.) The thin excuse for the spending amounted to little more than some impressive-sounding labels: independent research and development (IR & D) and bid and proposal expenses (B & P).

When Senator Proxmire questioned this and suggested that the Pentagon ought not to be giving such birthday presents, the Pentagon struck back with a heavyweight draft report produced on the Rand Corporation's letterhead. The Rand draft report was widely distributed, especially on Capitol Hill, in the spring of 1987. The DoD wanted its case dignified, so the corporation performed as requested, with arguments so devious and full of syllogistic error as to make Richard Nixon blush with envy. In effect the Pentagon's acquisition spending czars had rented the Rand Corporation's letterhead.

Rand proposed looking at the size of each grant as a measure of the grant's "surrogate" contribution to national security: the more money laid out in grants, the more national security we got. (But did we get 100,000 tons of national security, FOB, for each billion we paid?) Of course, we needed as much national security as we could get, presumably to store away in the Pentagon basement for a rainy day.

After the report was published, my associates and I asked the Rand experts if they could come up with an example of benefit the country had received from the billions of dollars spent on the IR & D and B & P boondoggle. They couldn't. That fact, however, didn't stop Robert Costello, the Poindexter-Packard acquisition czar, from sending his people to Capitol Hill to argue, on the basis of the Rand absurdity, for removal of the ceiling on the IR & D and B & P birthday gifts.

It worked. The June 6, 1988, issue of *Federal Contracts* reported (page 1108): "For the first time since 1983, the House Appropriations Committee has approved a funding measure for the Defense Department that does not contain a ceiling on independent research and development and bid and proposal costs."

This breakthrough was aided by a barrage from the MAC Group, hirelings of the military contractor trade-and-lobbying associations, the Aerospace Industries Association (AIA), the Electronic Industries Association (EIA), and the National Security Industrial Association (NSIA). The "MAC Report" (from the initials on its letterhead) was more officially — and stultifyingly — titled "The Impact on Defense Industrial Capability of the Changes in Procurement and Tax Policy, 1984–87." It was prepared by a group of obedient scholars, prominent among whom were Harvard Business School professor Robert N. Anthony, former comptroller of the Department of Defense, and his colleague Joseph L. Bower.

The report was a fairly inept attempt to roll back the various reforms in Pentagon spending habits that had been effected between 1984 and 1987, reforms that had been essentially halted by the Poindexter-Packard coup after modest progress in the right direction.

The report's "analytical" approach was based on a highly suspect presentation of cash flow. (It should be explained that the contracts used for examples were asserted to be real ones, though they were not identified.) Ordinarily, a cash flow statement is the simplest kind of financial analysis; every small businessman who ever got a loan from a bank knows how to put one together. A cash flow analysis does not contain accrued or booked revenues, and it doesn't show accrued costs. What it does display are cash collections and disbursements. Cautious bankers know that money owed, or "accrued," to the business might never turn into cash, since not everybody pays his bills. The bankers also want to make sure that the business has enough money coming in to pay current bills plus a sufficient surplus to make loan repayments to the bank.

Professor Anthony, in his textbook *Management Accounting*, said this about cash flow statements: "Transactions that do not involve a flow of cash are eliminated." Yet in the MAC report he changed the rules for the big contractors. In its "cash flow model logic," the MAC group showed presumed cash collections on the credit side of the ledger and presumed "incurred" costs on the debit side. I say "presumed" because the figures were simply furnished by the contracting companies and may or may not have had anything to do with reality.

When I asked Russ Aney, one of the authors of the report, what was meant by "incurred" costs, he said that meant accrued or booked costs. This altered the meaning of "cash flow" dramatically. Many of these costs are "accrued" on the contractor's books months before he pays the bills for them, so the contractor's cash requirements looked much larger than they really were. This didn't seem to bother the faculty members because it bolstered the case they'd been assigned to bolster.

The other noticeable feature of the report was its candor. It made no attempt to hide the fact that it was trying to justify larger IR & D and B & P handouts for the giant contractors.

One of MAC's loudest complaints was about "lower allowable cost recovery." I asked Aney what he was really talking about. I asked him if the "lower" part meant recent congressional restrictions and the "allowable cost" part meant paying room and board for dogs like Fursten, sending flowers, paying strolling musicians, and the like. He said yes.

I then asked him whether the companies were still indulging in these amenities even after the government stopped paying for them.

"What other assumption could one make?" said Aney.

In the upper brackets of executiveville, it's important to maintain the quality of life even if the ungrateful taxpayer won't foot the bill any longer.

Finally, from Harvard, came another fearsome broadside: the MAC report warned that if the 1984–1987 reforms were "allowed to run their course," we could expect the dire result of "increased competition." And that would lead to the worst of consequences — "the potential for a low-cost culture." Not a single strolling musician in sight.

The bombardment was joined by Georgetown University's Center for Strategic and International Studies (CSIS), which delivered a treatise titled "U.S. Defense Acquisition: A Process in Trouble." As the title suggests, the authors conceded what nobody in his right mind could deny: there were troubles in boondoggleland. "There has been influence peddling. Kickbacks have been made. The revolving-door syndrome has been abused. Patently unrealistic promises have been made." And so on. CSIS even dared to admit that some of the spare parts and support equipment were overpriced, but it went on to rationalize such scandals by writing that the tools were bought "in strict accordance with regulations." There was no mention of the glaring flaws in the regulations (see especially Chapter 12), much less any proposal for correcting them.

Did Georgetown's staid Jesuit fathers know what was being committed under their aegis? The report produced a remarkable piece of flimflam when it blamed the soaring weapons costs of the Reagan years on "program instability," which was further explained as "the cost of stretch-outs." According to this bit of sophism, alterations in a weapons funding program in midstream drove costs higher than expected.

As I described in Chapter 10, however, the astronomical unit cost increases — both realized and projected — were recognized by the Pentagon's advance planners during the period January to May 1984, when the Reagan spend-up was going full steam. Out-of-control contractor costs and even wilder projections of costs to come drove unit prices up so steeply that even the Reagan money pump fell behind.

And the CSIS solutions? They were, it turned out, based on the false gospel of David Packard, that is, to retain and attract "professionally competent [military] acquisition personnel" and then to appoint not one, but two *blue-ribbon commissions!*

The first of these commissions was supposed to "examine the role of Congress through all stages of the acquisition process." That, of course, could postpone any real reform until doomsday. The second commission, charged with monitoring progress of the reforms and restoring "national confidence," would have a life of five years in the grand tradition of Chet Holifield.

When I finally reached the end of the CSIS report and read the list of its creators, I had a sudden epiphany. The turgid style and the abundance of error were explained: the chairman was none other than that old apostle of pork, James Schlesinger. I noted sadly that the co-chairman was Representative Les Aspin. I hoped he was there only as a reserve piano player and that he didn't know what was going on upstairs.

Finally, among the scholarly artillery, came the sound of Big Bertha. Under the copyright of the President and the Fellows of Harvard College, the Harvard Business School Press published *The Defense Management Challenge.* Its principal author was my old friend and associate, Dr. J. Ronald Fox, the Jaime and Josefina Chua Tiampo Professor of Business Administration at the B-school. Along with his academic credentials, Ron could point to almost thirty years of experience in Pentagon procurement.

I had met with Fox and his assistant author, James Fields, and had described some of the lessons to be learned through case studies of overpricing on tools and spare parts. On my recommendation, Dingell's investigators and the PMP had opened their files to Fields. I expected a worthwhile analysis that would get to the roots of procurement troubles.

When I saw the finished book in June 1988, I was momentarily gratified to find that the section "Problems in the Defense Business" began with a look at overpriced spare parts and tools. But after five and a half lines the sag set in. I was faced with a warning of sophisms to come: "These allegations cause many Americans to question DoD's management capability as well as the integrity of the defense industry."

Dismayed, I wondered if Major Ketcham and Colonel Roberts were co-authors. Cover up the truth, they suggested, so the taxpaying suckers won't get wise:

> Although [the media] rarely — if ever — explained that the high prices frequently had to do with the allocation of overhead costs and the rigor of military requirements as much as or more than they do with implied contractor overcharges.

Government regulations require that overhead costs (i.e., costs associated with more than one program) be distributed equally among a
contractor's products. Under this system, prices for small items are
artificially inflated and those for large items artificially reduced.
Overhead costs have to be absorbed one way or another, but if the
allocation system results in pricing anomalies and is not adequately
understood or explained by the media, the public is misled.

Could Professor Kelman's snake oil still have buyers? In dismay I called
Chuck Spinney, who said he had reviewed Ron's manuscript and had
advised Ron to delete the "equal allocation of overhead" fallacy.

Colin Parfitt followed up on the very queer "government regulations
require" line. Where were those regulations to be found?

They were in the FAR [Federal Acquisitions Regulations] or the DAR
[Defense Acquisition Regulations], Ron said. "You can look them up."

They weren't and you couldn't.

The fact that the Pentagon and its academic footmen had to keep the
old lie alive suggested that none of the DoD flacks had enough
imagination to invent a new lie to justify exorbitant prices. There was
no defense.

I still believed that Ron Fox was a basically honest man, but I had no
choice except to confront him about the distortions in his book. With
some mortification, he said I should remember that "distributed
equally" could have several meanings. It might mean equal *percentages*
of overhead. Brightening, he said that was, in fact, what he'd meant all
along.

Just what we'd always been talking about, I said. Isn't it true, I asked,
that the overhead, fat and all, is distributed proportionately to measures
of direct costs — hours or dollars — of the products in question? He
agreed.

Fox would not agree, however, that one major thesis of his book —
namely, that Pentagon critics use false reports because they are against
national defense — was wrong. A close reading of *The Defense Management Challenge* revealed where the cheating really lay. Consider page
31:

In some cases, the news reports contained outright distortions, by
omission. The $3,046 coffee maker was designed for the huge C-5A
aircraft, which carries as many as 365 people. Major airlines have
purchased similar coffee makers for $3,107.

This has to be taken as a blatant attempt to mislead. First, the C-5A
pot was priced at $7,622. (After Lockheed was publicly embarrassed,
the replacement pots came in at "only" $3,046.) Second, it would be

dangerous flying if anybody tried to cram 365 people into a C-5A. Third, the coffee pot in question is a *ten-cup* model.

The authors went on to damn "the inaccurate or incomplete reporting by the news media" and "the theatrics of a congressman or senator" as he displayed a pair of grossly overpriced duckbill pliers. "Sensationalism and entertainment," said the Harvard report, an attempt "to discredit efforts to achieve a defense buildup." After such amazing misrepresentations, one can only ask whether the Harvard motto *Veritas* has lost all meaning.

The hero of the book was, predictably, David Packard: "one of the ablest Pentagon managers" (page 134) and "dedicated to improving the acquisition process" (page 49). And there are, indeed, many noble Packard quotes that sternly denounce contractor inefficiency and non-enforcement of contracts. The authors did not point out, however, that these were hindsight quotes, delivered as Packard was leaving office and were the diametric opposite of Packard's actions. The ruinous effects of Packardism in office were not considered: the "capable" officers in charge of programs (and up to their ears in money), the Poindexter-Packard "streamlining" that meant "contract now, ask questions later." "Self-policing" meant looking the other way while the scoundrels make off with the loot. And how could a book purporting to discuss "the defense management challenge" overlook the fact that the streamlining has resulted in a huge shortfall between the President's fiscal guidance, much less what funds Congress will supply, and what the Pentagon plans to spend? And the most painful part is that the fighting part of the Air Force certainly — and perhaps the other services as well — will emerge from the $2 trillion Reagan spending binge *smaller* than it was before Reagan.

The mischief that such irresponsible academics can do is not immediately apparent. The effects of false teachings on the students don't show up for years. But the bad thinking in those specialized publications and university press books does trickle down to unsuspecting journalists. It may influence politicians as well. In the 1988 election year, the for-rent intellectuals around Harvard Square were being sought out by the spending coalition because of their presumed closeness to Democratic candidate Michael Dukakis.

In spite of my feelings about the book, I went to the publication party for *The Defense Management Challenge.* I got there late, but I soon found that the party had split into two factions; when Ron Fox was introduced as the author whose book would counter the criticism of Pentagon buying habits, the establishment Pentagonists cheered. The underground types just sulked. Looking around at the crowd, I had the depressing feeling that no matter who won the election, the same corps of rationalizers would still be there in the Pentagon, running the same old sick system.

While Colin Parfitt and I were driving home that night, I was reminded of Colonel Joe Warren's long-ago comment on an earlier shuffle of administrations: "Same old whores, just new beds."

Even with the apparent success of the big push to make Pentagon management look respectable and the decline in morale in the economizers' ranks, I was still hopeful of a revival in our fortunes. Despite the propaganda barrage, real improvements in Fort Fumble's wasteful system were minimal. The first new crack in the façade would cause the latent public discontent to erupt again.

On May 31, 1985, communications specialist Richard Pollack had reported, in a privately distributed letter, pollster Peter Hart's assessment of a new trend:

> There has been a dramatic change in public thinking on the military budget. Support for higher arms spending has dropped dramatically. This is due to the sharp cutbacks in social spending and the many reports on corporate fraud and abuse. As Peter Hart put it, popular outrage over fiscal irresponsibility at the Pentagon "comes roaring out of the polling data."
>
> The fact that Johnny Carson is making jokes about the Pentagon's toilet seats and ashtrays confirms this analysis. You can't make jokes about something like this unless popular feeling and concern are very widespread. This attitude on military spending is a complete about-face on how the public felt just a few years ago.

Even at the height of public support for the Pentagon, in October 1980, 78 percent of the sampled public believed that the Defense Department didn't use its ample sums efficiently. And by 1988 cynicism was rising. It was a sleeping campaign issue with great potential, but no candidate for the nominations seemed to be acute enough, or opportunistic enough, to seize upon it.

But in 1986 a former Navy employee, now working for a contractor, warned the Naval Investigative Service that a consultant was trying to sell contractors inside information from the Pentagon. An FBI investigation was begun under the supervision of William Weld, head of the criminal division at the Justice Department. Attorney General Meese was not informed, and the inquiry not made public until mid-1988.

The Justice Department, which had behaved with such suspicious partiality for nearly eight years, now proved to have its own underground — a prosecutor who was willing to listen to a closet patriot, and a sizable investigative force to follow up. No thanks, of course, to Edwin Meese, Ronald Reagan, Caspar Weinberger, or Frank Carlucci.

The sudden revelation reminded us that there is one very old-fashioned check on malfeasance even in a system as vast and complicated as the Department of Defense. And, for those who could see the lesson, it was also a reminder of the kind of mentality that feared and hated the results of simple honesty.

On June 14, 1988 — the day before Ron Fox's book party — FBI agents with search warrants descended on at least five Pentagon offices and on dozens of contractors' and consultants' offices in twelve states and the District of Columbia. Later news put the number of grand jury subpoenas at about 275. The two-year investigation, code-named "Operation Ill Wind," was a wide-ranging examination of bribery, bid rigging, and insider trading in the defense industry.

Former Secretary of the Navy John Lehman and consultant Melvyn R. Paisley (ex-chief of Navy research and development) were among the former high Pentagon officials under suspicion. Henry Hudson, the U.S. attorney in Alexandria, Virginia, who was overseeing the investigation, was scrutinizing such well-known corporations as McDonnell-Douglas, Martin Marietta, Litton Industries, Unisys, Hercules, Pratt and Whitney, and Norden Systems.

I first heard of the raids when Peter Stockton telephoned to ask if the office of my fellow deputy in the Air Force, Victor Cohen, was being searched. William Weld and FBI directors Webster and Sessions had shrewdly — considering the Meese Justice Department's record in such past cases as those of George Spanton and Bob Golden, not to mention Ollie North — kept the operation under deep cover. Among the very few people on Capitol Hill who I know had prior knowledge was Kris Kolesnik.

In October 1985, Kolesnik's boss, Senator Grassley, had tried to investigate similar allegations but had been blocked by the Justice Department on the grounds that it was pursuing its own investigation of the case. Nothing had come of Justice's supposed effort, however. Congressman Dingell, too, had warned Caspar Weinberger of some alarming indications, but Weinberger had ignored them.

Most members of Congress professed to be shocked at the news. Senator John Warner of Virginia, senior Republican on the Armed Services Committee, probably spoke for the majority of Congress in his unintentionally recorded remarks to Senator Sam Nunn on June 16, picked up by an open WUSA-TV microphone. "I'm shook to my shoes about this fraud case," Warner whispered, adding, "Bribery is rampant."

Senator Grassley, on the other hand, spoke for me and my allies when he said that the congressional expressions of disbelief reminded him of a scene in *Casablanca* with the French police captain, Louis Renault (Claude Rains). Sitting in the front room of Rick's saloon, Renault is informed that gambling is going on in the back room. He says, "I'm shocked!" Just then a porter hands Renault a sheaf of currency, saying, "Your winnings, sir." The *Washington Post*'s Herblock cartoon here

"Shocking!" copyright 1988 by Herblock in The Washington Post.

reproduced is a good example of what many journalists thought of the "shock."

I was somewhat surprised by two aspects of the scandals. The first was that the FBI (and as later came out, Assistant Attorney General William Weld) was able to avoid having their project killed by Ed Meese, which they accomplished by not telling him about it.

The second mildly surprising aspect was the extent of alleged transactional bribery. My perception was that transactional, or "fee for service," bribery had been relatively rare in Pentagon acquisitions. Ordinarily the spending coalition buys the *servant*, so it has no need to buy specific services. The co-opted servants are obedient ("responsive," in the jargon) and understanding, real "team players." For the military, especially, the prospect of a plush, revolving-door retirement job gives the coalition a real hold on all but the most principled and selfless officers. Most are pushed out of the service in their mid-forties by the up-or-out system, and they need jobs for that expensive phase of life, what with growing families and staggering college costs ahead. They need good jobs, and the door at Defense Boondoggle Systems, Inc. (DBS) is open. As for simple black-bag bribes, most officers would regard them as both demeaning and unnecessary. There are so many fraternal, back-scratching relationships within the officer corps, including both active-duty and retired officers, that an ex-colonel at DBS can get the tip he wants without a bribe.

After the first shock the media stories of Pentagon scandal began to widen. Three congressmen were implicated, according to press reports, and names of more contractors and consultants began to surface. Reports cited specific examples of suspicious bid rigging, such as that on a $70 million Marine Air Traffic Control system. On July 1 Defense Secretary Carlucci announced that nine Navy contracts — none for major weapons systems — were "tainted" and would have their funding frozen.

Most of the Pentagon-industry spenders were, like Warner, "shook to their shoes" — whether at the revelations or from the fear of being caught themselves only time would tell. The academic barrage they had instigated now seemed as feeble as the noise of firecrackers the ancient Chinese armies used to frighten the enemy. Nevertheless they tried to put on a bold face and offer explanations.

Because most of this happened on Weinberger's watch, he was questioned closely on a couple of TV panel programs. His defense, echoed in a statement by Reagan, was that "there are a few bad apples in any barrel" and that, with millions of people working for the Department of Defense, it wasn't surprising that a small minority were on the take. The corollary was that there was nothing wrong with "the system." That the system invites bad apples and makes bad apples prosper richly is, of course, part of the thesis of this book.

Another exculpatory, partial explanation of the scandals was voiced by Representative John Spratt, a member of the House Armed Services Committee (as quoted in *Time*, June 27, 1988), when he spoke about the contracts process: "You almost have to be an insider to understand it." *Time* went on to say that the consultant companies, or "rent-a-general" agencies, hire former procurement officers who "know both the procedural intricacies of how contracts are processed and the technical needs of the services." *Time* added, "Without these middlemen, the military's complex procurement system might not work at all."

If, instead of the insider system, we tried honest, old-fashioned competition — such as that envisioned by Senator Grassley's Creeping Capitalism — the greasemen wouldn't have a foothold. They would have little to sell, and bid rigging would be much more difficult, especially if we had good internal checks and balances.

The way the system "works" and to whose advantage it works was becoming more and more apparent. If and when the details of Project Ill Wind are fully exposed, the public will be more surprised by what is legal than by what is illegal. As I had illustrated in my June 4, 1987, congressional testimony, the Pentagon had all but destroyed its traditional, time-tested safeguards against corruption. Along with that, the Reagan team had suppressed that greatest of all controls: the impulse of honest men to tell the truth in public. The First Amendment's guarantee of free speech is not only the best of all legitimate management controls; no other works without it. Ex-Secretary Weinberger might be reminded of Sherlock Holmes's dialogue with Colonel Ross, speaking of a watchdog: " 'Is there any point to which you would wish to draw my attention?' 'To the curious incident of the dog in the night-time.' 'The dog did nothing in the night-time.' 'That was the curious incident,' remarked Sherlock Holmes."

In addition, the combination of loose procurement rules and government acquiescence in rip-offs leaves many a crook untouched. As exposure followed exposure, the Packard doctrine of contractor "self-governance" or self-policing looked more and more ludicrous. Solemnly accepting the Packard rules on their face value, the Dingell staffers and I inquired as to whether any contractor had turned in a self-arrest form when the scandal broke. None had. We had previously asked Derek Vander Schaaf, the Pentagon's deputy inspector general and self-policing advocate, if he had been busy distributing the self-policing forms. Apparently he hadn't. On July 6, 1988, the House Armed Services

Committee laughed out loud when Vander Schaaf testified that thirty-nine of the forty-six contractors who had signed up for the self-policing program were under investigation.

Secretary Carlucci moved quickly in the crisis. He appointed an internal review committee headed for the moment by his general counsel, Kathleen Buck. And he called in the oldest hand of all, David Packard, to go once more into the breach. On June 22 the *Washington Post* reported that Carlucci had asked Packard to examine the issues involved and to advise the Pentagon on ways to handle them.

One of the issues was very close to home. Kathleen Buck already knew that Secretary Frank Carlucci had a continuing financial stake in one of the companies under investigation. Between his Pentagon job as deputy secretary in the early 1980s and his appointment as Reagan's national security adviser, Carlucci had been elected to the board of Unisys Corporation, a major investigative target. He served on that board for two handsomely rewarded years.

In addition, this two-year stint earned him $82,482, to be paid over an unspecified number of years, starting when he left federal service, according to the financial disclosure statement Carlucci filed with Buck on November 9, 1987. Carlucci's disclosure form also included the following entry: "Pursuant to Unisys (Sperry) Corporation directorship, will receive pension plan payments ($14,300 to be paid annually effective 11/90)." These payments depend on Unisys still being in business by then, a circumstance heavily dependent on the actions of Secretary Carlucci.

After the June 1988 scandal broke, reporters began asking for copies of Carlucci's financial disclosure forms, whereupon another version appeared, this one dated May 16, 1988, and also approved by Buck. The earlier, obvious conflicts were changed, but not too neatly and certainly not convincingly. The new disclosures said that the $82,482 Unisys would pay Carlucci had been "cashed out." Actually, it appeared that Carlucci had cashed in. The disclosure form did not specify how much the serving secretary of defense received from the investigative target, but David Evans reported in the July 6, 1988, *Chicago Tribune* that the payoff was nearly $96,000.

In addition, Carlucci's new disclosure stated that his Unisys pension plan was being replaced "with an annuity with Travelers [Insurance Company]." No details were forthcoming, but the arrangements elicited these observations in Evans's July 6 article:

> The report does not say if the transfer is, or was, made by a single lump-sum payment from Unisys, or if Travelers will receive a series of payments.

A series of payments would leave Carlucci with a continuing financial stake in the fortunes of Unisys, presenting a conflict of interest if he makes decisions on defense issues regarding the company. Carlucci has not made a public statement about how he will handle Unisys matters.

If a lump-sum payment was made, Carlucci may be in a similar situation to that of Melvyn R. Paisley, the former assistant Navy secretary who is one of the principal targets of the FBI investigation.

Paisley received a lump-sum "golden handshake" of $183,000 from the Boeing Co. when he left the company to join the government.

The U.S. Court of Appeals recently declared the payment was a conflict of interest, overturning a lower court ruling.

Where was General Cappucci, who saw conflicts of interest even where there were none, when we really needed him?

Finally, another talent pool was available to help out in the Pentagon inquiry. On the June 26 ABC "This Week" program already mentioned, Don Fuqua, head of AIA, the contractors' organization, volunteered that the CEOs of the giant corporations were willing to come to the Pentagon to help Packard smite their archenemy, Low-Cost Culture. What with Carlucci's own general counsel, an array of contractor moguls, and David Packard heading the parade, the malefactors would be begging for mercy.

On the other hand, they might be falling out of their chairs with laughter.

17

☆ ☆ ☆

Our Corporate State

A LONG AND CURIOUS article titled "The Morning After" appeared in the
October 1987 issue of the *Atlantic Monthly*. Its author, Peter G.
Peterson, was an investment banker, former government official, and
chairman of the Council on Foreign Relations. It was curious in that
much of its analysis was so accurate and its conclusions so wrong.
Those conclusions represent, in some interesting ways, a lot of the
confused thinking of the 1980s.

Peterson wrote, "We now find that the budget deficits and an evapo-
ration of the public's pro-defense consensus are drawing an ever-
tightening circle around all our strategic options." That, of course, is only
half the story. What is needed to complete the thought is a better understanding of the Reagan-era fiscal disasters that helped to evaporate the
consensus.

Among other symptoms of fiscal illness, Peterson noted the collapse
of our trade balance in manufactured goods "from a $17 billion surplus
in 1980 to a $139 billion deficit in 1986." His solution? "First, we must
tame the federal budget deficit." Obviously, but where do we start
cutting? At the Pentagon? That's not impossible, according to Peterson,
if fate would give us a lucky break: "Real defense spending has been
effectively frozen for the last couple of years, and we may be at a
crossroads in foreign policy which will allow us to make substantial
future savings in security expenditure."

In looking forward to, presumably, a new era of détente with the
Soviets, Peterson overlooked the fact that the greatest pacific develop-

ment in American foreign policy over the past forty-two years — the withdrawal from Southeast Asia — was followed by an enormous increase in military spending. Peterson used the standard Establishment evasion: We can't control the huge expenditures at the Pentagon, but with a more benign foreign policy, expenditures may recede in some natural ebb of the tide. The reader will note that this argument rests on a supposed cause and effect that have no necessary connection.

Meanwhile, what to do? "We must," Peterson said, "increase federal revenue" by adding a huge sales tax on gasoline and a "five-percent value-added [sales] tax on all products." Presumably working people, who are hit hardest by such regressive taxes, would then be too broke to buy Japanese cars and televisions, and thereby the trade deficit would be reduced.

While in our nightly prayers we were supposed to wish for a change in foreign policy that might miraculously slow the Pentagon's upsurge in spending, where could we actually economize? The answer: in "non-means-tested entitlements," of which Social Security, a favorite Peterson target in the past, was the largest.

But wait. Social Security was not adding to the budget deficit; the Social Security trust fund was running a huge and growing *surplus*. According to the February 18, 1988, *Washington Post*, the Congressional Budget Office estimated that the surplus in the trust funds (Social Security was the largest of these) was likely to be $97 billion in fiscal 1988, as opposed to a *deficit* of $245 billion in the nontrust-fund part of the federal budget, or the Federal Funds Schedule. Chart 17-1 shows the role of the Social Security surplus in masking the size of the overall federal deficit and making the black hole look less deep than it is.

As of this writing, government actuaries estimate that Social Security surpluses will, unless there is an economic collapse, rise to the trillions before the inevitable downward trend when the Baby Boom generation begins to retire in the 2010s. The constant danger, of course, is that an administration faced with the hungry demands of the Pentagon will begin reneging on the deal with the old folks.

In his *Atlantic Monthly* article, Peterson pointed out that at the end of 1981 we were the world's largest net creditor nation, with foreigners collectively owing us $141 billion more than we owed them. By the end of 1987, Peterson forecast, we would be closing in on a negative $400 billion, with our net foreign debt projected to reach $1 trillion by the early 1990s. As Chart 17-2 shows, by 1988 the federal government's bonded debt was growing exponentially. It was becoming interest-driven; that is, we were borrowing money to pay accrued interest, which, as Senator Grassley has often pointed out, is a classic economic definition of bankruptcy.

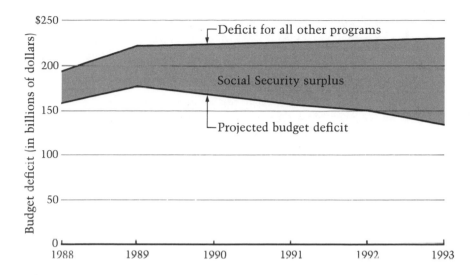

Chart 17-1. How the Social Security surplus masks the size of the federal deficit. Source: Congressional Budget Office.

So Congress had to take some action. It did that with the budget summit of 1987, making a modest start on the Peterson prescription. But in doing so it actually *added* more than $10 billion to the military budget set by the House Budget Committee and almost $5 billion to that approved by the Senate!

Since the two houses usually reconcile their budget figures by splitting the difference, the Senate Budget Committee staff focused on the midpoint of the difference between the two bodies, as shown in the summit outcome. This produced an increase for the military of $6.676 billion and a cut of $1.587 billion for everybody else, which meant a net *increase* of $5.089 billion in overall obligational authority. When this was translated into projected spending, the Pentagon outlays budget went up $5 billion from fiscal 1987 to 1988 and a whopping $8.5 billion for FY 1989. Most of that new $13.5 billion was for acquisitions.

In the end the Merlins of the budget announced a projected reduction in the deficit. But how? First they used the trust fund surpluses as camouflage. Next they whistled up some hoped-for increases in revenues from 1987 to 1989 — $119 billion, partly from higher Social Security taxes and partly from projected increased revenues from general taxation.

The summit's action seemed insane: the only scare loose in the world was a peace scare. Congress had decided that we were not going to initiate a war in Central America. Mikhail Gorbachev was behaving less like an Evil Emperor and more like a politician eager to make arms reduction deals with Ronald Reagan. There was no known increase in The Threat. It had been demonstrated to all Pentagon insiders that we could drastically reduce unit costs for weapons while improving their quality. So why the big increases in the military budget?

The secret was that the planners in the DoD had continued to stick to their ascending plan even during the slowdown called the Freeze. Over the previous twelve years Congress had appropriated so much

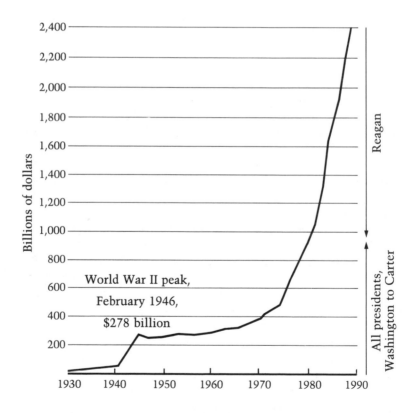

Chart 17-2. U.S. public debt, 1930–1988. Source: Office of the Secretary of the Treasury, May 3, 1986.

more than the Pentagon was able to unload that there was a huge backlog of unspent money. Spending did rise, just more slowly. Meanwhile, back at their computers, the planners and programmers looked into their crystal screens and saw visions of new billions after the Freeze nonsense was forgotten.

Their guiding horoscope was a kind of five-year plan. Back in 1961 the Robert McNamara Whiz Kids created something called the Program Planning and Budgeting System, or PPBS. Managers used it to make their future cost projections, which were combined into the Five Year Defense Program, or FYDP. This latter, with its year-by-year estimates for each element, was intended as fiscal guidance for the president.

Needless to say, the negotiations that produced the FYDP were horrendous, with great politicking, re-estimating, trimming the losing programs and expanding the winners, adjusting and reallocating the adjustments. My friends in the office of the secretary of defense estimated that all this consumed at least a million manhours per year in the Pentagon. And though it was far from perfect, PPBS did bring some order to Fort Fumble's feeding frenzy.

Then in 1986 an odd thing happened. The price tag on the future plans vastly exceeded even Ronald Reagan's permissive guidelines, the sum of the parts being much greater than the acceptable total. Weinberger and his baffled aides finally gave up trying to reconcile the figures, and thus there was no balanced FYDP in 1987.

Under strictest secrecy, they were able to get away with the concealment, sharing the facts only with Pentagon insiders, big contractors, and tame members of Congress. This was management breakdown on a huge scale, involving hundreds of billions of dollars in mismatched projections. But it passed unnoticed in 1987, and in 1988, under the Poindexter-Packard plan, no reconciled FYDP was required.

It was a hefty time bomb that Cap Weinberger had wrapped up to present to the new administration when it took office in January 1989. A new management team would "discover" that the Pentagon "needed" as much as $400 billion more than previously planned for the ensuing five years in order to avoid immediate mass layoffs, contract terminations, and base closures — all nightmare prospects for even the most fiscally responsible president.

The obvious course of that point would be for the president to announce to the country that in this crisis the nation's security and economic health were at stake. He would call upon everybody to make sacrifices until he could bring order out of chaos. In the meantime Pentagon spending would have to remain at the current level, or even higher.

The only thing that prevented Weinberger's ruse from succeeding was the vigilance of one senator, Lowell Weicker, and his staff assistant, Charlie Murphy. Informed members of the Pentagon underground passed the news to Murphy in early 1987. I learned of it at about the same time, but I was crippled by the straitjacket of Poindexter-Packard and the new secrecy gag rules, which threatened me even though I had not signed the SF 189. More important, almost everybody else had gagged themselves, which greatly reduced the flow of information.

My arithmetic showed that the Air Force alone had a five-year price tag that exceeded the Reagan guidance by $24.5 billion and exceeded our expectations of what Congress might appropriate by $72.8 billion. I tried repeatedly to get my new military bosses to discuss the issue, arguing that the sooner we squeezed some appreciable amount of fat from our programs, the better off we would be when we faced the budget discrepancy.

They had a sudden and interesting deafness. It took me a little while to realize that what the top Pentagonists were aiming for was fiscal chaos. They actually believed that chaos would benefit them and their contractor allies by forestalling any new spending discipline. It would be a license to steal.

I had some clues about this that would have been amusing under any other circumstances. In one staff meeting when I was trying to get some useful discussion of our overriding problem, I was silenced so that the meeting could devote itself to the price of haircuts in Air Force barbershops. In another meeting I was cut off in favor of a discussion dear to the heart of the chief of staff of the Air Force: leather flying jackets for pilots. In the year 1987 pilots no longer actually wore leather jackets (our open-cockpit biplanes had all been retired), but in their off-duty hours, such jackets would give them a kind of heroes-of-the-Dawn-Patrol look greatly admired by the chief of staff.

Specifications had been drawn up for the purchase of North African goatskins, which were supple and soft and supposedly had more sex appeal than other goatskins. But the North American goat breeders were horrified. What about the Buy American act? What about the fact that American goatskins were almost half again larger than the foreign kind? Shut up, Fitzgerald, this is a lot more important than any $73 million budget shortfall.

I then appealed to General Claudius Watts to declassify information about the serious budget mismatch, but while the bureaucrats stalled, Senator Weicker brought the news. In the meantime a secret deal — a kind of defense summit — had been in the works. Apparently, part of that deal was to replace Weinberger with Frank Carlucci. Carlucci, the rumor went, looked more "reasonable" to the public and Congress and would probably be a more plausible front for increased Pentagon spending.

On January 10, 1988, the *Washington Post* published a chart that gave a graphic view of the budget mismatch before the summit deal (see Chart 17-3). The exact details of the deal have not been made public at this writing, but the essentials were these: the Reagan administration had projected spending at the 1987 level plus 3 percent annual growth plus inflation; the deal changed that to 2 percent plus inflation, compounded annually. The trade-off was an accelerated increase in the congressional funding line. Instead of rising to $300 billion by 1997, congressional funding would get to that figure by 1990, seven years sooner. All this, of course, would be the problem of the new president. It was a true banana-republic solution: postpone it to *manana*.

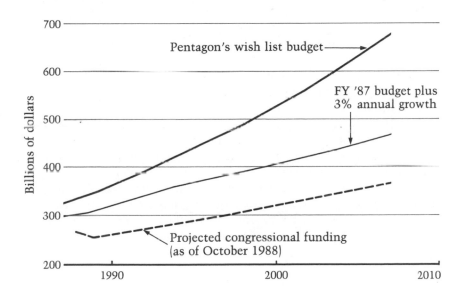

Chart 17-3. Defense Department budget projections. Source: System Planning Corp., prepared for the Commission on Long Term Strategy but not included in the commission's report to the Pentagon and the president.

Peter Peterson was only one of many economists and critics who commented on the defense spending crisis. Seymour Melman wrote a monumental book on the subject, titled *Profits without Production* (1983). A key passage noted that "the Pentagon has effectively displaced cost-minimizing with a system of cost- and subsidy-maximizing," a demonstrably correct proposition that David Packard and Ronald Reagan have hailed as a virtue.

Gordon Adams and David Gold, in a July 1987 study financed by the Rockefeller Brothers Fund and the Circle Fund, tried to counter Melman's view with a kind of apologia. Defense contractors' prices were comparatively reasonable, they said: "Cost-maximizing practices within defense industries appear to have contributed to significant growth in weapons systems costs. However, defense sector price indexes compiled by the Department of Commerce indicate that inflation within defense industries is only slightly higher than inflation in civilian sectors *with similar products*" (emphasis added).

The point is that the comparison is tainted. The industries with "similar products" were already infected with cost-maximizing by the defense giants in their midst. Thus it was only natural that the infected sectors should be only slightly behind the disease carriers. Adams and Gold did not even begin to address the problem of a manufacturer whose cost for making one toilet pan was $600. He could not sell his product in *any* truly competitive market, domestic or foreign; his only conceivable buyer was the Pentagon.

Melman and his colleagues had noted the important "lost opportunity" factor, which is one way that military spending drains the general economy. Engineers who devote many hours to designing a plain three-inch piece of wire are not using their time to design products that might compete with Toyota or Sony. Worse, engineers long employed in such boondoggles rust and lose their skills. Adams and Gold missed those points entirely. They also failed to understand the additional drain caused by the lax and slovenly work habits so endemic to defense industries — and so easily spread to "civilian sectors with similar products."

Another attempt to answer the great "why-can't-America-compete-any-longer?" question arrived in a 1988 treatise titled "The Case for Manufacturing in America's Future," prepared under the general supervision of Colby H. Chandler. Mr. Chandler was chairman and CEO of Eastman Kodak, a sizable military contractor. The paper began with the sensible but obvious thesis that American manufacturing now compares badly with that of the rest of the world and that we thus have reason to worry about our competitiveness. Chart

17-4 (constructed from data compiled by the CIA) illustrates the situation.

After that beginning, Chandler and company headed for the deep end. They decided that "our competitiveness plummeted due in large measure to an overvalued dollar." As patient readers of this book know by now, our "competitiveness" began to decline in 1965, and whatever the state of the dollar — high in 1985 or low in 1988 — the overall trend in our balance of trade has been down. Obviously we can improve the balance of trade if we take less for our goods and pay more for imports, thereby reducing the American standard of living. But this is a self-flagellating solution to the major problem of competitiveness.

Chandler's article, in fact, gave evidence that our competitiveness did *not* plummet solely as a result of an overvalued dollar. He included a chart of values ("U.S. Real Exchange Rate") based on an index for the

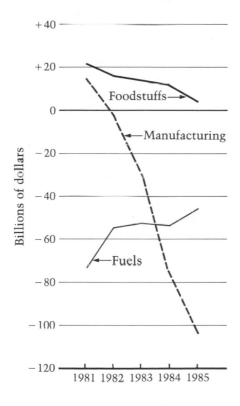

Chart 17-4. Changes in components of the U.S. trade deficit. Source: Central Intelligence Agency.

years 1970–1988 and compiled by Morgan Guaranty Trust. It compared the prices, in dollars, of nonfood manufactures in the United States, to prices for the same goods in other countries, in their currencies. In 1970 (the year before our first modern-day trade deficit), the index stood at 112. By 1987 it had dropped by 17 percent to 93. In other words, the dollar had lost only 17 percent in relative value while our balance-of-trade figures were in a free fall. The correlation Chandler's authors sought just wasn't there.

Chandler had a Petersonian remedy, though: boost consumer taxes, especially the value-added kind. That would raise the price of American manufactures at home and "all imported goods would be taxed, so that consumers would not detect any differential between the retail prices of domestic and imported goods." It was a marvelous soak-the-poor-to-support-the-rich program — the rich being anybody who profited from military contracting and the poor being all ordinary taxpayers.

Chandler went on to give apparently impressive figures on increases in defense manufacturing jobs: over a million new ones in 1977, 1980, and 1985. As manufacturing employment in general decreased by 1.29 million from 1980 to 1986, defense employment went up by 740,000. Without defense industries to bolster the job market, he stressed, employment would be at its lowest since 1965.

So a lot more people were working in defense, but what were they producing? Chandler said nothing about output of useful products, nor even whether all that employment culminated in the noneconomic objective of outgunning the Evil Empire.

The *ergo* at the end of all this was that military acquisitions were wonderful medicine for our economic health: "Just as the manufacturing sector benefits the most when defense spending increases, it will be the largest loser as spending declines." And, making the prognosis of many a quack doctor before him, he uttered the words most likely to make Congress turn faint and helpless: "Defense cutbacks will . . . lead to rather concentrated employment reductions."

Like Adams and Gold, Chandler was not quite in the real world. As many of our giant corporations became less and less able to compete in foreign — or domestic — markets, Congress gave them massive intravenous injections of military money. Unfortunately, as Chart 17-5 demonstrates, that was no cure. If anything, Congress anticipated the steep drop in our competitive ability. The upward-zooming line of "total obligation authority for DoD acquisition" actually preceded the downward slide of the trade figures because the former is done by fiscal year and the latter by calendar year. Prior to 1977, then, the obligation figures appeared on July 30 and the trade figures at year's end. Further-

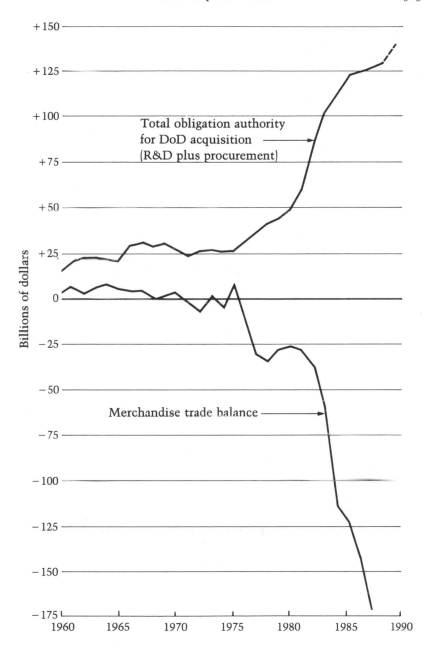

Chart 17-5. *Defense acquisition costs versus U.S. balance of trade, 1960–1988, in current dollars. Source: Office of the Secretary of Defense and the Department of Commerce.*

more, the obligation authority is simply a permission to spend. The actual spending usually comes a year or so later.

In their simplistic surveys of economic problems, Chandler and other writers overlooked another subtle aspect of the "lost opportunity" factor Melman had pointed out. This was the deterioration brought about by underemployment in defense industry. When a contractor warehoused a team of engineers in order to take advantage of the "full absorption accounting principle," he was letting talent rust. That principle encouraged corporations to keep technical teams together even if they had to be given busywork. The degradation of so many American engineers may be the most devastating hidden effect of our reckless military spending. When I was an engineering student and young engineering practitioner, we were indoctrinated with the idea that engineering is applied economics. Defense manufacturers seem never to have heard it.

Still another strain of military-contractor infection that began to spread through the general body of the nation from the 1970s on was cost justification, which the academics in charge of B-school management training adopted in all its manifestations. The cost-plus-percentage-of-cost concept (politely called "pass-through") spread into the campus courses and from there into many areas of business and industry, most rapidly in administered-price industries.

The health-care industry became one of the chief sufferers. The feverish rise of health-care costs starting in the late 1960s went hand in hand with the hospitals' adoption of cost-plus pricing. Along with that, physicians' billings were now based on an elaborate pricing system that (like the military contractors') was based on an average of past billings — an average that kept moving higher and higher. The same disease spread to the quasi-public corporations such as the Postal Service, Amtrak, and Comsat.

For a long time I have felt like an eyewitness to the systematic disintegration of everything that made America competitive in the industrial world of the twentieth century. From the factory floor to the boardroom to the rarefied air of high government offices, a slackness of mind has set in. To be tough-minded, economical, and bent on winning is no longer the fashion.

Not that these shoddy, new habits are unresisted or universal; some stubborn and honest people do remain in corporations and the government. In my own area of concern, performance measurement systems are still in place even after years of battering from the cover-up troops. Should-cost worked when we were allowed to use it properly. Whenever we could pry loose enough information to do technical audits, they were valuable. We clung to the concept of work measurement for factories and managed to preserve it in principle. The times when we could persuade the big spenders to permit some competition for a contract, it paid off.

Competition had some interesting facets. In 1985 Congress passed a "reform" act called the Competition in Contracting Act, or CICA. One of its immediate effects was to allow the Pentagon to change the definition of "competitive" in its reporting. Before CICA, competition meant advertised solicitations and sealed-bid responses. Under the new system, even if the rivalry was no more fierce than two sumo wrestlers running the hundred-yard dash, any vying qualified. One striking case of CICA's effects was when a little competition brought the bid from one of our worst-case contractors down by about 80 percent. This contractor still couldn't make, say, a plastic toilet pan for less than $1,000 apiece, and if he ever tried to compete in the world market, the most insignificant Japanese company would eat him up.

And CICA failed to do anything about the grand swindles that hid under the Pentagon's label of competition. A splendid example of this was demonstrated by Ronald Brousseau, Sr., whose remarks were first secretly recorded by the FBI and later amplified in a guilty plea, according to Peter Stockton, who was following the case.

Brousseau was a Northrop buyer who took kickbacks on purchases for the B-2 Stealth bomber. This machine was headed for a $500 million price tag (each), and Brousseau explained part of the reason. Original bids would be "bumped," or increased, so that the seller could pay a kickback, about 25 percent of the bump, and keep the rest. Brousseau explained how he got away with it for so long: "Nobody questions dollars or anything like that. As long as I can show competition or courtesy competition or bullshit competition you know. That's all I gotta be able to show is competition." (All these quotes come from the U.S. Attorney's sentencing memorandum.)

Brousseau's prosecutor further illuminated the practices, describing "courtesy competition" as "a fraudulent arrangement between a buyer and a group of sellers who agree that the suppliers will take turns being the low bidder." Everybody inflates his bid so that the low bid is still fat enough to provide a kickback and a nice cushion of profit for the winner.

It's a beautiful scam, and if it weren't for the occasional FBI operative with a body mike, a safe one. The big corporate contractors have let their own internal controls wither away until they no longer have much ability to check on such schemes. The auditors and purchasing systems evaluators have the comforting multiple-bid documentation to show that competition has taken place and the rest doesn't matter. Brousseau summed it up when he said, "Don't get greedy. You know, a nickel [5 percent] here and a nickel there. Everybody's gonna get fat and everybody's gonna be happy."

Peter Stockton shortly thereafter interviewed a supplier who said he'd been shaken down by most of the big corporate names in his industry. He was willing to testify that what Brousseau had done was common practice in military contracting. But the Edwin Meese Justice Department wouldn't grant Stockton's source immunity in return. The department promised to take some action, but that action never came. Not surprising, inasmuch as Brousseau himself received only light punishment, according to Stockton.

Another subtle and seldom-perceived danger was the growth of the military into a gross and mighty bureaucracy, one of the scariest developments of the 1980s. Reagan, after outbidding Carter with contract gold for the favor of the military party, then supplanted civilians with the Praetorian prefects of procurement. In this he was only following the example of the Emperor Lucius Septimius Severus, who, as he lay dying after a pointless campaign in North Britain, advised his two sons and heirs, "Make your soldiers rich; don't bother about anything else."

Reagan raised the pay and allowances of the military brass to unprecedented levels. With their handsome raises and tax-free allowances, supplemented by taxpayer-financed personal servants, drivers, homes, and executive airplanes, generals and admirals live in multimillionaire style. Even Air Force colonels, so thick on the ground that special jobs have to be concocted for them, cost the taxpayers 40 percent more than equivalent-grade civilians doing the same work. And many, of course, are headed for retirement rewards as executives in the contractor companies they have been cozy with while in uniform or as consultants ("rainmakers" in trade jargon) making sure the big contractors don't want for business.

Edward Gibbon, in his *Decline and Fall of the Roman Empire*, noted that "an hundred thousand well-disciplined soldiers will command, with despotic sway, ten millions of subjects." Instead of the gladius and the pilum, the dominating weapons of our own military party are rich contracts, jobs, assured profits, power, and prestige. And one more: the power to deny jobs to people in many areas of our society. For example, the loss of a security clearance is often tantamount to the loss of a work permit. I don't intend to imply by this that the military alone is running an "invisible government." The military side of the spending coalition has thus far been satisfied with its perks and has remained a servant of the corporate side. But if one day the power should shift, we are in for more serious trouble.

Where the military exercises a scarcely visible governing power is in its use of National Security Decision Directives (NSDDs). These, as we have seen, can be promulgated by a militarized National Security Council staff and okayed by the president's auto-pen. (And remember, the *Nixon v. Fitzgerald* decision put the president out of reach for civil damage suits.)

In 1988 The Threat seemed to have lost much of its old black magic, what with *perestroika*, a medium-range ballistic missile treaty, and the withdrawal of troops from Afghanistan. A Russian landing on Long Island did not seem imminent. The administration started a frantic search for sinister foreign enemies — even little Threats — to make continued big military spending seem respectable. But Ortega failed the test, then Noriega failed to build as hoped and even became an embarrassment.

A move was made to throw our armed forces into the war against the drug smugglers, but that was handicapped by increasing evidence that our national security apparatus, or parts of it, had tolerated certain smugglers in certain very suspect ways. In any classic scenario of power taking, the military would be happy to move into enforcement, but our military wanted none of the drug-policing role. Narcs have a hard, nasty job and few showy victories.

Another circumstance that separated the United States from the classic banana republic was our highly developed industrial and economic base, dominated by corporate oligarchies rather than oligarch families. The privileged Pentagon contracting corporations took for granted that they would give to their government customer in accordance with their ability, or their mood of the moment. The grateful government would see to it that the ever-malleable contracts were changed to conform to the giants' actual products. And the big corporations would be compensated in accordance with their need, as documented by their actual spending.

Just as the Pentagon contractors' bad work habits and worse management practices were encouraged and spread throughout the United States' corporate body, so did the notion of corporate communism. *Every* big corporation seemed to think it had a right to be kept alive, no matter how poorly it performed. The sloppier and more unsuccessful the management, the more it insisted on bailouts and protection from competition. The very thought that favored giant business firms should compete for the trade of consumers with free choice was somehow abhorrent to the defenders of privileged status for the big corporations. The suggestion that a changing economic climate demanded that dinosaur companies adapt or die bred panic. The pampered giants had become so grossly fat, so lethargic, and so nonproductive that their most strenuous efforts were periodic campaigns for more public money and more protection.

The evolving corporate welfare system was brilliantly described and analyzed by two British academics, R. E. Pahl and J. T. Winkler, in "The Coming Corporatism" (*Economic Affairs*, March-April, 1975). By their definition, corporatism is a political-economic system under which government guides privately owned businesses toward four goals: order, unity, nationalism, and "success."

Order, they said, "meant the elimination of the anarchy of the market in all its forms (including extreme success or failure for capital or for labor). This desire for stability emanates from a revulsion against the market processes that lead, on one hand, to the collapse of major companies in important industries . . . and, on the other, to excessive speculation and windfall profits."

Unity is the "substitution of cooperation for competition. This desire for collaborative effort arises from a revulsion against the perceived wastefulness of competitive struggles." Nationalism is the "elevation of 'general welfare' to complete priority over self interest or sectional advantage."

"Success" is the "attainment of national objectives established by the state. . . . it means giving conscious direction to the economy by establishing priorities and targets and by restricting work done toward alternative objectives. First and foremost, this means the control and concentration of investment and of the allocation of resources."

The authors were writing about corporatism in Britain; American academic writers prefer the more palatable "industrial policy." Pahl and Winkler had a less bland description: "Let us not mince words. Corporatism is fascism with a human face." They went on to say, "An acceptable face of fascism, indeed, a masked version of it, because so far the more repugnant *political and social* aspects of the German and Italian regimes are absent or only present in diluted form." Corporatism, they said, takes over "the core elements of the *economic* strategy" of old-fashioned fascism. "Corporatism is a distinct form of economic structure. It was recognized as such in the 1930s by people of diverse political backgrounds, before Hitler extinguished the enthusiasm which greeted Mussolini's variant." That is true; many economists of the 1930s admired Mussolini's reorganization of the Italian economy along corporative and syndicalist lines. By setting up special parastate agencies or "corporations" to replace failing or inadequate private enterprises, he was able to control the important economic sectors. Elitists everywhere found that laudable.

Hitler, with a much more highly industrialized nation, built on and to a great extent integrated the existing large corporations into the government system. The smokestack barons of the munitions industry benefitted greatly, of course.

At first both Italy and Germany seemed to have produced an economic marvel. They had created markets for troubled industries and made jobs for many more workers. Hitler's *wehrwirtschaft* (roughly, "defense economic system") was very much like our own parastate cartel of giant defense contractors in many respects. It appeared to be a splendid tonic for the economy. Another similarity was that the smokestack barons supported this new order and gave it direction. The *Wehrwirtschaftführer* role played by Alfried Krupp was similar to that of David Packard in our own day.

Despite the rosy look of prosperity from making more guns than butter, the German and Italian arms economies were nonproductive in a classic economic sense. They did not add much of anything to the infrastructure or to the quality of life, and they weren't competitive in foreign markets. And that meant even more subsidies and protectionism.

In the end, going to war was the only cure. In *Hitler's Secret Book*, the Führer despaired of competing with the productive capacity and efficiency of the United States, and he spoke of us as "emerging in all fields as the sharpest competition to all European nations fighting . . . for the world's markets." He added, "Despite [America's] enormous wages, it no longer seems possible to undercut her prices."

It is tempting to array all the similarities between the 1930s corporate state and today's American military-industrial complex and use them as a predictor of things to come. However, I think the threat we face is from a peculiarly American version of corporatism. In this, our strengths are also our weaknesses. Hitler, Mussolini, and Tojo had no chance of making their vast slave empires work in the long run — the home bases were too small and inadequate. Ours, in contrast, is the largest economy in the world; if we decided to, we could live very well within our own borders, with perhaps a few raids abroad to secure strategic materials or to prevent Grenada from falling into Cuban hands.

Or to teach somebody like Khadafi a lesson. The morning after the April 1986 bombing of Libya by the USAF, my associate Tom Amlie appeared live on Cable News Network and explained that the raid was necessary: "It's that time of year." In other words, military budget time. "The budget's in trouble; aid to the Contras is in trouble," Tom said. And Khadafi was an ideal enemy. As Tom pointed out, he was "not a Christian, he talks funny, and he is probably guilty of most of the things we accuse him of." Tom then got the hook from CNN, but he had made his point.

Most Americans have a deep respect, almost reverence toward the military, from memories of Washington at Valley Forge to the Marines at Iwo Jima. They don't realize that the combination of Pentagon Praetorians and big-corporation executives has nothing to do with heroism and, in fact, almost nothing to do with war except for the occasional bloody spasm to provide an emotional excuse for more big spending. The only thing the soldiers, sailors, and pilots in combat arms service have in common with the Praetorians is the uniform.

It was only natural that corporatism in America should flourish during the eight-year lease of the White House by a sleepy old actor who loved multimillionaires, but it had been well started under his predecessor, whose notable contribution was a scheme called the President's Executive Interchange Program.

In a personally signed directive, Carter told us that this program was "a positive force for marshalling our human resources. Through this effort, both the public and private sectors jointly contribute to greater sensitivity and responsiveness in the interest of all Americans."

No, he was not offering a sensitivity-training course. He was very gently trying to give us a kind of Mussolini message: "Boundary lines between government and business are blurring. The activities of both have become increasingly similar. Each recognizes the need for closer cooperation to achieve its goals." Those goals were:

> To exchange management expertise and innovative techniques; To develop a cadre of executives of experience in both sectors [government and private] who could be called to serve on government advisory panels and in higher appointive positions in future administrations.

It was the perfect definition of institutionalized conflict of interest, which is one of the "unifying" aspects of corporatism.

If Carter's interchange program should reach full flower, imagine the pool of executives and generals who could be called to serve on blue-ribbon commissions. Since not all Pentagon acquisition practices have been made legal, and since some of them still leak out and get a bad reaction in the press and from Congress and the public, we'll need blue-ribbon commissions for some time to come. *Somebody* has to drag the red herring, paint the whitewash on, pull the wool, stack the deck, and otherwise get the world to overlook whatever must be overlooked.

The Carter-era and Reagan-era moves for tighter "national security" secrecy is another support for corporatism (as well as for larceny). Congressman Jack Brooks gave a stirring description in testimony before the House Post Office and Civil Service Committee on October 15, 1987:

> Most of the [security] classification, in my judgment, is not to keep our enemies from finding out information. It is to keep the American people and the Congress from finding out what in God's world various agencies are doing and how they are throwing away money, wasting it. They preach economy and they throw money away like dirt, and lie and cheat, and hide, and dissemble. . . .
>
> Now, that's what their real complaint is, that the people and the Congress might find out what they are doing. Reprogramming money, wasting money foolishly, not enforcing the law, not enforcing safety provisions, all sorts of things, and they just do not want anybody in a position to know to say publicly that, yes, this did happen. They want these people to shut up and go away.

Yet the secret part of the government keeps adding bulk. Tim Weiner, who won the Pulitzer Prize for his reporting on the "black," or supersecret, budget told a meeting of the Fund for Constitutional Government on April 20, 1988, that one measure of this was the increase in funding for secret programs during Reagan's first seven years. When Reagan took office, the price tag for intelligence and secret military activities was about $12 billion a year. In 1988 it had risen to $35 billion a year. The military portion of that amount had gone from about $2 billion to $18 billion, an increase of 900 percent. That jump suggests how much more the Pentagon, under Reagan, had to cover up. For instance, the Stealth Bomber fiscal atrocities, some of which are beginning to come to light at this writing.

The corporate state always encroaches on individual rights. And one sign of corporatism victorious is court decisions against individual rights in favor of government "security." There is the pernicious practice of making a security clearance and a work permit one and the same, in imitation of the KGB. Take the 1987 case of *Navy v. Egan.* Egan, a shipyard worker, was denied a security clearance and thus had his job taken away without due process. A majority of the U.S. Court of Appeals panel agreed that Egan was entitled to a fair trial, but Chief Judge Markey dissented. The man *couldn't* have a trial, he ruled, "because there is no law to apply." The security clearance process, Markey wrote, was "predictive . . . judgmental and neither factual nor legal." For the millions of people who needed security clearances to keep their jobs, the single test was the judgment of "responsible military officials."

Markey added that the officials derived their power from the president, and his power flowed from "the President's constitutional mandate to provide for the national defense, U.S. Const., Art. II, Section II." Interestingly, Article II, Section II says nothing of the sort.

When the case went to the Supreme Court on February 23, 1988, the court upheld Judge Markey. This logic, if carried to its conclusion, could permit the (mostly secret) NSDDs to usurp the legislative power of Congress, as usually happens in corporate states. The Reagan administration's push in this direction can be measured by the estimated three hundred or more of these edicts that Reagan issued between February 1981 and mid-1988.

The most dangerous sign of the times in 1988, however, was the slowly gathering consensus in favor of a big budget increase to finance a new spendthrift era at the Pentagon. The *Washington Post*'s lead editorial on April 10, 1988, denounced candidate Jesse Jackson's military spending proposals as a "caricature of a policy" that "no president would try, or, if he did, would not be allowed by either party in Congress to pursue."

And what proposal by the Reverend Mr. Jackson so frightened the *Post*? A budget freeze like the one sponsored by those dangerous left-wingers Senator Charles Grassley and Representative Denny Smith. The editorialist's notion was a strange anomaly for a newspaper with an excellent reporting staff and plenty of stored information to show what damage irresponsible military spending has done. I called the editorial office to ask for clarification, but I was given no answer.

The adverse consequences of the Pentagon's addictive boondoggling to our economy and true military capability are serious indeed, but the damage to our country's moral fiber is catastrophic. Our Constitution and our laws have been subverted to excuse wrongdoing and to rationalize the wasteful system. Concealment of misdeeds had become an official virtue, and suppression of truth national policy. Sophistry reigns in "intellectual" circles. Government officials, from the majestic office of the president to the lowest, sleaziest procurement office, lie routinely and with impunity in defense of the system. So do leaders of business and academia. Some, though thankfully not most, working people have succumbed to the lure of easy money, of what was called blood money in my youth.

So, the blocks, beams, and lintels of a corporate state are already at the construction site and the foundation has been laid. Anyone who has seen the marble structures built in Rome between 1922 and 1943 will know what it is going to look like. But looks are deceiving: this is meant to be a prison for most of us.

I have a hunch, however, admittedly an overly optimistic hunch, that it will never be built. Part of that hope comes from the fact that the military party is so blunder-prone that even its rites of *omertà* can't keep the truth from getting out eventually. The June 1988 disclosures of widespread bribery and bid rigging in the acquisition community are just one example. But, even more important, I conjecture that ordinary Americans will stop this sinister architecture from being built on our soil. To use an old and unfortunately debased word, it's truly un-American.

Here is the voice of one working man who figured it out. Greg Nelson, a Lockheed employee, published this view in the October 1987 issue of *The Union Member's Review:*

> We are the only ones worried about layoffs. Lockheed is trying to make as much money as possible right now. They love Star Wars because it's so easy to make big bucks inventing things nobody can check on. Unlike Lockheed, IAM [International Association of Machinists] members are in it for the long term. We want secure jobs and a good retirement. Is that what we get with Star Wars? What does your work experience tell you? Most folks who work here know that producing useful things with all these tax dollars is not what Lockheed is all about. That's why Lockheed is more interested in attendance than production. They don't care what we make, as long as we show up, so they can justify their budget. That's the real "Lockheed way."
>
> What happens when people find out what their tax dollars have been wasted on? They are gonna be pissed, and we are gonna get the axe. It's up to our union to show the way out.
>
> Why doesn't Lockheed and its governmental sugar-daddies care about production? First, they're all getting rich off this scam. They won't get laid off when we do. Second, the government doesn't really need this stuff. It's just the best way to get rich quick. If they really needed all these nuclear bombs and killer satellites, they wouldn't run this place the way they do. They'd fire three-fourths of the white badges [management people] around here and set this place up to get some work done.
>
> They tell us what we make is vitally important for national Defense. If that's true, looking at the way they run Lockheed, we're in big trouble.
>
> Never underestimate the blindness of greed. Beware of the man who gets more money the more he claims to defend the country. That's the guy who got so many people killed in Vietnam. War industries got rich while we were dying, and for what?

I happen to think that a lot of Greg Nelsons have the strength to overwhelm a few David Packards. But if we are going to stop the corporate state from rising on our land, we had best remember the words of the late Supreme Court Justice William O. Douglas, who wrote (in *The Douglas Letters*):

As nightfall does not come at once, neither does oppression. In both instances, there is a twilight when everything remains seemingly unchanged.

And it is in such twilight that we must be most aware of change in the air — however slight — lest we become unwitting victims of the darkness.

White House Memorandum, January 20, 1970

MEMORANDUM

THE WHITE HOUSE
WASHINGTON

January 20, 1970

ADMINISTRATIVELY CONFIDENTIAL

MEMORANDUM FOR: MR. HALDEMAN

FROM: ALEXANDER P. BUTTERFIELD

RE: A. Ernest Fitzgerald

I may be "beating a dead horse" at this late date ... but it was only a few days ago that Alan Woods called to ask if we had arrived at any particular Administration line regarding Mr. A. E. Fitzgerald. And someone else (I can't remember who) asked the same question at about the same time.

You'll recall that I relayed to you my personal comments while you were at San Clemente, but let me cite them once again -- partly for the record -- and partly because some of you with more political horse sense than I will probably want to review the matter prior to next Monday's press conference.

   -- Fitzgerald is no doubt a top-notch cost expert, but he must be given very low marks in loyalty; and after all, loyalty is the name of the game.

   -- Last May he slipped off alone to a meeting of the National Democratic Coalition and while there revealed to a senior AFL-CIO official (who happened to be unsympathetic) that he planned to "blow the whistle on the Air Force" by exposing to full public view that Service's "shoddy purchasing practices". Only a basic no-goodnik would take his official business grievances so far from normal channels. As imperfect as the Air Force and other military Services are, they very definitely do not go out of their way to waste government funds; in fact, quite to the contrary, they strive continuously (at least in spirit) to find new ways to economize. If McNamara did nothing else he made the Services more cost-conscious and introspective -- so I think it is safe to say that none of their bungling is malicious ... or even preconceived.

   -- Upon leaving the Pentagon -- on his last official day -- he announced to the press that "contrary to recent newspaper reports" he was not going to work for the Federal Government, but instead, was going to "work on the outside" as a private consultant.

ADMINISTRATIVELY CONFIDENTIAL

ADMINISTRATIVELY CONFIDENTIAL

- We should let him bleed, for a while at least. Any rush to pick
   him up and put him back on the Federal payroll would be tantamount to an admission of earlier wrong-doing on our part.

-- We owe "first choice on Fitzgerald" to Proxmire and others'
   who tried so hard to make him a hero.

cc: Mr. Ehrlichman
     Dr. Kissinger
     Mr. Klein
     Mr. Colson
     Mr. Nofziger
     Mr. Magruder
     Mr. Ziegler

FBI Memorandum, Two Versions, May 23, 1978

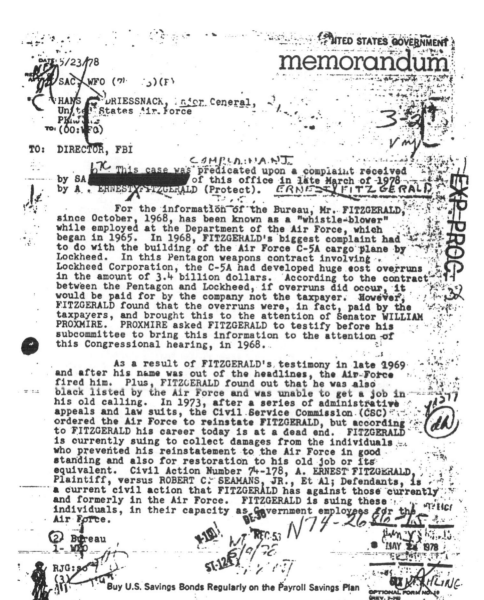

UNITED STATES GOVERNMENT

memorandum

DATE: 5/23/78

FROM: SAC, WFO (7 3)(F)

HANS DRIESSNACK, inior General,
United States Air Force
Pla. J...
(OO: FO)

TO: DIRECTOR, FBI

COMPLAINANT

This case was predicated upon a complaint received by SA ▓▓▓▓▓ of this office in late March of 1978 by A. ERNEST FITZGERALD (Protect). ERNEST FITZGERALD

        For the information of the Bureau, Mr. FITZGERALD, since October, 1968, has been known as a "whistle-blower" while employed at the Department of the Air Force, which began in 1965. In 1968, FITZGERALD's biggest complaint had to do with the building of the Air Force C-5A cargo plane by Lockheed. In this Pentagon weapons contract involving Lockheed Corporation, the C-5A had developed huge cost overruns in the amount of 3.4 billion dollars. According to the contract between the Pentagon and Lockheed, if overruns did occur, it would be paid for by the company not the taxpayer. However, FITZGERALD found that the overruns were, in fact, paid by the taxpayers, and brought this to the attention of Senator WILLIAM PROXMIRE. PROXMIRE asked FITZGERALD to testify before his subcommittee to bring this information to the attention of this Congressional hearing, in 1968.

        As a result of FITZGERALD's testimony in late 1969 and after his name was out of the headlines, the Air Force fired him. Plus, FITZGERALD found out that he was also black listed by the Air Force and was unable to get a job in his old calling. In 1973, after a series of administrative appeals and law suits, the Civil Service Commission (CSC) ordered the Air Force to reinstate FITZGERALD, but according to FITZGERALD his career today is at a dead end. FITZGERALD is currently suing to collect damages from the individuals who prevented his reinstatement to the Air Force in good standing and also for restoration to his old job or its equivalent. Civil Action Number 74-178, A. ERNEST FITZGERALD, Plaintiff, versus ROBERT C. SEAMANS, JR., Et Al; Defendants, is a current civil action that FITZGERALD has against those currently and formerly in the Air Force. FITZGERALD is suing these individuals, in their capacity as Government employees for the Air Force.

(2) Bureau
1- WFO

RJG:so
(3)

REC-53 N74-26 86 15

MAY 24 1978

WFO 74-303

In April, 1974, then Lieutenant-Colonel HANS H. DRIESSNACK, named also as a defendant in this civil action by FITZGERALD, produced a sworn affidavit dated and signed 4/18/74. Through discovery in this civil action, FITZGERALD's attorneys were able to produce an unsigned affidavit by DRIESSNACK with numerous corrections that eventually became his swch affadivt of 4/18/74.

After reviewing FITZGERALD's civil suit at the U.S. District Court House during April and May, 1978, SA ███████ came across the affidavit of General DUWARD L. CROW dated and signed on 4/19/74. Through the chain-of-command, DRIESSNACK had reported to CROW on 5/7/69 allegations that FITZGERALD was involved in a conflict of interest as a civilian with the Air Force, and the private managment firm, Performance Technology Corporation (PTC), which FITZGERALD was formerly President. CROW forwarded DRIESSNACK's allegation on FITZGERALD to his immediate superior, General MC CONNELL, Chief of Staff, which initiated an investigation by the Air Force's Office of Security (OSI).

In DRIESSNACK's signed affidavit of 4/18/74, he states, "I did not discuss these matters again with General CROW (after the meeting of 5/7/69) nor did I ever discuss them with other defendants in this case after the OSI interview."

It is the opinion of WFO that by DRIESSNACK altering his unsigned affidavit into its present form of 4/18/74, and the fact that both DRIESSNACK's and CROW's affidavits appear to be similar, it does give the appearance that DRIESSNACK "discussed these matters with General CROW" prior to submitting the final form of his affidavit dated 4/18/74. If this is the case, WFO feels DRIESSNACK perjured himself.

SA ███████ discussed the above with Assistant U.S. Attorney (AUSA) DONALD E. CAMPBELL, Major Crimes, Washington, D. C., and he advised the facts warrant that a preliminary investigation be instituted at this time.

FBI Headquarters is requested to grant WFO the authority to investigate captioned matter. For the information of FBI Headquarters, Major General DRIESSNACK is currently Director of the Budget for the Air Force, and the complainant, A. ERNEST FITZGERALD, a well-known figure in the Washington, D. C. area, has strong ties with Senator WILLIAM PROXMIRE.

WFO indices negative regarding DRIESSNACK.

WFO 74-303

In April, 1974, then Lieutenant-Colonel HANS H. DRIESSNACK, named also as a defendant in this civil action by FITZGERALD, produced a sworn affidavit dated and signed 4/18/74. Through discovery in this civil action, FITZGERALD's attorneys were able to produce an unsigned affidavit by DRIESSNACK with numerous corrections that eventually became his sworn affadivt of 4/18/74.

After reviewing FITZGERALD's civil suit at the U.S. District Court House during April and May, 1978, SA GOLDEN came across the affidavit of General DUWARD L. CROW dated and signed on 4/19/74. Through the chain-of-command, DRIESSNACK had reported to CROW on 5/7/69 allegations that FITZGERALD was involved in a conflict of interest as a civilian with the Air Force, and the private managment firm, Performance Technology Corporation (PTC), which FITZGERALD was formerly President. CROW forwarded DRIESSNACK's allegation on FITZGERALD to his immediate superior, General MC CONNELL, Chief of Staff, which initiated an investigation by the Air Force's Office of Security (OSI).

In DRIESSNACK's signed affidavit of 4/18/74, he states, "I did not discuss these matters again with General CROW (after the meeting of 5/7/69) nor did I ever discuss them with other defendants in this case after the OSI interview."

SA GOLDEN discussed the above with Assistant U.S. Attorney (AUSA) DONALD E. CAMPBELL, Major Crimes, Washington, D. C., and he advised the facts warrant that a preliminary investigation be instituted at this time.

FBI Headquarters is requested to grant WFO the authority to investigate captioned matter. For the information of FBI Headquarters, Major General DRIESSNACK is currently Director of the Budget for the Air Force, and the complainant, A. ERNEST FITZGERALD, a well-known figure in the Washington, D. C. area, has strong ties with Senator WILLIAM PROXMIRE.

WFO indices negative regarding DRIESSNACK.

- 2 -

National Security Decision Directive 102, September 5, 1983

UNCLASSIFIED

September 5, 1983

U.S. RESPONSE TO SOVIET DESTRUCTION OF KAL AIRLINER   (U)

INTRODUCTION

This directive defines the measures the United States will undertake to respond to the Soviet Union's shooting down of a Korean Airlines civil airliner, an act that resulted in the loss of 269 lives. This action demands a serious international and U.S. response, with primary focus on action by the world community. This Soviet attack underscores once again the refusal of the USSR to abide by normal standards of civilized behavior and thus confirms the basis of our existing policy of realism and strength.   (U)

OBJECTIVES

o   Seek Justice. We must consult with, and help to lead, the international community in calling for justice. Civilized societies demand punishment and restitution to deter, and raise the costs of, future egregious acts. We have a responsibility to impress upon the world that the Soviets, at a minimum, owe the international community:

   --   A full account of what happened, an apology, an admission of responsibility, and appropriate punishments to those responsible. (U)

   --   Immediate access to the crash site for joint efforts by Korea, Japan, and the United States to recover the bodies of their citizens and, if possible, the wreckage of the Korean airliner. (U)

   --   Firm assurances that the USSR will not use destructive force against unarmed aircraft in the future, including necessary alterations in Soviet procedures for handling cases in which aircraft mistakenly cross its airspace. (U)

   --   Agreement to provide compensation for the benefit of the aggrieved families and KAL. (U)

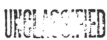

UNCLASSIFIED

Partial Text of
NSDD 102

2

o   **Advance Understanding of the Contrast Between Soviet Words
     and Deeds**. Soviet brutality in this incident presents an
     opportunity to reverse the false moral and political
     "peacemaker" perception that their regime has been
     cultivating. This image has complicated the efforts of the
     Free World to illuminate the USSR's true objectives.   (U)

ACTION

In order to realize the objectives above, the United States will
take the following bilateral and multilateral actions in the
areas of diplomacy, aviation security and safety, and regional
confidence building:

o   **Diplomacy and Justice**. The following steps should be
     continued or undertaken immediately to mobilize the
     international community:

     --   Conduct intensive efforts to secure coordinated
           international action.   (U)

     --   Seek maximum condemnation of the Soviet Union in the
           U.N. Security Council and provide wide dissemination of
           statements made in these sessions.   (U)

     --   Announce that the US-Soviet Transportation Agreement
           will not be renewed and suspend all discussion on the
           issue of consulates in Kiev and New York and on a new
           exchanges agreement.   (U)

     --   Continue to conduct a search in international waters,
           in consultation with Japan and Korea, for the remains
           of the aircraft. Assure the government of Korea that
           we will vigorously support their request to conduct,
           participate in, or observe salvage operations.
           Indicate our clear willingness and desire to assist the
           government of Korea in recovering the bodies and flight
           recorder as appropriate and in accord with
           international law.   (U)

     --   Make joint request with the government of Japan for
           Soviet authorization for access to Soviet territorial
           waters and airspace to search for remains of the downed
           aircraft.   (U)

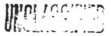

3

-- Initiate a major public diplomatic effort to keep
   international and domestic attention focused on the
   Soviet action and the objectives outlined above. (U)

-- Develop an omnibus U.S. claim against the Soviet Union
   for compensation for the loss of life and property.
   Offer to present to the USSR similar claims on behalf
   of the Korean victims. Also coordinate claims with the

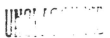

UNCLASSIFIED

4

> governments of other countries with citizens on the
> aircraft to dramatize the USSR's responsibility for its
> actions.   (U)

--   Reaffirm the existing U.S. sanctions against Aeroflot
     that predate the Soviet attack on KAL.   (U)

IMPLEMENTATION

The Secretary of State, in concert with the Secretary of Defense,
the Secretary of the Treasury, the Secretary of Transportation,
the Director of Central Intelligence, the Chairman of the JCS,
the Director of USIA, and the Administrator of the FAA, will
develop a coordinated action plan to implement the provisions of
this Directive. This plan should include a legislative, public
affairs, and diplomatic strategy and be forwarded to the
Assistant to the President for National Security Affairs by
Wednesday, September 7, 1983. (U)

Under the direction of the Secretary of State, an interagency
group will continue to evaluate and explore additional
possibilities for international and U.S. actions consistent with
this Directive. The first report on this continuing effort
should be forwarded to the Assistant to the President for
National Security Affairs by September 14, 1983. (U)

Index